Essays on Regional Economic Development

Edited by

Greg Coombs

South Australian
Centre for Economic Studies

Adelaide and Flinders Universities

The South Australian Centre for Economic Studies

SACES is a professional, independent, joint university economics research body.

Bibliography

Essays on Regional Economic Development

ISBN No. 1 86254 539 1

1. Regional economics. 2. Regional economics - Case studies. 3. Australia. - Economic conditions. 4. South Australia - Economic conditions. I. Coombs, Greg. II. South Australian Centre for Economic Studies.

338.90994

South Australian Centre for Economic Studies
PO Box 125
RUNDLE MALL SA 5000
AUSTRALIA

Telephone: (+61-8) 8303 5555
Facsimile: (+61-8) 8232 5307

Email: velice.langcake@adelaide.edu.au

Contents

Contents (Continued)

Page

Contents (Continued)

Contents (Continued)

Page

Foreword

The progressive integration of international markets, reflecting open trade policies and declining costs of transport and communication, is driving fundamental change in the competitiveness of regions. The goal posts are shifting: the community talks more of the importance of the quality of life than of income growth. The game is getting more competitive: aspirations of the community are rising to penetrate new international markets and stretching for best practice, rather than being content with local markets and local practices. The community wants greater choice in what they consume and a broader diversity of experiences. New rules are emerging for the game: there is no protection for regions, and no bale-outs. We talk of new ways to organise production, a greater role for civic leadership and collaboration, stimulating innovation and the integration of work and leisure. There are new umpires: the economic regulators and other overseers of corporate boards.

These changes are so fundamental, and there is no doubt that some regions will rise and others will decline. What can the constituents of regions do to stimulate growth of their jurisdictions? What is the role of government? How important is innovation to growth? These questions have been the source of discussion, research and publication for many years. Fortunately, consensus is being reached, and progress is being made to understanding the factors that facilitate regional growth and development.

This book is mainly concerned with presenting current thinking on factors that may influence regional and industry growth, and what strategies and policies should be adopted by industry, government and the community. The focus is mainly on South Australia and its sub-regions, although the principles and case studies have applications more broadly.

Most of the current literature on factors influencing economic growth is based on large closed economies reflecting, to a significant degree, the origins of the research in the US and UK. This book seeks to explore economic growth from the stand point of a small regional economy, critically examining the basic assumptions of the literature and recasting the results under changed assumptions.

Importantly, this book will draw on the research and insights that the South Australian Centre for Economic Studies has gained through a broad range of commissioned assignments undertaken over the last few years, and in particular, reports on provincial cities, industry studies in the information technology, electronics and defence industries in South Australia and various assignments into economic conditions. The book will also utilise studies of the impacts of national policies and key investments to illustrate regional diversity and regional advantage.

This book is intended for the policy advisers and decision makers, not necessarily equipped in the field of economics. Accordingly, the aim is to provide a clear interpretation of the theory and apply it in the specific regional context, rather than advancing the theory.

The first section offers five chapters on the contemporary theory and empirical evidence on factors influencing the growth of small regional economies. The intention is to provide the reader with a framework for thinking about regional issues and to offer a guide for the remainder of the book, which deals with practical applications. The discussion draws on earlier literature reviews by the Centre (Research Papers No. 97/1 to 97/4) and updates that work for more recent important contributions to the field of regional development. There is renewed interest in the literature on the capacity of small regions to effectively engage in economic policies and to stimulate regional growth which is discussed. In particular, Chapter 1 introduces the concept of a small regional economy and why globalisation is effecting these regions. Chapter 2 presents current thinking on economic growth theory, emphasising the role for policy and institutions. Chapter 3 discusses generally accepted basic factors that influence growth and development and Chapter 4 considers the catch-up factors for regions including governance, the role of government, organisation of firms, social cohesion and culture. Chapter 5 tackles the economics of innovation and the importance of R&D to growth.

From this framework, the book offers a potted picture of a socio-economic profile of a small regional economy, namely South Australia. A potted picture because the intention is to emphasise certain important aspects of the South Australian region. Chapter 6 puts the State and the sub-regions in the context of the nation, and discusses the forces of urban agglomeration. The following two chapters consider the endowments of the South Australian economy and identify triggers and events that have influenced its growth path. Human capital is also considered by placing emphasis on the needs of an advanced economy. The characteristics of the structure of the South Australian economy are covered in Chapter 9, followed by a discussion in Chapter 10 on the degree of openness of the economy to trade.

The book then turns to exploring South Australian regional development through several case studies. Firstly, in Chapter 11, is a discussion of the regional impact of a national policy on greenhouse gas emissions which illustrates that South Australia is structurally different from the rest of Australia. Chapter 12 considers the impact of an international investment in space technology on the Woomera region which draws on endogenous growth theory to analyse the potential for new knowledge spillovers to be captured by local firms through State policy. Chapter 13 takes a fiscal policy perspective, through discussion on the impact of globalisation on intergovernmental fiscal transfers between national and regional government. This chapter examines the methodological differences between the Australian and Japanese systems with a view to encouraging stronger resource strategy and planning in Australian regional government. In Chapter 14 we visit the economics of co-operation and consider two South Australian economic development initiatives, the water industry and the Multi Function Polis. A synthesis of the book is presented in Chapter 15.

Overall, there are many actions that communities can take to influence the growth and development of their region, but to match the pace of other regions and forge ahead requires an intimate knowledge of both the region's own attributes and the external environment. A regional growth path involves a sequence of incremental adjustments responding to a changing set of signals. How well those signals are read and how well a region responds is the key to navigating the path.

Acknowledgments

On behalf of the South Australian Centre for Economic Studies, it is a pleasure to recognise the very substantial financial contribution and support of the South Australian Government to this book incredible patience, support and understanding for a script that was a long time in the making.

Jonathan Pincus, the George Gollin Professor of Economics and Convenor of the Academic Board at Adelaide University and his anonymous associate provided the intellectual guiding hand, and we are most grateful to them for sharing their insights in the making of this book.

Much of the book is built from the experience gained by the Centre in the normal course of undertaking commissioned assignments for government agencies most notably, those agencies in South Australia. Apart from the authors themselves, insights from those experiences were drawn from Janine Molloy, Jim Hancock, Michael O'Neil, Kevin Kirchner and Steve Barrett who are (or were) members of the Centre's research staff.

Finally, warm thanks are extended to Cheree Metcalfe and Velice Langcake who spent many long hours word processing the countless drafts, always smiling and helpful.

Greg Coombs
Adelaide
October 2000

List of Contributors

Rini Budiyanti is a Research Economist at the Centre, and received her PhD in agricultural economics from the Department of Agricultural Economics, Oklahoma State University, USA. Her publications (as an author and co-author) include "Rural Development: Towards an Integrative Policy Framework", *Journal of Regional Analysis and Policy,* Nebraska, USA, Vol. 26, No. 2 , "Measuring Regional Economic and Welfare Impacts of Sport Fishing Expenditures in Oklahoma", in Proceedings of the Sixth International Computable General Equilibrium Modelling Conference, University of Waterloo, Canada, 1995. Dr Rini Budiyanti's expertise and interest are in areas of benefit-cost analysis, input-output analysis and computable general equilibrium modelling.

Greg Coombs is the Managing Director of the South Australian Centre for Economic Studies. He has extensive experience in public finance as a senior public servant in Commonwealth and State government central fiscal agencies and has expertise in public economics and economic development. Apart from managing the Centre, he has overseen and researched many economic assignments including the economic impact of climate change policy, small business tax issues, national competition policy and reform of government enterprises. He has also undertaken APEC economic governance assignments on the Philippines and Thailand.

Anthony Kosturjak is a Research Economist at the Centre. He joined the Centre in January of 1999 after completing his Economics degree at the University of Adelaide (with first class honours). Through his studies he has developed a keen interest in development and environmental economics issues, economic history and international trade. While at the Centre, Anthony has participated in various projects and research covering a wide range of topics including resource, regional and development economics.

Steve Whetton is a Research Economist at the Centre. He gained his Honours Degree in Economics from the University of Adelaide in 1997 and has been working with the Centre since then. His research interests include applied and theoretical macroeconomics, agricultural and resource economics as well as the political economies of East Asia. While at the Centre he has been involved in projects concerning tax, employment and small business policy, econometric analysis and the evaluation of government programs, environmental and agricultural economics and growth theory.

About The Centre

The South Australian Centre for Economic Studies, established in 1983, is a joint research unit of Adelaide University and Flinders University of South Australia.

The Centre operates under a constitution, and the governing body consists of highly respected members of the academic, business and public sector community in South Australia.

The role of the Centre is to provide research and consultancy services of significance to the community on issues where economists can make a valuable contribution. The Centre also produces a regular, three times a year, the *Economic Briefing Report,* for its 80 or so corporate members. This report provides in-depth analysis of South Australia's economic conditions, outlook and medium term issues, in the context of national and international affairs.

Section 1

Factors Influencing the Growth of Small Regional Economies

Chapter One
Small Regional Economies

Regions have always had a role to play, but their role has grown in importance. Global dynamics have changed, and small regions are emerging as the engines of growth. This chapter deals with some preliminaries: definitions of small regions, a brief look at long — run growth of South Australia and, importantly, what is it about globalisation of the world economy that puts the spot light on small regions to rise or fall.

Definition of a Small Regional Economy

The term 'region' does not have a precise meaning. In practice, the actual meaning given to the term is essentially purpose driven. However, in all instances the purpose implies some spatial dimension, based on some set of characteristics common to 'the region' and uncommon or not applicable to "outside the region". Regions rarely coincide neatly with practical jurisdictions. The term 'region' can be applied in an international context to refer to trading partners in a distinctive part of the world economy (such as the Asia Pacific region or the European Community). In a national context a region may be defined by a political power to influence policies and institutions such as the region of Australia. At the sub-national level, the term may be used to refer to a 'state', 'territory', 'province', 'precinct', 'barangay' or 'planning zone' over which a government or its agency has authority. The term may be used to refer to an area on the basis of its pattern of settlement (e.g., metropolitan and non-metropolitan regions) or predominant type of economic activity (e.g., grape growing, forestry, tourism regions). Yet another definition of a region can be given by socio-economic purposes (e.g., income group, ethnic background). In fact you can define a region on many bases.

'Region' is essentially a geographical word, indicating that the globe, or the continent, or the nation, or the State, etc., has been divided into parts according to some principle. For example, 'the Pacific region' (in the international context) consists of all countries lapped by that ocean, or at least the literals of those countries. It is possible to treat each state of Australia as 'a region', but we prefer, as did the South Australian Regional Task Force (SARTF), to consider South Australia as a 'region of regions', each based around some useful distinguishing characteristic. Too crude for our purposes is the popular use of the term "regional South Australia" to refer to all of the non-metropolitan area: non-metropolitan South Australia contains diversity, which can usefully be distinguished.

Different regional economies display considerable diversity in their physical characteristics. Regions vary in their size, location, climate and natural resource endowments. These characteristics essentially represent fixed attributes or givens for particular regions: in contrast to developed attributes such as port facilities or quality of government. Since they can be quite significant influences on a region's opportunity set, the question arises: How do these attributes affect the attractiveness of regions as locations for activity? One of the most distinctive features of patterns of settlement and activity within nations is their extreme unevenness. As Krugman (1991) observes, "Step back and ask, what is the most striking feature of the geography of economic activity? The short answer is surely *concentration*."

Economic geographers and regional economists (Richardson (1972) and Butler and Mandeville (1981)) refer to three different approaches to the definition of a region. In particular: uniform or homogeneous regions; nodal or functional regions; and planning regions. All with the exception of the last definition are operational regions.

A *homogeneous* region is based on the view that areas can be identified according to certain uniform characteristics. These characteristics are determined by the particular interest of the observer, for example, similar production structures, per capita incomes, unemployment levels, common socio-economic characteristics, similar occupational distributions of the labour force, geographical factors such as dominant natural resource, topography or climate. Non-economic criteria are also applied such as uniformity of social attitudes, culture, political outlook or race.

The main problem in defining regions on the basis of homogeneity is that the boundaries of such regions tend to be blurred.

The *nodal* or *functional* region is defined in terms of the interactions or functional linkages between different components within a space. The interactions are measured by flow phenomena, the heaviest flows being to and from the node. In contrast to homogeneous regions, nodal regions consist of heterogenous units, but are bonded with each other, functionally. Examples of the flow phenomena are communications traffic, patterns of journey to work, freight and passenger movements, migration flows, origin of graduates from educational institutions, central location of community facilities.

The main problem with this nodal definition is that determining the controlling centre or nucleus of the nodal region tends to detract from defining the boundary of the region. In addition, even when functionality and interrelationships are clear, dependencies are not. For example, a rural town may be the nucleus of the grape growing region. If the town were eliminated, the region could survive by transporting grapes elsewhere. Conversely if the region were eliminated could the town survive - the flow phenomenon does not alone answer the question of dependency.

Planning regions are defined in terms of the coherence and unity of economic decision making and are normally designated by a particular authority. Such authorities include governments which determine state and local government boundaries and political electorates. If planning regions are defined indiscriminately or the pattern of economic activity changes over time or the controlling authority loses influence over the region (say because of new external factors) then planning decisions will become ineffective and the region as defined becomes irrelevant.

Regions are also defined in terms of *operational* characteristics of service providers, for example, post codes which reflect operational characteristics specific to postal services, and defined also for the collection of data such as the ABS statistical divisions.

In general, the impact of globalisation on regional economies makes it more difficult to identify regional boundaries in a geographic sense. As transport and communications costs decline, the exchange of trade and information from anywhere in the world makes location less important. Globalisation is redefining regions according to the comparative advantages offered. The Barossa Valley reflects a comparative advantage in wine, Silicon Valley reflects a comparative advantage in information technology and the Beneton region in Italy reflects a comparative advantage in art and design in clothing and furniture and so on.

Importantly, comparative advantage cannot be defined if factors of production are mobile. In a classic work, Ohlin (1933) suggested that forces that create regions be put not only on political boundaries, but also on the extent of factor mobility. In the case of the Barossa Valley, the suitability of the soil and climate are important comparative advantages in growing high quality grapes for wine. These factors are immobile, at least until biotechnology masters the growing of grapes in buildings using artificial means. In Silicon Valley, information technology labour is world class and highly mobile. Forces that counter-veil to return these workers in the region are to do with the benefits and synergies of clustering.

Large regions tend to be more influential than small regions, because they have a greater command over economic activity. Small open regional economies:

- are more likely to be price-takers because they do not command a large enough portion of the global market to influence prices;
- tend to specialise in a limited range of competitive outputs because they have a limited range of natural endowments and other relatively immobile factors of production;
- may have a small market for their domestic products because of the relatively small scale of local agglomeration or the demand for local products does not match the needs of the international market;
- exhibit cultural traits enabling the region to complete effectively in some environments but not others (e.g., 'laid-back' Californians of Silicon Valley compared with the 'buttoned-up' New Englanders from Massachusetts influence relative capacities to recognise the need for and respond to change); and
- have regional governments that have diminished influence to create the 'right' conditions for growth and development because of the greater force of external factors.

The smaller is the regional economy, the more likely that the above restrictions will hold, and the fewer are the resources available to those economies to work with to achieve and sustain international competitiveness. However, the preceding statement is a generalisation and tiny regions can sustain international competitiveness. For example, the aboriginal community of Kalumburu, a remote settlement of about 300 people in the Northern coastal region of Western Australia, sells artwork to collectors from Europe who fly-in directly to the settlement to see the exhibits contained in rusty sheds kept by the elder women folk. It is the unique and primitive characteristics of those paintings that determine the comparative advantage of this region.

In defining a region, one is inevitably faced with the problem of the boundary, that is, defining where the boundary lies between one region and another. Some boundaries can be readily defined: the boundary between South Australia and other states of Australia. But other boundaries between regions can be far less clear. Where, for example, does the Adelaide metropolitan region end and the rural area begin. Should the boundary be determined by population density or land use or some other factor, and, if it were determined by the first, then what is the measure of density to be applied.

Boundaries can be dynamic or static. Regions grow and contract, and the structure of economic activity can change. The defining factor will greatly influence the dynamic nature of a boundary - population density, even the boundary of government jurisdictions can change, and in some circumstances, better information and data can influence a boundary.

In general boundaries are purpose-driven: influenced by the operational characteristics of service providers or the particular field of interest. A postcode boundary is suitable for defining and segmenting the operations of Australia Post for the delivery of mail articles, but may not be suitable for assigning a risk category for the purposes of calculating the risk premium to be attached to a motor vehicle policy. Nor is a postcode boundary necessarily suitable for defining metropolitan and non-metropolitan regions. Similarly, the State border between South Australia and Victoria may not be suitable for determining the bounds of the "green triangle". As will be developed in later chapters, a boundary of most interest is the jurisdictional boundary which determines the limits of the influence of government policy and institutions - a major factor influencing the growth of regions.

Regional Development and Regional Growth

Regional development, a broad concept, involves regional communities in improving their economic, social, cultural and environmental well-being by fully utilising the potential of a region's resources including its people. This concept covers all the intrinsic qualities of well being. Regional economic development has been described as dealing with 'policies, programs and ... institutions concerned with encouraging local economic growth and employment which operate at the sub-State or Territory level' (Beer and Maude, 1997). Regional economic development has been thought of as a pre-condition for regional development generally because without sustainable economic activities, regions stand little chance of creating the wealth needed to achieve a higher quality of life. However, economic development will not be captured unless there are the required social, cultural, environmental and other non-economic characteristics of regional communities. To some extent these characteristics feed from each other, and to what extent is a problematic issue both in causation and measurement.

Regions are not independent of extra-regional policies. Although wine typifies both the Barossa Valley region and the Bordeaux region in France, it must be remembered that these regions remain influenced by overlapping policies such as national, state and local taxation as in the Australian case.

Regional economic development requires change to occur before growth occurs. Development implies changes in economic incentives, attitudes and ways of thinking about problems which lead to reorganisation, reform and structural change. As Jones (1987) states "Modern studies do show that development and growth run together, in the sense that structural change is positively associated with income growth".

As discussed in the previous section, regions can be defined according to purpose, and these purposes may change over time. Regions evolve or regional political boundaries are adjusted to reflect changing regimes, which makes regions uncertain vessels into which to pour inter-temporal analysis.

Regional economic growth is a much narrower concept than regional development (although they are often used interchangeably). The most common measure of economic growth is real per capita income where income is either measured by Gross Domestic Product (GDP) or Gross National Product (GNP), and adjusted for inflation. Many researchers including Pomfret (1997) point out that there is a widespread scepticism over whether average per capita income adequately represents the level of economic development. To illustrate the point, by simple per capita income comparisons for 1985, the United Arab Emirates had GDP/capita of $19,627, exceeding all other countries in the world, and about 40 per cent higher than for Australia. Such a ranking does not accord with the popular perception of an economically developed country: United Arab Emirates, an oil producer with a small population, essentially had two sub-economies: wealthy oil producers and peasants.

A problem, for cross-regional comparisons of economic growth, is that the domestic price and exchange rate bases for calculating income are often distorted and hence do not reflect true value. An example will help. Vietnam's real per capita income is about US$400 in 1994 which is only about $^1/_{20}$th of Australia's. This does not imply that the standard of living for the Vietnamese people is only $^1/_{20}$th of that of Australian people. If you take a haircut in Minh Phung Street in the China Town district of Ho Chi Minh City (Saigon) you will pay about 10,000 dong. That's about $1.20 via the market exchange rate. In Adelaide, South Australia, the same haircut using similar pair of scissors and that same glowing smile will cost between $15 and $20. In Vietnam, wage levels and price levels are both lower, and, crudely, their proportional difference is what represents purchasing power. Moreover, the non-traded sector and family 'trading' is a feature of exchange in the Vietnamese economy that extends well beyond haircuts. For traded goods, prices and wages will tend to be equalised in world markets at the currency exchange rates. For non-traded goods, both prices and wages tend to be lower, and the relative difference reflects local productivity. In a normal basket of consumption goods (consisting of both non-traded and traded goods) then exchange rates will understate money income levels. As Pomfret (1997) states, even in market-based economies, the exchange rate tends to overvalue the domestic currency. So, overall, income levels may be adjusted significantly when estimating the domestic units of currency needed to buy as much as a dollar buys in the United States, that is, by adjusting for Purchasing Power Parity (PPP). Temple (1999) observes, in the case of India, that relative income is improved by a factor of two and a half meaning that, as a proportion of US per capita income, India is closer to 5 per cent under PPP calculations rather than the 2 per cent indicated by exchange rate-based comparisons. The Viet-Australia and India-US comparisons are fairly stark. The intra-regional story in South Australia is much less so (to some albeit unknown extent), and partially explains why income levels in country regions are lower than those of metropolitan regions.

Another problem is that income per capita figures cover only the formal economy. The informal economy may be substantial, but we do not know the size. The informal economy consists of illegal transactions, barter and consumption of own produce. During the depths of the 1997 South East Asian economic crisis, children in North Eastern villages of Thailand were engaged to receive opium from growers across the border in Cambodia. The incomes from this trade enabled the children to buy survival goods (CIE and Coombs, 1999), but such transactions were illegal and therefore not recorded in the GDP figures of either country. The opium trade over the South Australian borders is somewhat less lively, but the barter trade between families and neighbours in country South Australia is still important - less so for survival but more for sociable activity. As a worker in local fish processing factory at Streaky Bay in the late 1960s, I observed fish process in a workers receiving base rate minimum wages for on-call and overtime work and the 'top-up' wage came in lashings of filleted whiting and crustaceans. Consumption of own-production is also important. The largest own-consumption activities are owner-occupied housing and home management (child care, cooking, cleaning, gardening, etc.), and particularly in rural regions own-consumption of food and beverage production is important. The informal economy is larger in poorer regions than wealthy regions, and that the trade fluctuates with economic cycles. This tends to overstate the gap between the wealthy and poor, but we do not know by how much. Nonetheless, income per capita is a widely used measure because it is simple, and PPP is a research-intensive procedure not without its problems.

High per capita income levels in aggregate for a region indicate the potential for high living standards. But high standards of living for individuals in the region depend on access to incomes, which depends on the distributive mechanisms which in turn depend on a broad array of factors including cultural interpretations of social equity, wages policy, systems of property ownership etc. In other words, high per capital income figures may disguise inequity in the region.

The United Arab Emirates is no longer the leading country on the basis of per capita income, the fall from the number one rank reflects a fall in oil prices during the mid 1990s, and more particularly, an inability to develop an alternative industries exhibiting a comparative advantage that could fill the gap when ail prices fluctuate. This is an uncomfortable signal to those regional economies that rely on a narrow range of commodities.

Table 1.1
OECD Countries — GDP Ranking's

Country	Ranking	
	GDP/Capita (1994)	GDP/Hour (1992)
Australia	12	14
Canada	7	9
France	8	1
Germany	5	5
Japan	3	17
New Zealand	16	6
United Kingdom	15	12
United States	1	2

Source: Gruen (1996), page 369.

Finally, to illustrate how fragile are the ranking's of countries on a narrow concept like GSP per capita, let us consider, as Gruen (1996) has, changing the denominator from GDP per head to GDP per hours worked. This might be regarded as a crude measure of quality of life because fewer hours at work are more hours available for non-pecuniary activities such as "smelling the roses". A striking feature of the comparison between rankings is the change for France and Japan. It would seem that if the French spent less time in bed, then their economy could be first, instead of eighth, or putting it the other way around, the French enjoy a higher quality of life because they work fewer hours a week. In contrast, the Japanese are at the other end of the spectrum. Japan falls from 3rd to 17th, taking into account the very long hours worked. Australia's ranking slips a little on the basis of hours worked: Australians work longer hours than the 'average' OECD country member. If the recent survey on Australia is any guide (The Economist, 2000), Australia may have slipped a little further down the ladder -"Australians may still be better than most at enjoying themselves, but they have less time for their pleasures, and sometimes 'mateship' loses out in the struggle up the greasy pole".

Long Term Trends in Economic Growth

There is no doubting the importance of growth. As Barro and Sala-i-Martin (1995) point out, to appreciate the consequences of apparently small differentials in the rate of growth when compounded over long periods of time, consider what the world's leading country the US would have looked like under different growth rates assumptions. The average annual growth rate in GDP/capita between 1870 and 1990 for the US was 1.75 per cent. If the growth rate instead has been 0.75 per cent, that is 1 percentage point less, the US real per capita GDP in 1990 would have ranked 37th out of 127 countries and been similar to Mexico, Hungary and less than Portugal and Greece: a 'world' of difference. To bring this point a little closer to home, consider Australia. In 1870, Australia's per capita income was $3,143 in 1985 prices and the average annual growth rate between 1870 and 1990 was 1.22 per cent. At this rate of growth, Australia's rank fell from the highest income country to 9th followed by Japan, Finland and Denmark.[1] Others might rank differently according to the methodology applied. For instance Barro and Sala-i-Martin (1995), adopting data from Maddison, ranked Australia 12th behind Japan, Denmark and Finland. If the average annual long term growth rate had been about 1.47 per cent, just slightly more than the actual rate, then Australia would have retained its number one status. If the average Australian annual growth rate had been 1 per cent less, then real per capita GDP in 1990 would only be $4,101 and would be keeping company with Czechoslovakia, Brazil and Fiji.

By way of further contextual information, some stylised facts about economic growth of countries and regions are as follows.

Constant Growth

Per capita output grows over time, and its growth rate does not tend to diminish. Kaldor (1961) and Barro and Sala-i-Martin (1995) support this view. Their data suggests that for 16 developed countries, the average per capita growth rate has been 1.9 per cent per year over roughly a century and for 15 less developed countries the growth rate has been 1.4 per cent over a similar period. Pomfret (1997) supports this trend and notes that the world economic growth rate in the second half of the twentieth century has been much more rapid than in the previous era. As Barro and Sala-i-Martin (1995) point out, growth of the developed economies has slowed between 1970 and 1990 to 2.2 per cent compared with what the authors call the great productivity slow down; but the slowing was from an unprecedentedly - high rate. Nordhaus (2000) supports the importance of higher living standards. "Hence the economic value of improvements in living standards due to deduced mortality is 40 per cent of [US] consumption over the period [1975 - 1995], or about 2 per cent per year".

1 Penn World Tables.

A brief diversion is warranted here as Australia is an atypical case, as Table 1.2 shows.

Table 1.2
Long Term Growth Data - Australia

Year	GDP/Capita (1985 $US)	Population (Millions)	Ratio to US GDP/Capita	Annual Growth Rate of GDP/ Capita (%)(1)
1870	3,143	1.62	1.40	n.a.
1890	3,949	3.11	1.27	1.14
1910	4,615	4.38	1.02	0.78
1930	3,963	6.47	0.70	-0.76
1950	5,970	8.18	0.69	2.05
1970	9,747	12.51	0.76	2.45
1990	13,514	17.81	0.74	1.63

Source: Barro and Sala-i-Martin (1995), p. 364.
Note: (1) Over 20 year intervals.

In 1870, Australia's GDP/capita was the highest in the world, and exceeded the United States GDP/capita by about 40 per cent. Australia's high incomes reflected resource abundance spread among a small population. At that time, Canada's GDP/capita was only about $^1/_3$ of Australia's. By 1910 the United States had caught up, achieving growth through mass production of homogenous products based on comparative advantages in natural resources, particularly minerals for strategic modern industries, and superior corporate organisational structures. Over the twenty years to 1930, and particularly during the depression years, Australia was hit hard, recording a contraction in per capita incomes, unlike the other 16 developed countries which managed moderate growth rates over the same period. Australia recorded solid growth rates from 1950 to the 1990s, but it did not match the pace of other developed countries. By 1990, Australia's GDP/capita was only about $^3/_4$ of the United States and lower than Canada, West Germany, Sweden, Switzerland, and probably lower than Japan and Norway, and ranking approximately 8th or 9th out of 122 countries.

Reflecting on the point made earlier that GDP/capita measure does not tell the whole story, McLean and Pincus (1983) conclude, using alternative measures, that Australian living standards did not stagnate between 1890 and 1940. Increases in life expectancy, a shorter working week, earlier retirement were all substantial improvements in living standards not directly reflected in the measured GDP. Conservatively they estimate that living standards may have doubled over the half-century.

Table 1.3
Real Income World Ranking, 1990

Country	Real GDP/Capita (1985)	Rank	Real GNP/Capita (current Int. Prices) (1990)	Rank
USA	18,054	1	21,827	1
Canada	17,173	2	20,752	2
Switzerland	16,505	3	20,729	3
Luxembourg	16,201	4	19,636	4
Norway	14,902	5	16,345	19
Hong Kong	14,849	6	17,431	9
Sweden	19,762	7	18,029	6
W. Germany	14,628	8	18,600	5
Australia	14,445	9	17,517	8
Japan	14,331	10	17,625	7
Finland	14,059	11	17,080	11
Denmark	13,909	12	17,217	10
France	13,904	13	16,956	12
Iceland	13,362	14	16,293	15
Belgium	13,232	15	16,533	13
UK	13,217	16	15,741	16
Netherlands	13,029	17	16,096	19
Austria	12,695	18	15,560	18
Italy	12,488	19	15,307	19
Singapore	11,710	20	14,389	20

Source: Penn World Tables; 1990 data.

Convergence or Divergence

There is considerable debate over the issue of whether poor countries are catching up with rich counties. In (neoclassical) theory, if all economies were intrinsically the same except for their starting capital intensities, then convergence would apply in an absolute sense. Temple (1999) concluded that poor countries are not catching up with the rich countries, and to some extent, the international income distribution is becoming polarised. This is not to suggest that there have not been notable exceptions such as Korea, Botswana, Hong Kong, Taiwan, Singapore and Japan which have over the last 30 years made the transition from lower middle income to high income countries. But there have been many disasters also. Former USSR countries have experienced a contraction over the past 25 years and most of sub-Saharan Africa and Eastern Europe have barely registered positive growth. The United Nations

Development Programme (UNDP) and other international aid agencies seize on these observations to stem the declining availability of aid funding and urge more effort to improve pro-poor policies.

Barro (1997) suggests, in his more moderate view, that there is evidence of conditional convergence. The growth rates of advanced economies are tending to cluster, but the less developed economies do not appear to be experiencing such a pattern. Something is holding them back. If economies differ in various respects - including propensities to save and have children, willingness to work, access to technology and government policies - then the convergence force applies only in a conditional sense.

However, Henderson (1999) is very critical of the UNDP's position of the economic performance of countries. In the table below, Henderson shows that over the past 25 years, more than half of the world's population has resided in countries experiencing growth rates of about 2 per cent or better. The proportion of the world population experiencing income growth is unprecedented.

Table 1.4
Per Capita Growth - Sectors of the World Economy, 1973-1998

Sector (No of countries)	Average Annual Compound Growth Rate	Percentage Share	
		World GDP	World Population
Western Europe (12)	1.75	17.9	5.5
Western Offshoots (4)	1.66	23.4	5.5
Japan	2.28	8.0	2.2
Western Europe Periphery (17)	2.12	2.7	1.1
China	5.40	11.2	21.1
India	2.91	4.9	16.5
Other Dynamic Asia (7)	4.41	7.8	6.2
Sub-Total	**n.a.**	**75.9**	**58.1**
Sluggish Asia (31)	1.47	2.6	9.8
Latin America (44)	0.93	8.8	8.5
Middle East (16)	0.49	4.0	3.8
Eastern Europe (12)	0.34	2.0	2.1
Africa (57)	0.04	3.3	12.7
Former USSR (15)	-1.84	3.5	5.0
World Total	**1.25**	**100.0**	**100.0**

Source: Henderson (1999).

Finally, as discussed earlier, much of the debate about growth turns on the basis of measurement. As Castles (1999) points out, if you take the UNDP Human Development Report for 1999 and re-express real incomes in terms of purchasing power (PPP) instead of GDP then the experience of poor countries is not so bleak: the ratio of PPP income of the richest $^{1}/_{5}$th countries to the poorest $^{1}/_{5}$th counties has fallen since 1990.

At the regional level within countries, the evidence in favour of convergence is stronger. Barro and Sala-i-Martin (1995) consider convergence of US regions (47 states or territories), European regions (90 regions across 8 countries), Canada (12 provinces or territories) and Japan (47 prefectures). The econometric studies show that the poor regions of these countries tend to grow faster per capita than the rich ones and that convergence is absolute. Unfortunately, unpublished research work by the SA Centre for Economic Studies concluded that there is insufficient data to produce econometrically reliable results to test for convergence between South Australia and the other Australian States. However, available data on South Australia's growth rates has been reproduced below. The trend would suggest that convergence is not apparent although there is a strong correlation in the fluctuations. That is, South Australia tends to follow Australia's ups and downs, with the downs being relatively more severe for South Australia, and the ups being not so strong. Consequently the average rate of growth over the 130 years since 1870 is lower in South Australia by about 0.4 per cent per annum compared with the whole-of-Australia average. This does not sound significant, but it is. If South Australia had matched the pace of Australia over that time then GSP would have been $63,095 million compared with $40,493 million actually achieved by 1999. In per capita terms that gap is $15,138 per head.

Economists' theories of what makes economies grow have suffered many set backs, and there are many problems with data sets. However, the empirical evidence suggests that, with some notable exceptions, the poor countries seem to be making some progress to catching up to the rich ones. At the regional level, the empirical evidence is more positive: regions within developed countries are converging, but again there are some notable exceptions. This suggests that there are some persistent problems which are holding back poorer countries and under-performing regions in developed countries. What those problems might be is the topic of the rest of this book. However, before turning to this, the remainder of this chapter offers some insight to whether or not regions can take action to catch up and stay ahead in the growth race.

Table 1.5
Real GDP Levels and Growth Rates - South Australia and Australia, 1881 to 1999

Year	Real GSP/GDP ($ Million) (1997-98=100)		Annual Growth Rate (Per Cent)	
	South Australia	Australia	South Australia	Australia
1870	757	7,100	-	-
1880	1,711	11,627	8.49	5.06
1890	1,621	17,105	-0.54	3.94
1900	1,826	18,715	1.20	0.90
1910	2,844	27,296	4.53	3.85
1920	3,035	26,120	0.35	-0.44
1930	2,297	33,910	-2.75	2.64
1940	4,665	56,252	7.53	5.24
1950	6,630	83,525	3.63	4.04
1960	9,110	129,063	4.15	4.45
1970	16,739	223,885	5.27	5.52
1980	22,266	294,777	2.73	2.88
1990	33,441	440,584	4.15	4.10
1999	40,493	591,546	2.15	3.33
Average	n.a.	n.a.	**3.13**	**3.49**

Note: Using 1880 as the starting year, the average rate of growth over 120 years would be lower in South Australia by 0.7 per cent per annum. If South Australia had grown at the same rate as Australia, GSP would have been $87,064 million. The per capita gap is $31,192 per person.

Source: Vamplew, W. et al, (1984 and 1987), Maddison (1995), and SACES calculations.

Can Small Regional Economies Influence Their Growth

Throughout this book we will return to one of the most fundamental questions about regional growth and development: to what extent do small regional economies steer their own boat and to what extent do they just ride the currents of economic change. If the answer is the former then what are oars - the characteristics, policies and processes - that effect gains for their own communities.

Evidence about the capacity of small regions to engage in policies to promote growth and respond to changes in the external environment is a theme of this book. Without such an affirmative position then discussion about factors that influence growth has no carriage for formulation of regional policy. If small regions can change their course of direction and move against the economic tide of the nation then clearly the mechanisms for economic growth must be available and working effectively. Given that there are further chapters in this book, then the authors clearly believe that there is scope for collective regional action to influence their destiny, but there has at least been some doubt about this. For the time being, some general evidence is presented to give the reader some reassurance that oars are available to influence regional outcomes which will be re-enforced and clarified in later chapters.

Research on growth policies for sub-regional economies nearly died out in the 1970s after Musgrave (1959) and Oates (1972) almost convincingly argued that sub-national governments have no appropriate role in these policies, with the implication being that sub-national governments could do nothing to stimulate growth in their regions.

The conventional wisdom, forcefully put by Oates (1968, 1972), was that central government can best resolve the stabilisation and distribution problems. The main arguments were presented to support this view are:

- sub-national government fiscal policy for both tax and expenditure programs is not capable of influencing growth because of the highly open structure of sub-national economies;
- cyclical economic conditions tend to be parallel in highly interdependent sub-national areas, so cyclical movements become mostly national in scope;
- sub-national governments do not have access to monetary policy, an important tool for economic stabilisation and growth;
- high labour and capital mobility can offset the benefits of state development policies; and
- central control of the growth and stabilisation function is necessary to ensure proper co-ordination of policies.

Support for regionally based growth policies can be traced to Engerman (1971) in which he argued that national stabilisation policies would have widely different effects on sub-national regions depending on the industry structure, economic diversity, and trend growth rate in the region. Engerman also indicated that sub-national employment policies could be more effective in reducing employment than comparable policies applied on a nationwide scale.

During the past several years the conventional wisdom has been questioned, initially by Gramlich (1987) and Fisher (1993), and more recently by Fox and Murray (1997) and Fisher (1999). Fox and Murray draw on the empirical evidence of these studies and, in general, they argue that the points above are either invalid or are equally true at both the sub-national and national levels.

Openness of State Economies: Fiscal policy multipliers (and the impact of regional fiscal policy) are argued to be small because sub-national economies are very open. Gramlich (1987) determines that the propensity to spend on interstate produced items in the United States is low in many States (e.g., California).

Linkages Between Regional Cycles: State impacts of national shocks may not be correlated. For example, oil price shocks being a win for producers and a loss for non-producers. Econometric evidence using employment data Marston (1985), Ziegler (1972) indicate that growth patterns are materially different from region to region.

Factor Flows: Labour migration could offset the need for stabilisation policy. Marston (1985) results indicate that migration to higher wage areas should not necessarily be expected because higher wages are intended as compensation to keep workers from migrating from the high unemployment that often characterises these areas. The conclusion is that cycles are long because the migration of unemployed workers from high unemployment rate areas to low unemployment rate areas operates very slowly.

Co-ordination of Fiscal Policy: Fox and Murray do not seem to offer much by way of a counter-argument, other than to say that national governments may not be effective in implementing national stabilisation policies.

Regional Monetary Policy Effects: Carlino and De Fina (1996) give three reasons why monetary policy can be expected to have a different effect across regions: 1) mix of interest-sensitive industries (manufacturing and construction); 2) small banks find it more difficult to obtain attention sources of funding during periods of tight monetary policy, i.e., mix of small banks within regions; and 3) small borrowers are more likely to use banks as their lending source - mix of small borrowers.

In the South Australian context, the key practical issues are the degree of the openness of the economy and the mobility of resources. Measures presented in section 2 of this book suggest that there is some scope for effective regional policy. Regions can have unique cyclical conditions and regional governments may want to do something about it, but they need to be aware of their limitations and that they may do better to focus more on medium term structural pre-conditions for growth.

There has also been much public debate at the policy level over the role of regions in economic development. The broad policy position might be summed up by suggesting that the promotion of economic development is a major objective of all governments, and all three tiers of government are significant players in Australia. The contemporary debate is over the extent to which sub-national governments should move beyond the establishment of a sound economic policy and regulatory framework and the efficient provision of essential social and physical infrastructure to a more active role in promoting development by industry.

There are serious doubts about the role of industry assistance policy in achieving conventional targets of regional growth. The Industry Commission study, *State, Territory and Local Government Assistance to Industry* (1996) expressed serious reservations about one of the most popular forms of regional development policy, namely, selective industry assistance. The principal issue was that regional governments tend to lose sight of the fact that the allocation of resources to industry assistance has an opportunity cost in that these resources could have been used for some other (more) beneficial purpose. There were other reasons cited: mis-specification or mis-assessment of the net benefits of the assistance; lack of clarity about the regional objectives of the assistance initiatives; potential to create unfavourable public perceptions about the government processes; lack of transparency; disproportionately large share of project risks falling to the public sector; and length and cost of the process for assessing assistance, potential for inequitable treatment, the capacity to create incentives for lobby groups. Giesecke and Madden (1997) present empirical evidence on the small regional economy of Tasmania using computable general equilibrium modelling techniques. They show that the use of fiscal or industry assistance instruments lifts GSP by only minor amounts even when large assistance packages, relative to the tax base, are involved. National microeconomic reform policies were found to provide a relatively stronger regional stimulus than industry assistance packages, although other studies indicate that results may vary depending on the structure of small regional economies. The Industry Commission's study also reported on the problem of competitive bidding for industry attraction to the point of arguing that such practices be outlawed. However, Groenewold and Hagger (1997) use modelling techniques to show that its possible for States to gain an economic advantage by engaging in competitive bidding with the very important proviso that they play the game sensibly.

The abandonment of the Commonwealth Regional Development Programme in the 1996-97 Budget because of the absence of a 'clear rationale' for Commonwealth involvement in regional development was further expression of doubt about the usefulness of regionally based development policies. However, the Commonwealth is now reconsidering its role in regional policy. At the State and Territory level, most governments are also placing greater emphasis on regional development policy and strategy.

Government's interests may be largely driven by the rise in community concern about the economic and social issues facing regional communities, evidenced by significant disparities within and between regions such as those reflected in the nicknames of 'rust belt' and 'sun belt' regions. Poverty and disadvantage are geographically concentrated in the nation's rural areas and outer suburbs of major cities.

In addition to the swell of public opinion, there is also emerging a common understanding of the active role that regions can play in facilitating economic development. Firstly, there is the realisation that regional development is not the exclusive province of government, but the interaction between business, community and government. There is a reconfirmation that each player contributes directly (rather than passively through taxes) to development, as the benefits are shared throughout the region by the trade linkages and that each player has the capacity to contribute including, importantly, the capacity to take a leadership role. Secondly, there is the recognition that the true competition for a region is other regions which shift the incentives away from local firms competing locally for government assistance unless the region as a whole benefits. Thirdly, regions tend to have common interests and aspirations in production - not necessary homogeneous, but related - which facilitates stronger networking and organisation to respond to the external environment.

Globalisation and Regionalism

Most importantly, the dynamics are changing. Globalisation is a term describing the progressive spread and intensification of economic, social and cultural exchange between countries. Industries and enterprises increasingly transcend national boundaries guided by best available markets for inputs and outputs as well as compatible political regimes.

In respect of the economic aspects of globalisation, there remains debate over the importance of the impact on regionalism and the role of the nation-states. However, there is evidence that globalisation is driving the intensification of regionalism and diminishing the role of nation-states (see, for example, Bergsten (1997), Sideri (1996) and Ohmae (1995)). Nonetheless the question of the impact of globalisation warrants some analysis.

The growing interconnection between countries consists of two elements. The first element can be called intensified interdependence, that is, a growth of imports and exports between countries. The second element involves a qualitative shift towards an integrated world economy that is no longer based on autonomous nation-states. Instead there is a consolidated global market-place for production, distribution and consumption. This market dominates the numerous national economies contained within it (Hirst and Thompson, 1992). The two aspects of economic globalisation are illustrated in diagram 1.1.

As the diagram suggests there is no argument about whether or not globalisation is happening. But the extent of the intensification of interdependence versus the degree of the qualitative shift of the market integration remains open to debate.

Three perspectives over the impact of economic globalisation on regionalism and the consequent importance of the role of the nation-states are:

- economic liberals: see evidence of a strong qualitative shift, so it is now "possible to produce a product anywhere, using the resources from anywhere, by a company located anywhere, to be sold anywhere" (Friedman, 1993). Under this view, globalisation means that the nation-state disintegrates to smaller and more numerous components each representing a cluster of communities or regions with common 'tribal' identities (e.g., language, culture) and comparative advantage;

- mercantilists: see little evidence of the qualitative shift towards a global economic system, but see an intensification of interdependence between countries. They reject the claim that corporations have lost their national identity (see Reich, 1992) and support the view that corporations remain closely linked to their countries of origin. Mercantilists argue that the economic liberals fail to take account of the increased capacity of nation-states to respond to the challenges of economic globalisation. Technological developments that foster globalisation have helped increase the state's capacity for regulation, surveillance and to tax citizens; and
- neo-Marxists, such as Cox (1994), view economic globalisation as having both intensified interdependence and involved a qualitative shift to a new global economy. The nation-states are losing power over the economy, but instead of fragmenting, they are forming much larger macro-regions driven by a need to exercise global military power backed up with economic strength. The macro-regions, the most important of which is the USA, in the Americas, Japan in East Asia, and the European Union are the new political-economic frameworks of capital accumulation. Globalisation is seen as a form of capitalism because it perpetuates the hierarchy of class domination and the expropriation of the natural and human resources of weaker countries and the power of peoples. The neo-Marxists also stress the uneven nature of regional development, and the increasing concentration and convergence of the leading industrialised countries.

The debate over the effects of economic globalisation on regional economic development will be influenced heavily by the course of future events, particularly through the impact of technological change and measures by nation-states to liberalise trade and finance. Empirical evidence tends to support strongly the intensification of trade, and there is some, but much weaker, evidence that global trade is becoming more integrated and progressively weakening the nation-states.

From diagram 1.1 there is no doubt that there is 'more or the same': global exports have risen dramatically between 1985 and 1997, and that the developed countries have maintained their share of the world export market. The 'qualitative shift' is less apparent. Using US trade figures, exports from US non-bank firms to their foreign affiliates are over one third of total US exports. Thus intra-firm exports are very important component of exports, but, surprisingly, the proportion has not grown over time. Similarly, imports from US non-bank firms from their foreign affiliates represent about 40 per cent of all US imports, but that level stagnated between 1977 and 1989.

Particularly with the intra-firm trade data there are limitations and problems, and therefore the data must be regarded as indicative only. The best definition would reflect the level of control and ownership. There is also the problem of transfer pricing, and the obvious issue that the data is now ten years old.

Diagram 1.1
Economic Globalisation - Global Exports and Intra-Firm Trade

Economic Globalisation	**More of the Same**	**Indicator: Global Exports - US$**		
		1985	**1990**	**1997**
		1,606.3	2,848.5	5,490.4
		Indicator: Percentage of Global Exports from Developed Countries		
		1985	**1990**	**1997**
		63.6	65.5	65.6
	Qualitative Shift	**Indicator: Intra-Firm Trade (as % of total US Trade)**		
		Exports		
		1977	**1982**	**1989**
		35.8	33.1	33.5
		Imports		
		1977	**1982**	**1989**
		39.5	36.7	41.4

Source: United Nations (1999) and OECD (1993, page 18).

Returning for a closer look at the economic liberalists' view, they would argue that the reason for the rise of regionalisation is basic. The volume of trade between countries is negatively related to the economic distance between them. Economic distance consists of geographic distance (reflecting transport costs, time zone limitations etc.), plus trade barriers. The liberalisation of trade through global integration of markets makes geographic distance, which is purely regional specific, the more important determinant of cost-competitiveness. Trade barriers are country and/or product specific not region specific. Removal of trade barriers exposes the remaining factors determining comparative advantage and these factors tend to be specific to the region. Trade barriers are broader than tariffs and the integration of markets involves compatible transport systems, standardised customs entry, comparable standards for packaging and quality and, at progressively deeper levels, the surrender of national sovereignty on commercial and property law procedures for dispute resolution, common monetary systems and compatible systems of government (e.g., trading with non-capitalist regimes).

Another factor intensifying the importance of regions is the declining cost of transport and communications. Lower costs have taken the importance of location out of regions - brought them closer together - which has greatly improved the accessibility of markets to firms and increasing the tradeability of a wider range of goods and services. Progressively, regional competitiveness relies on the attributes of the products of the region, not on distance to the market.

New information technologies and telecommunications have reduced the cost of information but, more importantly have greatly improved the quantum and speed of access to information. This has enabled more complex and time sensitive transactions. On these bases, the OECD (1998) states that the intensity of markets for knowledge, technology and the capacity to innovate are driving economic growth. Regions that are able to provide a suitable environment and structure of incentives for these drivers will prosper. As Henton, Melville and Walesh (1997, p. 11) point out, it is not clear where new information technologies will lead us, but what is clear, is that the information revolution has a decentralising power that makes regions - and relationships that link players within regions - more and more important.

Globalisation is an uneven process, reflecting the differential pace of change across different countries. The capacity of a region to embrace the opportunity globalisation offers reflects the length of the adjustment period and the significance of the reduction in trade barriers, both in terms of the size of the reduction and the relevance to the regions' range of products. Multilateral removal of barriers will reduce the cost of the regions' inputs or replace regionally produced inputs with foreign inputs.

Changes in consumer tastes are also working to raise the importance of regions. Throughout the 20th century, mass production has been the means of achieving low cost production. Economies of scale has ruled. However, at least in developed economies, real incomes have risen which provided the means for communities to experience the benefits of diversity and variety and these experiences have permeated the tastes of consumers, and their propensity to seek out new experiences. Niche markets, boutique services are growing strongly. One of the fastest growing industries in South Australia in the mid to late 1990s is the local bakery. The variety of breads has exploded. The community demands variety, even in the most basic of consumables. Smaller production runs, with a broader array of items is becoming more and more important. Regions no longer need to mass produce to reach lowest possible costs. They do not need a large domestic market. Higher cost, shorter production runs are viable so long as the producer can convince consumers that the quality or uniqueness of the product can justify a higher price.

Regions are emerging as the natural units of competition, defined less by the economies of scale in production, but rather by their ability to match the changing and diverging tastes of consumers through smaller production runs and at the same time offer at low cost a co-hesive environment for production and meeting community needs. A region, more than a nation-state, tends to:

- have a clearer identity which is both distinct from other regions and is not defined arbitrarily by a border;
- produce an array of products that tend to be related by the combination of inputs, production processes or interlinked by complementarity; and
- are networked locally and with the international market but with fewer points of contact than for nation-states, which means that cooperation and collaboration are more likely to form and are less likely to break down. The network facilitates the exchange of information and response to the external environment.

The Challenge: Finding the Path, Matching the Pace

Small regional economies can be defined in many ways - by borders, common socio-economic characteristics or common products and are a geographical expression that is purpose driven. Small regions tend to be heavily influenced by the external environment.

Regional economic development is a broad expression reflecting not just growth of incomes, but the quality of life. Although difficult to measure, this concept embraces health, learning, experience, variety, work and leisure quality, security and confidence about the future.

World economic growth has tended to be stable at around 2 per cent per annum over most of the 20th century. There is debate over whether the poor countries are catching up to the rich countries, but this is considerable evidence that sub-regions within countries are converging.

Australia has not matched the pace of economic change over the past 130 years since 1870, when Australia was the world's richest economy in per capita terms. South Australia has not kept pace with Australia. Although a broadly affluent society, South Australia has limited levers to pull to effect the catch up process, but small regional policies can make a difference. Targeted industry assistance is not the answer. Mirco-economic reform policies are a stronger stimulus, but most importantly regions need to recognise that the global dynamics are changing.

Regions are emerging as the natural units of competition, defined less by the economies of scale in production but rather by an ability to match the changing and diverging tastes of consumers through small production runs of specialised products.

There is an overwhelming sense that small regional economies are being increasingly exposed to powerful external factors. Regions will need to assess the impact of global forces on them. They must charter a course, find a new passage to growth by building on their regional advantages and hope that they are smart and nimble enough to survive and prosper in a rapidly changing global environment.

References

Barro, R.J. (1993), *Macroeconomics,* Wiley, New York.

Barro, Robert J. (1997), *Determinants of Economic Growth: A Cross-Country Empirical Study.* The MIT Press, Massachusetts, London, England.

Barro, Robert J. and Sala-i-Martin, X. (1995), *Economic Growth,* McGraw-Hill, New York.

Beer, A. and Maude, A. (1997), *Effectiveness of State Frameworks for Local Economic Development,* Prepared for the Local Government Association of South Australia, Adelaide.

Bergsten, C.F. (1997), "Open Regionalism", Institute for International Economics, Working Paper 97-3.

Butler, G.J. and Mandeville, T.D. (1981), *Regional Economics: An Australian Introduction,* University of Queensland Press, St. Lucia, Queensland.

Castles, I. (1999), *Facts and Fancies of Human Development,* Academy of Social Sciences in Australia, Symposium on 8 November 1999.

Carlino, G.A. and De Fina, R.H. (1996), "Does Monetary Policy Have Differential Effects?", *Business Review,* Federal Reserve Bank of Philadelphia, March/April, pp. 17-27.

Centre for International Economics and Coombs, G. (1999), *Impact of the Asia Crisis on Children: Issues for Social Safety Nets,* August, Commonwealth of Australia, AusAID Special APEC Governance Papers.

Cox, R.W. (1992), *Towards a Post-Hegemonic Conceptualisation of World Order: Reflections on the Relevancy of Ilon Khaldun,* in Governance without Government: Order and Change in World Politics, eds. J.N. Rosenaw and E.-O. Czempial, Cambridge University Press, Cambridge, pp. 132-59.

Engerman, S.L. (1971), *The Reinterpretation of American Economic History,* e.d. by Fogel, R.W. and Engerman, S.L., Harper and Row, New York.

Ethier, W. J. (1998), "The New Regionalism", *The Economic Journal,* July.

Fisher, R.C. (1993), "Macroeconomic Implications of Subnational Fiscal Policy: The Overseas Experience", in *Vertical Fiscal Imbalance and the Allocation of Taxing Powers,* ed. D.J. Collins, Tax Research Foundation, Sydney Australia.

Fisher, R.C. (1999), *Intergovernmental Fiscal Relations*, Kluwer Academic Publishers, Boston.

Friedman, M. (1993), *Why Government is the Problem*, Stanford University, Stanford, California.

Fox, W.F. and Murray, M.N. (1997), "Intergovernmental Aspects of Growth and Stabilisation Policy", in *Intergovernmental Fiscal Relations*, ed. R.C. Fisher.

Giesecke, J.A.D and Madden, J.R. (1997), "Regional Government Economic Policy: Assessing the Policy Instruments", *Australasian Journal of Regional Studies*, Vol. 2, No. 1.

Gramlich, E. M. (1987), *Sub-National Fiscal Policy, Perspective's on Local Public Finance and Public Policy*, Volume 3.

Groenewold, N. and Hagger, A.J. (1997), Competitive Bidding and the States: Winners and Losers, *Australasian Journal of Regional Studies*, Vol. 3, No. 1.

Gruen, F. (1996), "The Quality of Life and Economic Performance", in *Dialogues on Australia's Future*, ed. P. Sheehan, B. Grewal, and M. Kumnick. Centre for Strategic Economic Studies, Victoria University.

Henderson, David (2000), "Facts and Fancies of Human Development", *Academy of Social Sciences*, Occasional Paper 1/2000, May.

Henton, D., Melville, J. and Walesh, K. (1997), *Grassroots Leaders for a New Economy*, Jossey-Bass Inc.

Hirst, P. and Thompson, G. (1992) "The Problem of Globalisation", *International Economic Relations*, National Management and the Formation of Trading Blocs, Economy and Society, 21/4, pp. 357-94.

Industry Commission (1996), *State, Territory and Local Government Assistance to Industry*, Canberra, APS, (draft).

Jones, C.A. (1987), *International Business in the Nineteenth Century: The Rise and Fall of a Cosmopolitan Bourgeosie*, Wheatsheaf, Prizhaton, Sussex.

Kaldor. N. (1961), "Capital Accumulation and Economic Growth", in *The Theory of Capital*, eds. F.A. Lutz and D.C. Hague, New York: St Martins.

Krugman, Paul R. (1991), *Geography and Trade*, MIT Press, Cambridge Massachusetts, Leuven University Press, Leuven Belgium.

McLean, I.W., and Pincus, J.J. (1983), "Did Australian Living Standards Stagnate between 1890 and 1940?", *Journal of Economic History*, March, Volume XLIII.

Maddison, Angus (1995), *Monitoring the World Economy 1920-1992,* Development Centre of the Organisation for Economic Co-operation and Development.

Marston, T. (1985), "Two Views of the Geographic Distribution of Unemployment", *Quarterly Journal of Economic,* February.

Musgrave, Richard A. (1959), *The Theory of Public Finance: A Study in Public Economics,* McGraw Hill, New York.

Nordhaus, W., (2000), *New Directions in National Economic Accounting,* American Economic Association Papers and Proceedings, May.

Oates, W. E. (1968), "The Theory of Public in a Federal System", *Canadian Journal of Economics,* February.

Oates, W. E. (1972), *Fiscal Federalism,* Harcourt Bruce Jovanovich, New York.

Ohlin, B. (1933), *Interregional and International Trade,* Cambridge, Harvard U.P.

Ohmae, K. (1995), *The End of the Nation State: The Rise of Regional Economies,* The Free Press.

Organisation for Economic Co-operation and Development (OECD) (1993), *Intra-Firm Trade,* Trade Policy Issues, Number 1, Paris.

OECD (1998), "Technology, Productivity and Job Creation", *The OECD Job Strategy,* Paris.

Pomfret, Richard W.T. (1997), *Development Economics,* Prentice Hall, London, New York.

Reich, R. (1992), *The Work of Nations: Preparing Ourselves for the 21st Century Capitalisation,* Vintage, New York.

Richardson, Harry W. (1972), *Input-Output and Regional Economy,* Wiley, New York.

Sala-i-Martin, X and Barro, R.J. (1995), *Technological Diffusion, Convergence and Growth,* Economic Growth Center, Yale University, New Haven, Connecticut.

Sideri, Sandro (1996), *Globalization and Regional Integration,* Institute of Social Studies, The Hague, Netherlands.

SA Regional Development Task Force (SARTF) (1999), *Report to the South Australian Government,* Published by the SA Government.

Temple, J. (1999), "The New Growth Evidence", *Journal of Economic Literature,* Vol. 37, No. 1, March.

The Economist (2000), "Australia Survey", September 9-15th, p. 69.

United Nations (1999), *Trends and Policies in the World Economy,* New York.

Vamplew, Wray (ed) (1987), *Australians, Historical Statistics,* Broadview, NSW.

Vamplew, W., Richards, E., Jaensch, D. and Hancock, J. (1984), South *Australian Historical Statistics,* University of New South Wales, Kensington.

Ziegler, Oswald L. (ed) (1972), *The World and South East Asia,* Oswald Ziegler Enterprises, Sydney.

Chapter Two
Contemporary Theories of Economic Growth

Some regions are wealthy and others are not. The contrast is obvious when comparing different countries across the globe such as Australia with Mozambique, but is also obvious when comparing the wealth within South Australia such as between the Marla aboriginal community in the North West and the Eastern suburbs of Adelaide. What is the underlying theory that explains such divergences, even within a small regional economy such as South Australia?

One might be tempted to say that the reasons for the observed divergences in wealth boil down to two.[2] One is that we are so good and they are so bad. We are hard working, intelligent, well governed and efficient and they are lazy, crazy, lawless and inefficient. The other is to argue that we are so bad and they are so good. We are ruthless, exploitive, greedy and manipulative and they are weak, innocent, abused and vulnerable. These characteristics - good and bad - can be found in all communities. While it's not apparent which is the true force, it is clear that the way forward to prosperity calls for different strategies.

2 The theme is adopted from Olson (1996).

Throughout the long pursuit of the understanding of regional economic growth and development, theories have been submitted and elevated to 'laws' only to be demolished. As Temple (1999) says "It is certainly true that, taken as a whole, the growth literature can seem something of a disappointment". The search for a single all embracing theory, that magic formula for all countries to follow, continues relentlessly, but remains elusive. Some would argue that there is no such thing as an all embracing theory, but instead, subscribe to an alternative but no less fundamental view there are different paths to economic development. Each path reflecting the characteristics of the region and its relationships with other regions. And that such a path is time dependent. What worked for South Australia at the turn of the century may not work today for creating a better future.

The purpose of this chapter is not to advance a new theory on regional development, nor form an opinion on the most relevant theoretical framework for explaining why such regional economies grow. Instead, the purpose here is much more modest: to introduce the topic of regional growth by describing the current thinking from leading economists and economic historians. That is, to set the scene, the framework, for the next chapter that describes generally accepted key factors for regional development. The basic theme of this current chapter subscribes to the view that economic policies and institutions do matter, and, indeed, matter a great deal. A brief history is offered to remind us of the struggle to understand the forces that drive economic growth. This is followed by a discussion drawing heavily on economic development literature to accentuate basic points which is then interpreted for regions.

And in the Beginning

And in the beginning there was Adam Smith who said, in his 1776 publication *The Wealth of Nations,* that growth would take care of itself. The 'invisible hand' of the market would sort things out. People would make choices that would maximise their returns and the market would reward needed products of labour, knowledge and timing and punish the opposite. This is a natural process that would lead to the augmenting of wealth.

Economics attracted the tag of the dismal science from Malthus and Ricardo who developed theses on the limits of growth. Malthus argued that in the long run the population would increase beyond the limits of subsistence. In his world, natural and man made disasters - disease, famine and war - would limit population growth and that the natural equilibrium would be not more than the subsistence level. He permitted a slight possibility that the population would self-impose restraint on re-production but such restraint was no force against the human urge. Ricardo saw the same future, but from a different angle. As the demand for food increased, ever poorer land would be used to cultivate crops. The effort from labour required to produce each bushel would increase, driving up the price which in turn would put pressure on wages to rise. Profits would fall, inflating land rents and crowding out other uses of capital to meet the urgent need to produce food. Growth would slow, and ultimately, reach a stationary state. These are the most cited constructions to the classical paradigm. We know, of course, that in the heady days of the post-eighteenth century that the threats of yesteryear have passed - new staple crops, growth enhancing fertiliser, virgin lands and improved transport have not only sustained the population but the surpluses have been exported. The lessons of the classical paradigm have not been dismissed, but it seems, set aside. There were the occasional lone voice, warning of exhaustion of resources, but the technological innovations of the industrial revolutions have transformed economies to continual growth.

John Stuart Mill carried forward the classical view by describing economic growth as the race between increases in population and the capital stock. One could increase the living standards of the poor by reducing the rate of procreation below the rate of capital accumulation. He extended the debate by arguing a role for the Government: the obligation of providing the understanding and incentives that the poor needed to moderate their fecundity. Mill's public program depended heavily on education. He was also an early proponent of women's liberation by pointing out that liberated women would contribute significantly to limiting family sizes.

Karl Marx is the last of the classical figures, and qualifies as a classical economist despite his dissident views about the social desirability and future of capitalism. Marx espoused a theory of value based on the cost of production. He contributed to the notion of stages of development — federalism, capitalism, socialism and communism — and he was around at the time of the British industrial revolution to observe structural transformation. Marx was not optimistic about capitalism or the importance of technological change. He argued that workers' wages would be driven down to subsistence level by labour displacing machinery and that only the capitalists would reap the surplus from production. Instead of a growth trajectory, Marx saw a series of economic cycles punctuated by crises which become increasingly severe leading to the workers expropriating the capitalists and creating the vacuum to be filled by communism.

By the late 19th century, writers focused on free trade and protectionism debates. Problems of economic growth seemed to have lost their urgency although concerns were being raised (Jevons, for example) that the exhaustion of resources such as coal might interrupt economic growth. Marshall introduced a mathematical approach which was taken up by Ramsey, Von Neumann and others by the late 1920s and 1930s.

Schumpeter's contribution in the early 1900s concentrated on innovation as the engine of growth. Innovations include new products, new methods of production and business organisation, and new markets. Schumpeter returned to economic development during the years of World War II contributing to the understanding of routinised innovation through R&D laboratories and large corporations. He introduced concepts of disequilibrium in markets and the role of corporate rent in funding innovation necessary for the development of new products. The more formal modelling work originally developed by Harrod and Domar, led to a widely accepted view that the rate of growth was determined by the rate of savings. Rostow, a highly respected British economist estimated savings ratios for Britain, and claimed that the jump in savings in about 1780 launched Britain into sustainable economic growth. The proposition that there existed a simple relationship between savings and growth was grasped by the World Bank and other aid providers in the 1950s as there seemed to be a simple but powerful policy prescription to assist developing countries out of poverty. However, the 'big push' to get developing countries to increase their savings ratios to stimulate economic growth lost credibility as the impotence of the policy was realised, and Rostow's expert measures of savings turned out to be 'rubbery'.

The starting point for modern growth theory is the classic article by Ramsey (1928) which drew on the foundations of household budget optimisation, consumption theory, asset pricing, and the business-cycle theory to explain growth. Ramsey's work is the genesis of the so called neoclassical approach under which income is modelled as a specified function of capital and labour. These models were developed by Harrod, Domar and later by Solow, Swan and others. The main focus is on equilibrium and departures from equilibrium. These models inherently analysed departures from equilibrium as being temporary phenomena and concluded that a steady-state (no growth) was inevitable. However, by the 1950s, evidence was accumulating that economic growth was being experienced for long periods. This was backed up by statistical analysis from the World Bank and others on developed countries. By 1957, Solow was arguing that something other than labor and capital was driving growth (shifting the production function) which was preventing the effect of diminishing returns to scale, that is, something exogenous to the model. The theory of economic growth stagnated.

Romer (1986) and Lucas (1988) found a way of explaining growth which created a new wave of research. They argued that what was causing increasing returns to scale, that is, driving growth, was R&D, human capital and anything that created favourable externalities.[3] The so called endogenous growth theory or new growth theory has its basis in earlier work on externalities, that is, public good theory to explain forces generating growth. The work is theoretical, and Romer, Lucas and their followers have not yet fully explored such policy

3 The essence of a favourable externality, whether in production or consumption, is that their benefits are not fully reflected in market prices.

implications as the benefits of increasing education nor seek to provide empirical evidence to prove the theory. Moreover, their contributions, albeit sound, do not explain adequately the real world. Over the late 1990s new research has been undertaken which has permitted some consensus on the theory of growth, which is covered in the sections that follow.

Big Bills Left on the Sidewalk

Much of contemporary economic thinking over the last quarter century rested on the idea that any gains that can be obtained are in fact picked up. This is the Efficient Markets Hypothesis - the disequilibrium wage adjusts to eliminate involuntary unemployment. Profit maximising firms have incentives to enter markets that are highly profitable, driving down profits and, conversely, firms exit markets that not profitable driving up profits for remaining firms until normal profits are reached. Under this hypothesis there are no bills left on the sidewalk.[4] However, current thinking is to the contrary: big bills are indeed left on the sidewalk.

Borders delineate regions having different economic policies and institutions. To the extent that economic performance cannot be explained by endowments, then they tell us something about the extent that societies have attained their potential. With income levels varying by 20 times between rich and poor regions, at the highest level of aggregation, Olson (1996) argues that there are only two explanations:

- differences in the availability of productive resources per capita: poor regions are poor because they are short of resources, and in particular, land and other natural resources, human capital and latest technology; and
- differences in public policies and institutions that are better or worse at providing the structure of incentives that brings forth productive cooperation.

How important are these two possibilities in explaining differences in economic performance? Several aspects of Olson's arguments are discussed. In sum, these suggest that differences in policies and institutions are much more powerful than differences in resources in explaining differences in regional growth.

Availability of Productive Resources

Firstly, let's consider access to productive knowledge. To the extent that productive knowledge takes the form of unpatented laws of nature and basic science, it is a non-excludable public good available to every one without charge. Non-purchasers can however be denied access through patents or copyrights, or because knowledge can be embodied in equipment. Knowledge and the

4 This term is coined in Olson's article.

processes must be purchased by poor countries from rich countries. So which country captures the gains? The rise of Korea suggests that almost all gains can be captured by the poor countries.

Secondly, is poverty in the poor countries largely due to overpopulation, that is, a low ratio of land and other natural resources to population?

Suppose we shifted workers from low income countries to high income countries. What would happen to world income? What would happen to changes in relative wages and the marginal productivity of labor? Lets assume that both countries are on their production frontiers so that marginal product of labor is equal to the wage rate (MPL=w). When workers migrate from low wage to high wage countries, world income rises by the difference between the wage received by the migrant worker in the rich country and what that worker earned in the poor country. However, the world as a whole is not on the production frontier, even if all of the countries in it are because, for the migrant worker, MPL<w. That is, although the migrants wages have risen the stock of knowledge and productivity has not changed much. At best, superior capital has enhanced their productivity but only a little. Also, the migrant would be willing to work for less. There would still be an incentive for migration even if the rich countries took half the increase and gave it to the rest of the citizens.

The results of large migrations do not support this proposition. The out migration from Ireland did not lead to a rapid growth of per capita income in Ireland. Also the immigrants from Ireland to US and Britain tended to earn as much as the other peoples, and any differences in human capital could not explain the increase in wage that the immigrants received when they go to a more productive country. It is not the ratio of land to labor that has mainly determined per capita income in Ireland. In another case the migration of Latin Americans to the US did not diminish significantly differences in per capita incomes. Temple (1999) argues that population growth does not seem to have the large negative effects that are frequently conjectured.

Also, many of the most densely settled countries have high per capita incomes, and some of the most sparsely settled are poor. Some studies even show a positive correlation between density and per capita income.

Thirdly, can poor regional performances be blamed on lack of natural resources? The ratio of natural resources to population does not account for variations in income because most economic activity can now readily be separated from deposits of raw materials and arable land. Transportation technologies improved and products that have a high value to weight have become more important. Silicon Valley is important for computers not for deposits of silicon, London and Zurich are not banking sectors for their fertile land.

Fourthly, is the issue of diminishing returns to capital. If the countries of the world were doing their best, that is, on the frontiers of neoclassical production functions, the marginal product of capital would therefore be many times higher in the low income countries than the high income countries. Capital is scarce in low income countries. Lucas (1990) estimates that if an Indian and an American worker supplied the same amount of labor then the marginal product of capital would be 58 times higher in India than America. This analysis would suggest that such large differences in return should generate a huge migration of capital from high income to low income countries. That is, capital should be struggling just as hard to get to the third world as labor is struggling to get to the high wage countries. Countries are not on their frontiers we observe the uneven distribution of capital around the world. Shortcomings in economic policies and institutions in low income countries keep capital from earning returns that reflect scarcity. Foreign investors are sometimes unwelcome, or investments are too risky. Furthermore, capital and labor can be found to be moving in the same direction contrary to neoclassical theory.

Given the uneven allocation of capital and the strong relationship between capital mobility and the economic policies and institutions of countries, capital cannot be taken to be exogenous in the theory of economic development.

Fifthly, can differences in per capita income be explained by differences in the human capital per capita? Included in 'human capital' are cultural or other traits (e.g., Protestant work ethic, national traits that make them hard workers, frugal savers and imaginative entrepreneurs) as well as skills and education.

Poor countries are alleged to be poor because their populations lack these positive traits, which are hard to change because they are built on centuries of social accumulation.

Although a plausible explanation of regional performance, "culture" is also a vague cause of poverty. Some types of culture personal culture - is marketable, and captured in the wage rate. The second type of culture - civic culture - is a public good. This capital includes, for example, the knowledge about how one should vote: about what public policies will be successful. Civic culture is not normally marketable and only affects incomes by influencing public policies and institutions. The distinction between personal and civic culture is useful for some natural experiments.

Newly arrived immigrants have approximately the same marketable human capital or personal culture they had before they migrated, but the institutions and public policies that determine the opportunities that they confront are those of the host country.

The very act of immigration does not itself immediately change the personal characteristics and skills of the immigrant, but can radically change the opportunities. As a result, immigrants to the US from low-income countries enjoy large rise in earnings from low levels typically earned in their own countries, to achieve levels equal to about 55 per cent of American. The rise is not to be explained by self-selection, that is, the most productive immigrate. On the contrary, immigrants are disproportionately drawn from those earning incomes low by home-country standards. The conclusion drawn by Olson was that the rise in earnings is due to the institutions and public policies of the U.S.

These natural experiments do not tell us much about the public or civic cultures of different peoples, except that they strongly influence wealth.

Olson argues that neither 'old' growth theories nor 'new' growth theories predict the relationships actually observed: the fastest growing countries are never those with the highest per capita incomes but always a subset of the lower income countries. That is, poor countries on average have had poorer economic policies and institutions than rich countries, but have the opportunity for rapid catch-up growth, if only they can change policies and institutions.

As Olson (1996) points out, endogenous growth models do not predict that the most rapid growth will occur in a subset of low income countries; those models apply best to the 'leading' economies.

Large differences in per capita income across countries cannot be explained by differences in access to the world's stock of productive knowledge or to its capital markets, nor by differences in the ratio of population to land or natural resources nor differences in the quality of marketable human capital or personal culture.

Borders of Public Choice

Olson's second point is that there is evidence that national borders, which delineate different institutions and economic policies, are decisive for its economic performance. This evidence contradicts the view that societies produce as much as their resource endowments permit.

Furthermore, an assertion contradicted by the facts is that the quality of a nation's economic institutions and policies is inversely related to the size of its public sector. Temple (1999) supports this view. In addition, he adds that government spending on infrastructure is beneficial for growth. There is strong evidence that economic performance is determined by the structure of incentives for good economic behaviour which are created by institutions and policy. Furthermore, gains from specialisation and trade cannot be made without efficient cooperation between firms and institutions. Institutions must enforce contracts impartially, otherwise the gains are of those transactions are lost. Property rights are important. Trade policies are important.

Temple (1999) cites studies finding a negative effect of high inequality on growth. Many studies have moved away from political economy arguments to examining the effects of inequality on fertility rates, investment in education and political stability. Notably, there does not appear to be empirical evidence to link democracy and growth. The nature of the regimes, whether authoritarian or democratic, is not as important as are the incentives. That is, are those running autocratic regimes motivated by on self-interest and accumulating wealth or are they orientated to national economic goals.

Abramovitz and David (1986) share Olson's view that a key factor influencing growth is social capability. Social capability refers to those attributes of people and economic organisation that influence the responses of people to economic opportunity. It includes a society's culture and the priority it assigns to economic attainment. It also covers the rights, limitations and obligations involved with property and the incentives that create effort, investment, enterprise and innovation, policies that govern particular forms of organisation (corporations, financial institutions), provision of public services including education and research. Nelson and Wright (1992) identify social capability as a major determinant of a region's technological leadership, because it influences the strength of networks required not only to educate people but to combine education effectively with leading edge applications - management and organisation, experience and strong recognition of the interplay between public, private and the university sectors are what is needed.

An interpretation of this literature is that the structure of incentives does not emerge spontaneously from rational decisions by individuals. What drives the effective management of a region's economic and social resources is collective or community actions. These actions are based on five elements: sound government policies and administration; human rights; democracy; rule of law and participatory civil society. In sum, these five elements represent what has now been widely termed as governance.

Diagram 2.1 below identifies the main components of good governance. How well a region is able to combine these components determines the strength of the incentives within the regional community to maximise the opportunities for growth and development. Under good governance, resources are directed to productive outcomes rather than being wasted on a range of destructive activities (e.g., war, civil unrest, subversive behaviour, industrial espionage, corruption) or rent seeking behaviour (e.g., lobby groups, monopoly pricing, competitive favouritism, political manipulation). Although these are problems experienced in developing countries, they are also very much part of the developed world.

Diagram 2.1
Governance

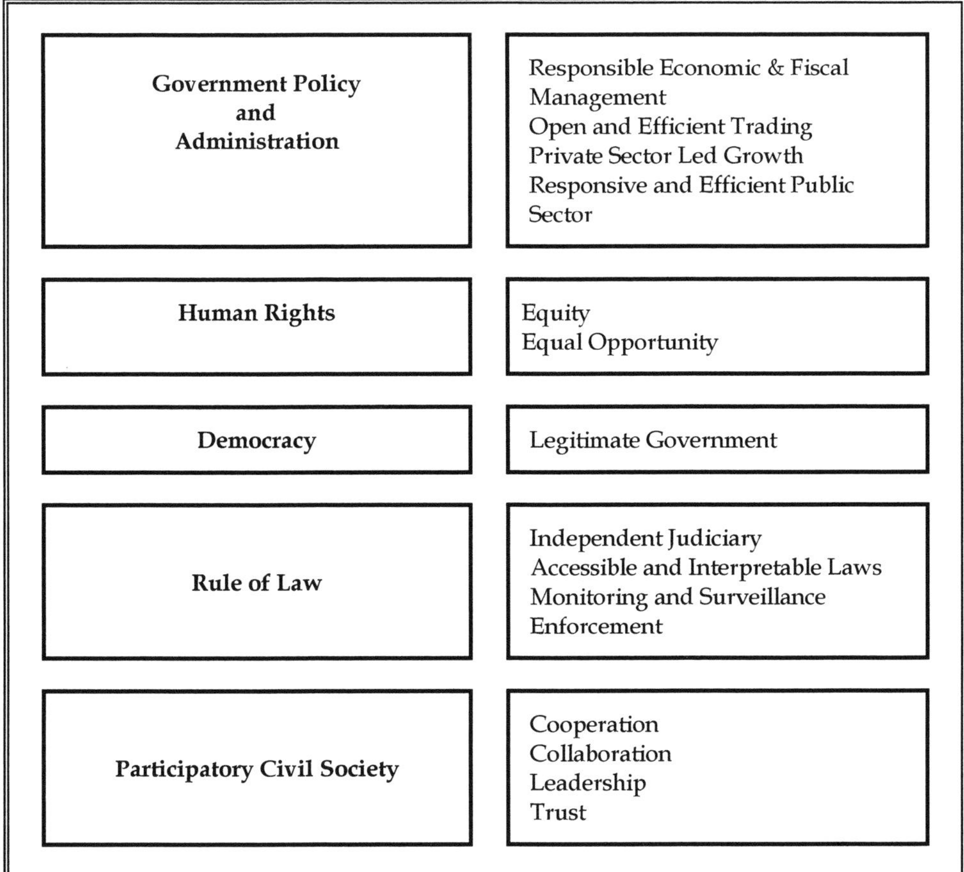

Poor governance strikes at the effectiveness of some of the oldest of our institutions through a lack of accountability; weak measures of performance; inability to effectively implement rewards for good behaviour and penalties for bad behaviour these undermine and divert resources from productive activities.

An Interpretation for Regions

Much of the forgoing discussion is based on the economic literature of developing countries but to a significant degree it is applicable to regional economies in developed countries such as Australia.

The regional interpretation focuses on the following elements: (i) the fundamental drivers of growth of countries approximate the drivers of regional economies; (ii) returning to Temple (1999), each region has its own path to development (absolutely and inter-temporally); and (iii) although national and regional systems have different roles, they are linked. These elements are discussed in turn.

On the first element, most of the forgoing discussion is focussed on countries. However, growth economists have also sought understand growth of regions within countries. Regional analyses help identify the forces that drive long-run growth. Firstly, regions share attributes that are difficult to control for in cross-country studies yet also provide for heterogenous economic attributes and experiences. Secondly, the growth of the national economy is frequently viewed as the outcome of the development of a number of regional economies and their progressive integration.

Studies have been undertaken in several countries to examine for evidence of convergence of growth across regions or states. Barro and Sala-i-Martin (1995) studied 48 states of the U.S. over the period since 1880, 46 prefectures of Japan since 1930 and the regions of eight European countries since 1950. The results indicate absolute convergence[5] - that is, regions that have roughly similar tastes, technologies and political institutions - will tend to reach the same steady state positions. The results also showed that the income gap closes at around 2-3 per cent per year of all countries studied, and this implies that it takes about 25-35 years to eliminate one half of the initial gap in per capita income. Mitchener and McLean (1999) used personal income data for US States over six census years from 1880 to 1980 to test for convergence of regional economies. Using nominal per capita income figures their study has found that, the gap between the lowest and highest income states has narrowed since 1880. Proximate causes of regional variations in real income were shown to be the masculinity ratio, age structure, industrial structure, labour market variations and resource abundance.

While the general message of these studies is that states are converging there are persistent factors which are retarding the rate of convergence, and baring major shocks, it may take some decades for convergence to be absolute. Attempts were made for this book to utilise Australian regional data to assess factors influencing differential growth of regions but there are insufficient observations to identify statistically reliable results. However, it is still worth focussing attention on why South Australia is consistently growing at rates lower than the national trend, that is, are there persistent factors retarding convergence. The shift share analysis presented in Chapter 9 clearly points to a different economic structure as a key factor.

Secondly, it should not be surprising to find that there is no unique path to growth and development. A brief excursion into economic history serves the point. In the 17th Century, Europe and Japan had attained similar levels of economic development. Jones (1997) says "Japan [in 1865] was as European as if

5 If a poor economy grows faster than a rich one, it will catch up with the rich one in terms of per capita income or product. This property corresponds to the concept of B convergence.

it had been towed away and anchored off the Isle of Wright". By the 17th Century, there had emerged an economic structure of market urbanisation, monetisation, internal trade, rising agricultural productivity and regionally patterned rural industry. However, there was almost no contact between Japan and Europe until that time, and Japan strictly forbad foreign trade. Japan's developments were not a natural outcome of market forces but of administrative absolutionalist decree requiring samurai to settle in castle towns and the daimyo spend half the year in Edo. The enforced urban growth led not to civil retreat but to an expansion of the market encouraging economies of scale and opportunity for the private sector to flourish. In Japan, political liberty was not necessary for economic progress. Japan's population to land ratio was above subsistence level - reflecting planned population control through infanticide as well as the unplanned effects of epidemics and geophysical eruptions. Development paths can be different reflecting starkly contrasting approaches or different time periods.

In another example, Abramovitz and David (1996) describe technological leadership in the United States as an emerging process whereby technological paths changed overtime, firstly with the explosion of the rich virgin land of the new prairies, to the minerals-intensive, tangible capital-using and scale-dependent production of the nineteenth and early twentieth centuries and then to the new capital - augmenting techniques and shift toward investment in intangible assets: information-intensive education and organised R&D.

Each path reflects the characteristics of the region. The endowments it has to work with offer an initial advantage, but the ability to sustain of growth lies in the capacity to solve the particular types of problems it confronts (e.g., poor water quality, remoteness from world markets) which in turn drives the particular technological path and particular technological strength (e.g., dryland farming). The nature of the problem may also determine the degree and nature of involvement by government (e.g., a focus on transport infrastructure, agricultural emphasis on education). The path may also reflect the relationship between the region and other regions - a feeder relationship as might describe the trade relationship between South Australia and the Eastern States reflecting structurally dissimilar economies, mutual trade (between say the Easter States where economies are structurally similar), strictly competitive such as the Barossa and Hunter Valley wine areas and adversarial (Kosovo and the neighbouring regions).

The third of the general issues for regions is the interplay between national and regional economic communities. That is, having acquired a clear understanding of the factors influencing the growth and development of a country, there is then a question of understanding which parties are best able to utilise the factors to achieve the outcomes - the national or the regional economic communities.

What happens at the national level is clearly important for regions. National economic communities cover national government and other entities with national perspectives - firms and community groups. Broadly, the role for these communities is that of signalling, integrating and creating a common economic basis. One of the most critical roles is signalling, that is, identifying and highlighting the priorities and challenges facing the economic community. For government this may involve shaping attitudes toward industry, promoting competition through national policy and monitoring trends in the external environment. For industry it may be to shape attitudes toward government involvement in the community, determining the best combination of regional inputs for international competition and for the community it may be to foster change towards equality and reduction of poverty. Integration implies a strengthening of links between the common policies for the nation and the regions, promotion of inter-firm networking and transmission of knowledge from external sources.

What happens at the regional level is clearly important for the nation as a whole. Regional economic communities work at the micro level drawing on the regionally specific endowments and searching for solutions to regionally specific problems. Driving down the cost of production has always been important, but the emphasis now is on new products and services that are unique or superior in the global market place. Such an emphasis underscores the importance of encouraging industry clusters and networking as a means of exchanging new information and ideas, fostering entrepreneurship, establishing incubator industries and other means of establishing closer connections between pure research, applied research and new product commercialisation. Regional governments have a role in facilitating these conditions and providing the basic infrastructure. Overall, both at the national and regional levels, here must be a capacity to identify change in the external environment, to transmit new information and for the 'working parts' to assess and then coordinate the response.

Three Wise Economists

Contemporary theory on economic growth can perhaps be circumscribed by three overlapping pieces of wisdom from three prominent economists. The first piece of wisdom, ascribed to Eric Jones (1993), is that economic growth is like a combination lock. Certain things must be in place before it happens. A region may have some of the right factors, but if one or more of the remaining factors are missing or inappropriate then the others may not be enough to permit sustained growth. This emphasises the role of substitutes. If you don't have the human capital and you can't wait 20 years to develop it, then hire it from another region.

The second piece of wisdom, ascribed to James Riedel (1986), is that regions should do what comes naturally. His insights are drawn from the East Asian growth miracle. Economic growth has been fostered because workers, business people and the community have been left alone to get on with the job. Relaxation of government control and reduced intervention in markets seem to work.

The third piece of wisdom, ascribed to Mancur Olson (1996) and discussed at some length earlier in this chapter, is that big bills are left on the sidewalk. There are opportunities. They have not been picked up through arbitrage. Some things about our society are holding us back, we are not on the production frontier. Its not so much the size of our populations or our technologies or our natural resource endowments that are holding us back. Borders of public choice that delineate economic institutions and policies are what make the difference. Institutions and policies create a system of incentives for good and bad economic behaviour. Our institutions and policies are what we make of them, and they reflect our society and culture, how hard we work, the way we organise to produce, how we conduct our relationships with others, and our attitudes to development of ourselves and the others.

References

Abramovitz, M. and David P.A. (1996), "Convergence and Deferred Catch-Up: Productivity Leadership and the Warming of American Exceptionalism", in *The Mosaic of Economic Growth*, eds. R. Landaw et al. , U.P., Stanford.

Barro, R.J. and Sala-i-Martin, X. (1995), *Economic Growth*, McGraw-Hill.

Dorfman, R. (1991), "Economic Development from the Beginning to Rostow", *Journal of Economic Literature*, Vol. 29, No. 2, June.

Engel, C. and Rogers, J.H. (1996), "How Wide is the Border?", *American Economic Review*, Vol. 86, No. 5, pp. 1112-1125.

Jones, E. (1993), *Coming Full Circle: An Economic History of the Pacific Rim*, Boulder Westview Press.

Jones, P. (1997), *The European Miracle*, Cambridge Press.

Lucas, R. (1988), "On the Mechanics of Economic Development", *Journal of Monetary Economics*, Vol. 22.

Mitchener, K.J. and McLean, I.W.(1999), "US Regional Growth and Convergency 1880-1980", *Journal of Economic History*, Vol. 59, No. 4, December.

Nelson, R.R and Wright G. (1992), "The Rise and Fall of American Technological Leadership", *Journal of Economic Literature*, Vol. 30, No. 4, December.

Olson, M. (1996), "Big Bills Left on the Sidewalk: Why Some Nations are Rich and Others Poor", *Journal of Economic Perspectives*, Vol. 10, No. 2, Spring.

Riedel, J. (1986), "Economic Development in South East Asia: Doing What Comes Naturally?", National Centre for Development Studies, ANU, Working Paper 86/1.

Romer, P. (1986), "Increasing Returns to Long Run Growth", *Journal of Political Economy*, Vol 94, No 5, pp. 1002-37.

Temple, J. (1999), "The New Growth Evidence", *Journal of Economic Literature*, Vol. 37, No. 1, March.

Chapter Three
Influences on Regional Growth — Basic Factors

In this chapter and the next, we consider the main factors influencing regional development. Drawing on the main themes of the literature, the more basic factors are discussed in this chapter. These factors tend to be the proximate causes of growth, but none generates satisfactory policy prescriptions. Although the discussion generates more questions than answers, it serves to remind us of the complexity of the issues we are dealing with, and enables a progression to the more relevant factors for advanced regions such as South Australia covered in the next chapter.

Main Themes in the Literature

A review of the literature on the growth of small regional economies can be found in a set of four research papers by SACES (1997). The main contemporary theories described in those papers that are generally considered to have some relevance to the debate about influences on the growth of small regional economies can be categorised as follows:

- new economic growth theory;
- the competitive advantage of nations;
- economic development geography and new industry policy;
- strategic trade theory;
- forces of globalisation and their implications for governance and for business strategy;
- social capital and trust; and
- some other important strands of thinking, notably complexity theory.

New economic growth theory postulates that long-run growth is the result of technological progress. Romer (1990) and Lucas (1988), for example, identify three elements that are thought to drive technological progress namely: investment in physical capital, human capital and research and development.

The theory of the competitive advantage of nations developed by Porter (1990) identifies four broad attributes, and the interactions between them, through which nations achieve international success in a particular industry, namely:

- factor conditions: the quantity and quality of resources used in production;
- demand conditions: the nature of home demand of the industry's product or service;
- related and supporting industries: the extent to which supplier and related industries in the region are internationally competitive; and
- firm strategy, structure and rivalry: conditions in the region governing how companies are created, organised, managed and the active of domestic rivalry.

In addition to these four elements, Porter maintains that the role of chance and of government influence a regions' advantage. Chance events include, for example, extraordinary invention, political decisions of external governments and war. Porter indicates that governments are thought to have an important role in shaping factor conditions. Governments provide funding and facilities to develop skilled human resources, basic scientific knowledge, economic information, infrastructure and health care. Porter recognises that many skills are either industry or firm specific, but that the role of government in providing education and training to update industry is "perhaps the greatest long-term leverage point available".

The literature on economic development geography (see Krugman 1979, 1980, 1981) and particularly, *new trade theory,* emphasises the spatial element of the economy. That is, it compares the centripetal forces that drive the scale economies from agglomeration of economic activity at the margin with the centrifugal forces that drive the dispersion of economic activity.

Strategic trade theory emphasises regional interdependency, that is, the actions of one region in the international market may have implications for the competitiveness of another region (Brander and Spencer, 1985).

Ohmae (1995) argues that globalisation will force nation-states to give way to region-states where regions are defined by clusters of related industries or natural economic zones. Thus growth involves enabling direct dialogue between industry and their consumers globally, encouraging knowledge intensive industry, eliminating industry protection and facilitating industry and regional adjustment and providing efficient and high standard infrastructures.

Putnam (1995), Fukuyama (1995) and other writers in the field of *social capital and trust* emphasise the importance of civil society which binds the economy. Well behaved societies are low cost and efficient organs of economic co-operation. Excessive resources are not consumed on formal contracts law enforcement, administering justice and social services.

Complexity theory (for example, see Arthur, 1994) emphasises the importance of random factors, technological lock-in and path dependence in explaining growth.

All of these stands of thinking on economic growth are relevant to regions, but none offer an embracing theory nor a comprehensive set of prescriptions for economic agents that is accepted by all parties. Nonetheless, from this literature on contemporary growth theory, main factors that have emerged to explain comparative regional economic performance are differences in:

- capacity to expand factors of production and improve the efficiency of resource use;
- patterns of export and domestic demand;
- capacities to exploit and benefit from critical events or triggers to development;
- the life-cycle of main products and technologies of the region;
- natural endowment advantages and disadvantages;
- the extent to which firms achieve competitive advantage;
- frameworks for governance and government strategies and policies; and
- cultural values and social cohesion.

At the most basic level it would seem that working with one's comparative advantage and adjusting to changes in the external environment is the mainstay of a region, but the ways in which comparative advantage is maximised and the characteristics of a dynamic regional economy are the keys to growth and development. The problem is not dissimilar to a boat race. The first task is to stay afloat, checking the hull and the engine for any signs of weakness - in maintaining and improving competitive advantage of products and services.

The second task is to determine the direction of travel, avoiding major adverse external events and riding the currents through by making a series of adjustments. Clearly these are a set of activities in which all regions must engage to stay in the race.

Of the factors identified above, the first five are considered to be the pre-requisites for staying afloat, the survival or basic factors. All regions should be operating on these factors. There is nothing new or unique about them and these factors existed before globalisation took hold. Nonetheless, they are briefly discussed below to serve as a reminder of their importance. But there is a second set of factors which enable regions to catch-up or keep ahead of other regions in achieving growth and development. These are the factors which drive innovative and entrepreneurial regions. These factors deal more directly with the development of new products and services that are unique to the international market place and emphasise networking; enterprise facilitation, industry clusters, fostering entrepreneurship, forming of strategic alliances, access to and information exchange.

The *basic factors* are further discussed below and the *catch up and staying ahead factors* are covered in the following chapters.

Production and Efficiency

An important basic source of differences in the growth of regions arises from supply-side influences, consisting of two broad categories: differences in rates of growth of factors of production (e.g., labour and capital) and differences in growth of productivity between regions.

Under this approach, investors and workers are assumed to search for the most profitable or attractive regions for their investment and employment. In practice, the flows of mobile factors of production are affected by the characteristics of a region's immobile factors of production (such as the availability of suitable land, quality of natural resources and economic infrastructure and government policies), which influence expected returns for mobile factors of production.

The implications are that wage rates will be relatively high in regions with a high capital-to-labour ratio, but at on the margin, return to capital investment will be low. This implies that labour and capital will flow in opposite directions - labour will migrate to high-wage regions while capital will be attracted to low-wage regions. Low-wage regions will tend to have higher growth of output per head and to enjoy higher rates of capital accumulation and greater increases in wages than other regions. Inter-regional flows of labour and capital will continue until returns are equalised across regions. The basic model predicts the convergence of regional per capita incomes.

Empirical verification of this theory is made difficult by data limitations. While a number of studies support the view that labour and capital movements are a response to factor price differences between regions so that convergence occurs (Barro and Sala-i-Martin, 1991 and 1992), others challenge whether convergence of incomes does in fact occur (Baily and Schultze, 1990; Helliwell and Chung, 1991; Sheehan, 1992). The BIE (1992) suggest that the empirical results seem inconclusive, with evidence of convergence and divergence across countries and over different time periods.

Moreover, this analysis at best describes the proximate causes for economic change in regions, but does deal with at the fundamental causes of superior or inferior capital and labour productivity. On the surface though, it could be inferred that a low cost environment (high quality infrastructure, skilled workforce, political stability) and a mobile workforce would encourage productive efficiency.

The Role of Export and Domestic Demand

The output and income of a region are affected by the demand for its products. Variations in demand from both export markets and domestic markets, therefore, influence a region's growth performance.

The Role of Export Demand

The export or *economic-base approach* to explaining growth differentials stresses the role of external demand in shaping a region's growth performance. A region comprises two sectors: an export sector and a support sector. Export industries are the key source of income. The remaining industries comprise supporting industries linked by 'derived demand' to the export industries. Increases in external demand provide a direct stimulus to the export sector which in turn induces an expansion of the support sector.

The structure of demand and the region's endowment of factors determine the 'leading' industry or industries. As the leading industry expands over time, it forms *backward* and *forward* linkages with other related and supporting industries, stimulating their growth. Because of these linkages, development diffuses throughout the region to other industries and, to the extent that industries in other regions are linked to the leading industry, to neighbouring regions (North, 1955). These developments can give rise to spin-off benefits, such as agglomeration economies, that yield cumulative benefits for a region. The influence of these on a region's growth is taken up in the next sub-section.

In small regional economies, export markets are usually larger than domestic markets and thus can confer greater benefits on the region. The products exported by a region depend on its comparative advantage - determined either by its technology, or its abundance of factors - and the set of relative prices in the international market place.

The ability of a region to take advantage of the growth of its 'leading' industry or industries will depend on its ability to respond to the changes in demand and supply. On the demand-side, a region will have to develop new markets or products. On the supply-side, a region may face the emergence of competitors and so the need to improve its competitiveness.

The literature on export-led growth does not throw much light on what conditions are conducive to the formation of linkages between the exporting and other industries. It is possible that some activities will remain as 'enclaves' in the economy, providing little more than basic employment opportunities while appropriating raw materials. For example, the Argle diamond mine near Kunnunurra in the North East region of Western Australia has almost no impact on the regional economy. Labour is flown in and out of the region, capital goods are brought in and the small volume high value output is transported mainly to Eastern States.

Where a regional economy is highly dependent upon the success of one or a few specialised activities, such as mining and agriculture, price variability can lead to fluctuations in income and growth. This is unlikely to be a long-term problem, unless it reflects a secular decline in prices and the region's industries are unable to adapt. Also, the pattern of a region's international trade can be distorted and gains from trade potentially lost through protection and other trade interventions. Although regions can expect to benefit from trade, the same openness also makes them dependent on performance and policies of their trading partners.

The Role of Domestic Demand

For some regions, the demand for their outputs will be determined by the needs of neighbouring regions. The growth of a neighbouring urban region redirects the pattern of inter-regional trade as well as attracting both labour and capital. Thus for many regions, the growth of a central metropolitan region may prove more important to their development than export demand. In terms of national trade, this is 'import substitution' since goods are directed towards domestic rather than to international markets. Import substitution impacts on the national trade balance by reducing exports and imports. These combined effects would make the country (or region) appear to be less 'internationalised' because foreign trade is a smaller proportion of total output. Yet, a region with low trade intensities may still be internationally competitive if its industries successfully out-bid foreign suppliers for the domestic market.

In the Australian context, the most populous states New South Wales and Victoria have the lowest ratios of primary (and total) exports-to-gross-state-product ratios (BIE, 1994b, 1993), because Sydney and Melbourne are large, and trade within the states is self-contained.

Critical Events and Triggers

The *cumulative causation* explanation of regional growth from the economic development geography literature suggests that growth is an inherently unbalanced process, so that over time regions tend to experience diverging rather than converging per capita incomes. This view of the growth process owes its development to Myrdal (1957) and Hirschman (1958). This explanation of growth uses the notion that some initial development or occurrence gives rise to a 'kick' or 'trigger' which advances the development of a region. For example, a large rise in world mineral prices may make mining increasingly profitable. This creates a variety of investment opportunities in resource-based regions and triggers an influx of labour and capital. This 'trigger' determines the growth path of the region, until another shock or event changes that path. The immigration of capital and labour, in turn, increases the scope for localisation and urbanisation of the economy. Firms agglomerate to growing regions because of the lower costs of doing business. As more firms and households locate in the growing region, its size and share of the economy increases, reinforcing its localisation and urbanisation advantages. This process gives rise to the 'virtuous circle' of self-sustaining or cumulative growth. Moreover, as noted by Hicks (1959), the advantage derived from growth itself encourages the development of 'internal momentum' in the favoured region.

The other side of the coin is that the decrease in population in less-favoured regions caused by emigration reduces the demand for goods and services in that region. Lower demand detracts from the achievement of scale economies which in turn reduces the return to other factors of production and consequently stimulates their emigration. The virtuous circle of growth in agglomerating regions can only be achieved by imposing a 'vicious circle' on other regions. Regions that lose out in this process may thereby be prevented from industrialising (Kaldor, 1970) or advancing. Labour and capital emigration from non-advancing regions constitute the *backwash* effects of the advancing region (Myrdal, 1957). Wittwer and Bright (1997) illustrated the backwash effect by measuring the negative economic impact on South Australia arising from mining booms occurring elsewhere in Australia.

The backwash effects need not lead to the deterioration of the region because there is potentially another factor at play. The growing region may increase the demand for the products of the advancing region and there may also be a diffusion of technical knowledge. These constitute *spread* effects. There is evidence that this effect operates. When Victoria and New South Wales experience a boom then South Australia benefits through the trade linkages as a feeder service. The net effect of the backwash and spread effects are very difficult to measure. According to the cumulative causation explanation, divergences in regional growth are the predominant tendency because backwash effects exceed the beneficial spread effects, so that the cost of doing business in growing regions continues to fall relative to the cost of doing business in other regions. Given this, the favoured region's growth amplifies the divergences between it and the other regions as it draws more resources. This increases the scope for additional scale economies, generating a further round of specialisation and internalisation of externalities.

These cumulative processes have a tendency to 'polarise' economic growth across regions. In other words, economic growth is a regional experience rather than a uniform national one. Perroux (1950) argued that *growth poles* are formed around the success of individual 'leading' industries, which have established forward and backward linkages with other firms and industries in their vicinity. The growth of leading industries encourages the growth of other industries. The economic success of the secondary industries and their ability to attain competitiveness, such as through R&D and specialisation, allows them to reinforce growth in the leading industry. These mutually reinforcing effects encourage the evolution of self-sustaining industrial clusters (Hermansen, 1977).

There is evidence of divergence of growth rates between highly agglomerated regions and less-agglomerated regions (BIE, 1994a). There tends to be high concentrations of activity and population in metropolitan regions, and low concentrations in other regions. High concentrations of activity are also associated with high levels of per capita income. According to the Industry Commission (1993), each of Australia's capital cities has average per capita incomes higher than their state averages, and the per capita incomes in Australia's largest centres (Sydney and Melbourne) are greater than the average for the other capital cities. Moreover, Sydney's per capita income grew quicker than the Australian average, and the gap between it and Australia's poorest regions widened, between 1986 and 1991.

Not only are there significant differences in the distribution of economic activity, but over time these differences have become more pronounced. The faster growth of metropolitan regions demonstrates their economic advantages; for many classes of firms, these are better places to do business. Manufacturing, capital city and remote resource-development regions experienced growth in per capita income, relative to agricultural, agricultural/warm climate coastal, agricultural/manufacturing/warm climate coastal and other regions. (BIE, 1994a).

Self-sustaining growth does not continue indefinitely since no region is able to grow without limit. Limits to growth can be imposed by such things as *congestion* and the *capitalisation of externalities* into land prices. As the costs of operating in agglomeration rise, dispersion of activity to other places becomes more attractive. The share of Australian population residing in Sydney and Melbourne has declined slightly in 1999 compared with 10 to 20 years ago, indicating that congestion factors are influencing location decisions. But the population is not turning to Adelaide. Instead the share of the Australia population has risen in Brisbane, Perth, Gold Coast and the Sunshine Coast.

However, even if one accepts that the theory of critical events and triggers is a powerful explanation of regional growth, the theory does not lead to policy prescriptions.

In the *cumulative causation* model, different shocks affect regions and industries differently. There is no reason to expect any one region or industry to experience systematically favourable or unfavourable shocks from 'national' events. As the shocks even out over time, one is left wondering what are the underlying or deeper factors that are driving the regional advantage.

At best, the theory suggests that a region should diversify its activities so that the impact of any one adverse event would be minimised. Although a sound policy, this only leads to the next puzzle of how do you successfully diversify a region.

Life Cycles of Main Products and Technologies

The growth of economies can be explained in terms of the cyclical behaviour attributable to the main product life-cycle (Vernon, 1966), technological diffusion (Pred, 1965; Norton and Rees, 1979) and the role of institutions and governments as sources of secular growth and decline (Olson, 1982; Blandy *et al*, 1994).

Economic cycles occur in all economies. Cycles vary in length and magnitude, from local business cycles and seasonal employment cycles. Our concern is with the former since we are interested in the rise and decline of regions. Examples of longer-term regional life-cycles in the U.S. include the recent revival of the industrial North-East and central-North-West after a period of sustained decline in the 1970s and 1980s, and the absence of strong growth in the West and South in the 1990s, although they had experienced rapid growth over the same early period (Greenwood, 1985).

The *product life-cycle* approach argues that a region will move through different stages of development as the competitive and technological conditions of its output change over time. Initially effort is placed in the R&D of products and production processes, and employment is largely confined to skilled labour. The product is sold in a *seller's* market where limited competition guarantees large profits to the innovating firm and region. In the *maturing product* stage, production methods are gradually streamlined, considerable effort is placed in product differentiation, product prices fall as competition increases, and new production technologies quickly make earlier production techniques obsolete. In the *product standardisation* stage, production technologies are simplified and 'stabilised', know-how becomes more dispersed, and production is mostly handled by unskilled labour.

However, the ability of the product-cycle model to explain regional cycles is limited since firms can often relocate production between regions and countries. Instead of regions experiencing different stages of development as the nature of their output changes, firms are able to export entire production stages of a product's life-cycle to those economies which are most able to produce cost-effectively. Labour-intensive stages of production are located in countries where the cost of labour is low. Ideas and creativity-intensive activities of the first stage involve highly skilled and creative labour, and are likely to be located in mature regions with a tradition in research, design, product development and marketing.

The potential for regional specialisation in certain product stages, involving sustained investment in machinery, equipment, and infrastructure, as well as education, training and R&D, may bias the industrial structure of some regions towards certain activities. This can be a positive force, for example there are many regions in Switzerland, Germany and the United States which tend to specialise in the *new product* (or innovation) stage of the life-cycle (Porter, 1990, p. 570). In the U.S. high-technology industry, these include Route 128, Massachusetts and Silicon Valley, California. However, this industrial bias can be a negative force. Migration and progression between stages are inherently difficult, and it is possible to envisage a region which is 'locked' into a particular stage of the product cycle. High investment costs which are sunk can keep industries and regions in an economic activity even if it is clearly unprofitable to expand capacity or diversify into related areas (Pindyck, 1991; Dixit, 1992). Throughout the 1970s, motor vehicle manufacturing in the U.S. remained largely concentrated in the state of Michigan because of the 'sunk' costs involved in the original investments, although other manufacturing activities tended to spread to the South and West.

Related to the product life-cycle is *technology diffusion*. Growth of regions is created by the technology 'gaps' created between firms and their competitors. In the first stage of development, firms undertake high levels of R&D investment. The second stage is characterised by very high growth rates as the region's firms reap the short-run monopoly profits from the limited competition imposed by the technology 'gap'. In the third stage the innovation becomes common knowledge (such as through product standardisation) and is diffused to competitors in other firms and regions who then subsequently close the technology 'gap' (Pred, 1975; Mansfield *et al*, 1977; Grossman and Helpman, 1991; Kokko, 1992).

However, life-cycles explain patterns of growth, but do not explain the deeper or underlying factors influencing regional advantage or the capability of a firm to change product as it reaches the end of its economic life.

Natural Endowments

Resource-rich Australia had the highest per capita income in the world in the late nineteenth century but has since declined relatively. Resource-poor Singapore, Japan and Switzerland have high per capita incomes. Resource-rich Mexico, Nigeria and Venezuela went bankrupt. Resource-poor Chad has one of the lowest per capita incomes in the world. If you were looking for a pattern, there is not one. In fact there have been quite reputable studies (for example, Sachs and Warner (1995) of the Harvard Institute) suggesting that there is a negative relationship between natural resources and growth. On the surface this presents a puzzle because you might expect that natural resources would raise wealth and the purchasing power over imports, so that resource abundance might be expected to raise an economy's investment and growth rates as well.

Natural endowments can play an important role in explaining the competitive advantage of regions, but it depends on how well natural endowments are combined with human resources, knowledge, capital and infrastructure.

Natural endowments include the abundance, quality, accessibility, and market value of a region's land, water, mineral, or timber deposits, hydroelectric power sources, fishing grounds, and other physical traits. Climatic conditions can be viewed as part of a region's physical resources as can a region's location and geographic size. Location, relative to other nations that are suppliers or markets, affects transportation costs and the ease of cultural and business interchange. The time zone of a nation relative to other nations may also be significant in a world of instantaneous global communications. London's position between the United States and Japan is often identified as an advantage in financial service industries, because London-based firms can do business with both Japan and the United States during a normal working day.

Looking a little deeper into the puzzle shows that failures of resource-led developments suggests many of the economic and political factors that may have played a role in the disappointing performance of resource-abundant economies. An explanation, drawn from the early social science literature by Bodin[6], is that "easy riches lead to sloth", but this explanation does not help much. Another explanation is that resource-rich economies are subject to more extreme rent-seeking behaviour than resource-poor economies. Although this is some evidence of this, one would still need to argue that the distribution of the rents is inferior to a broader distribution of incomes, and that the inferior distribution led to retardation of economic growth.

In the economic literature of the 1940s and 1950s there was an argument that resource based growth would be retarded by a long run decline in the world prices of primary exports relative to manufactured goods. The so called Prebish and Singer hypothesis has its basis in the gradual shift away from resource

[6] Jean Bodin is a sixteenth century French philosopher.

based inputs to production, suggesting that minerals are becoming less important in the world economy. However, the hypothesis led to the policy prescription that countries should focus on state-led industrialisation, but such policies foundered everywhere.

More recently, the importance of natural resources in economic growth has been considered in the context of the 'forward and backward linkages' in the domestic economy. That is, the extent to which natural resource extraction draws on local inputs for the processing of minerals and production of other commodities and the extent to which these products and processes reach final stages and are consumed in the domestic economy, has a bearing on the economic growth of a country.

Underlying this approach is that the manufacturing sector provides a more complex division of labour which leads to a high level of income and standard of living. A second component to this argument is provided by Matsuyama (1992) who considered the case of a two sector economy consisting of agriculture and manufacturing. The manufacturing sector is characterised by learning-by-doing and leads to spillovers of new knowledge - inducing growth. Despite the agricultural sector being internationally competitive, the economy's growth is retarded because the sector draws resources away from growth enhancing manufacturing sector.

The linkages and spillovers argument is fundamental to the origins of the American industrial success. America's initial advantage was abundant natural resources, but what drove economic growth from the mid 1800s to post WWII was the way in which those resources were utilised. America's high labour incomes and enormous domestic market with regularly homogenic tastes and preferences enabled capital-intensive mass production techniques. The efficiency of mass production was augmented by transnational transport systems. The capital intensity of the mass production established a technological path for Americans whereby learning-by-doing created the intimacy of the technology needed for innovation and creation of new knowledge. Later, the virtues of more formal education and organised R&D became important and enabled America to project economic growth well beyond that afforded alone by natural resources. Superior forms of corporate structure, organisation and management techniques, legal systems and work ethic all played a role.

The discussion above serves to identify that the importance of natural resources rests not so much with what you have but how well you use it, that is, the degree of integration of the extraction or utilisation of those resources with the processes leading to final consumption. The strength of the linkages, both forward and backward, between the extraction process and final consumption are what drive growth. Importantly, the ownership of resources determines the direction of the flow of profits.

Conclusion

In this chapter we have examined the main factors that have been advanced in the contemporary regional economic growth literature to establish which factors are basic to understanding regional growth and which offer a deeper more fundamental understanding upon which policy prescriptions can be developed.

The basic factors of labour and capital productivity, the role of export and domestic demand, critical events and triggers, life cycles and natural endowments are all relevant in describing why some regions grow and others do not, but offer little by way of guidance on how to improve regional growth. These factors are the proximate causes, not the deeper more fundamental factors. At best, they point to the need for diversification of economic activity, low cost efficient infrastructure and government services, the need to identify export markets particularly where the domestic or local market is too small to reap economies of scale. These are useful hints for the policy maker, corporate adviser and community leader but there is no prescriptive power in the analysis.

References

Arthur, W.B. (1994), *Increasing Returns and Path Dependence in the Economy*, Ann Arbor, University of Michigan Press.

Baily, M., and Schultze, C. (1990), "The Productivity of Capital in a Period of Slower Growth", *Brookings Papers on Economic Activity: Microeconomic Issue*, Brookings Institute, Washington D.C.

Barro, R.J. and Sala-i-Martin, X. (1991), "Convergence Across the States and Regions", *Brookings Papers on Economic Activity*, Number 1, Brookings Institute, Washing D.C.

Barro, R.J. and Sala-i-Martin, X. (1992), "Convergence", *Journal of Political Economy*, 100(2).

Blandy, R., Carne, S., Johnson, D. and Kenyon, P. (1994), "Economic Growth and the Victorian Economy: A Medium Term Perspective", Institute of Applied Economic and Social Research, Working Paper Series 5/94.

Brander, J.A. and Spencer, B.J. (1985), "Export Subsidies and International Market Share Rivalry", *Journal of International Economics*, 18, pp. 83-100.

Bureau of Industry Economics (BIE) (1992), "Recent Developments in the Theory of Economic Growth: Policy Implications", Occasional Paper 11, AGPS, Canberra.

Bureau of Industry Economics (BIE) (1993), *State Economic Performance 1980-81 to 1990-91*, Australian Industry Trends, 18 (May): 12-22.

Bureau of Industry Economics (BIE) (1994b), "State Economic Performance 1980-81 to 1990-91", Occasional Paper, AGPS, Canberra.

Bureau of Industry Economics (BIE) (1994a), *Partnerships for Development and Fixed Term Arrangements: An Evaluation*, AGPS, Canberra, December.

Dixit, A.K. (1992), *Optimal Trade and Industrial Policies for the U.S. Automobile Industry*, in Imperfect Competition and International Trade, ed. G.M. Grossman, MIT Press, Cambridge Massachusetts.

Fukuyama, Francis (1995), *Trust: The Social Virtues and the Creation of Prosperity*, Hamish Hamilton.

Greenwood, M.J. (1985), "Human Migration: Theory, Models and Empirical Studies", *Journal of Regional Science*, 25(4): 521-544.

Grossman, Gene M. and Helpman, E. (1991), *Innovation in the Global Economy*, MIT Press, Cambridge Massachusetts.

Helliwell, J.F., and Chung, A. (1991), "Macroeconomic Convergence: International Transmission of Growth and Technical Progress", NBER Working Paper, Number 3254 and Reprint Number 1710, National Bureau of Economic Research, Cambridge Mass.

Hermansen, T. (1977), "Development Poles and Development Centres in National and Regional Development: Elements of a Theoretic Framework", in *Growth Poles and Growth Centres in Regional Planning*, ed. A. Kuklinski, United Nations Research Institute, Geneva.

Hicks, John R. (1959), *Essay in World Economics*, Clarendon Press, Oxford.

Hirschman, A.O. (1958), *The Strategy of Economic Development*, Norton, New York.

Industry Commission (1993), *Impediments to Regional Industry Adjustment*, Volumes I and II, Report No. 35.

Kaldor, N. (1970), "The Case for Regional Policies", *Scottish Journal of Political Economy*, November, pp. 337-348.

Kokko, A. (1992), *Foreign Direct Investment, Host Country Characteristics and Spillovers*, Stockholm School of Economics, Stockholm.

Krugman, P. (1979), "Increasing Returns, Monopolistic Competition and International Trade", *Journal of International Economics*, Vol. 9, pp. 469-479.

Krugman, P. (1980), "Scale Economies, Product Differentiation and the Pattern of Trade", *American Economic Review*, Vol. 70, pp. 950-959.

Krugman, P. (1981), "Trade, Accumulation and Uneven Development", Journal of Development Economics, Vol. 8, pp. 149-161.

Lucas, R.E. (1988), "On the Mechanics of Economic Development", *Journal of Monetary Economics*, Vol. 22, No. 1.

Mansfield, E. et.al. (1977), *The Production and Application of New Industrial Technology*, W.W. Norton, New York.

Matsuyama, K. (1992), "Agricultural Productivity, Comparative Advantage and Economic Growth", *Journal of Economic Theory*.

Myrdal, G. (1957), *Rich Lands and Poor*, Harper and Row, New York.

North, P.C. (1955), "Location Theory and Regional Economic Growth", *Journal of Political Economy*, Vol. 63, pp. 243-258.

Norton, R.D., and Rees, J. (1979), "The Product Life Cycle and the Spatial Decentralisation of American Manufacturing", *Regional Studies*, 13:141-151.

Olson, M. (1982), *The Rise and Decline of Nations: Economic Growth, Stagflation, and Social Rigidities*, Yale University Press, New Haven.

Perroux, F. (1950), "Economic Space: Theory and Application", *Quarterly Journal of Economics*, Vol. 64, February, pp. 89-104.

Pindyck, R.S. (1991), *Econometric Models and Economic Forecasts*, McGraw-Hill, New York.

Porter, M.E. (1990), *The Competitive Advantage of Nations*, Macmillan Press, London.

Pred, A. (1965), "Industrialisation, Initial Advantage and Metropolitan Growth", *Geographical Review*, Vol. 55, No. 1, pp. 158-185.

Putnam, Robert (1995), "The Strange Disappearance of Civic America', *The American Prospect*, Winter.

Putnam, Robert (1995), "Bowling Alone: America's Declining Social Capital", *Journal of Democracy*, 6.

Romer, P. (1990), "Endogenous Technological Change", *Journal of Political Economy*, Vol. 98, No. 5.

Sachs, J.D. and Warner, A. M. (1995), "Natural Resource Abundance and Economic Growth", National Bureau of Economic Research, Working Paper 5398, December.

Sheehan, P. (1992), "Economic Theory and Economic Strategy: The New Growth Models", Paper delivered at the 21st Conference of Economists, University of Melbourne, July.

South Australian Centre for Economic Studies (SACES) (1997), "The Development of Regional Economies Project", Research Papers No. 97/1 to 97/4, April.

Vernon, R. (1966), "International Investment and International Trade in the Product Cycle", *Quarterly Journal of Economics*, 80(2): 190-207.

Wittwer, G., (1997), *Calibrating Intra-Domestic Substitution Elasticities in a Multi-Regional Model of the Australian Economy*, South Australian Centre for Economic Studies, *mimeo.*

Wittwer, G. and Bright, M. (1997), *The Effects of a Mining Boom on the South Australian and Australian Economies*, South Australian Centre for Economic Studies.

Chapter Four

Influences on Regional Growth — Catch Up Factors

In this chapter we move from the proximate causes of regional development to the deeper more fundamental factors. These factors drive at the establishment of incentives for good economic behaviour exercised through strong democratic relationships between the relevant stakeholders: governments, firms and the community. The factors take us beyond the traditional tools of micro and macroeconomics analysis to the less precise fields that govern the fabric of our society and our culture. Social and cultural factors drive the way we organise our institutions, our relationships with stakeholders and the way in which our region relates to the global community.

Governance

Governance not Government

Governance is the exercising of political, economic and administrative authority to manage a region's affairs comprising a complex range of mechanisms, processes, relationships and institutions through which citizens and groups articulate their interests, exercise rights and obligations and mediate differences. Governance promotes sustainable economic development through efficient government, effective civil society and a successful private sector.

Good governance consists of effective and well co-ordinated efforts directly to achieve the best results through a harmonious blending of natural, material, human and financial resources for increasing the socio-economic welfare of the population.

In particular, good governance is participatory in that members of governance institutions have a voice in the decision-making process based on democratic traditions. Procedures and methods of decision making are transparent to ensure effective participation. Good governance promotes equity and equality of treatment based on non-discrimination, and strengthens indigenous mechanisms. Based on the rule of law, good governance engenders and commands respect and trust.

A key element of good governance in advanced regions is building partnerships, embracing all relevant stakeholders in the community and forming strategic alliances around a set of goals and plans to achieve those goals. These strategic alliances recognise the strengths and weaknesses of the various partners as well as developing synergies for results-oriented activities. That is forging the linkages between those stakeholders which are both strong and flexible. These partnerships are both vertical and horizontal. Vertical in linking global, national and local institutions, processes and people. Horizontal in linking government, civil society and the private sector at each level.

Partnership relationships for good governance are characterised by five elements:

- inclusiveness: widening the scope of participation to include all relevant stakeholders;
- experience sharing: finding commonalities and comparing perspectives;
- strategy: linking stakeholders pro-actively to maximise outcomes and economies of scale;
- employment: building capacity of all stakeholders and in the inter-relationships;
- consensus building: developing mutually supportive policies, processes and operations; and
- continuous improvement: establishing moving targets of success and measures of approaching success and building successes.

Governance, rather than being government-led, is a process of managing public affairs in a participatory manner. Partnerships cover a wide variety of linkages, such as citizen-to-citizen, government-to-government, government-market, and between local communities.

So far in this discussion, the emphasis has been on governance not government. Although the government's share of economic activity is substantial in regional economies, it is not the level of fiscal stimulus of that promotes sustained growth but what matters is how well the government can foster and strengthen the linkages between all relevant stakeholders through that fiscal stimulus.

Roles of Governments

The history of involvement by Commonwealth and State governments in Australia in regional development has been characterised as a centralist approach. That is, government policy has been largely about delivering services to regions, and supporting regional development more generally through nationally imposed policies, strategies and initiatives, rather than being responsive to and supportive of specific regional priorities, preferences and needs.

Promoting regional differentiation in central government policies and responses potentially consumes substantial resources and outcomes are uncertain. However, treating the nation or a State as if it was homogeneous in most critical policy respects, made administration of policies and programs easier. And, in earlier economic times, this approach may not have been of serious concern to regional communities because the economic environment was stable or at least predictable.

However, in the context of increased diversity in the forces on regional communities and the consequences of them, a centralised view of regional needs, and one-size-fits-all responses, is generating inferior economic and social outcomes.

Both the Commonwealth and the SA State Government are reviewing their regional policies. The central message must be that regions want to be *partners* in promoting their economic and community development, rather than having policies and initiatives, and supporting advisory or administrative structures, imposed on them.

The model of inter-governmental relationships that has evolved in the Hunter Valley region, and is now being adapted to South Australia's Upper Spencer Gulf Region, provides an indication about directions for adversely affected regions. The model is potentially applicable to regions that would be booming, if it were not that they are constrained by lack of infrastructure or perverse policies. At the core of these models are:

- a joint agreement between Commonwealth and the respective State governments that they have a shared interest in regional development;
- a protocol governing how the Commonwealth and each State will collaborate to promote regional development; and

- provision within the protocol that both central spheres of government will consult and cooperate with regional leaders (in government and the community) in the design of policies and strategies to support regional development.

Such an approach should lead to decentralisation or devolution by Commonwealth and State governments to regional and local organisations of economic and community development strategy and implementation.

The notion that regional development is a "joint task" of governments is consistent with trends in other advanced economies. Three examples, of many, are offered here. In Austria, functions such as housing are shifting from the central to the Länder level, and local governments are playing a larger role in economic expansion and social change. There is a jointness between federal and Länder level governments about macroeconomic management and reduction of regional and social disparities. In Canada, the Federal government has withdrawn from labour market training, forestry, mining and recreation, and has proposed a much strengthened partnership with the provinces on such items as food inspection, environmental management, social housing and tourism. In Denmark, responsibility for social security with shifted to municipalities and regional planning and secondary schools moved to the counties. In Iceland, responsibility for primary education was transferred from central to local government (OECD, 1997).

The key element would be to remove the typical assumption made by regions that the role of Federal and State governments is principally to provide funding (whether for infrastructure or investment attraction). Furthermore, regions would be primarily responsible for strategy formulation, in consultation with governments as well as other major stakeholders.

What governments would take responsibility for would include agreement to:

- support regional strategies that "make sense" to them;
- more effectively coordinate their planning, management and delivery of services and support within and across regions;
- look for opportunities to devolve (or at least decentralise) to local and regional organisations functions that could strengthen the capacities of regions to promote their economic and community development, with appropriate parallel devolution of financial resources; and
- recognise the need for variations in approaches and strategies to allow for regionally "tailor-made" strategies, rather than trying to impose centrally designed approaches.

Government Policy and Strategy

From the theme of the previous chapter, there are a number of policies of a more basic nature that are necessary to promote or at least not constrain regional growth and development. Firstly, the provision of efficient, low cost public services and infrastructure. Secondly, adoption of an efficient taxation system, and a fiscal policy using the budget as a stabilising mechanism which neutral in the long term. Thirdly, governments should address market failure by providing social goods where the private sector does not produce or under-provides. Fourthly, there is a distributive role, to ensure that wealth and income accumulate in what the society considers a 'fair' or 'just' state of distribution. These four major functions reflect the standard role adopted by governments in developed countries. Beyond these factors lies a more influential role for government to actively promote the ability of regions to compete in the global market place. This role is strongly based in government policies and strategies to position regions for success.

Government policy can influence the 'growth paths' of regions. In a report which discussed the poor relative performance of South Australia, the consultants to the State government, Arthur D Little International (1992), observed:

> The problem is not the current recession; it is much deeper and more fundamental. South Australia in the past was able to maintain its standard of living by producing and selling goods and services mainly in the local Australian market. Now the Australian market is opening up to international competition and the performance standards of the past are giving way to a requirement for world class performance. The bases of economic success have been fundamentally changed by the process of globalisation. For the first time, the world has seen global scale industries that are able to organise ... on a worldwide basis. With the dismantling by the federal government of Australia's tariff protection, South Australia's tradeable goods and services will need to be competitive with the best the world can offer.

In other words, government has a significant role to play in determining the business environment, and therefore the 'growth path' of the State economy in previous years. But globalisation of the world economy and the increased level of competition have meant that the State government's role has changed markedly. The report also observed that:

> ... the protected environment in which business has developed has created a dependency on government that is not conducive to firms being aggressive or competitive in international markets.

The South Australian experience is not atypical. It provides an example of a region whose economic future is dependent upon government, as well as the wider community embracing the challenge of undergoing economic change. Government and its institutions can and do influence the capacity and willingness of firms and households to respond positively to change by changing the fundamental business climate in which they operate.

The willingness of government and the wider community to change can affect the ability of the region to adopt to the changing economic conditions. Olson (1992) examines the role that institutions and political organisations have in the determination of national and regional policy. Regions whose governments are able to react quickly and responsively to the changing economic circumstances have tended to generate higher rates of growth. Whereas governments which are in 'gridlock', and unable to influence policy to any major extent, often occur in countries and regions with low rates of growth and relative incomes.

Government policies and strategies that better position regions for competing globally involve the following actions:

- increase the role of the most responsive sector of the economy, the private sector, to provide services. This involves creating a competitively neutral environment, transferring resources from the public to private sector and adopting light handed regulation of the economic activities;
- facilitate the exchange of information between stakeholders through information networks, conferences and clusters;
- government procurement of leading technologies to assist in fostering economies of scale for infant industries;
- gather, analyse and disseminate information about the environment external to the region when that information has multiple purposes and uses for units in regions;
- encourage a participatory approach to regional decision making through transparency and clear criteria;
- diversify regional activity (limited only by sustainable long term outcomes) by adopting immigration polices drawing on people to supplement shortages in skills, international business networks and entrepreneurial skills and linking to existing regional activities;
- match accountability with control, and devolve government activity by deconcentrating (central government represented at the regions) and decentralising (transfer of responsibilities to lower tiers of government and non-government or semi-government bodies);
- provide incentives for good economic behaviour by rewarding excellence, and, just as importantly, rewarding significant and sustained improvements;
- up-skill the community particularly in technology, entrepreneurship, management, professional ethics and relationship building. Education should be promoted as a life-long experience; and
- promote the region by show-casing, marketing, staging events and creating a distinctive feature or feeling about the region.

The Government of South Australia has produced a document "Directions for South Australia 2000-01" which builds on the previous years' annual statement and has produced several related publications including a statement of economic directions emphasising longer term priorities and a policy statement on innovation, science and technology. The Directions 2000-01 document has seven key themes:

- education and life-long learning;
- employment and economic development;
- regional communities;
- culture, lifestyle and the environment;
- health and communities;
- justice and safety; and
- government reform.

The document expresses the importance of many of the elements described earlier, emphasising the need for partnerships, innovation and learning as well as the basic requirements of efficient infrastructure, high value added export orientation. The initiatives are many, and broad based, and, in principle, there is not a single one which does not contribute in a positive way to the State's future. Although not a criticism, these policies are being adopted everywhere. The true value therefore lays in their potency and consistency of application over time.

In that context some elements of the directions statement warrant emphasis:

- accentuation of regional and State identity through cultural diversity, broadening the production base and lifestyles. A greater emphasis on immigration of diverse groups of peoples with capacity to generate incomes though partnerships (business or community). Visual differentiation is also important;
- policies to promote regionalism, and, in particular, clarifying the roles of national, State and local government in regional development including fiscal transfer systems to local government;
- raising the level of community debate over regional development issues by hosting international conferences. That is, adopting the view of looking for the people with answers, rather than trying to solve problems locally; and
- adopt stronger incentive based methods for allocating resources. The establishment of a fund for supporting best practice in each of the key ssues for the region.

Some activities warrant extra discussion as follows.

Direct Assistance to Industry: "...with few exceptions, assistance to industry is not an effective means of promoting economic development in Adelaide, or of improving the standard of living of Australians as a whole" (Industry Commission 1996). However, Kenyon and Kincaid (1991) find that "...common-good policies - such as innovation and infrastructure investment - motivated by competitive pressures are likely to have generally beneficial effects". A key problem with direct assistance to industry is the secrecy of the activity. The 'Commercial-in-confidence' classification does not encourage the community to see the government as acting the community's interests.

Degree of Openness: The extent to which an economy engages in trade free from restrictions such as tariffs and quotas is known as the openness of an economy. Although there has been much anecdotal information that suggests that countries open to trade grow faster, only recently (Edwards, 1998) have economists been able to prove the connection empirically. The main problems have been collecting a large enough data sample and identifying the best indicators of openness. However, Edwards constructed nine different indices of openness for 92 countries and identified that their relationship with growth to be significantly positive and robust to the choice of measure.

There are several reasons why openness is important:

- particularly for small economies, openness permits specialisation and expansion of production beyond domestic demand. This has been emphasised by Australian trade theorists who played a big role in arguing twentieth century could be traced to protectionist policies;
- external competitive pressure is exerted on domestic industry to improve efficiency. This factor is regarded generally as a very important influence on growth, but problems arise if local industry is not ready to cope with the competition;
- investment decisions are likely to improve because revenue flows are based on world prices which is a better reflection of the opportunity cost of resources; and
- capital mobility is likely to improve because funding decisions can based on the most efficient use of those funds.

Importantly, openness also plays a more fundamental role in promoting growth. The more open an economy is to trade and other international economic transactions, the more receptive it is likely to be to new knowledge and innovation. This hypothesis, as with almost anything to do with the spread of ideas, is difficult to test rigorously. However, one of the most striking features of the high performing East Asian economies has been their degree of participation in the world economy. Entrepreneurs in Hong Kong, Singapore, Taiwan and South Korea copied technology and adopted it, so that they became the most efficient suppliers of labour-intensive manufactured goods in the world. In the larger, second generation high-performing Asian economies, a salient feature has been the concentration of economic growth in coastal areas particularly parts where the effects of openness are strongest (e.g., the coastal provinces of China or greater Bangkok in Thailand). Meanwhile, the majority of the developing world was pursuing inward-oriented development strategies and failing to achieve self-sustaining economic growth. The centrally planned economies were the extreme case; the limited trade within planned economies was no substitute for exposure to global competition.

Australia pursued inward-oriented development policies for most of this century. Thanks to the country's rich resource endowment living standards were the world's highest in 1890 but declined steadily throughout the 20th century. The South Australian economy shared this experience; being part of the Australian "customs union" was better than being an isolated unit, but being sheltered from global competition was not conducive to rapid growth. However, it could be argued that a country must be strategic about the degree and timing of openness. To some extent, the benefits of openness depend on how others play the game. At one extreme you could be the only open economy and others would place barriers against your exports and wipe out your local industry through subsidised imports. That is why openness is a global issue, and one in which policies must be unified so that all countries can step forward together. Small regional economies cannot afford to act in isolation. For a small open regional economy inward-looking development is a poor option, but the question remains of how South Australia can make the most of its opportunities to grow rapidly with an outward-oriented strategy.

Lucas (1988) points out that openness has the advantage of "learning by doing and seeing" which enhances the incentives for dynamic behaviour to achieve best outcomes.

A final point is that, if a country does not specialise in high growth industry but has free trade, the country could be locked into a low growth trap because it will specialise in industries with lower capacity for growth. Free trade can be a 'double edged sword' — the less open the economy the less likely that there will be a leakage of the knowledge to foreigners, on the other hand, openness can lead to a leakage of knowledge from foreigners to the home country. The issue of the degree of openness is not covered in the literature.

Degree of Regional Autonomy: Hill and Roberts (1995) argue that there is both theoretical and empirical support for the hypothesis that regions with the fastest rates of growth in Europe will be those with the highest degree of regional autonomy.

The economic arguments in favour of the devolution of government and its primary responsibility, namely, the efficient allocation of public resources, are well known. Basically, autonomy relies on the notion that decisions are best made by those whom decisions affect. That is, regions have distinct economic characteristics that ensure that their interests are inevitably poorly served by a nation-state that imposes national policies on disparate regions.

Hill and Roberts compared variations of income in regions in the UK and Europe with the degree of autonomy of those regions (measured by the allocation of funding from central to regional government).

The study identified a research agenda more so that providing strong evidence for the relationship. To extend research past the provision of anecdotal evidence, definition and measurement problems must be overcome. Hill and Roberts suggest that defining some scale of regional autonomy per region and seek to establish the empirical relationship between this and regional economic development (probably using GSP growth as an indicator). Econometric problems need also to be overcome including assessment of relative autonomy, pooling problems of using data across regions and over time and correctly specifying other factors influencing growth.

Quality of life: This is a slippery concept which requires careful research before it features as a policy instrument for attracting activity to a region. There are several authors such as McLean and Pincus (1983) that note the GDP per capita is not necessarily a good measure of the standard of living, and others, such as Crafts (1997), who have examined alternative measures notably the World Bank's Human Development Index which attempts to augment income measures for health and education standards.

However, as these authors point out, the concept is 'sticky'. Firstly higher standards of living are usually only achieved with rising incomes - society has chosen to utilise newly acquired wealth by reducing the length of the working day, etc. That is, quality of life and incomes are highly connected. Secondly, while it is true that Adelaide is a 'more affordable' location to live than most other capital cities, the majority of people still prefer to pay higher rents and put up with congestion because of the broader benefits of agglomeration - networking, diversity and opportunity - and higher incomes. Thirdly, while corporate decision makers are always looking to cut costs, head offices are hard to attract on that basis because of intangible factors - business networks, family ties of the corporate leadership group. It took 20 years to fill the office space in the Empire State Building because it was built on 42nd Street in mid-Manhattan whereas the hive of corporate activity was in the Southern area of Manhattan.

Nonetheless, the quality of life has intuitive appeal as a factor to influence the location of business and the labor force. It may be on the list of influential factors, but its rank is not known, and may change according to the nature of the interested party. Parents, making decisions about their child's university education may be highly influenced by fees, housing affordability and crime rates, but the corporate executive may place far more weight on business networks and transport costs and only after these are satisfied would housing affordability and crime rates have an influence in location decisions. Much more research is required in this field.

Education: The new growth theory's emphasis on ideas and human capital suggests an important role for educational institutions in promoting economic growth. The precise role will vary from location to location, depending *inter alia* on the level of economic development and on comparative advantage. In East Asia a crucial ingredient of success of the four tigers (Singapore, Hong Kong, South Korea and Taiwan) was the high literacy levels (relative to other low-wage countries). The tigers made the transition to manufacturing and then moved up the production ladder from cheap goods to quality manufactures, and then to services. The tigers invested heavily initially in secondary and then tertiary education consistent with the needed quality of production.

Australia already has universal primary education, but lags countries at similar income levels in secondary school completions. The Year 12 completion rate in South Australia is rising quickly but is not matching the pace of the rest of the nation. Nevertheless, in South Australia's current advanced stage of economic development, tertiary education is likely to be the critical for the services.

It is worth emphasising that much human capital formation occurs outside formal education, within the family or by on-the-job training or in informal settings. Training in specific skills is important. As the economy grows and the structure changes, new skills are needed. New entrants into the workforce (and existing workers whose skills are becoming less relevant) need to acquire these skills. This is uncontroversial, but it can also be overemphasised. Manpower planning, which was popular in education ministries around the world in the 1960s, is in eclipse because the planners had poor predictive capabilities the market could reduce specific demand/supply mismatches.

The Role of the University Sector in Promoting Global Partnerships

Second only by the Church, universities are the oldest institution of the global community. Universities, as an institution have weathered the test of time and flourished despite charges of irrelevant curriculum and socio-economic elitism. As Dr Hideo Sato, Acting Director, The Leadership Academy, United Nations University says "Indeed, universities are our national treasurers, if not global treasurers, for the incubation of ideas, innovations, initiatives and experiments" (United Nations, 1999).

One point of this view is that Universities are for the most part training people for life, which is why the role of broadening the mind takes precedence over the inculcation of specific skills which may themselves be redundant within a decade.

The IT&T Faculties/Departments with which the Centre held face-to-face discussions as part of its study for Department of Employment, Training and Youth Affairs (DETYA) on Unmet Demand for IT&T Education (SACES, 2000) were selected primarily on the basis of their relative graduate outcomes (i.e., within their region). A significant majority of these Faculties/Departments indicated that, given the 3 to 4 year lag between commencement and completion for most undergraduates, to meet industry skill needs students must be taught fundamental skills that will allow them to quickly learn new computing languages etc. Simply training in areas of current industry skill needs (such as current programming languages) will lead to students having skills that are likely to be out of date by the time they graduate.

Industry is also demanding graduates who are 'job ready', or who have significant practical experience in the type of activities which graduates would be expected to undertake in the workplace. In order to address this, most of the successful Faculties/Departments included at least some requirement to develop industry related skills such as written and oral communication in their graduates. Some Faculties/Departments offer specific courses (either optional or compulsory) on industry related skills such as communication and project management. Virtually all also include a 'real life' project, which is generally performed for an external client with students expected to demonstrate their ability to apply their skills to a practical situation. Others include semester length industry internships in their degrees, rather than the short (6-8 weeks) placements required for a course to receive IEAust accreditation. These Departments believe that the internship better prepares the student to work in industry and reduces the burden on companies which offer internships by ensuring that the student is there for enough time to become a net benefit to the sponsor.

Universities can make contributions to growth both as research centres and as educational institutions. Such co-operation already takes place on a significant scale in Australia. Governments have fostered such co-operation by providing seed money and continuing grants to co-operative projects. It also happens on an unaided basis when university researchers find common interest with private sector workers in related fields, and such collaboration can be mutually beneficial, or when private sector firms hire university staff as consultants.

A less direct link between educational institutions and growth is implicit in Porter's view of innovative activity (Porter, 1990). Better educated people are more open to new ideas and hence to making innovations. Literacy is the first huge step in widening horizons, but secondary and tertiary education continue this process. Specific knowledge may be helpful in giving educated people a basis to spot how an idea might be applied in a new context, but more importantly is the educational function of training people how to think, how to connect and how to see things from a different perspective.

It would appear that although the hypothesis has not been subject to rigorous testing, the USA's continuing technological edge derives from precisely these elements of its educational system. While Asian countries have successfully upgrade their workforce so that they can adopt and adapt ideas from elsewhere, the USA retains high income levels and technical leadership through its record of dramatic and continuous innovation.

Such innovations in frontier industries seem to occur in geographical clusters (Silicon Valley in California and Route 128 in Massachusetts are the best-known examples), supporting the view that educated people provide externalities. Better educated people not only innovate more, but are more innovative when surrounded by other well-educated people (a concept not unfamiliar to universities). Such clusters do not have to be in the most educationally advanced country, but can be fostered elsewhere, as has occurred around Lyons in France, Emilia-Romagna in Italy, Silicon Valley in California, Glen in Scotland and Bangalore in India.

The United Nations has been actively promoting the role of universities during 1999. The comments below are intended to remind South Australia's three universities of the benchmarks thought to be regarded as important by the global community. Universities should:

- demonstrate effective governance and meaningful contribution to society[7];
- have a sense of mission and responsibility to prepare future leaders[8];
- provide the 'right kind' of education, develop bodies of knowledge about societies and phenomena beyond their immediate geographical horizons;
- develop internationalised or globalised curriculum based on a multicultural (not ethnocentric) approach;
- develop interdisiplinary approaches because no policy problem can be resolved in a mono-disciplinary perspective; and
- rise above national interests and ideological conflicts in order to contribute to wider understanding global problems.

Overall, the United Nations (1999) see that universities are expected to adopt:

- new approaches in educational methodologies, including distance learning;
- interdisciplinary curriculum focussed on practical social issues;
- voluntary activities to expose students to the real world;
- continuous updating of their teaching materials, making them more transnational and multi-cultural in nature, including twinning arrangements, international educational exchange, associations with

7 Dr Emil Javier, President, University of the Philippines.

8 Professor Hideo Sato, on behalf of the United Nations University Rector.

regional and global academic bodies and participation in a myriad of development activities; and

- self-governing strategies as a model of good governance, while working harmoniously with local governments and private organisations to resolve issues.

As Pratt and Poole (2000) point out in the Australian context, there are various interpretations to the implications of globalisation on the university sector. A variant on the interpretation by the United Nations is what the authors call 'neo-liberal ideologies exhorting and cajoling governments and their broader societies toward more market-like behaviours', or, in other words, reduced public funding. Whether globalisation or Australian competition policy is forcing Australia universities to seekout international markets is arguable, but what the authors argue strongly, is that increased entrepreneurialism (applied research for sale) and international teaching activities are putting academics under high stress and morale is low. These concerns are not raised to deny that commercial pressures can make universities more efficient and effective. However, universities in South Australia lack a corporate structure and are new players in business entrepreneurialism, and accordingly need to tread with caution to preserve the qualities espoused by the United Nations while they gain sustainable momentum to acquire substitutes for public funding.

The Extent to which Firms Achieve Competitive Advantage

Governments and the tertiary sector play key roles in governance, but for the most part it is the firms that produce the output. In the previous chapter, the emphasis was of efficiency of production. This is of course important. But the emphasis in this chapter is on the capacity of firms to produce for a global market where best practice is the only practice that matters for survival. Innovation and entrepreneurship are key elements to get ahead of the pack and stay there.

Romer (1990) and other new economic growth theorists argue that externalities generated by new knowledge explains economic growth. New knowledge can come about through investment in:

- human capital in terms of general education and on-the-job training;
- physical capital; and
- innovative activity and R&D.

From a firm's perspective, the primary factor influencing the type and amount of investment undertaken by the investor is the rate of return generated on that investment. The extent to which externalities of such investments are captured by other firms will depend critically on achieving an acceptable rate of return on their investment by capturing this knowledge and using it for their production purposes. Notably, the presence of externalities will mean that returns captured by the investing firm are lower than would otherwise be and therefore the level of investment will be sub-optimal.

The current state of thinking on the link between new knowledge spillovers and regional economic growth is incomplete. While it is apparent that some form of subsidisation would enable firms to undertake the optimal amount of investment, there is little empirical evidence to support the extent of government intervention nor adequate guidance in the literature covering areas of investment that generate the most important source externalities. Furthermore, the literature offers little insight how much it matters if the economy in question is large or small, open or closed. Nonetheless, several elements appear important.

Investment

Investment in human capital can be partitioned into general education and specific knowledge. General education is not enough to ensure growth because this form of knowledge is too raw, not readily transformed into returns adequate to justify investment. Specific knowledge is closer to the production process, but how close it needs to be is not clear from the literature. On one hand, the knowledge must be general enough to enable externalities to be created but on the other hand specific enough to enable the knowledge to be put into practice.

The growth in human capital may be inhibited by the labour market because individuals may be discouraged from investing in their own human capital, but the literature offers little guidance.

Physical investment is considered to generate externalities, although new growth theories have recently tended (Romer, 1990) to de-emphasise the importance of externalities associated with physical investment.

Investment in innovative activity is thought to have a role in generating positive externalities, but again the literature provides no guidance on what sorts of innovative activity are more important.

Economic Rent

Dynamic rent seeking by firms provides a further source of explanation as to why some regions grow faster than others. Burns (1996) concludes that competition must involve firms seeking to obtain and sustain for as long as possible, finite periods of market power. This domination will in general require that an organisation outperforms its competitors in at least one of the following dimensions: architecture; capacity to adjust and innovate; reputation; and ownership of strategic assets. The knowledge and insights of the dominant firms are eventually replicated by other firms and the market power is lost. To stay dominant the lead firm must find another opportunity to extract a rent.

This 'leapfrog' explanation of corporate strategy explains the dynamics about why some firms (and regions) grow, and provide an interesting extra dimension to the externalities argument offered for growth. The market power and externalities arguments can be seen as complementary and possibly sequential - the investment is undertaken by the dominant firm which then exploits the market power temporarily - meanwhile the new idea has spread to other firms who then capital the externalities and drive down the dominant firms rate of return on that investment to normal levels.

As opposed to basic research which may need to be publicly provided, innovations which lead to new goods or services, or new processes for producing or marketing goods and services, come primarily from the private sector. Given the non-excludability of new ideas, how can private firms be expected to make the investment of time and money needed to generate new ideas?

There are two distinct views of this process. The first is a view by Schumpeter (1942). This view, emphasises the large fixed costs involved in research activity, and points to giving the successful innovator a period of monopoly power during which it can recoup the costs and make a profit. This is recognised in patent and copyright laws. There is, however, a cost to this approach as the innovator is under no pressure from competitors, so that consumers benefit from the new product's availability but suffer from high prices and lack of product improvements during the monopolistic period. Such a conflict underlies trade policy disputes between the USA wanting to give pharmaceutical firms incentives to innovate and India which wants new drugs to be available to its people at low prices. Patent protection, while rewarding an initial innovator, can prevent further improvements if the original patent is sufficiently broadly specified and the innovator rests upon its laurels; a classic example was the lack of improvement in photocopiers while Xerox had wide patent rights, followed by the blossoming of improvements after the original patents expired.

The alternative view, associated with Porter (1990), is that innovation is driven by competitive pressures, especially from local rivals. Porter based his analysis on observations of the clustering of dynamic industries in specific locations in the USA and in Northern Italy. Entrepreneurs are especially driven by observing local competitors doing well, because they cannot blame special advantages of foreigners for their own lack of success. An important element of Porter's view of technical change is its emphasis on brainwaves leading to improvements, rather than on major technical breakthroughs. To return to East Asia, the Porter hypothesis underlies the economic dynamism of much of the region as entrepreneurs had new ideas about how to cut costs or improve quality in making clothes, toys, sporting goods, etc. (They were not inventors as such). An important element in dynamic economies has often been the crossover effect whereby an entrepreneur picks up ideas from another industry by competition to innovate and to keep innovating; those that make a big enough innovation or stay ahead of the game long enough will be rewarded with fact profits, while those who are unobservant or fail to connect opportunities go out of business.

Although the views of Schumpeter and Porter have opposite policy recommendations, they are not incompatible. The Schumpeterian view captures the innovative process in capital-intensive activities like pharmaceuticals where research and development costs are large and the outcome is readily copied; either subsidies or patent protection are desirable. The Porter view captures the innovative process where brainwaves can be quickly implemented, such as computer software or other light industries; unimpeded entry and exist are desirable.

Capacity to Engage in Strategic Trade

Small regions may be poorly placed to play strategic trade games. However, many small regions are non-trivial in the production of and trade in specific commodities.

As Dixit (1984) writes, small countries seem poorly placed to play games where the trick is to threaten to make your firms larger. First, to the extent that other countries believe that the small country would not risk excessive specialisation in production, they would not find the small countries threat to do so credible. Second, small countries may be more restricted in their ability to expand output if some factors are specific or in limited supply. Third, 'the budgetary costs of a given absolute amount of subsidy will loom larger in the calculations of a smaller country.'

However, one approach may be where domestic firms who do not have a dominant market share in the industry, but are still able to capture rents. This is possible when barriers to competition exist, such as the firm having a brand name. If small firms are not seen to pose a significant threat to the market share of larger firms, then it is unlikely that the larger firms will compete with them for rents. Thus the strategy for these small firms is to restrict their own growth in production. This may be achieved through export or production taxes.

The real test of its application in the small region context depends whether suitable firms exist for targeting. The necessary characteristics are that firms must be able to earn substantial and lasting rents. This requires that there be an initial period with substantial barriers to entry. These barriers do not appear to exist in the Australian agriculture or mining industries and early processing industries, that comprise most of the value of Australia's exports.

Transmission Mechanism

The transmission mechanism from new knowledge to related applications has an important bearing on the speed at which new knowledge is used and how much is lost in the transmission. Technology transfers, foreign investment and trade are all ways in which knowledge is known to be diffused internationally but there is little agreement on which forms are the best or whether the best form is purely circumstantial.

Capacity of regions to use firm networks is another strand of thinking that is depicted by Saxenian (1994) which will enable regions to adapt to ever changing competitive environments.

During the 1970s, Northern California's Silicon Valley and Boston's Route 128 attracted international acclaim as the world's leading centres of innovation in electronics. Both were celebrated for their technological vitality, entrepreneurship and extraordinary economic growth. With common origins in University-based research and postwar military spending, the two were often compared. However, enchantment waned during the early 1980s, when the leading producers in both regions experienced crises of their own. The performance of these two regions diverged. In Silicon Valley, a new generation of semiconductor and computer start-ups emerged alongside established companies. Route 128, in contrast showed few signs of reversing the decline. Silicon Valley has now gone on to double its employment in high technology since 1975 whereas Route 128 employment increased albeit slowly from 1975 to 1985, and then declined.

These regions used similar technology, consisted of firms of similar size and were geographically agglomerated and clustered. Each region generated countless new firms and technologies. The key difference between Silicon Valley and Route 128 is that the industrial systems of Silicon Valley were built on regional networks which were flexible and technologically dynamic whereas Route 128's industrial system involved experimentation and learning confined to individual firms.

The difficulties of Route 128 are to a great extent the product of its history. The region's technology firms inherited a business model and a social and institutional setting from an earlier industrial era. When technology remained relatively stable over time, vertical integration and corporate centralisation offered needed scale economies and market control. In an age of volatile technologies and markets, however, the horizontal coordination provided by interfirm networks enables firms to retain the focus and flexibility needed for continuous innovation.

Regional institutions and business culture are difficult to change. An industrial system is the product of historical processes that are not easily imitated or altered. However, managers and policy-makers need to overcome their outdated conception of the firm as a separate and self-sufficient entity; they need to recognise that innovation is a collective process as well as an individual one. Adopting a business model that breaks down the institutional and social boundaries that divide firms represents a major challenge for Route 128, but it is decidedly less daunting than the challenges faced by regions with less sophisticated industrial infrastructures.

However, Silicon Valley, must not assume that the greater flexibility of its industrial network guarantees its continued success. The semiconductor crisis of the mid-1980s underscores potential weaknesses of the decentralised system. Network systems, like all forms of productive organisation, are fragile constructs that must be continually renewed and redefined to meet new economic challenges. The individualistic approaches of Silicon Valley entrepreneurs have, for most of the region's history, limited their ability to respond collectively to challenges or to build cross-cutting institutions that would sustain regional interdependencies.

This has left the region vulnerable to the adoption of autarchic strategies or to a deterioration of its skill base and infrastructure. The difficulties of Apple Computer - which failed to open up the proprietary architecture for its Macintosh personal computers - are a reminder that even once-innovative companies can succumb to betting on a product. Apple, in the words of one analyst, "built a fortress to protect themselves, but found out they are isolated from the rest of the industry", and began losing share in a market they had helped to create.

This danger is particularly great in recessionary times, when firms are often tempted to compete by simply cutting costs rather than differentiating their products and services or creating new markets. Firms may also be tempted to resort to litigation rather than negotiation and innovation to solve their problems. Similarly, cuts in public funding for education, research, and training, or tax policies that discourage venture capital, or transport congestion or soaring housing prices may undermine the institutions and infrastructure that support the region's network-based system.

Social Cohesion and Cultural Values

Drawing on the work of Putnam (1995) and Fukuyama (1995), the level of trust and social cohesion in society is an important feature which allows individuals and organisations to interact in an optimising way. The authors argue that social capital is not something that can be directly formed by policy - a healthy civil society depends on people's habits, customs and ethics which can only be shaped indirectly through conscious political action and must otherwise be nourished through increased awareness and respect for culture.

The competitive advantage of social capital is difficult to pin down because the arguments are not to do with radical contrast such as civil war and peace but more pervasive aspects of society as expressed through religion, language, institutions and their origins. Nonetheless, advantages may arise from lower transaction costs for firms as deals can be made on trust without draconian formal contacts, increased ability of groups of small organisations to co-operate by forming new associations as technology and markets change. High levels of social capital can reduce crime rates and enable governments to re-direct resources to further regional advantage.

On a related theme, Pomfret (1994) identifies what he terms 'cosmopolitanism' as an important attribute explaining the rapid growth of East Asia, particularly along the coastal areas where most interaction with foreigners has occurred. Porter (1990) also identifies social capital as a factor that may influence the way in which firms are created, organised and managed as well as the nature of domestic rivalry. Some of the most important aspects are attitudes toward authority, norms of interpersonal interaction, attitudes of workers toward management and vice versa, social norms of individualistic or group behaviour and professional standards.

Factors influencing the accumulation of social capital are not well understood in the economics literature. Putnam (1995) has identified that higher levels of education foster trust and social cohesion. But there is no evidence that popular notions about suburbanisation, the impact on family of women in the workforce, labour mobility, television and other media are detracting from social capital.

Temin (1997) of the Massachusetts Institute of Technology argues that the Anglo-Saxan cultural characteristic of individualism in contrast with the Japanese cultural characteristic of collectivism is an important factor differentiating how production is organised. As society's preferences or consumption change over time different will be produced which will influence the type of organisation best suited for those products.

Individualism draws a close link between the effort of an individual and an outcome. This concept was fundamental to the early theory of the firm - Adam Smith's pin factory - in which small scale firms would organise individual endeavours in a process to produce a pin. Specialisation involved the individual's concentration on a certain aspect of the production process which yielded the necessary gain in efficiency. Individualisation involved a competitive process not just with other individuals but in a share of the surplus between owners of capital and labour. Individualism was well suited to the British Industrial Revolution. Individualism was also well suited to the American process oriented mass production of goods for a huge population with near homogenous tastes which successfully carried America into the twentieth century, through the battlefields of WWII and the 'heady' days of the 1970s. Japanese growth is not an application of British or American technology. The Japanese used different methods to organise production. As Dore (1973) saw it,

Japanese workers are more likely to work as members of a team. The team aspect of Japanese business extends beyond the shop floor to governance of the firm. The J-firm is more like a coalition of stakeholders consisting of stockholders and a body of quasi-permanent employees locked into implicit contracts. In a cultural sense, employees were owners or fixtures which involved long-term investment not only in the employee but in the employee's family. In contrast with Anglo-Saxan individuals in competition, Japanese mode stresses the cooperative nature of production both within the working group on the factory floor and between the management of the firm. Output is the joint product of the team in contrast with the individual, and the jointness of this production is most suitable for customised products.

The organisation of production is changing rapidly, away from the mass production on which America is build toward customised products and shorter production runs that fit more easily into the Japanese than the American corporation. This is not a prediction of American decline. American firms have adopted Japanese strategies of unifying the interests of employees and shockholders and the Japanese firms are laying-off workers, but the network orientation to the organisation of production especially in intensive knowledge industries, information technology, communications, electronics firms, and the increasing emphasis on customised products reflecting rise of purchasing power is now a driving force. The cultural trait of individualism is undergoing a metamorphic: it is more an expression in customised consumption and in the process of production.

Cultural characteristics play an important role in the organisation of regions. If the products of a region are customised for niche markets or are knowledge intensive then there is a strong case for network organisation. This may not be the cultural ethos of the region. The thrust of Henton et al. (1997) is on civil entrepreneurship, a network concept involving the bringing together of a community to solve problems and forge ahead. It was a call for managed change to cultural traits that were inhibiting advancement. Importantly, Henton's call was suited to that region, but that does not mean all regions should choose this path.

Microsoft is the flagship of the new knowledge armada but it is not a demonstration that new software can be created on the internet by remotely located employees communicating by email. Microsoft resides mostly in a single place - a suburb in Seattle. As Bill Gates says:

> "...all our being...[is] here on one site, so that whatever interdependencies exist you can see that person face to face...[is] a major advantage" Temin (1997).

In exploring the question of what factors drive welfare-maximising outcomes in small, regional economies, it is important to recognise that such economies have some characteristics that may apply anywhere in the world. But conversely, an economy may have a particular pattern of production based on natural endowments, ongoing innovations or accidents of history that will not change dramatically. Therefore, a policy that might promote a desirable outcome in one circumstance may not work in another, due to its questionable relevance.

Conclusion

There are some general observations about regional development that are now generally accepted.

Firstly, in a globalised world, promoting regional development is increasingly a key element in promoting national development. Inter-regional linkages often have overtaken national linkages as the focal point of economic and social development opportunities. People appear to be establishing a stronger attachment to their regional and community bases - in contrast to national and State governments - as a source of support in the face of increased uncertainty, instability and stress associated with competing globally.

Secondly, regional development is about more than economic development. While the word "sustainability" has usually been attached to environmental and natural resource issues, in its widest sense it encapsulates all factors that affect the capacity of a regional economy to remain viable and vibrant - whether these relate to natural resources, the skills base of the region, its administrative and political support systems, the vitality of its sports, or strength of cultural and social cohesion.

Thirdly, regional development critically depends on the regions leading the process of developing strategies and plans for realising their potential or redressing the factors that have been pulling them down. This does not imply that regions and communities can do it all for themselves. Rather, the international evidence points to the fact that regions which have turned around their fortunes, or who have most fully capitalised on new opportunities arising from global change, have done so in large part by recognising that they have themselves the capacities needed to influence their future economic and community development. What they need is collaboration and support from State and national governments.

Fourthly, there is nothing unique about the drivers of regional development, although differences in the relative significance of some of them have emerged as a result of both the rapid growth of the information economy and changes in broader economic factors. That is, like all economies, regional economies basically grow or decline according to the demands for, and supply of, the natural and human resources they have access to, and the investments that businesses are prepared to make in them as a result. The expansion of the wine industry within the Riverland region is a case in point.

Fifthly, the basic or proximate factors that support regional growth include the availability and quality of transport, efficiency of land use, energy and housing infrastructure. But the more fundamental drivers of regional development, those that enable regions to catch up and stay ahead, lay in the institutions, policies, social and cultural values of the community, and the way in which firms and individuals organise to work together and relate with the external environment. Those factors form the structure or framework within which incentives are created for good or bad economic behaviour. The stronger the incentives for good economic behaviour the more likely:

- individuals will work near full levels of effort and potential;
- individuals and firms will co-operate and collaborate;
- resources will be devoted to productive outcomes and less likely that resources will be devoted to rent seeking, subversive behaviour, protracted legal actions, crime and destruction; and
- there will be trust in the society.

Finally, what recent thinking would emphasise, more so than in the past, is the role of regional leadership, the increased significance of innovation and technology transfer at regional level, the significance of not just education and skills development but also adaptability to changing needs and demands, and the significance of the development of strategic clusters and networks as a basis for the development of industry.

References

Arthur D. Little International (1992), "New Directions for South Australia's Economy", Final Report of the Economic Development Strategy Study prepared for the Government of South Australia.

Burns, M (1996), "Business Strategy in the Competitive Environment: Does Regulation Inhibit Success?", Industry Commission Conference, July.

Crafts, N.F., (1997), "The Human Development Index and Changes in the Standard of Living: Some Historical Comparison'", *European Review of Economic History*, December.

Dixit, A. (1984), *International Trade Policy for Oligopolistic Industries*, Economic Journal, 94, supplement, pp. 1-16.

Dore, Roland (1973), *British Factory, Japanese Factory: The Origins of National Diversity in Industrial Relations*, Allen & Unwin, London.

Edwards, S. (1998), "Openness, Productivity and Growth", *Economic Journal*, 108, March, 383 - 98.

Fukuyama, Francis (1995), *Trust: The Social Virtues and the Creation of Prosperity*, Hamish Hamilton.

Henton, D., Melville, J. and Walesh, K. (1997), *Grassroots Leaders for a New Economy*, Jossey-Bass Publishers, San Francisco.

Hill, S. and Roberts, A. (1995), "Economic Development and Regional Government — Wales, Britain and Europe", *Australasian Journal of Regional Studies*, Vol. 1, No. 1.

Industry Commission, (1996) "State, Territory and Local Government Assistance to Industry", Report No. 55.

Kenyon, D. and Kincaid, J. (eds) (1991), *Competition Among States and Local Governments: Efficiency and Equity in American Federalism*, The Urban Institute Press, Washington D.C.

Lucas, R.E. (1998), "On the Mechanics of Economic Development", *Journal of Monetary Economics*, Vol 22, No. 1.

Matsuyama, K. (1992), Agricultural Productivity, Comparative Advantage and Economic Growth, *Journal of Economic Theory*.

McLean, I.W. and Pincus, J.J. (1983), "Did Australian Living Standards Stagnate between 1890 and 1940?", *Journal of Economic History*, March, Volume XLIII.

Olson, M. (1992),*The Rise and Decline of Nations: Economic Growth,* Stagflation, *and Social Rigidities,* Yale University Press, New Haven.

Porter, M.E. (1990), *The Competitive Advantage of Nations,* Macmillan Press, London.

Pratt, G. and Poole, D. (2000), "Global Corporations "R" Us? The Impacts of Globalisation on Australian Universities", in *Australian University Review,* Vol. 42, No. 2, 1999 and Vol. 43, No. 1, 2000, Double Issue.

Putnam, Robert (1995), "The Strange Disappearance of Civic America", *The American Prospect,* Winter.

Romer, P (1990), "Endogenous Technological Change", *Journal of Political Economy,* Vol. 98, No. 5, pp. S71-S102.

Sachs, J.D. and Warner, A. M. (1995), "Natural Resource Abundance and Economic Growth", National Bureau of Economic Research, Working Paper 5398, December.

Saxenian, A. (1994), *Regional Advantage,* Harvard University Press.

Schumpeter, J.H. (1942), "Capitalism, Socialism and Democracy", Chapter VII.

South Australian Centre for Economic Studies (SACES) (2000), *Unmet Demand for IT&T Education.*

Temin, P. (1997), "Is it Kosher to Talk About Culture?", *Journal of Economic History,* Vol. 57, June.

United Nations (1999), *Building Partnerships for Good Governance,* New York.

Chapter Five

The Economics of Innovation

High Technology industry and its intersection with the rest of the economy have increasingly become a focus of attention, both for academic research and for policy makers. In this chapter we will explore two areas of intersection between high technology industries and the broader economy; evidence on the extent of spillovers from R&D (one of the suggested underpinnings of new growth theory) and theoretical frameworks for analysing the locational decisions of high technology. The latter discussion will focus on explaining the observed high densities of high technology firms in particular regions, such as Silicon Valley.

R&D Spillovers

As discussed in Chapter 2 of this book, much of the early theory of economic growth was concerned with diminishing returns to inputs - land, labour and capital - which would eventually lead to a steady state level of income per capita. However the "New Economic Growth Theory" (also called Endogenous Growth Theory), which has its origins in Romer (1986), argues that economic growth can continue indefinitely. Romer emphasises the importance of spill-over benefits of R&D investment. An R&D spillover occurs when knowledge which was created by one firm is transferred to other firms (in the same or related industries), and when the real resource cost of the transfer is very low. There is a kind of increasing returns involved in R&D: it can be costly to create knowledge, but cheap to disseminate it. The patent system is a testimony to this difference in costs, as well as to the difficulty that firms have in preventing the unauthorised transfer of ideas or discoveries to other firms. Indeed, it can be costly, even impossible, for firms to prevent such transfers, even when patents apply. (In technical jargon, economists call this characteristic of knowledge 'non-exclusivity'.)

Although innovation in industry can lead to product innovation, the literature on spill-over benefits from R&D tends to concentrate on process innovation. There are two main sources of R&D spillovers into the production process. The first is spill-overs to other firms due to the non-excludable nature of much basic research. This spill-over can involve foreign firms, but most studies concentrate on calculating the home-country benefits. Research spillovers are not confined to technical developments; they can also include things such as improved management or production technologies. The increasing predominance of new manufacturing techniques, such as Just-in-Time manufacturing, suggests that this type of research spill-over can be as important as research which leads to new products or capital goods. The second source of R&D spillovers is through companies receiving higher quality and/or cheaper goods and services due to the R&D investments in their supplier industries.[9] Advances in inputs improve the competitiveness of industries that use those inputs. This benefit is significantly larger for those industries further down the chain of production and those that use technologically sophisticated inputs such as the chemicals and aerospace industries and low for those industries at the forefront of technology such as scientific equipment and computer manufacturers.

Studies on the estimated social and private Rates of Return (RoR) for domestic R&D investment usually produce large numbers. Estimated private RoRs for R&D are generally in the order of 20-30 per cent, with the net estimated social RoRs usually being twice as great (e.g. Bernstein and Nadiri, 1988; Nadiri, 1991). The rates of return to an industry of R&D in other sectors can also be substantial with estimates ranging from 5 to 100 per cent for various industry sectors (e.g. Bernstein and Nadiri 1988; Suzuki, 1993). These significant differences between private and social RoRs for R&D would suggest that R&D investment would be sub-optimal in the absence of subsidies or other public policies. The very large social RORs imply that public policies have been too cautious and not supportive enough, but, as some authors point out, at the margin, under supply of R&D is likely to be reduced because firms need their own R&D effort to be able to utilise the products of other firms.

---

9 Griliches (1992) argues that the latter source of R&D spill-over should not be properly thought of as a true spill-over; instead he argues that it causes a problem for measuring the real price of capital equipment. He argues that capital price indices should include an allowance for increased quality in their real price levels and so quality improvement should be measured as a decrease in the real price of capital goods rather than as a spill-over from other industry R&D.

R&D spillovers are not constrained to any particular region, particularly with the increasing international flows of information through the internet, and several studies have attempted to calculate rates of return to countries of foreign and world R&D. Coe and Helpman (1995) estimated the rate at which Total Factor Productivity (TFP) in various countries increases as a result of changes in the domestic and foreign stock of knowledge. These calculations were performed for all of the G7 countries and 15 smaller OECD economies, with the rates of change in TFP being used to calculate Rates of Return (RoR) to R&D expenditure. An approximation of foreign R&D capital stock for these calculations is produced by import-weighting the R&D capital stocks of a country's trading partners; i.e., if 15 per cent of country X's imports come from the USA then 15 per cent of the US R&D capital stock is included in the foreign R&D capital stock of country X.

The average own RoR for R&D capital in G7 countries was 123 per cent and for the 15 smaller OECD countries it was 85 per cent. Additionally they estimated that on average investment in R&D in G7 countries had a worldwide RoR of 155 per cent, this being effectively the benefit to the world economy through increasing the total stock of knowledge. In order to calculate the rate of return of G7 R&D expenditure in other countries, the R&D expenditure of each of the G7 countries was entered into the production function of the other OECD country in proportion with their bilateral import shares from the G7 country.

Engelbrecht (1996), like Coe and Helpman, used an elasticity approach to calculate the rates of returns of R&D investment within and between selected OECD countries. Engelbrecht postulated that Coe and Helpman's elasticities for R&D are inflated because they did not consider the potential impact of Human Capital on total factor productivity. To rectify this Engelbrecht repeats Coe and Helpman's estimation procedure with the addition of a term to reflect the stock of human capital in each country (average years of education for persons in labour force aged over 25). Due to data limitations the sample period was reduced to 1971-85 and Denmark was omitted. This Human Capital value was a significant feature of the change in TFP, and for comparable years the elasticity's of TFP to foreign R&D stock were roughly halved. If this were reflected in the estimated rates of return over the whole sample period it would reduce own country rates of return for R&D investment to 40 to 60 per cent, which is more in line with the estimates from micro-level studies.

As was noted previously both the private and social rates of return to R&D investment seem to be very substantial; these are however likely to be overstated due to several data limitations. At the firm level, R&D statistics only include the cost of the research itself, not the associated costs of translating this innovation; such as re-tooling production plants, market research, marketing, etc. At the national level, whilst non-capital and non-labour improvements to total factor productivity should give a reasonable idea as to the benefits of innovation, R&D expenditure is only one factor in the development of innovation. A range of other factors such as microeconomic reform, changes in industrial organisation techniques, and reductions in the distortions in international trade are also likely to increase Total Factor Productivity. Hence, any use of R&D as the only source of innovation will lead to R&D's benefits being overstated.

Unfortunately failure to account for improvements in human capital was not the only limitation to the work on international spillovers. Keller (1996; reported in Jorgenson, 1996) found that the size of spillovers from international R&D were even higher when, instead of being assigned according to actual trade data, the import shares used to calculate foreign R&D capital stocks were chosen randomly. Returning to our earlier example; in Coe and Helpmans' calculations 15 per cent of US R&D capital stock was included in country X's foreign R&D capital stock because 15 per cent of country X's imports were sourced from the US. In Keller's calculations however, a randomly calculated proportion of US R&D stock (e.g., 12 per cent) was used instead. If the data supported Coe and Helpmans' hypothesis then it would be expected that this random assignment would on average lower the estimated size of spillovers from international R&D stock as the stock of foreign R&D available to country X would be incorrectly specified in Keller's calculations. The fact that estimated spillovers actually increased after this random assignment suggests that the current data available is not of sufficient quality for the evidence of international R&D spillovers to be reliable.

Work by Jorgenson and others has suggested that a significant proportion of what has been traditionally inferred from national accounts as (and hence ascribed to spillovers) is in fact an accounting error due to the failure to adjust measures of capital and labour stocks for their quality. For example Jorgenson and Stiroh (1999) estimate that for the USA from 1990 to 1996, of the 2.36 per cent average annual growth in output, only 0.23 per cent was ascribable to TFP growth. This suggests that improvements in the quality of the capital stock are the most significant benefits which result from other firms' R&D. High technology goods have made a significant contribution to this growth, with computer outputs accounting for 16 per cent of US GDP growth from 1990-96.

This work suggests that whilst productivity improvements have been a factor in economic growth their total impact has been significantly less than that of growth in the stock and quality of labour and capital services, and hence the government does not need to alter investment choices to maximise national economic growth. Despite this evidence that national growth is essentially determined by the cost and quality of capital and the quantity and quality of labour, regional growth may be more policy amenable. In the case of regional growth the question is not just why growth occurs, but also why it occurs where it does. The following two sections discuss economic theories on the locational choice of firms and the reasons for variations in economic performance.

Clusters and the Location of High Technology Firms

In recent times there has been a significant focus on the reasons behind the locational decisions of firms, particularly those in so-called 'sunrise industries'. Much of this research has occurred in the United States and has focussed on industries such as semi-conductors and electronics.

Markusen, Hall and Glasmeier (1986, pp. 132-143) make several observations about more general attractions for high-tech industry: major airports with good national and international passenger and air cargo activities; areas with good natural amenities in particular mild and sunny climates; areas offering attractive housing at reasonable prices; areas with educational and cultural advantages, including good educational opportunities, an array of specialised cultural services, low levels of pollution, and good recreational opportunities; regions which are weakly unionised and have low wage rates and high unemployment rates; a high degree of internal accessibility and connectivity, as for instance areas with well developed highway systems; well-established infrastructure of specialised business services; anti-regulatory, free-enterprise ideology; centres of industrial R&D which will tend to locate close to the headquarters of major industrial corporations; concentrations of federally funded fundamental scientific research; and areas with high concentrations of defence spending.

Markusen et al. tested their hypothesis with respect to the location (both of plants and jobs) of the American high tech sector in 1977 and the changes in the location between 1972 and 1977. Most variables had their expected signs although not all were significant. Of those sectors which performed as expected were; climate index (+), educational opportunities (+), the presence of existing business services infrastructure (+), and defence spending (+) all had high confidence levels.

The relative importance of factors that influence the choice of location of high-technology firms was explored by Ó hUallacháin (1990). He used data from all 264 US statistical regions to study possible causes of manufacturing location over the period 1977-1984. There were several findings. The most statistically significant variable influencing the location decisions of high-technology manufacturing was the presence of similar firms, although the coefficient was less than unity implying some diminishing returns in agglomeration economies. Pre-existing firms were significant for all high-tech sectors. Other generally significant variables were local market strength (+) and wage rates (-). Defence expenditure (+) and the presence of research parks (+) were significant for communications equipment. Climate was significant for electronic components. Government economic development expenditures were not significant for any sector. The presence of research parks may have as much to do with access to subsidies than access to synergies from co-location of firms in parks.

Boddy and Lovering (1985) investigates the relative success of the Bristol sub-region in the UK at attracting high technology investment. They found the region had a higher than average proportion of employment in the defence/aerospace industries. From interviews with firms the authors believe that a combination of the presence of highly skilled labour [managers and engineers] and an environment which will attract and retain this labour, and the availability of production labour [skilled (wirers) and unskilled] determined firm location. They found that the presence of defence/aerospace industries in a region creates a pool of highly skilled production labour, hence encouraging electronics firms to locate in these regions.

Fingleton (1994), in a study of the spatial location of high tech industries in the UK, finds that these industries were not distributed spatially like other industries. The results are only normalised by introducing a dummy variable for the presence of aerospace industries, this means that the presence of aerospace industries in a region serves to encourage the establishment of other high tech firms.

One common conclusion of these studies is that high-technology firms tend to locate near similar firms, forming industrial complexes or clusters. Electronics and communications equipment manufacturing, in particular, have a tendency to cluster around defence or aerospace facilities. This tendency could be brought about by either companies being independently attracted to a particular area because it exhibits those features which attract high tech firms, or it could be due to the existence of agglomeration economies; or government subsidies.

Aydalot (1988) identified a range of mechanisms underlying the development of high technology complexes in various regions in the United States and Europe, only some of which involve agglomeration economies. Factors which have been influential in the locational choice of high-technology firms, and hence in the initial establishment of a high technology industrial complex are:

- location through government decisions (such as technology parks);
- attraction through government incentives;
- attraction through the image of the area;
- attraction through local demand for high technology products;
- internal spin off within the region;
  - from knowledge centres such as universities; and
  - from local firms (as occurred in Silicon Valley);
- high rate of internal firm creation;
  - local socio-professional adapted structure; and
  - local profit opportunities.

Just because a high-technology cluster comes into being in a region does not mean that there will be sustainable benefits for the region such as agglomeration economies (or to put it another way, just because a few high technology firms are attracted to a region does not mean that it is destined to become a new Silicon Valley). Aydalot also lists a range of factors which positively influence the operation and growth of a high technology industrial cluster once it has been established. These are the factors which maximise the benefits to the region of the presence of innovative industries:

- local customers;
- local suppliers;
- sub-contracting on a local basis;
- local inter-firm cooperation;
- local scientific/technical links.

Keeble (1988), writing about the UK's experience, identified different factors in location decisions in high technology companies between R&D intensive operations, and production facilities. The location of R&D intensive high-technology operations is predominantly driven by two key factors: the locational preferences of highly qualified professional staff relative to their current location; and the local scientific research capacity. With regards to the first, human capital is becoming the critical input to production in industries which have in many cases seen average product life cycles fall from 10-15 to 3-5 years. There is a significant body of evidence that 'high tech' workers place a high value on the quality of the local environment, and as they are in strong demand they can afford to be "choosy" as to where they work and live. Local scientific research capacity is important as it provides a pool of existing experienced researchers, a steady flow of new graduate recruits, a supply of new research developments which can be 'spun-off', and a source of technological innovation through informal and formal research linkages. The final significant factor in R&D focussed activity location in the UK was proximity either by motorway or high-speed rail connection to London, with its international airports and financial markets.

For Britain, Keeble reports that R&D and mass production activities have been increasingly distinct in their geographical location. In the case of mass production new investment has increasingly focussed on peripheral areas of Britain, such as Scotland and Wales. Keeble asserts that this is primarily driven by government regional policy, with 80 per cent of foreign owned computer electronics firms reporting (Kelly 1986, quoted in Keeble) that regional policy incentives had been a major factor. Keeble also suggests that labour market advantages (such as female production workers and a pool of locally trained para-professional employees) act as a secondary incentive for new investment location.

Keeble's work suggests that agglomeration economies are more likely to be a factor in the location decisions of research focussed firms, whereas the location of production facilities would be more likely to be driven by cost, factors, and to a lesser extent labour supply.

The tendency of high technology firms, particularly R&D intensive activities, to locate in existing industry clusters cannot simply be due in all cases to the characteristics of the region. If this were the case then firms would cease to locate in a region once negative externalities of firm location (such as increased pollution) reduced the attractiveness of the area as a residential location. Instead it has been observed (Saxenian, 1985) that firms continued to locate in Silicon Valley even after pollution increased significantly, overcrowding increased commuting times and house prices increased substantially. This suggests that, at least in some cases, agglomeration economies are a significant factor in the locational decisions of high technology firms.

What has been revealed by research into the nature of agglomeration economies associated with clusters of high technology industry? Firstly, the local labour market within a high-tech cluster is a repository of skills directly relevant to a wide variety of employers, and, conversely, employees have access to a wide variety of employment opportunities (Scott, 1993). Secondly, job search and recruitment costs are minimised because of the high density and degree of familiarity with the labour market (Scott and Angel, 1987). The first and second points above apply equally to the provision of sub-contractor services. The third factor is the availability of local educational institutions geared explicitly to the training of qualified labour (Scott, 1993). The benefits of tailored education are not limited to the existence of advanced degree courses, but also include the availability of adjunct professors to high-tech firms and the willingness to provide tailor-made course work and facilities (Henton, Melville and Walesh, 1997). Fourthly, Fingleton (1992, 1994) emphasises that not only are high-tech firms drawn to an existing cluster but new firms are "*spawned from existing firms or from related research-orientated institutions in the area...This spawning process is the outcome of product and process diversification and innovation associated with R&D activity*". This source of agglomeration economy is very concentrated in areas which contain R&D intensive facilities. There would seem to be little prospect for spin-off companies to be created in clusters which only include manufacturing facilities, as little or no innovation occurs in the area. Finally, the economies of scale which exist in a cluster enable the creation of firms to provide highly specialised business services Fingleton (1992, 1994). The existence of these firms then serves to further increase the attractiveness of the cluster for firm location.

The identification of factors influencing the formation of clusters should allow conclusions to be drawn as to whether a particular investment is likely to result in an industry cluster being formed or strengthened. Two judgements could potentially be made. Firstly, it should be possible to analyse an investment proposal by a large high technology firm to assess whether the nature of the investment and its location have the potential to engender a cluster by creating agglomeration economies. Secondly, existing industry complexes could be examined to determine if agglomeration economies exist (and hence whether they are likely to be self-sustaining and continue to attract new firms), or whether they are simply a feature of a region's comparative advantages or government policies. This analysis could be applied to any industry sectors which had shown a tendency for geographical concentration, although the relative importance of different impacts will obviously vary.

Innovative Milieus

Whilst the research on clusters examines why existing clusters formed, and details a range of externalities which lead to cluster formation, it does not explain why clusters don't come into existence in every region where these benefits exist, nor why some clusters are provide greater benefits than others. Hence, the economic growth literature needs to be broadened to capture the relationship between the cluster and the region it is located in.

The concept of the "Innovative Milieu" was developed by a group of European scholars centred around the GREMI (Group de Recherche Européen sur les Milieux Innovateurs). It essentially seeks to provide an explanation as to why some regions with clusters of firms in innovative industries (or the preconditions of a cluster) grow rapidly and sustainably and others do not. This approach focuses on the links between innovative industries and the broader macro and political economy of the region.

The central theoretical components of innovative milieus as an explanation for variation in regional economic performance (Camagni 1995, p. 318-19 and Aydalot, 1988) are based on what are normally considered to be factors in national economic development. However, these factors are enhanced by proximity and the economic and cultural homogeneity of a region. The central theoretical components highlighted by Camagni (1995, p. 319) are:

- highly specialised division of labour (first outlined by Adam Smith);
- processes of 'learning by doing' and 'learning by using' (developed by Arrow), which produce broader benefits than can be captured by individual firms due to the high labour mobility within an innovative milieu expanding the pool of available talent for each firm;
- the externalities generated by industry clusters (discussed previously in this chapter), particularly the specialised labour and subcontracting markets;
- Schumpeterian entrepreneurship enhanced by longstanding and specific skill sets available in the region's labour force and by the imitation possibilities offered by the regional 'cluster' of activity; and

- the cross fertilisation process which occurs in clusters of related industries, generating systems of integrated and incremental innovations.

It is also essential that these components are matched by an efficient regional economy, particularly one where the Schumpeterian process of 'creative destruction' (the switch towards new industries through resources being freed up by the decline of old industries) is facilitated (through measures such as training of retrenched employees) rather than hindered by government.

A distinguishing feature of innovative economic communities such as Silicon Valley is not just that they have clusters but that they have mechanisms to engage their clusters and understand what they need from the community (Henton, Melville and Walesh (1997).

Henton et al. believe that for a region to be successfully innovative the cluster must be able to 'intersect' with the economic community through "civic entrepreneurship". These entrepreneurs understand the needs of the cluster and know how and where to get what they need. These needs may include access to head office finance facilities, readily accessible residential areas of appropriate quality, airports that offer direct access to other regions, access to information networks, responsive government police with strong IT skills and other combinations of services suited to the needs of the cluster. To offer such services the economic community needs a critical mass to be able to provide the diversity of needs at costs competitive with other economic communities.

Aydalot (1988) observes that typically the focus of cluster development is on the firms as the only innovative actors in the economy. Aydalot extends the discussion by contending that the truly self-sustaining clusters of high technology industry are where innovative firms come into being (or locate in) regions that are themselves innovative and flexible (either at the government or the societal level). If an innovative firm locates in an area which is not flexible enough to enable its innovation then it is not as likely to succeed, and a cluster of similar firms is certainly unlikely to develop. Similarly an innovative government, or a research intensive region will not produce an innovative region without entrepreneurs. These observations have led to the development of the 'innovative milieu' approach, with research focussed at the GREMI (Group de Recherche Européen sur les Milieux Innovateurs). Essentially this suggests that resources are not enough, nor is good policy, nor is an entrepreneurial business sector. Instead an innovative region only develops when there is a combination of these factors.

Aydalot also observes that research on clusters and innovative regions tends to examine the issue through the lens of Silicon Valley. Instead, he contends there are three primary patterns of innovation, and the features required for one are not necessarily required for another. Aydalot's three patterns of innovation are:

- the restructuring of a pre-existing industrial environment;

- large firm corporate restructuring; and
- the 'production' of knowledge.

Collaborative Economics (1999) advance similar views based on experiences in the USA. They describe the four cornerstones of innovation as being: *assets; networks; culture;* and *community*. However *regional leadership* (either public or private sector) is essential to draw these factors together, thereby enabling innovation. It is regional leadership that creates the networks and interconnections (such as between basic research in universities and entrepreneurs) to fully utilise the region's assets and seek to influence the culture and community of the region so that it supports rather than resists innovation. They outline four key roles for regional leadership in the development of an innovative region:

- building fundamental economic assets, such as education, research capacity and venture capital;
- creating networks connecting entrepreneurs to regional assets, and expanding the connections between entrepreneurs;
- promoting a culture of innovation, both by marketing individual innovators to the community as role model, and also educating the community as the need for, and benefits of, increased flexibility; and
- making quality of life a key asset for the region.

This once again reinforces the point that a region cannot become innovative just by relying on its existing assets (such as quality universities) or by attracting inward investment from high-technology firms. As Saxenian (1994) wrote, it is "not the ingredients but the recipe". This is the role Collaborative Economics see for regional leadership; to ensure a region maximises the benefits from its intellectual and innovative assets. As an example, Collaborative Economics (1999) compare Houston and San Diego: "Houston's resources in bioscience and communications dwarf those of San Diego, yet San Diego is currently generating many more entrepreneurial start-ups in these sectors." Collaborative Economics see the regional leadership of San Diego as being the difference between the relative success of the two cities in capitalising on their university's research base. In particular they highlight the culture within the University of California - San Diego which encourages (and trains) academics to recognise ideas with commercialisation potential and either follow the idea through to commercialisation, or alternatively brings in private entrepreneurs to handle this process; the availability of local risk tolerant venture and angel capital; and the strong links between the university and the local business community.

Camagni (1995), based on the experience of lagging regions in Europe, has developed a methodology of identifying Innovative Milieus from historical data, and detailed the various transition paths which can lead to the establishment of innovative milieus in lagging regions. The two data sets used to measure the presence of an innovative milieu are the productivity growth rate (used as a proxy for innovation) and the growth rate in local employment (used as a proxy for the local capacity to generate development). This conceptual framework can be outlined diagrammatically by comparing the lagging region to the national or supranational (in the case of Europe) averages for these two factors, with Camagni's diagram shown as Figure 5.1.

The diagram can also be used to determine the current situation of a lagging region, by plotting these indicators against the national average, placing it in one of four basic states. The bottom left-hand quadrant is a situation of stagnation, with neither innovation nor local capacity at the national average. The upper left hand quadrant indicates that innovation is occurring, but that a local milieu is not developing, the lower right hand quadrant is the reverse case, indicating that local capacity and interconnectedness is being developed but that innovation is not occurring. The final state is the upper right hand quadrant, which indicates the presence of an innovative milieu, as both innovation and local capacity are growing at a rate above the national average. In this diagram the area above the negatively sloped diagonal represents GDP growth relative to the national level, and the area below the line relative GDP decline.

Growth generated solely by the attraction of inwards investment which does not 'connect' to the existing structures of the local economy is not necessarily beneficial. As Camagni (1995) puts it: "... as in the Mezzogiorno or the Irish case, ... without the true involvement of the local socioeconomic fabric, externally driven growth seldom generates a sustained development process in the long term. In contrast, it more easily creates 'cathedrals in the desert' (or 'cathedrals desertifying their immediate environment,' due to the shock exercised on the local wage structure). This is essentially an example of the Dutch disease problem, caused in this case by 'windfall' investment rather than a resource discovery.

Similarly local economic capacity and interconnectedness cannot be sensibly increased without attention also being paid to innovation. If a local government simply concentrates on increasing local employment, without an associated increase in labour productivity then the economy will remain in stagnation; although in this case as a mendicant economy reliant upon government financial aid or legislative protection.

The lesson in this for policy makers is that the no single approach to increasing growth is likely to produce sustainable benefits. If the government is attempting to produce growth by attracting external investment then to ensure the Dutch disease problem does not emerge they should also work on expanding local economic capacity, either by targeting investment that fits the existing industry structure, or by providing training etc. to ensure the local economy possesses the skill to link with, and take full advantage of the external investment. If the government is attempting to produce growth by increasing local capacity, interconnectedness or employment then they also need to ensure that productivity growth also occurs. This could be done by actions such as ensuring that government policies do not interfere with the transfer of resources away from declining industries, or by the provision of training to increase the quality of labour.

Figure 5.1
Possible Development Trajectories from Stagnation for Lagging Regions

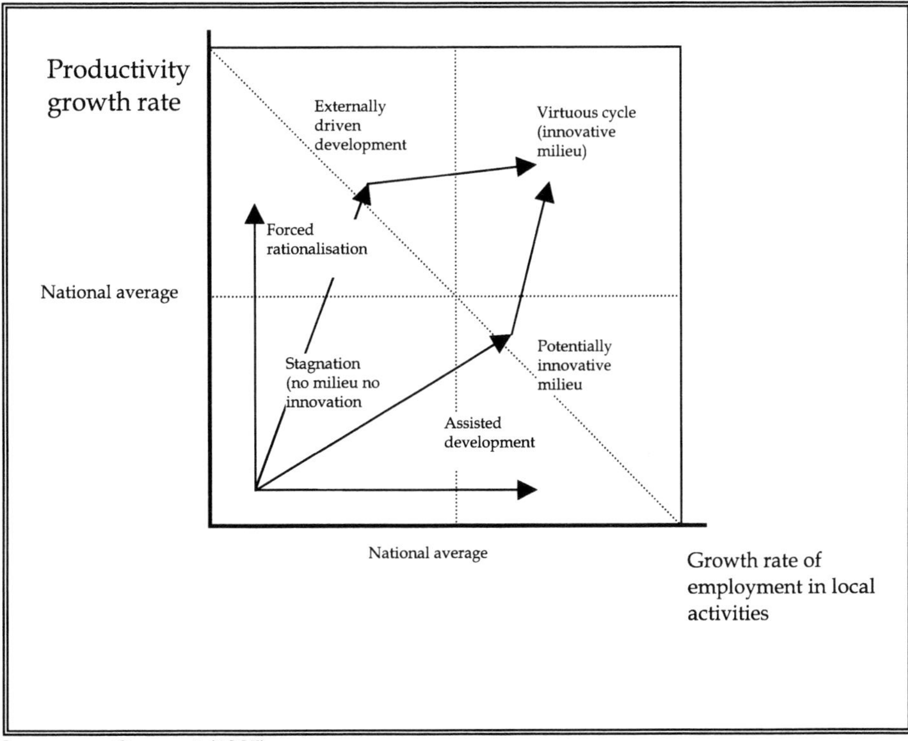

Source: Camagni (1995).

There are four possible trajectories from stagnation for a region in response to a shock, either from government policy or industry location decisions. The first is by significantly increasing productivity by rationalisation of industry, usually driven by external pressures. This leads to a sub-optimal condition, forced rationalisation, where the failure to improve employment means that GDP growth remains below the national average. The second growth trajectory is through the stimulation of local employment, usually through government assistance. This growth path leads to a sub-optimal condition, assisted development, where indigenous employment is increasing above the national average but productivity growth is low and hence GDP growth is below the national average.

There are however two growth trajectories which can move the region into an above average growth condition. The first of these is externally driven development due to investment (and subsequent transfer of knowledge) from outside the region. This investment significantly increases regional productivity due to the new activity, but only leads to limited employment growth as this new activity is not fully integrated with the regional economy. The second positive growth trajectory stems from strong increases in local employment due to the synergies between local firms (a potentially innovative milieu) but relatively limited innovation (and hence productivity growth).

These two positive growth trajectories can, if the appropriate policies are introduced by governments or "civic entrepreneurs", be transformed into an innovative milieu. In the case of externally driven development what is needed is policies to integrate the new activity into the region. This can be achieved by policies such as encouraging local firms to change their focus to provide specialised business or sub-contracting services to the new activity; introducing policies that encourage and enable the creation of new firms to provide complementary services to the new activity; encouraging technological transfers between the new activity and the region; and ensuring local institutions enable firms to 'spin off' from the new activity's R&D effort. In the case of potentially innovative milieus what is needed is policies to encourage innovation in the existing integrated industry structure. This could be done by policies such as subsidising corporate R&D effort, encouraging and enabling research institutions and researchers to commercialise their results and increasing the quality of public education and R&D in the region.

Policy Implications of Innovative Milieus for Regional Leaders

This work on Innovative Milieus by GREMI and on Regional Leadership by Collaborative Economics suggests a strong role for regional governments (state and local) in the development of their regions, by addressing any factors in their region which inhibit the development of an innovative local economy. This could involve:

- improving the resource endowments of the local economy by physical or human capital investment;
- improving the flexibility of the local economy by:
  - increasing the efficiency of government regulations and service delivery;
  - increasing community awareness of, and support for, the need for improved economic flexibility;
  - providing retraining to persons employed (or recently employed) in declining industries to smooth the transition to new areas of economic activity;
- encouraging the development or entry of specialised business services companies;

- building the educational capacity of the region;
- building the research capacity of the region;
- building connections between local businesses;
- building connections between local business and research institutions;
- building connections between local business and educational institutions;
- strategically attracting firms from outside the region where the attracted firm could enable the success of existing business by either providing business services which were not previously available or by making use of them as suppliers or subcontractors, or by transferring technology;
- marketing the capabilities and endowments of the region to firms outside the region; and
- market the quality of life of the region to skilled individuals and entrepreneurs.

E-Commerce: Challenges & Opportunities for Governments and Regions

The earlier parts of this chapter examined the importance of R&D to economic growth and the conditions that may encourage innovation. In this section, the discussion turns to a particular innovation, namely e-commerce, to understand its impact on regional economies.

Scale of E-Commerce

In their June 2000 economic outlook publication, the OECD highlight e-commerce as an emerging area of innovation which could have a significant impact on the structure of the economy. Broadly speaking, e-commerce involves sales which are transacted over the internet (or through another system for linking computers) whether the goods or services in question are delivered electronically or physically. E-commerce is a new area of activity for the internet, but it has developed rapidly since commercial use of the internet was first permitted in 1991. Estimates for the value of e-commerce in 1999, reported by the OECD (2000) vary from US$70 billion to US $1,000 billion and projections for 2003 from US$1,244 to US$4,600 billion.

Currently e-commerce is dominated by business to business transactions, which the OECD estimates account for 70 to 85 per cent of total e-commerce. Whilst business to consumer transactions are expected to increase their share of the total, the International Data Corporation (1999, reported in OECD, 2000) projects that even by 2003 business to business will still be the dominant form of transaction. Although it has grown rapidly, US data (Boston Consulting Group, quoted in OECD, 2000) suggests that consumer e-commerce expenditure is still only a small proportion of retail sales, 0.5 per cent. E-commerce does have much higher penetration in some retail sectors, 15 per cent for financial broking, 9 per cent for computer hardware and 5 per cent for books and event tickets. It also has a broader influence than its market share would suggest as it is also used as a tool for gathering information.

Economic Implications of Increased E-Commerce

The OECD considers that the principal economic impact of increased use of e-commerce by business and consumers is likely to be reduced prices - through disintermediation, reduced 'bricks and mortar' capital investment, and increased competition - and improved information and coordination. Disintermediation is the process whereby one or more of the layers in the product distribution chain are able to be bypassed due to the new technology. It could involve, for example, a manufacturer selling directly to a consumer or to a retail chain.

The extent to which disintermediation will occur depends on the level of information held by consumers and consumer preferences. For example to take the book sector, potential barriers to disintermedian could include lack of knowledge held by purchasers as to the publisher of a specific book, a desire to browse various books before making a purchase decision, or to purchase books from more than one publisher.

E-Commerce and Taxation

One of the most significant potential areas for increased use of e-commerce to impact on macroeconomic policy is the potential for tax erosion. As many OECD countries receive a significant proportion of their government revenues from consumption taxes (particularly value added taxes) e-commerce has the potential to erode these revenues by shifting expenditure away from the consumer's home country. The OECD (1998 and 2000) considers that consumption taxes are the most susceptible to erosion as consumption shifts to e-commerce. The risk to tax revenue comes from the fact that it is logistically difficult to assess a consumption tax on goods purchased in another country as the retailer (who normally collects the tax is outside the jurisdiction of the consumer's country). Whilst it would be theoretically possible (and indeed legislation exists for this in most countries) to collect consumption taxes from the consumer at the point of entry to the country, Soete and Ter Weel (1998) identify several problems. Firstly, the significant volumes of mail entering most countries would make examining each incoming package logistically difficult and involve high collection cost. Secondly, even if it were practical to examine and value each incoming item many countries have *de minimis* provisions in their customs legislation which would put many consumer purchases outside the tax net. Finally, in the case of the provision of digital goods (such as computer programmes) over the internet the supplier may not even know the country of residence of the consumer.

Goolsbee (1998) has found that in the US (where retail sales taxes vary between, and often within states) the probability of purchasing on-line, after controlling for factors such as education, income regional "technological sophistication" and individual familiarity with technology, is highly dependent upon local sales tax rates. In the national sample the elasticity of the probability of buying on-line with respect to the tax price is 2.3, and the elasticity of on-line expenditure was 3.6. These results imply that applying existing levels of local sales tax to e-commerce sales would reduce the number of online purchases by 20-25 per cent and online expenditure by 25 to 30 per cent.

This research has two policy implications for government. Firstly, the research suggests that domestic consumption taxes are an important factor in consumer's decisions to shop online. This implies that as more of the population become familiar with the possibilities of e-commerce that the extent of tax erosion will increase. Secondly, there are implications for tax administration in countries which levy a consumption tax. As the expenditure elasticity of e-commerce expenditure is quite high when a greater proportion of consumption occurs on-line the situation could exist that increasing consumption tax rates actually reduced revenue due to the expenditure switch.

Potential Impact of E-Commerce on Australia

The Centre for Policy Studies at Monash University was commissioned by the National Office of the Information Economy (NOIE) to model the impact of increased use of e-commerce on the Australian economy. As this is one of the first attempts to model the potential future impact of e-commerce on an economy, and e-commerce is still in its infancy in many sectors of the economy, the degree and nature of the impacts are uncertain. The team from Monash approached this problem by establishing an Industry Reference Group to provide advice on the likely impact of e-commerce on various sectors of the economy, these results were then fed in to the MONASH Computable General Equilibrium Model of the Australian economy.

The Monash results were that the direct impact of e-commerce would be to increase Australian GDP by 1.6 per cent relative to the base case scenario by 2007. As a result of indirect impacts (also known as multiplier effects), the total impact on the economy would be to increase GDP by 2.6 per cent. The major source of this GDP increase is disintermediation of both consumer and producer purchases. There are additional smaller benefits from time savings in consumer and producer purchases and increased promotion of certain industries such as tourism in overseas markets. The increase in employment is less than the increase in GDP, as real wages increase and jobs are lost in some sectors, particularly in the retail sector due to the process of disintermediation. The model results also suggest that the Australian dollar will appreciate due to the increased capital flows and investment from overseas due to the increase in GDP.

A weakness with the Monash modelling appears to be its lack of consideration as to what happens in the rest of the world. The rate at which other countries adopt e-commerce, and the benefits which they derive from it, are likely to effect the level of benefits Australia receives. It is likely that the benefits derived by Australia from e-commerce would be greater than estimated if we were at the forefront of e-commerce adoption, and lower if we were a relative laggard. Adoption of e-commerce in the rest of the world, and the consequent cost saving and efficiency gains, are likely to increase Australian welfare, and probably GDP as well.

How accurate is this estimated level of benefit likely to be? Other work (such as OECD, 2000) supports the areas listed above as the principal sources of potential benefit from increased use of e-commerce. However, whether or not e-commerce produces the quantum of impact suggested by the Centre of Policy Studies depends upon a variety of factors, most notably the accuracy of their estimates of industry level cost savings through disintermediation (provided by their Industry Reference Group).

There are also other factors which may lead to the actual benefits being lower than projected. The Centre for Policy Studies does not appear to have factored in the potential impact on government revenues from tax erosion due to a shift in retail spending overseas as e-commerce becomes more prevalent. This would lead to either reductions in government spending or increases in taxation, offsetting some of the gains from e-commerce.

The second potential offsetting factor (reflecting modelling assumptions) is whether the Australian dollar would actually appreciate due to the increased investment, and indeed whether Australia would actually be able to attract sufficient capital inflows to sustain its increase in activity of 2.7 per cent. If the productivity gain was confined to Australia then Australian capital would become relatively more productive and hence be more attractive to investment. This would increase capital flows and therefore cause the Australian dollar to appreciate. However other countries will also increase their efficiency due to increased use of e-commerce. This suggests that Australia would only increase its proportionate share of world capital - and hence the Australian dollar would only appreciate - if it achieved greater than average productivity gains due to e-commerce. If Australia's productivity gains were roughly average for the world economy then it is likely that the currency would not appreciate. If Australia achieve below average gains due to e-commerce then it may not be able to increase its inflow of capital sufficiently to achieve the projected growth rate as other countries would be more attractive investment destinations, and the currency would depreciate.

Finally, the Centre for Policy Studies did not take into account the fact that the world economy as a whole will increase its productivity due to increased use of e-commerce. This will increase demand for many of Australia's exports, and decrease the cost of import to Australia, increasing consumer welfare and decreasing production costs. This would tend to increase the gains to GDP from those estimated by the Centre for Policy Studies.

Discussion of Regional Impacts

The Centre for Policy Studies also calculated the impact of e-commerce on the states and territories by using the industry level impacts calculated by the model, and data on their industry shares. These estimates suggest that, relative to the base case, all states and territories would experience higher GSP due to e-commerce. Those states and territories which have a relatively low share of commodity exports, the ACT, Victoria and SA, experience the greatest benefits, and those with a high share (WA and the NT) the least. This result is largely driven by the fact that the modelling assumes relatively low productivity gains for these sectors which are more than off-set by the estimated appreciation of the Australian dollar. If, as discussed above, the actual impact on the exchange rate is neutral or the Australian dollar depreciates then the benefits for these lagging states and territories will be much higher.

In calculating the impact of e-commerce on the various states, one issue ignored by the Centre Policy Studies is the potential for disintermediation to concentrate economic activity in the major financial centres, Sydney and Melbourne. For example if book retailing were to become substantially an e-commerce based industry, nationally there would be a drop in activity and employment in book retailing, an increase in activity in the wholesale trade and transport sectors, increased activity in other sectors of the economy as the resources previously devoted to book retailing are invested elsewhere, and an increase in consumption in other areas as prices for books have fallen therefore consumers can spend more income on other consumption goods. At the national level this should increase GDP (unless all book consumption switched offshore, in which case the net result would be uncertain) however this is not necessarily the case for a region within the country. In this example the increased employment in wholesale trade and part of the increase in transport would be more likely to occur in Sydney or Melbourne than in Adelaide, as South Australia receives a disproportionately low share of private investment.[10] It is also quite possible

10 Non-dwelling gross fixed capital formation per capita for the March 2000 quarter was $853 for SA compared with $1,278 for NSW and $1,180 for Victoria, ABS "Australian National Accounts: Quarterly State Details, March 2000, 5206.0.40.001" and "Population Projections, 1999 to 2101, 3222.0"

that the reinvestment of resources previous invested in book retailing would occur elsewhere.

There is also the possibility that there could be tax erosion from South Australia due to increased use of e-commerce, for example the growing use of internet share broking services could lead to the transfer of stamp duty revenue away from the smaller states. Similarly if the concentration of economic activity in the larger states increased due to e-commerce (as described above) then this could reduce tax revenues from sources such as payroll tax for the governments of smaller states. This would mean that governments in these states would face the invidious choice of either reducing government services or increasing other forms of taxation, both of which are likely to reduce community welfare.

References

Aydalot, P (1988), "Technological Trajectories and Regional Innovation in Europe", in *High Technology Industry and Innovative Environments: The European Experience*, eds. P. Aydalot and D. Keeble, Routlege, London, pp. 22-47.

Bernstein, J.I. and M.I. Nadiri (1988), "Interindustry R&D Spillovers, Rates of Return, and Production in High-Tech Industries", *American Economic Review*, 78(2), pp. 429-34.

Boddy, M. and Lovering, J. (1985), "High Technology Industry in the Bristol Sub-Region: The Aerospace/Defence Nexus", *Regional Studies*, 20:3, pp. 217-231.

Camagni, R.P. (1995), 'The Concept of Innovative Milieu and its Relevance for Public Policies in European Regions", Papers in Regional Science, 74:4, pp. 317-40.

Coe, D.T. and Helpman, E. (1995), "International R&D Spillovers", *European Economic Review*, 39:5, pp. 859-87.

Collaborative Economics (1999), "Innovative Regions: The Importance of Place and Networks in the Innovative Economy",. URL: http://www.coecon.com/

Dougherty, C and Jorgenson, D.W. (1997), "There is No Silver Bullet: Investment and Growth in the G7", National Institute Economic Review, No. 162, October 1997, pp. 57-74.

Dowrick, S (1995), "The Determinants of Long-Run Growth", in Productivity and Growth: Proceedings of a Conference held at the H.C. Coombs Centre for Financial Studies, eds. P. Andersen, J. Dwyer and D. Gruen, pp. 7-47.

Dowrick, S. and Gemmell, N. (1991), "Industrialisation, Catching Up and Economic Growth: A Comparative Study Across the World's Capitalist Economies", *Economic Journal*, 101, pp. 263-275.

Engelbrecht, H-J. (1996), "International R&D Spillovers, Human Capital and Productivity in OECD Economies: An Empirical Investigation", Massey University School of Applied and International Economics, Discussion Paper 96:1.

Fingleton, B. (1992), "The Location of Employment in High-Technology Manufacturing in Great Britain", *Urban Studies*, 29:8, pp. 1265-1276.

Fingleton, B. (1994), "The Location of High-technology Manufacturing in Great Britain: Changes in the late 1980s", *Urban Studies*, 31:1, pp. 47-57.

Goolsbee, A (1998) "In a World Without Borders: The Impact of Taxes on Internet Commerce", NBER Working Papers, No. 6863 (forthcoming in the *Quarterly Journal of Economics*).

Griliches (1992), "The Search for R&D Spillovers", *Scandanavian Journal of Economics*, 94: Supplement, p. 29-47.

Henton, D., Melville, J. and Walesh, K. (1997), *Grassroots Leaders for a New Economy*, Jossey-Bass Inc.

Ho, M.S., Jorgenson, D.W. and Stiroh, K.J. (1999), "US High-Tech Investment and the Pervasive Slowdown in the Growth of Capital Services", forthcoming. URL:http://www.economics.harvard.edu/faculty/jorgenson/papers/papers.html.

Jorgenson, D.W. (1996), "Technology in Growth Theory" in *Technology and Growth*, eds. J. C. Fuhrer and J.S. Little, Federal Reserve Bank of Boston, Boston, pp. 45-77.

Jorgenson, D.W. and Stiroh, K.J. (1999), "Information Technology and Growth", *American Economic Review*, 89:2, pp. 109-115.

Jorgenson, D.W. and Stiroh, K.J.(2000), "Raising the Speed Limit: U.S. Economic Growth in the Information Age", *Brookings Papers on Economic Activity*, Vol. 2, 2000.

Keeble, D (1988), "High Technology Industry and Local Environments in the United Kingdom", in *High Technology Industry and Innovative Environments: The European Experience*, eds. P. Aydalot and D. Keeble, Routlege, London, pp. 82-95.

Markusen, A. R. (1983), "High-Tech Jobs, Markets and Development Prospects: Evidence from California", *Built Environment*, 9:1, pp. 18-27.

Markusen, A., Hall, P. and Glasmeier, A. (1986), *High Tech America: The How, Where and Why of the Sunrise Industries*, Allen & Unwin, Boston.

Monash University, Centre for Policy Studies (2000), *E-Commerce: Beyond 2000*, Commonwealth Department of Communications, Information Technology and the Arts, Canberra.

Nadiri, M.I. (1993), Innovations and Technological Spillover", National Bureau of Economic Research Working Paper: 4423, August 1993.

OECD (1998), "Taxation Principles and Electronic Commerce". URL: http://www.oecd.org/subject/e_commerce/ebooks/ecomm2_1.pdf

OECD (2000), "E-Commerce: Impacts and Policy Challenges", *OECD Economic Outlook*, 67: June 2000, pp. 193-203.

Romer, P. (1986), "Increasing Returns and Long-run Growth", *Journal of Political Economy*, Vol. 94, No. 5, pp. 1002-37.

Romer, P. (1990), "Endogenous Technological Change", *Journal of political Economy*, Vol. 98, No. 5, pp. S71-S102.

Romer, P. (1996), "The growth of Nations", *Brookings Papers on Economic Activity*, Comments on G. Mankin paper, September.

Ó hUallacháin, B. (1990), "The location of US manufacturing: some empirical evidence in recent geographical shifts", *Environment and Planning A*, 22:1, pp. 1205-1222.

Saxenian, A.L. (1985), "Silicon Valley and Route 128: Regional prototypes or historical exceptions?", in *High Technology, Space and Society*, ed. M. Castles, Sage, Beverley Hills, pp. 81-105.

Saxenian, A.L. (1994), *Regional Advantage: Culture and Competition in Silicon Valley and Route 128*, Harvard University Press.

Scott, A.J. (1993) *Technopolis: High-Technology Industry and Regional Development in Southern California*, University of California Press, Berkeley.

Scott, A.J. and Angel, D.P. (1987), "The US Semiconductor Industry: A Locational Analysis", *Environment and Planning A*, 19:7, pp. 875-912.

Soete, L and Ter-Weel, B. (1998), "Globalisation, Tax Erosion and the Internet", Maastricht Economic Research Institute on Innovation and Technology Research Memoranda, no. 26.

Suzuki, K. (1993), "R&D Spillovers and Technology Transfer among and within Vertical Keiretsu Groups: Evidence from the Japanese Electrical Machinery Industry", *International Journal of Industrial Organisation*, 11(4), pp. 573-91.

Section 2

A Profile of a Small Regional Economy: South Australia

Chapter Six
Cities and Towns

The concentration of economic activity resembles the pattern formed when oil is spilled on a tin tray. The oil agglomerates in large and small clusters, some close together, others far apart and separated by vacant areas. A map of South Australia resembles the oil on a tray. Patterns of dense urban settlements - cities and towns - separated by vast tracts of rural land. In this chapter we compare and contrast Australia's patterns of urban settlement, offer some views about the forces that bind or disperse human settlement and then take a closer look at the regions within South Australia.

Patterns of Activity Across Australia

It is not difficult to paint a picture of diversity in urban settlement. The density and pattern of economic activity vary remarkably across Australia. One third of the Australia population lives in one state and nearly 60 per cent live in two states. There are only 2.47 persons per square km of available space, but the vast majority of the population lives in dense urban settlements. Most urban settlements are on the coast, and particularly the East Coast. This feature is observable in other countries such as the United States, Canada and the member countries of the European Community, but Australia is one of the world's most urbanised populations.

Table 6.1
Patterns of Activity Across Australia, 1999

State & Territory	Population (%)	GSP or GDP (%)	Employment (%)	Population Density (Persons/Km^2)	Urban Pop. (%)	Capital City Pop. (%)
New South Wales	33.8	35.8	35.0	8.01	34.8	33.4
Victoria	24.8	25.5	26.2	20.72	25.3	28.2
Queensland	18.5	16.2	19.7	2.03	17.3	13.2
South Australia	7.8	6.8	8.0	1.52	7.9	9.0
Western Australia	9.8	10.7	5.7	0.74	9.9	11.3
Tasmania	2.5	1.9	2.3	6.88	2.1	1.6
Northern Territory	1.0	1.1	1.1	0.14	0.8	0.7
ACT	1.6	2.0	1.9	131.43	1.9	2.6
Australia	**100.0**	**100.0**	**100.0**	**2.47**	**100.0**	**100.0**

Note: Urban is defined by the ABS as towns with 1,000 or more people. 'Capital city' is defined by ABS as a share of state/territory population.
Source: ABS, (various issues; 6203.0, 5242.0, 3101.0, 1301.0) and SACES calculations.

By comparing the first column, population, of Table 6.1 with the 5th column, urban population, the general observation is that all states are urbanised to about the same extent. For example, of the total Australian population, 33.8 per cent live in New South Wales, and of the total Australian population living urban areas about 34.8 per cent live in New South Wales. And so on for each state. However, in comparing the first column with the last, then differences emerge in the urban densities of cities in contrast with other urban settlements. In Queensland, for example, urban settlement is spread throughout the region more so than in other states. The spread of urban settlement is apparent also in Tasmania. By contrast urban settlement South Australia, Western Australia tends to be more dominant in the capital city, and the ACT is the ultimate city-state.

Table 6.2 shows population changes in major urban areas. Three of the largest cities accounted for over half of Australia's population and fifteen cities or urban centres accounted for 70 per cent of the population in 1999. Adelaide is currently the fifth largest city after Perth, while in 1977 it was the fourth.

The pattern of population has also been changing in recent decades. Major urban centres grew faster than other urban centres from 1954 to 1976. This was largely due to overseas immigrants locating in capital cities and a general internal movement of people to large cities. Since 1976, population has tended to grow faster in smaller urban centres. This trend reflects the growth of urban areas such as Newcastle and the Gold Coast-Tweed. Relative to almost all other countries in the world South Australia is at the top end of the spectrum of the least distributed population. The 'rural drain' has almost reached its physical or natural limit.

A closer look at the distribution of the population according to the size of the urban centre shows some mixed trends. However, there is a clear drift of the population away from rural areas. In 1954, 21 per cent of the population resided in rural areas, but by 1996 this proportion had declined to only 11.7 per cent. The size of decline means that in absolute terms there are fewer people living in rural areas now than 40 years ago. Such a significant change warrants a closer look. Table 6.4 shows that the drift away from rural areas is broadly occurring, in recent times, across Australia at about the same rate. The intensity of drift has occurred mainly in NSW and ACT with a disproportionately low rural population relative to Australia, and to much lesser extent in Victoria. South Australia has 13.9 per cent of the population in rural areas, slightly above the proportion for Australia.

Relative to 1954 the proportion of the population in major urban centres has increased with the strongest growth being to cities of over 1 million persons. By 1996 there were 4 urban centres with populations over 1 million compared with 2 in 1954. The other interesting trend is the fragmentation of the population in small to medium size towns, that is, urban areas of between 1000 and 9999 persons. There are now 632 of these town settlements compared with 374 in

Table 6.2
Major Population Centres

City or Urban Area	Rank			1977		1986		1999	
	1977	1986	1999	Persons	Share (%)	Persons	Share (%)	Persons	Share (%)
Capital City									
Sydney	1	1	1	3,168.1	22.32	3,471.6	21.7	4,041.4	21.3
Melbourne	2	2	2	2,740.8	19.31	2,966.9	18.5	3,417.2	18.0
Brisbane	3	3	3	1,012.2	7.13	1,217.3	7.6	1,601.4	8.4
Perth	5	4	4	851.8	6.00	1,050.1	6.6	1,364.2	7.2
Adelaide	4	5	5	933.9	6.58	1,003.5	6.3	1,092.9	5.8
Canberra[a]		7	9	212.6	1.50	280.9	1.8	309.9	1.6
Hobart		10	11	165.8	1.17	182.1	1.1	194.2	1.0
Darwin		16	18			75.4	0.5	88.1	0.5
Other									
Newcastle		6	6			417.0	2.6	479.3	2.5
Gold Coast-Tweed		9	7			215.6	1.3	391.2	2.1
Canberra-Queanbeyan			8					348.6	1.8
Wollongong		8	10			233.0	1.5	262.6	1.4
Sunshine Coast		14	12			87.3	0.5	172.9	0.9
Geelong		11	13			146.4	0.9	156.1	0.8
Townsville		12	14			105.0	0.7	127.2	0.7
Cairns		17	15			74.2	0.5	114.0	0.6
Sub-Total				9,085.2	64.0	11450.9	71.5	14,073.0	74.2
Australia				**14,192.2**	**100.0**	**16,018.4**	**100.0**	**18,963.6**	**100.0**

Note: (a) 1977 and 1986 data included Queanbeyan (in NSW). Some data for 1997 not available.
Source: ABS, Cat. No. 1301.0 and 3101.0.

Table 6.3
Distribution of Population by Size of Centres in Australia

State and Territory	1954 %	No. of Centres	1966 %	1976 %	1981 %	1986 %	1991 %	1996 %	No. of Centres
Major Urban	54.5	6	61.6	64.5	63.1	62.9	63.7	63.9	14
1,000,000 and over	37.7	2	39.4	38.7	37.4	42.8	47.6	47.7	4
5000,000-999,999	5.6	1	12.5	18.3	18.1	11.6	5.7	5.5	1
100,000-499,999	11.2	3	9.7	7.5	7.6	8.5	10.4	10.8	9
Other Urban	24.3	414	24.3	21.2	22.5	22.4	23.6	24.4	737
50,000-99,999	2.9	3	2.9	3.1	3.9	3.8	3.0	3.1	8
10,000-49,999	9.0	37	9	8.5	8.6	8.8	10.7	11.2	97
1,000-9,999	12.4	374	12.4	9.6	10.0	9.8	9.9	10.1	632
Rural	21.0	..	16.6	13.9	14.1	..	12.7	11.7	921

<u>Notes</u>: Figures do not add to 100 per cent as migratory population is excluded.
.. indicates not available.

<u>Source</u>: ABS (Cat 1301.0, 2016.0), IRDB 1998, SACES calculations.

1954. The decline in the percentage share of the total population reflects a decline in the average size of these settlements within the population category. This diffusion of small settlements reflects a life style trend for certain segments of the population attracted to country living with urban amenities.

Table 6.4
Rural Drift by State

State/Territory	Proportion of Total Population in Rural Areas (%)	
	1991	1996
NSW & ACT	6.7	6.1
Victoria	11.8	10.9
Queensland	20.5	18.3
South Australia	14.8	13.9
Western Australia	14.7	13.6
Tasmania	27.7	27.3
Northern Territory	25.2	19.1
Australia	12.7	11.7

Source: ABS (Cat 1301.0, 2016.0), IRDB 1998, SACES calculations.

Table 6.5 shows that about 65 per cent of the Australian population work in the city and 35 per cent work in other urban centres or in rural regions. In South Australia, a higher proportion of the population work in the city, almost 75 per cent, and the remainder work in other urban centres or in rural regions. This reflects the fact that the city of Adelaide attracts a disproportionately larger share of the State population than the other State cities. A second factor is the structure of South Australian industry is different, reflecting a high manufacturing base which tends world-wide to be located within a rim about 10 to 30 km from a city centre and near long distance transport facilities.

Agriculture, forestry and fishing and the mining sectors have those industries that tend to employ workforces in non capital city regions across Australia, as might be expected. However, there are some important contrasts. In South Australia, a relatively small proportion of the workforce in the mining sector is found in the non-capital city regions. The main reason is that this state has a smaller mining sector and the Australian head office for a major mining company, SANTOS, is located in the city of Adelaide.

An immediate implication of this discussion on the broad pattern of settlement is that the pressures that have arisen from increased global competition are affecting different regions and communities in different ways, and in ways

Table 6.5
Employment by Industry and Location, Australia and South Australia, 1999*

Industry Classification	Australia					South Australia				
	Capital City		Balance of Aus		Total	Capital City		Balance of SA		Total
	000 Psns	% of Tot	000 Psns	% of Tot	000 Psns	000 Psns	% of Tot	000 Psns	% of Tot	000 Psns
Agriculture, Forestry & Fishing	86.3	18.8	372.5	81.2	458.8	7.3	15.3	40.0	84.7	47.3
Mining	29.8	37.4	49.8	62.6	79.5	1.8	58.3	1.3	41.7	3.0
Manufacturing	715.0	69.9	308.3	30.1	1023.3	72.5	77.3	21.3	22.7	93.8
Electricity, Gas & Water Supply	33.0	54.5	27.5	45.5	60.5	4.5	85.7	0.8	14.3	5.3
Construction	401.0	64.0	225.5	36.0	626.5	29.0	73.9	10.3	26.1	39.3
Wholesale Trade	355.5	72.6	134.3	27.4	489.8	26.8	79.9	6.8	20.1	33.5
Retail Trade	766.8	61.6	478.3	38.4	1245.0	71.8	74.5	24.5	25.5	96.3
Accommodation, Cafes & Restaurants	233.5	58.0	169.3	42.0	402.8	22.8	69.5	10.0	30.5	32.8
Transport and Storage	271.0	68.1	127.0	31.9	398.0	21.8	79.8	5.5	20.2	27.3
Communication Services	110.3	75.5	35.8	24.5	146.0	10.8	87.8	1.5	12.2	12.3
Finance and Insurance	240.0	81.4	54.8	18.6	294.8	18.3	88.0	2.5	12.0	20.8
Property & Business Services	689.3	77.1	204.8	22.9	894.0	56.8	87.0	8.5	13.0	65.3
Gov. Administration & Defence	231.3	69.1	103.3	30.9	334.5	18.0	78.3	5.0	21.7	23.0
Education	373.0	64.0	209.8	36.0	582.8	37.0	75.9	11.8	24.1	48.8
Health & Community Services	504.8	65.7	263.8	34.3	768.5	57.8	79.4	15.0	20.6	72.8
Cultural & Recreational Services	140.3	70.8	57.8	29.2	198.0	10.0	78.4	2.8	21.6	12.8
Personal & Other Services	210.8	66.0	108.5	34.0	319.3	22.8	78.4	6.3	21.6	29.0
Total	**5,391.3**	**64.8**	**2,930.5**	**35.2**	**8,321.8**	**489.3**	**73.8**	**173.5**	**26.2**	**662.8**

Note: * Averaged quarterly.
Source: ABS Census, Small area data.

which are different from those that they previously experienced, as are now illustrated.

Queensland, for example, has strengths in mining and tourism, and is an attractive retirement location. Services relating to and supporting these forces are growing also. Queensland has economic strength, but there are pressures on infrastructure from a fast growing population, and government policies are not directing support to the regions. Queensland is seeking to address these issues. For example, in the 2000-01 State Budget, 64 per cent of the capital program is being spent of projects outside the Brisbane region. However, Queensland has potentially the biggest task of all the states in addressing the impact of globalisation as its sub-region are large and diverse.

Western Australia's rising wealth is strongly connected with mining, but the issue for them is declining commodity prices. The Northern Territory has grown a great deal of strength out of its mining base and, at least until the recent Asian crisis, from cattle exports and from other trade with South-East Asia. But the Northern Territory has a very narrow base, it has relatively limited physical infrastructure and even, to some extent, human capital and social infrastructure.

By contrast, New South Wales, and particularly Sydney, is increasingly connected into world financial markets. The Australian Capital Territory is a 'city-state' dominated by the public sector and is attracting information technology and other knowledge-intensive industry and commerce. Victoria is developing a strong information technology industry. However, in Geelong, the stresses of declining trade protection are obvious, as they are, too, in South Australia with its traditional manufacturing base. There are, moreover, great differences between Adelaide and, for example, the old "Iron Triangle" Cities of Whyalla, Port Augusta and Port Pirie, which have not only a narrower economic base than Adelaide, but also much less robust social infrastructure as well.

The Forces of Urban Settlement

Variations across Australia in population density, the degree of concentration in urban areas and the location of employment suggest that there are some underlying forces at play which drive decisions about where to live and work. These are the forces that bind or disburse economic activity. The identification of these forces can be traced back to Alfred Marshall's 1890 publication on scale economies, geographic concentration and the spread of new knowledge as being the key elements. More recently, Krugman (1994) argues that the choice between living in an urban area and a rural area is the outcome of centripetal and centrifugal forces.

Centripetal forces encourage economic activity to agglomerate around a nucleus. These forces are in the nature of:

- natural geographic advantages of site. Harbours, rivers, good climate, and good soil nearby for food supply. The site for Adelaide was chosen for these advantages;
- market size. Access to markets (or forward linkages) and access to inputs (backward linkages) reduce the unit cost of operating in the supply chain from production to consumption. The accessibility of high quality labour is an important component of the access to inputs. Market size also offers opportunity for persons to pursue fields of professional endeavour more closely aligned to their career goals. Agglomeration provides for a variety of choice in consumption. For example, choice of clothing stores and restaurants; and
- pure external economies The opportunity for a third party to benefit from the interaction between two other parties. New knowledge can be more readily diffused, and then improved, adapted and simply copied by others.

An additional centripetal force is associated with the intensity and diversity of social activity and cultural experience, and opportunity to experience the product of human co-operation such as major public entertainment and sporting events.

Centrifugal forces dissipate or fragment economic activity. These forces are in the nature of:

- market mediated forces. These include the rise in property rentals, costs of building elevated structures at or near the nucleus of densely populated areas, costs of augmenting infrastructure to cope with population growth and the production cost of encroachment on high quality farmland; and
- non-market forces: Congestion costs such as waiting times, air and noise pollution, and impaired visual amenities.

In addition, the high density of populations may diminish social cohesiveness and invoke cultural clash. Community disharmony and individual isolation created through the breakdown of relationships sometimes leads to increased incidence of crime and civil disobedience. This environment involves a range of pecuniary and non-pecuniary costs which undermine the competitiveness of an urban settlement. Such costs include the increased incidence of crime and civil disobedience, lack of trust which increases the propensity for formal contractual relationships. Isolation within the community can involve increased costs with formal (in contrast with informal or family) social safety nets as people are less able to cope with their passage through life.

Another way of expressing these forces is that every town, city and region offer its own quality of life, and each individual weighs each characteristic of that quality of life to form an assessment of where they want to be. Assessments are also made by individuals acting alone or in a family group of the costs, benefits and risks of giving up the quality of life in one region for that offered in another. The quality of life reflects a very broad array of characteristics, covering political, economic, environmental, social, cultural and family aspects of living.

The balance between these forces is different for each person in each region. For example, a region rich in agricultural, mineral and marine life would draw larger proportion of the population into rural areas, but a region specialising in financial services is likely to find the city to be densely populated. Nonetheless, despite the problems with big cities, almost everyone lives in them meaning that the centripetal forces are very strong. Alternatively there is considerable inertia which is discussed later in this section.

These forces can strengthen or weaken overtime as a result of random shocks, major external events or changes brought about by technology, social attitudes and culture.

Short-shock factors can tip the balance. For example, Cyclone Tracy ravaged Darwin in the 1960s and forced people to relocate to other cities for suitable accommodation. Some of those people never returned to Darwin after it was rebuilt. Adelaide acquired a permanent re-allocation of economic activity.

Technology is an interesting example which may be either a centripetal or centrifugal force. Access to information through the internet and the capacity to undertake transactions using communication services may reduce the cost of living in rural areas. Access to entertainment, health and education services will mean people are able to enjoy greater benefits without travelling to urban areas. However, technology is accessible at a price, and rural communities have lower real incomes and are less able to pay than urban communities. Even assuming that access is equally available at the same cost to all persons, urban people may still enjoy a relative advantage by using technology because they can do more with that information. For example, studying university from the e-net may enable a rural student to complete the course without leaving home, but there is a cost in terms of the social-professional network that could have been more strongly established; and, after graduating that person will most likely need to move to an urban area to take up employment.

Social attitudes can influence location. For example, the promotion through the media of a rural living combined city work has encouraged a 'life-style trend' for the development of small amateur farming in the Adelaide outer reaches and expansion of the road network and calls for better public transport services.

The forces are very complex because 'feed back' mechanisms make it difficult to separate cause from effect. For example, the relationship between technology and demography. Medical technology is extending the average life span and the period of active retirement. The Southern Fleurieu Peninsula offers a life-style which has attracted significant numbers of retired persons to the region.

Medical technology (amongst other factors) has created a centripetal force for that region. But moving in the opposite direction, demography influences technology. Older people demand better medical technology, and the innovation necessary to drive breakthroughs in medical science are most likely to happen in the dense clusters of urban settlements where ideas and new knowledge are shared rapidly. The evidence for the location of medical technology breakthroughs is abundant. In a sense, there is some polarisation of settlement patterns reflecting the way in which communities use technology in work and leisure.

Regions also experience inertia. Inertia prevents or slows the process of change. Inertia by definition is a state of rest, but, importantly, it can be regarded as the net effect of opposing forces. Characteristics of inertia are:

- highly risk adverse attitudes to change. Rural communities near the poverty line may not be prepared to give up subsistence living with certainty for the chance of a better life;
- economic factors, such as immobility of the labour force (redundant skills, lack of opportunity in other regions) and relocation costs of moving from one region to another.
- social norms, such as the strength of family ties or a strong sense of identity with a region;
- cultural factors, such as the tribal customs in aboriginal communities; and
- resistance to outsiders who want to move in to their region because they might take their jobs or because of prejudice.

It is worth emphasising cultural factors, because they are often overlooked but play an important role. Kalumbaru and Oombulgurri are two aboriginal communities in the East Kimberley region of Western Australia. The communities are about 200km apart, Kalumbaru being on the Northern coast near Admiralty Gulf and Okmbulgurri being about 50km North West of Wyndam. These communities are amongst the most remote in Australia, and receive goods by a barge about every six weeks from Darwin. Oombulgurri is a well governed community, skilled in growing basic food crops and building houses and roads. The workforce, although under employed, have a sense of pride about what they do and there is a sense of achievement there. By contrast, Kalumbaru is a lawless and depressed community. Commonwealth authorities have failed spectacularly to up-skill the community. Almost all people in the community are unemployed. Water borne mites have permanently affected the hearing of many children in the region. Although Oombulgurri is a growing community (in 1999 the population was about 400 whereas a decade ago it was only about 150 people), it is not attracting people from Kalumbaru. The communities do not communicate. Family feuds dating back to the early 1900s, concern about preserving tribal heritage, a strong sense of risk aversion and heavy government subsidisation (unemployment benefits, transport etc.) are assisting to create not only a sense of inertia but mummification.

Sub-Regions of South Australia

In earlier chapters we identified that globalisation is a primary force influencing the economic futures of regions. Globalisation disturbs the balance between centripetal and centrifugal forces. Although South Australia is generally regarded as a small regional economy, a closer examination shows that South Australia comprises of a number of diverse sub-regions. These regions are differentiated by, for example, their access to natural resources, their historical patterns of development, their underlying economic and social infrastructure and changing market conditions. As globalisation operates on the attributes of the regions, then the impact on regions and their policy response will differ and differ markedly.

Table 6.6 shows the distribution of employment by sector for the sub-regions and Adelaide. Three quarters of the employment is found in Adelaide. Including the outer Adelaide regions, increases the proportion of employment to just over 80 per cent.

From the trends over time we know that the centripetal forces that seem to be bind the sub-regions are weakening. Some of the country urban and rural centres are loosing the battle. An important consideration is that broad national-state policies directed toward sub-regional areas are directed to only 20 per cent of the workforce. Each region is different, none representing more than 5 per cent of the workforce. These figures overwhelmingly suggest that policies need to be regionally based because broader national-state policies cannot meet the needs of small heterogeneous regions.

The Centre's analysis (SACES, 1998) of the economies of South Australia's six provincial cities (Whyalla, Mt Gambier, Murray Bridge, Port Lincoln, Port Augusta and Port Pirie) and more recently, the riverland towns (SACES, 1999), provided clear evidence of significant differences between them in current trends and future potential.

The population of provincial cities and riverland towns shown in Figure 6.1 reflect the long term growth in Mount Gambier, Port Lincoln and the riverland towns, the struggle for growth in Port Augusta and the decline of Whyalla and Port Pirie.

Table 6.6
Employment By Sector and Statistical Division, South Australia, 1996

Sector	Adelaide)	Outer Adelaide	Yorke & Lower North	Murray Lands	South East	Eyre	Northern	Off-Shore Areas & Migratory	South Australia
	(Persons)								
Agriculture Forestry Fishing & Hunting	4,670	5,355	4,099	7,219	5,497	3,537	2,722	6	33,107
Mining	1,296	210	147	59	93	84	1,617	0	3,506
Manufacturing	67,964	6,465	1,144	3,313	4,815	591	4,346	8	88,645
Services	362,958	29,178	9,701	16,724	16,601	8,819	23,035	233	467,249
Electricity Gas & Water	3,193	285	115	299	148	132	457	0	4,630
Construction	21,320	2,453	614	1,095	1,381	597	1,836	5	29,301
Wholesale Trade	25,841	2,099	705	1,942	1,472	528	987	7	33,581
Retail Trade	60,010	4,947	1,881	3,226	3,427	1,624	3,883	9	79,007
Accommodation, Cafes & Restaurants	17,949	1,867	741	1,060	1,117	661	1,646	9	25,050
Transport & Storage	16,058	1,382	450	844	842	533	1,542	131	21,782
Communication Services	8,494	613	259	320	289	163	411	0	10,551
Finance & Insurance	16,360	928	313	429	528	229	518	3	19,306
Property & Business Services	42,566	2,516	431	895	1,073	481	1,904	12	49,878
Government Administration & Defence	19,983	1,459	507	717	753	397	1,162	16	24,994
Education	33,120	2,773	1,062	1,498	1,517	1,030	2,433	8	43,442
Health & Community Services	53,157	3,895	1,373	2,041	1,818	1,308	3,454	11	67,057
Cultural & Recreational Services	10,651	750	126	384	328	149	445	3	12,835
Personal & Other Services	18,536	1,540	376	813	737	396	1,084	7	23,488
Non-classifiable economic units	3,979	348	131	223	315	102	319	0	5,417
Not stated	11,741	1,323	617	938	856	489	954	12	16,930
Total	**436,888**	**41,208**	**15,091**	**27,315**	**27,006**	**13,031**	**31,720**	**247**	**592,507**

Source: IRDB, 1998.

Figure 6.1
Population of Provincial Cities and Riverland Towns, 1961 to 1996

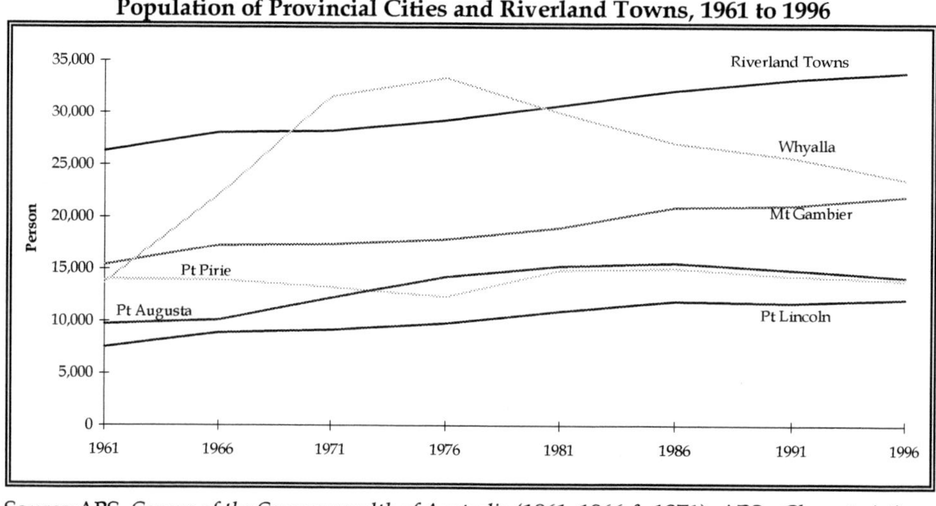

Source: ABS, *Census of the Commonwealth of Australia* (1961, 1966 & 1971); ABS, *Characteristics of the Population* Catalogue. no. 2203.0 (1976); IRDB (1998)

The main factors which account for variations in the economic performance of the provincial cities and the riverland towns are summarised as follows.

The Riverland has continued a strong path of recovery from the severe down-turn experienced in the recession of 1991-92, in contrast to the experience of several of the provincial cities. Public sector job losses in the riverland towns have been far less severe, while private sector employment growth has been relatively strong. The success story is, private sector investment in the wine industry and expansion of horticultural production and processing, which has been associated with significant public sector investment in irrigation systems improvement, environmental rehabilitation, storage (grain) and transport infrastructure. The expansion of the wine industry and more general diversification of the economic base of the riverland towns, has led in turn, to a strengthening of demand for higher qualifications and skills across the workforce.

In the case of Mount Gambier and Port Lincoln the explanation for the sustained economic growth performance is attributed largely to their dependence on primary industries, supply factors and physical attributes of the two cities. Economic diversification has taken place and continuing in the farming sector which has helped to support growth in the service sector in each of these cities. Both cities have lost public sector employees but have been more successful in attracting private investment in services and industries adding value to primary production. Much more still needs to be done.

In regard to Murray Bridge, the natural attributes of the region, climate and proximity to primary industries provide only part of the explanation for what has been relatively slower growth, but growth nonetheless. Murray Bridge has benefited from proximity to Adelaide, the use of state government incentives (subsidies to locate in or nearby to the city) and growth in exports and employment of several medium sized manufacturing companies. Parts of the primary industries sector have also been able to diversify into horticulture, viticulture, floriculture and newer broad acre crops. Private investment in wholesaling and meat processing (if it proceeds) will provide further stimulus to growth of employment.

For the three Upper Spencer Gulf cities - Port Augusta, Port Pirie and Whyalla - the economic pendulum has swung more strongly into the zone of disadvantage. The competitiveness of each of the cities is under threat. They are less reliant on agriculture and are more dependent on mining, manufacturing and selected services (electricity and water, rail, transport). The high concentration in these industries reflects supply factors in that each of the cities is located in close proximity to raw materials (coal, iron ore, minerals) or historically has been active in downstream processing of mineral commodities. Each of the cities exhibits a high degree of industry specialisation and reliance on one or two major employers.

The Upper Spencer Gulf cities have experienced net outward migration, higher levels of unemployment, a continuing loss of full time jobs and very slow growth in part time employment. The trend changes in the composition of employment mirror those in the national labour market but they have been more severe. The loss of male full-time employment and the more extensive cut-backs in public sector employment are unmistakable features of the difficult path of adjustment. A lack of jobs in country towns and rural centres has entrenched regional unemployment as one of the region's biggest problems.

Port Pirie has the highest rate of home ownership of all of the cities. Port Augusta and Whyalla, in response to opportunities afforded through the sale of SAHT stock, experienced the largest change in 'home ownership or being purchased' status over the period 1991 to 1996. In 1996 the status of 'home ownership or being bought' had increased to 55 per cent in Port Augusta (1986: 44 per cent) and to 51 per cent in Whyalla (1986: 34 per cent). Those renting had declined in the same period (Port Augusta 1986: 53 per cent to 41 per cent (1996) and in Whyalla (from 64 per cent to 46 per cent). Outward migration of the more mobile in the labour force contributed to a decline in rental status. The current level of properties for sale is still high. Notwithstanding, the mobility of the labour force is likely to be more restricted in the future with the positive trend towards increasing home ownership. All this suggests the need to continue with vigorous efforts to diversify the economic base of these three cities.

The burden of structural adjustment has fallen especially hard on the three Upper Spencer Gulf provincial cities, although employment losses are not confined to these three cities alone.

The recent Senate Inquiry into Regional Employment and Unemployment concluded that "each city or each region has its own specific difficulties. Although we could say that one of the worst contributors to unemployment in regional Australia is the cut-back in jobs - Commonwealth and State - the impact of that is different from region to region, the same with private investment."

Economic and community impacts are inseparable and are likely to be magnified in the Provincial Cities and in the towns and smaller rural centres. The major economic impacts over the recent years include:

- population decline characterises the cities of Port Pirie, Port Augusta and Whyalla, with slower growth in the other cities;
- declining local demand. Local demand exerts a strong influence on the level of services in each of the cities for education, health, retail and wholesale trade, financial services and consumer durables. Many of these services are dependent on certain levels of market and/or population thresholds, without which service provision becomes uneconomic;
- information technology, national competition policy, whole-of government tendering and procurement processes, further strivings for cost savings and for economy wide efficiency gains, may further seriously disadvantage/exclude regional providers and reduce market threshold levels;
- changes in employment have been associated with the loss of full time employment, most significantly for males, and slower growth of part time employment overall. This has occurred as the cities have engaged in the difficult task of diversifying their local economies;
- in the period 1991 to 1996 job losses have been more severe in Whyalla (1,600 positions), in Port Augusta (1,100 positions) and Port Pirie (600 positions). Whyalla is reported to lose a further 800 positions at BHP by the year 2000;
- State Government cutbacks have impacted markedly on employment (Mount Gambier 700, Whyalla 400, Port Augusta 275); and
- unemployment is shown to be regionally concentrated, to have increased in duration and there is a very strong probability that unemployment is concentrated by family type. The male, full time employment to population ratio has shown a significant decline, foreshadowing possible pockets of poverty in some regions.

The 'flow on' community impacts are often very subtle and are not always well understood by those outside the immediate zones of impact. The closure of a service or government agency in Adelaide may not be immediately noticed. A contract to supply may simply be transferred across the spatial economy of metropolitan Adelaide. In non-metropolitan regions and major centres the impacts tend to be magnified. Supply contracts lost to local maintenance staff, the local butcher and cleaners result in additional job losses in a city and a reduction in business activity overall.

All of these regions including those that are experiencing growth are vulnerable. As Table 6.7 indicates the human capital in these regions is not as strong as in the capital cities. Tertiary education skills are carried by only between 6.4 per cent and 10.2 per cent of the population in these regions, compared with 14.2 per cent of the Adelaide area. In keeping with the discussion of other chapters most particularly Chapter 8, these regions will struggle to cope with changing and changeable global competitive forces. Initiatives, such as the extension of university campuses to the riverland region may assist to upskill the workforce and overseas students and teaching staff may bring multiculturalism and new ideas.

Although criminal offence is only one measure of the social capital of a community, the measure is reflective of trust, respect for people and property, and to some degree the willingness of people to co-operate or otherwise engage in socially acceptable behaviour. On this measure, crime rates are higher in the provincial cities than in metropolitan Adelaide. A closer look at the riverland towns suggests a problem with crime also. The towns of Barmera and Renmark have crime rates of 201.7 and 167.2 per thousand, respectively, which are significantly higher than Adelaide. These results run contrary to the earlier argument that in highly dense settlements that social cohesion tends to be a centrifugal force. However, the external countervailing force in some of these regions is the social problems of higher rates of unemployment and a transient population (e.g., fruit pickers in the riverland).

The discussion above indicates several reasons why a regional development policy for South Australia cannot be a uniform "one size fits all" approach by the Commonwealth and State governments.

On the basis of interviews with persons from those provincial cities (SACES, 1998), a range of perceptions emerged about what people think about the quality of living in regional areas of South Australia:

- a perception that quality of life and well-being had declined;
- that it was not important to be a member of a political party;
- an over emphasis on economic policy to the detriment of social policy;
- a less fair society (than five years ago); and
- a strong disquiet concerning politicians and their ability to make decisions for the whole community.

These regions clearly expressed a sense of abandonment by policy makers and disillusionment with the political process and economic outcomes.

Table 6.7
Human Capital, 1996

	Riverland Towns	Mount Gambier (C)	Murray Bridge (RC)	Port Augusta (C)	Port Lincoln (C)	Port Pirie (C)	Whyalla (C)	Adelaide (ASD)
Higher Degree	0.2	0.3	0.2	0.3	0.4	0.2	0.6	1.0
Post Graduate Diploma	0.6	0.8	0.4	0.7	0.6	0.4	0.7	1.1
Bachelor Degree	3.0	4.2	2.4	3.2	3.6	2.7	4.6	6.5
Undergraduate Diploma	2.6	2.4	2.3	2.3	3.0	1.9	2.2	3.4
Associate Diploma	1.4	1.6	1.1	1.4	1.3	1.1	2.1	2.2
Sub-Total Degree/Diploma	7.8	9.3	6.4	7.9	8.9	6.3	10.2	14.2
Skilled Vocational	9.0	10.6	9.0	12.5	10.5	11.1	16.2	10.5
Basic Vocational	2.8	3.3	2.9	3.0	4.1	2.4	3.0	3.1
Inad Described	0.6	0.5	0.5	0.5	0.6	0.4	0.5	0.7
Not Qualified	69.4	67.0	70.7	63.4	65.6	70.8	60.5	61.5
Not Stated	10.3	9.4	10.6	12.6	10.4	9.0	9.6	9.8
Total	**100.0**	**100.0**	**100.0**	**100.0**	**100.0**	**100.0**	**100.0**	**100.0**

Note 1: Highest qualification, as a percent of population
Source: ABS, unpublished data.

Table 6.8
Social Capital[1], 1995

Region	Offence Against a Person	Offence Against Property[2]	All Offences
Riverland Towns[3]	12.1	13.3	136.1
Provincial Cities[4]	22.6	32.3	188.8
Non-metropolitan	12.0	20.7	116.8
Metropolitan	13.9	39.0	144.3

Notes:
1 Offences per 1000 persons.
2 Break and enter a dwelling.
3 Riverland Towns: Barmera, Berri, Loxton, Paringa, Renmark and Waikerie.
4 Provincial Cities: Mount Gambier, Murray Bridge, Port Augusta, Port Pirie, Whyalla and Port Lincoln.

Source: *Crime and Justice in South Australia, 1995*, Office of Crime Statistics and SACES (1999).

It is important therefore, that a more incisive and pragmatic understanding of the difficulties confronting the provincial cities is shared by decision makers. Forums for dialogue need to be constructed to develop meaningful results.

These perceptions also reflect on the adequacy of existing effort and current structures, relative to the adjustment difficulties the regions and the provincial cities are experiencing. There is evidence that some policies and programs (e.g., on procurement) may in their implementation act against achieving development outcomes. Such situations compound existing frustrations and impede constructive dialogue.

The SACES report also identified that provincial cities are aware of the changing environment: the impact of changing demographics, population flows, the developments in technologies and global trade and investment. The challenge for governments is to assist the provincial cities to respond to new opportunities and new threats, best encapsulated in the economic imperative to diversify the local economic base of the cities and associated regions.

The issue of diversification is a very difficult one which requires unremitting effort to restore and build stronger regional economies. It has been proven to be more difficult in the three cities of the Upper Spencer Gulf, but the six cities share similar challenges.

The State Government has responded to the call from the provincial cities (SAG, 1999). Key elements of the Government's response include:

- the introduction of new governance arrangements (establishment of a Regional Development Council and an Office of Regional Development and measures to strengthen the performance of Regional Development Boards), to provide more effective advocacy for regions and a whole-of-Government approach to addressing regional development issues;

- establishment of a Regional Development Infrastructure Fund to facilitate expenditure on infrastructure needed to realise regional growth opportunities (Improving regional information technology and communication systems has already been identifies as a priority);
- developing and retaining people in jobs through improved processes for identifying the skill needs of regionally-based industries and delivery of relevant and more accessible education and training services; and
- further research and analysis, led by the Office of Regional Development, on a number of issues including the development of partnerships between business, governments and local communities and options for more effective and integrated delivery of services to regions.

The Government plans to release a *Regional Development Statement*, which will provide a more detailed working blueprint for the implementation of a State-wide strategy to revitalise South Australia's regions and to help build the capacity of regional communities to plan and manage their own futures.

A key element of this strategy should be a clarification of the roles of the respective three tiers of government to ensure a united approach that involves no policy lap or gap.

However, the formulation of policy directed toward redressing the problems of the provincial cities, riverland towns and in general the rural areas, must be sensitive to the natural centrifugal forces which operate to drive people to move to other regions. The argument about regional development policy is no different to the arguments about industry development policy. Direct, targeted assistance and subsidisation will create an artificial environment which will not be sustainable in the long run and the cost of adjustment will be even higher further down the track. Regional development policy must recognise that these regions must be able to show that a comparative advantage exists or can be created from the changing environment brought about by globalisation.

Conclusions

In this chapter, we undertook a broad sweep of regional patterns in Australia to put the small regional economy of South Australia into context.

The pattern of urban settlement reflects the outcome of centripetal and centrifugal forces. For any region these forces will strengthen or weaken according to a broad array of factors. Globalisation is a major influencing factor.

South Australia's population is highly urbanised relative to Australia, and Australia is a highly urbanised country. Almost three quarters of total employment in South Australia is found in the capital city, and 80 per cent if you include outer Adelaide.

South Australia is a region of regions. Recent survey work by SACES shows that within the state's six provincial cities, there was a general perception of decline. These regions understand that the external environment is changing, but policies and programs by the three tiers of government were not helping sufficiently.

References

Krugman, P.R. (1994), *Peddling Prosperity: Economic Sense and Nonsense in the Age of Diminished Expectations*, W.W. Norton, New York.

Krugman, P.R., (1994), *The Age of Diminished Expectations: U.S. Economic Policy in the 1990s*, MIT Press, Cambridge, Mass.

South Australian Centre for Economic Studies (SACES) (1998), *Provincial Cities*, Various reports.

South Australian Centre for Economic Studies (SACES) (1999), *Riverland Towns and Provincial Cities.*

South Australian Government (SAG) (1999), *Statement of Economic Directions*, December.

Zann, L.P. (1995), *Our Sea, Our Future: Major Findings of the State of the Marine Environment Report for Australia*, Department of the Environment Sport and Territories, AGPS.

Zann, L.P. (1996), "State of the Marine Environment: Report for Australia", *Technical Summary*, Department of the Environment Sport and Territories, AGPS.

Chapter Seven

Endowments

From the perspective of the present day, all that has passed is an endowment. It is what we start with and what we have to work with to shape our future. Endowments cover everything from history, what is above the ground (i.e., climate) and below the ground, how far we are from our trading partners, our culture, human and physical capital and even the perceptions of others (including prospective investors) about our regional economy. All of these aspects have had some role in bringing us to this point today. The breadth of this topic cannot be covered in one chapter, but, instead, this chapter attempts to provide insight into selected endowments. In particular, by describing briefly the importance of turning points in the history of South Australia's economic growth, the importance of geography and certain demographic characteristics, and finally some issues with the management of one of our most important natural resources, namely the Murray River.

A Brief Economic History

1836 to 1868: Establishment and Consolidation

South Australia was proclaimed in 1836 and the first half century was a period of exploration by settlement. During this period the natural resource endowment and the biophysical constraints to settlement were largely determined. By the early 1840s a staple crop, wheat, had been identified and a wide variety of inventions and innovations had been developed so that it could be commercially grown and profitably exported. Copper discoveries in the 1840s further stimulated the inflow of labour and capital. Gold discoveries in New South Wales and Victoria increased the demand for South Australian goods and services, stimulating continued expansion of the Colony's rural industries (Gibbs, 1990).

1869 to 1900: Expansion and Retreat

In 1869 farmers were permitted to purchase land on credit for the first time, which facilitated the rapid Northerly expansion of the wheat growing districts (Meinig, 1988). The rapid expansion of wheat production was accompanied by large scale public provision of infrastructure and settlement, such that by the late 1870s South Australia was the 'breadbasket' of the British Empire. The droughts of 1880 to 1882 identified the Northern limits of wheat growing and the agricultural frontier retreated South, reserving the North for pastoralism. The droughts and capital restructuring that they precipitated in the wheat industry contributed to the South Australian economy slipping into recession during the mid-1880s (Figure 7.1). By 1890 a tentative recovery from recession was underway. However, the collapse of the Victorian boom dragged South Australian into depression for the rest of the century.

Despite the recession of the 1880s and depression of the 1890s, the South Australian economy began to diversify from its narrow dependence on wool and wheat. Silver was discovered at Silverton. Silver, lead and zinc deposits at Broken Hill were discovered in the early 1880s. This mineral wealth was located in New South Wales. Nevertheless, the South Australian government built a railway to the border and the ores were transported to Port Pirie. In 1895 iron ore was discovered stimulating the growth of Whyalla. Agriculture diversified. In 1887 an irrigation scheme commenced at Renmark along the upper Murray River. In 1894 a number of other irrigation schemes were commenced along the upper Murray. In the early 1880s swamps along the lower Murray were drained and dairying was developed. In the South East, the swamp drainage program gained pace and the region developed as an important agricultural and horticultural area (Gibbs, 1990).

1901 to 1920: Recovery and Adjustment

The years 1901 to 1920 was a period of recovery from drought and depression and adjustment to the new economic order imposed by Federation. Recovery from depression commenced in the mid-1900s in the wake of the Victorian recovery. Federation was something of a mixed blessing in South Australia. Prior to Federation a relatively large manufacturing sector had developed, mainly in Adelaide, behind fairly protective tariffs. When the inter-colonial tariffs were removed at Federation firms which did not enjoy a degree of natural protection, were unable to compete with interstate rivals and closed down. Significant interstate migration to Melbourne resulted from these closures, especially in the tobacco industry (Norris, 1975). The removal of the Colonial Victorian tariff also created new markets for many South Australian rural products (Norris, 1969). The opening of Australian Iron and Steel's blast furnace at Newcastle in 1915 stimulated iron ore mining and Whyalla (Gibbs, 1990).

1921 to 1939: Depression

During the early 1920s the South Australia enjoyed a brief period of prosperity as the economy continued to diversify in response to the increasing levels of protection offered by the Commonwealth Tariff. In particular, by the mid-1920s, Adelaide was the focus of the Australia motor body manufacturing industry (Broomhill, 1978; McFarlane, 1986). Despite the focus of the Commonwealth Government to stimulate industrialisation, South Australian government continued supporting further rural expansion and export led growth of commodities. South Australia slid into recession in 1926-27 and followed the rest of the country into depression in late 1929 (Figure 7.1). The Great Depression was most severe in South Australia. The depth of the Great Depression is more clearly evident in Figure 7.2. Official unemployment was the highest of any state, peaking at 35.6 per cent in 1932, compared to 29 per cent nationally, but the real level was significantly higher (Broomhill, 1978). Recovery commenced slowly in 1933-34, two years later than the national recovery. Pre-depression levels of State Domestic Product were not attainted again until after the outbreak of the Second World War, compared to 1937-38 nationally (Vamplew et al., 1984 and Schedvin, 1988).

The severity of the depression in South Australia was largely caused by the economy's reliance on rural exports as the engine of growth. Nevertheless, the government remained committed to further rural expansion during the early 1930s. However, by the late 1930's the government became committed to support import substitution industrialisation (McFarlane, 1986). Little was achieved in the late 1930s, however, the institutional framework within which post-war boom would be managed was developed. In particular, the South Australian Housing Trust was established in 1936 in response to local and national concerns about slum housing.

Developments during the war built on the moderate successes of the mid to late 1930 and laid the foundations for the rapid industrialisation that South Australia experienced in the post-war era. The strategic location of South Australia led the Commonwealth Government to choose Adelaide as the major site for the location of a number of large munitions factories. In addition, the existing industrial base was rapidly reoriented and expanded to meet the demands of the war effort producing military vehicles, aeroplanes, engineering equipment and artillery (Stutchbury, 1986). Pig iron production was expanded and ship building commenced at Whyalla.

Table 7.1
South Australian Economic Development

Economic Indicator	1861	1871	1881	1891	1901	1911	1921	1933
Population ('000)	126.8	185.4	275.3	315.2	358.3	408.6	495.1	580.9
Pop. growth rate	-	3.9	4.0	1.4	1.3	1.3	1.9	1.3
GDP $m	13.3	20.1	35.4	39.4	46.8	64.3	74.6	84.1
GDP growth rate	-	4.2	5.9	1.1	1.7	3.2	1.5	1.2
GDP per capita	105.1	108.1	128.6	124.9	130.6	157.5	150.7	144.8
GDP/cap. gwth rate	-	0.3	1.7	-0.3	0.4	1.9	-0.4	-0.3

Note: All growth rates in per cent.
Real GDP in 1910 prices, values have been converted to dollars.
Source: Vamplew et al (1984).

Figure 7.1
South Australian Real GDP — 1861 to 1938 (In 1911 Prices)

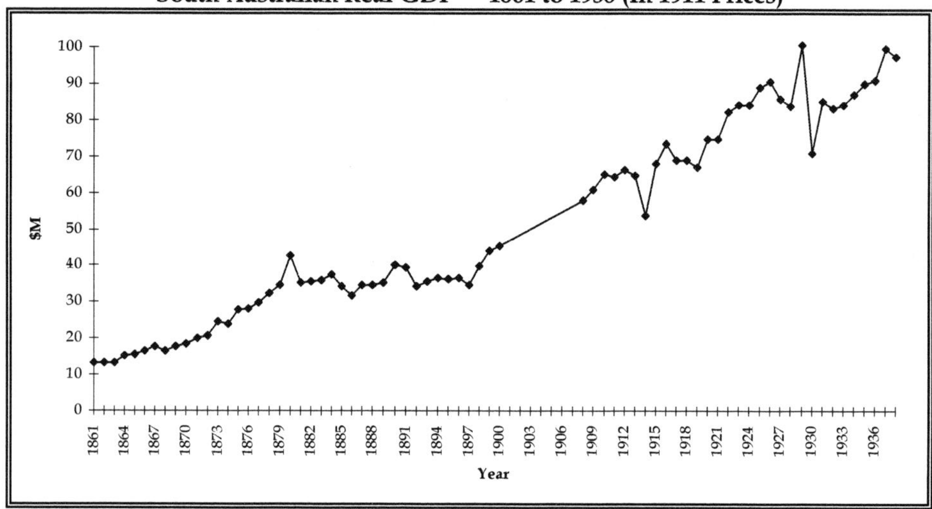

Source: Vamplew, W et al. (1994).

1946 to 1965: The Playford Era

During the post-war era the Australian economy was restructured by Commonwealth policies that fostered import substitution industrialisation. However, the Keynesian macroeconomic planning that was undertaken by the Playford Government went beyond anything that was happening at the Federal level (Stokes and Sharp, 1986; Rich, 1996). There were five main elements of Playford's macroeconomic planning. Firstly, the nationalisation of electricity generating and distribution system to guarantee that adequate electricity supplies would be made available to new industries. Secondly, the continued application of wartime restrictions to suppress consumer demand, inflation and wage pressures. Thirdly, the government stimulated immigration, especially skilled British migrants. Fourthly, the creation of a low cost and industrially stable environment for manufacturing in order to off-set the cost disadvantages of South Australia. To achieve this goal, the South Australian Housing Trust engaged in the large scale provision of low cost public housing for industrial workers reducing the cost of living and wages. Finally, the Trust became the economic development agency of the State government, acquiring and developing industrial land, providing infrastructure such as roads, railways, water and sewerage supply power and in many cases building factories to the specifications of the occupants (Stutchbury, 1986; O'Neil et al., 1996). The centrepiece of the Trust's achievements was the development of the industrial city of Elizabeth.

Figure 7.2
South Australian Real GDP Per Capita — 1861 to 1938 (In 1911 Prices)

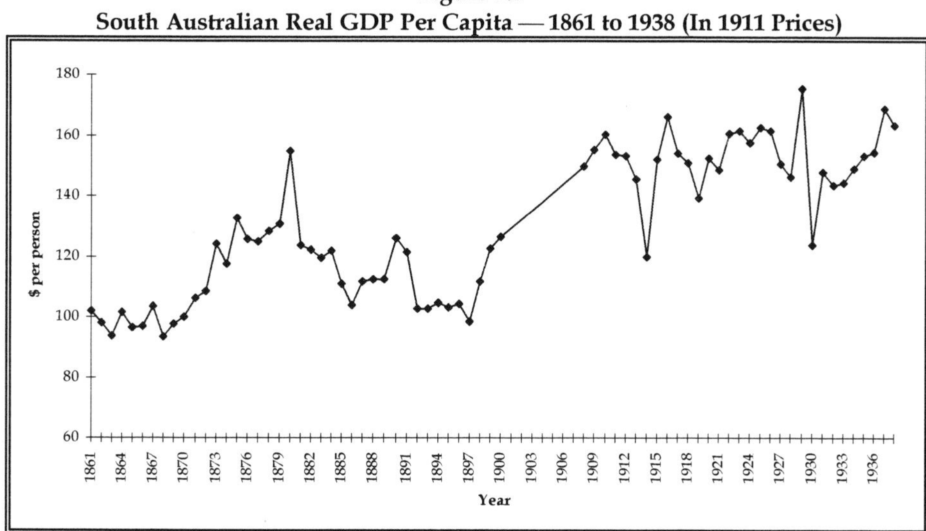

Source: Vamplew, W et al. (1994).

1965 to 1980: The Post-Playford Era

The mid-1960s was a turning point for the South Australian economy. A key ingredient of Playford's industrialisation recipe was the surplus manufacturing capacity built up during the war. But by the mid-1960s this excess capacity had been eliminated. Import substitution industrialisation policies had created a diverse and fragmented manufacturing sector both nationally and in South Australia. For many firms, government incentives to operate branch plants in South Australia no longer off-set the economic imperatives of consolidating production in a small number of sites in the Eastern states, initiating a process of rationalisation. The proportion of the workforce engaged in manufacturing peaked in 1966 employing 100,243 people or 26.5 per cent of the workforce. By

1988, manufacturing employment had risen to 103, 100 people, but the proportion of the workforce had fallen to 16.8 per cent.

The goal of government policy in the latter half of the 1960s and the 1970s was to further diversify the South Australian economy. The policies were remarkably similar to those pursued by Playford; the supply of cheap serviced industrial land, facilities and housing; the provision of other essential infrastructure such as water, transport and power; and financial assistance. These polices were largely unsuccessful, with the exception for the film making and tourism industries (McFarlane, 1986). However, the seventies were a decade of social rather than economic reform.

1980 to 1991: A Decade of Lost Opportunities

The 1980s represent something of a watershed in the South Australia's economic history. Government policy continued to support the diversification of the economy, but discontinued direct support manufacturing. The government attempted to promote tourism, through, for example, the construction of a casino, hotel and convention complex and an entertainment centre. Uranium mining and a petrochemical industries using Cooper Basin production were the key elements of a renewed focus on natural resource development. With respect to manufacturing, the focus was high technology industries and plans were made to expand Technology Park, establish the first Science Park in Australia, to make South Australia the hub of the nation's defence industries and to build a city of the future, the Multi Function Polis (McFarlane, 1986). The State Bank of South Australia was regarded as a key government asset and an instrument of growth, but the Bank grew too quickly and expanded into areas totally unrelated to the economic development of South Australia. The Bank's board was unable to control the Bank's activities and it collapsed in 1992, leaving the State Government, and moreover, the South Australian community, liable for debts of over three billion dollars.

Geographical Size, Climate and Natural Resources

Regional attributes, such as area, climate and quality of land and natural resources, tend to be quite different. These attributes confirm important economic advantages and disadvantages on a region, and significantly influence the concentration, nature of economic activity and the degree of competitiveness. These regional attributes tend to be fixed and non-transferable between regions although technological advances can limit adverse effects or enhance positive aspects of climate and natural resources through, for example, controlled climates, extractive technologies and low cost transport systems.

Table 7.2
Australian States and Territories - Area

State and Territory	Land Area	Marine Area[a]	Total Area		Coastline Length [b]	
	000s Km^2	000s Km^2	000s Km^2	Per Cent	000s Km	Per Cent
New South Wales	800.6	17.4	818.0	10.3	2.1	3.6
Victoria	227.4	14.4	241.8	3.0	2.5	4.2
Queensland	1,730.6	60.6	1,791.2	22.4	13.3	22.3
South Australia	983.5	31.5	1,015.0	12.7	5.1	8.5
Western Australia	2,529.9	74.4	2,604.3	32.6	20.8	34.8
Tasmania	68.4	27.0	95.4	1.2	4.9	8.2
Northern Territory	1,349.1	62.3	1,411.4	17.7	11.0	18.3
Australian Capital Territory	2.4		2.4	0.0		
Jervis Bay Territory	0.1		0.1	0.0	0.1	0.1
Australia	**7,692.0**	**287.6**	**7,979.6**	**100.0**	**59.7**	**100.0**

Note: (a) Commonwealth marine jurisdiction is 8.7 million km^2.
(b) Includes coastline of islands of 23.9 million km.

Source: ABS, Cat. No. 1301.0, Zann (1996).

Geographical Size

Australia is one of the world's largest countries with a land mass of over 7.6 million km^2. Being a continent, it also has one of the largest coastlines and marine regions. Australia's land mass is roughly equal in size to the United States (excluding Alaska), about 50 per cent larger than Europe and 32 times larger than the U.K.

In addition to the land mass, Australia has a 200 nautical mile Exclusive Economic Zone, proclaimed in 1994, which is over 11 million km^2.. This zone is one of the largest in the world. Jurisdiction over the exploration and exploitation of marine resources in this zone offers enormous economic potential for Australia (Zann, 1995).

South Australia has the fourth largest land mass with almost 1 million km^2, and also ranks fourth on coastline length. Size has a number of implications for the distribution of economic activity by influencing, for example, the cost of providing a variety of services such as roads, electricity, gas, and communications. In addition, marine area under State jurisdiction is 31,500 km^2 and adding South Australian waters under Commonwealth jurisdiction increase marine access to about 1 million km^2. That is, South Australia's marine resource endowment is about the same size as the states land mass. The potential harvest of natural resources both renewable (such as marine species) and non-renewable such as minerals is enormous.

Climate and Distance From Markets

Australia has a wide range of climatic conditions. However, the country's insular position and lack of significant natural features (such as high mountain ranges) make the continent less vulnerable to extremes of climate than other land masses of similar area. Most of the country is neither far enough North to be affected by tropical weather, nor sufficiently far South to be often visited by rain-bearing cold fronts. As a result, Australia has an extensive arid zone. The main exception to this pattern is the Eastern coast of Australia, which supports most of the nation's arable land and centres of population. South Australia's arid zone is very extensive. The location of activity in Australia has a clear relationship to climatic conditions and access to water and arable land.

A region's location shapes its attractiveness for people and activity. This occurs not just because of local factors tied to a location such as climate and natural resources but also because location in relation to other regions affects a region's accessibility to transferable inputs (such as materials and labour), as well as to centres of domestic and international demand.

South Australia is 983,482 square kilometres in size, or more than four times the size of Great Britain and almost two and one-half times the size of California.

South Australia in area is about 12.8 per cent of Australia. The Southern border of the State is the Southern Ocean, giving the State a coastline of approximately 3,816 kilometres (mainland coastline). The major port is Port Adelaide, but there are several other significant ports.

South Australia is a long way from anywhere. Saddled between Western Australia and the Eastern States, Adelaide is 2,104 km from Perth and 685 km from Melbourne. South Australia's single most important trading partner is the United States, some 13,142 km away (Los Angeles) with a time difference of 17.5 hours. Japan, almost as important is 7,800 km away.

About four fifths of the State receives less than 250 millimetres of rain annually on average. Nevertheless, some of this land is still the basis for an important pastoral industry. And there is growing optimism that one already announced mining project (i.e., the expansion of Olympic Dam in the state's far North) and other mining ventures in the arid North will make a significant contribution to the state's economy in the future. Such expansion may be constrained by available water resources, although the mining industry is optimistic that water-conserving technologies will overcome this potential constraint.

The geography and generally low rainfall of South Australia means that the adequate availability of water has always been a major challenge in progressing economic development. South Australia's only major river is the River Murray, which enters the State in the North East and meanders across approximately 300 kilometres, before finally flowing into the sea a little to the South of Adelaide. The river is an important source of water for domestic, industrial and agricultural use.

Distribution and Types of Natural Resources

There is considerable variation in the quantity and quality of natural resources across Australia. The distribution of water, arable land and vegetation, minerals and energy differs considerably between regions, and can also vary over time often because of human intervention.

While Australia is the world's driest continent, its ratio of water resources to population is relatively high. However, water resources do not always complement needs. Little more than a quarter of the continent contributes over 80 per cent of water runoff. In these areas, and in particular, Tasmania, the Northern parts of Queensland, the Northern Territory and Western Australia, water is relatively abundant. By contrast, water is relatively scarce in other regions, so the commitment of resources to usage, rather than management and storage, is very high. For example, the exploitation of water resources in the Murray-Darling basin is beyond practical limits, resulting in pollution and damage to the surrounding environment. Thus, while the East coast benefits from the most rainfall, run-off is relatively low, placing pressure on deposits in the form of rivers and lakes.

To a significant degree, the climatic conditions on the East coast contribute to the formation of natural vegetation across Australia (that is, the vegetation predating European settlement). While rains on the East coast sustain forests on highly arable land, much of Australia is vegetated by scrub and grasses that require water less frequently.

Land is relatively abundant in Australia but there is a problem with quality. The main types of land-use, area and value, are captured by the table below.

Of Australia's 769 million hectares about two-thirds of the land mass is used by agricultural establishments. Most of the area is used for grazing or is held under grazing licences. About three per cent of the land mass is dedicated to the more intensive production of crops, and another three per cent is used as sown pastures and grasses.

About one third of the land mass is classified as non-agricultural, and most of this area is unexploited. Such areas comprise of the sandy desert, sandy mallee country, and rugged and inaccessible regions in the Northern tropics.

South Australia's broad pattern of land use is similar to Australia as a whole, although the proportion of unexploited land is slightly higher.

There is a variety of agricultural commodities produced in Australia, which tend to be concentrated within particular states. Six commodity types account for about 80 per cent of agricultural production: wheat, coarse grains, sugar cane, fruit and vines, sheep and cattle. Wheat is found largely in New South Wales, Queensland and Western Australia, while Northern NSW and Queensland specialise in sugar cane. Fruit and vines, and coarse grains, are produces all over the country, but there is some concentration of these commodities in Northern Victoria and South Australia. Sheep production occurs largely in New South Wales, Victoria and Western Australia, while cattle are concentrated in Queensland, New South Wales and Victoria (ABS, State Year Books, Cat. No. 1301.0 to 1301.6).

Only about 1.4 per cent of land is dedicated to mining. In both area and percentage terms, mining occupies an extremely small part of Australia. Mining production involves a wide range of minerals. Coal is the dominant commodity by value, and is heavily concentrated in Queensland and New South Wales. Queensland also specialises in copper and iron ore, while New South Wales has large lead, zinc and copper deposits. Western Australia has large reserves of iron ore, bauxite and nickel, while Victoria derives a dominant share of the nation's oil and natural gas from the Bass Strait. South Australia has large natural gas and copper resources. The Northern Territory has large lead, zinc and bauxite reserves (State and Territory Year Books, various, 1993).

Table 7.3
Land Use, Quantity and Value, 1998

Land Use Quantity	Australia		South Australia		
	Million ha	**Per Cent of Total Aus**	**Million ha**	**Per Cent of Aus**	**Per Cent of Total SA**
Agricultural land [a]	463.80	60.30	57.50	12.40	58.50
Crops	21.50	2.80	3.30	15.30	3.30
Pastures and grasses	22.80	3.00	2.60	11.40	2.60
Others	419.50	54.50	51.60	12.30	52.50
Non-agricultural land [b]	305.40	39.70	40.80	13.40	41.50
National parks	53.49	6.95	20.37	38.08	20.71
Forestry reserve	14.82	1.93	0.10	0.67	0.10
Mining reserve	0.50	0.07		0.00	0.00
Defence land	1.86	0.24	0.36	19.35	0.37
Water reserve	1.10	0.14	0.02	1.82	0.02
Balance[b]	233.65	30.38	19.98	8.55	20.32
Total	**769.20**	**100.00**	**98.30**	**12.80**	**100.00**
Value	**$ Billion**	**Per Cent of Total Aus**	**$ Billion**	**Per Cent of Aus**	**Per Cent of Total SA**
Residential		74.80	27.90	4.90	67.10
Commercial	93.40	12.10	5.00	5.40	12.00
Rural	100.60	13.10	8.70	8.60	20.90
Total	**769.00**	**100.00**	**41.60**	**5.40**	**100.00**

Notes: [a] Total area of establishments with EVAO of $5,000 or more.
[b] Comprises conserved land, forestry, urban and unused land.
Source: ABS Catalogue No. 7113.0, 5241.0 and IRDB (1998).

Given the greater instability of agricultural and mineral commodity markets relative to the markets for other goods and services, the comparatively heavy reliance of some states/territories on these commodities makes their economies more susceptible to fluctuations in activity and incomes.

Land value in South Australia is much lower compared to nationally. South Australia occupies 12.8 per cent of the Australian land mass, but the value of South Australia's land is only 5.4 per cent of Australia's (Table 7.3). The value of South Australian land is under-represented in all three categories - residential, commercial and rural - but the largest gap is in the residential category. A variety of factors influence this gap including the size of the residential area relative to the Australian average, and lower urban density usually means lower property values.

The following sections explore the nature of these different types of regions in Australia, and provide some economic explanations for their existence.

Demographic Characteristics

Population

Within Australia, 85 per cent of the population lives in urban areas which occupy only 0.1 per cent of the nation's land mass. Moreover, the 10 largest urban centres account for 70 per cent of the nation's population and nearly 90 per cent of this is concentrated in just five urban centres with populations ranging from 1.1 million to 4.0 million. Over 60 per cent of the nation's gross domestic product is generated in two states - New South Wales and Victoria - which jointly account for less than 15 per cent of the nation's land mass.

As at December 1999 the population of South Australia was approximately 1.49 million, or 7.9 per cent of Australia's population. Reflecting its geography and historical development the majority of this population live in the more fertile South Eastern corner of the State and particularly in the capital city, Adelaide. The rest of the State is, in the main, very sparsely populated. In 1999, the population of Adelaide was approximately 1.09 million, or 73 per cent of South Australia's total population.

There have been three changes, since white settlement, in South Australia's ranking among regions in population level. In 1850, South Australia's population overtook that of Tasmania, to become the third most populous state. Queensland (proclaimed in 1859, compared to 1836 in South Australia) overtook South Australia's population in 1883 (ABS, Australian Year Book, 1966), lowering the ranking to fourth. And in 1982, Western Australia overtook South Australia, so that the latter became fifth in the ranking.

South Australia's population has grown slower than that nationally, with a consequent declining share of the national population over most of the past century (Table 7.4). As in Victoria, the only period during which the State's share of the national population increased was in the two decades after World War II.

A lower rate of international immigration may indicate perceptions about relative opportunities in South Australia. Closer examination of Table 7.5 shows that only two states, Western Australia and Queensland, plus the territories with their relatively small populations, have exceeded the national population growth rate. This points to a relatively simple explanation that accords with the pattern of growth that has been evident since white settlement: with their vast land masses, and consequent mineral and agricultural resources, Western Australia and Queensland have continued to grow quicker than the rest of the nation. Queensland has had the additional advantage of a rapidly growing international tourism trade over the past decade. And perceptions of a better climate and greater opportunities have resulted in a large migration of people to Queensland and New South Wales. Australia's resource base remains significant in the economy, the Northern sub-tropical and tropical state from Southern states, most notably Victoria with considerable human capital being directed into ongoing productivity improvements in the agricultural and mining sectors.

Table 7.4
South Australia's Share of the National Population

Year	South Australia	SA % of National	Australia
1881	276.4	12.3	2,250.2
1891	315.5	9.9	3,177.8
1901	358.3	9.5	3,773.8
1911	408.6	9.2	4,455.0
1921	495.2	9.1	5,435.7
1933	580.9	8.8	6,629.8
1947	646.1	8.5	7,579.4
1954	797.1	8.9	8,986.5
1961	969.3	9.2	10,508.2
1966	1,095.0	9.4	11,599.5
1971	1,200.1	9.2	13,067.3
1976	1,274.1	9.1	14,033.1
1981	1,318.8	8.8	14,923.3
1986	1,382.6	8.6	16,018.3
1991	1,446.3	8.4	17,284.0
1996	1,479.2	8.1	18,289.1
1999	1,493.1	7.9	18,963.6

Source: ABS, *Year Book Australia*, various years.

During South Australia's history, economic growth has exceeded the national growth, only in the two decades after World War II. During this time, manufacturing output grew more rapidly than job shedding per unit of output in manufacturing industries. This resulted in temporarily growing employment opportunities in states with a strong manufacturing base, including South Australia. There has been considerable debate about the impact of protection from international competition on manufacturing industries. In the twenty years from the mid-1960s when such protection was increasing in key industries including automotive production and textiles, clothing and footwear, manufacturing employment shrank both as a proportion of total employment and in absolute terms in Australia. Consequently, South Australia's population *share* has been shrinking continuously, following the abhorrent period after World War II.

Table 7.5
Composition of Regional Growth in Australia, 1985 to 1996

	Population (Thousands)		% Growth	% from	% Net	Composition of Growth	
	Dec 1984	Sep 1996	Cumulative	Baseline	Interstate Migration	% Net Overseas Migration	% Natural Growth Rate
New South Wales	5,431.8	6,207.9	13.6	-2.7	-3.8	8.6	8.8
Victoria	4,097.6	4,552.0	10.9	-5.4	-4.9	7.0	8.8
Queensland	2,547.1	3,373.2	29.9	13.6	15.0	5.0	9.9
South Australia	1,365.3	1,480.2	8.6	-7.7	-2.2	3.6	7.1
Western Australia	1,403.0	1,771.0	24.4	8.1	2.8	10.1	11.5
Tasmania	440.1	473.4	7.3	-9.0	-2.4	1.4	8.3
Northern Territory	145.3	179.8	20.6	4.4	-7.4	6.2	21.8
Aust. Capital Territory	247.1	308.2	22.1	5.8	4.8	2.8	14.4
Australia	15,677.3	18,348.7	16.3	0.0	0.0	7.0	9.3

Source: ABS (1997), *Australian Demographic Statistics* (3101.0).

Age Profile

Table 7.6 shows that as at 30 June 1999 South Australia has the largest proportion of the population 65 years or over of all States and Territories. The table also shows that South Australia's population is under-represented relative to mainland states in all working age categories 49 years and under.

Although South Australia has the oldest population in Australia, this needs to be brought into perspective. Firstly, on international comparisons, most of the advanced European countries and Japan have populations that are older. Northern America have relatively youthful populations but the differences are not enormous. Bos et al. (1994) report that the population aged 65 and over in OECD countries is expected to average 13.9 per cent of the population, that is, only slightly lower than for South Australia. Secondly, the age of the population relative to other states does not represent a major regional departure. For example, if South Australia had the Australian average population of 65 years or older, that is 12.2 per cent, then this implies that South Australia would have about 182,000 persons compared with 214,000 persons in this age group. The difference, about 32,000 persons, is not major in the context of the overall size of the economy.

What these figures suggest is that South Australia does not face any significant comparative disadvantage in the global economy from age structure. Our workforce is growing older, but the pace of change is not faster: most countries including our trading partners, are in the same situation. In East Asia, the age of the population is catching up, and as indicated above, Japan already has an older population.

However, the ageing of the population will have implications for government policy and, at the margin, how well governments here respond to the needs of the aged community relative to elsewhere may influence the contributions this group can continue to make to society and the location decisions of older people.

In the absence of a fundamental change that affects the demography of our region, South Australia's elderly will almost double by 2031. The older generation are expected to live longer and enjoy longer periods free of severe or even moderate disability. Retired persons will be more affluent. These characteristics are expected to change the structure of both the supply and the demand conditions for goods and services.

On the supply side, older people tend to be wealthy in terms of human capital. Many years of lifes experiences combined with good health will enable older people to continue to make valuable contributions to society through part-time employment and community building activities.

Table 7.6
Age Profile by State and Territory in Australia (As June 1999)

Age Group	NSW	Vic	Qld	SA	WA	Tas	NT	ACT	Australia
(Persons)	'000 Persons								
0-14	1,316	948	749	294	398	100	51	65	3,921
15-29	1,387	1,041	789	308	424	96	51	78	4,174
30-49	1,908	1,409	1,043	441	570	137	63	97	5,667
50-64	981	715	532	236	274	74	22	45	2,880
65 and over	819	599	399	214	196	63	7	25	2,322
Total	**6,412**	**4,712**	**3,512**	**1,493**	**1,861**	**470**	**193**	**310**	**18,964**
	% of Total Population								
0-14	20.5	20.1	21.3	19.7	21.4	21.3	26.2	21.0	20.7
15-29	21.6	22.1	22.5	20.6	22.8	20.4	26.7	25.3	22.0
30-49	29.8	29.9	29.7	29.6	30.6	29.1	32.5	31.2	29.9
50-64	15.3	15.2	15.2	15.8	14.7	15.8	11.3	14.5	15.2
65 and over	12.8	12.7	11.4	14.4	10.5	13.4	3.4	8.0	12.2
Total	**100.0**	**100.0**	**100.0**	**100.0**	**100.0**	**100.0**	**100.0**	**100.0**	**100.0**
	% Female								
0-14	48.8	48.7	48.7	48.7	48.6	48.8	48.2	49.1	48.7
15-29	49.4	49.3	49.2	48.9	48.7	49.7	47.3	48.3	49.2
30-49	49.9	50.4	50.0	50.2	49.6	50.7	47.3	51.1	50.1
50-64	49.4	50.0	48.8	50.3	48.5	49.8	43.2	49.5	49.4
65 and over	56.3	56.6	55.1	56.5	55.5	56.5	48.2	56.2	56.1
Total	**50.3**	**50.6**	**49.9**	**50.6**	**49.7**	**50.7**	**47.1**	**50.1**	**50.2**

Source: Australian Bureau of Statistics (Catalogue Numbers: 3201.0)

On the demand side, older people have higher propensities for spending on tourism, leisure, recreation, medical and health services, and particular preferences for the style and location of residences. Demand for education is likely to increase as the older people engage in 'life long learning'.

There are macro-economic implications. Savings rates will decline and there will be fiscal pressures arising from lower taxable incomes, pensions and public outlays for health, aged care and medical services.

In a slow growing population such as that in South Australia, the rate of change in the composition of the population is likely to out pace the rate of change in the composition of the infrastructure. In other words, the physical infrastructure will not age as quickly as the human infrastructure. The implication is that some infrastructure will become obsolete, and economic obsolence will be the arthritic catalyst more so than technological or physical obsolence. For example, the style and location of residential property, location of educational facilities and public transport are likely to become less suitable for older people.

The policy implications from this can range from encouraging older people to stay in the workforce and modifying existing residents to facilitating relocation through changes in tax laws on wealth, zoning requirements for higher density living, advice and counselling services to assist older people to relocate.

Ethnicity and Multiculturalism

A potentially far more important issue for South Australia than the ageing of the population is multiculturalism. The latter has significant implications for trade relationships and enriched quality of life.

Towards Multiculturalist Societies

Multiculturalism is a term that means different things to different people. It may signal an endorsement of mutual tolerance and a fair go, it may mean listening more to the migrant voice in an ethnic diverse country. Multicultural society is a form of society still in debate within the society itself.

People are different by nature. People think differently. They also have different life experiences. But by building upon the strengths of their differences, a group's outcomes often surpass the potential of each person alone. This is the fundamental benefit of multiculturalism. And to achieve a productive multicultural country, strong leadership and capacity to harmonise within a framework of strong governance is a must.

A fine example of a multicultural country is Brazil. Brazilian culture is never monolithic. It has been an amalgamation of traditional Iberian, indigenous, and

African values, as well as Western values developed in Northern Europe and the United States, such as equality, democracy, efficiency, and individual rights. Despite regional and social class variations, the Brazilian way of life has common traits with strong cultural values in favour of conciliation, tolerance, and cordiality. All the racial and ethnic groups that arrived in Brazil intermingled and intermarried, with few exceptions. This has led to increasing mixtures of all possible combinations and degrees. Many individuals are, therefore, difficult to classify in cultural terms. At times there are subtle or open conflicts, especially between norms of Mediterranean and Anglo-Saxon origin, or between practices of European versus Amerindian or African origin. However, Brazil is remarkable for unity in cultural diversity. (Library of Congress 1997). The longstanding government policy against racial discrimination, emphasising racial pride, has been able to unify the country together.

As we go to the 21st century, the world becomes increasingly a place of the multi-ethnic, and cultural diversity is a reality. A multicultural society creates a competitive advantage in a nation. The diversity presents itself as an invaluable human resource. The advantages include the range of language skills to facilitate external communication, communication styles to improve effectiveness, deepen international networks, improve knowledge other countries and external conditions and enrich life experiences that bring to the nation as a whole and the organisations within it to be more effective internally as well as with other countries. Workforces are most effective when they are as diverse as the local and global environments in which the organisation trades. They also contribute in stimulating economy with their supply and demand of diverse products.

Empirical research findings suggest that differences in deep-rooted cultural manifestations across countries play a significant role in the way in which economic and management issues are addressed and resolved (Morosini 1998). For example, Franke et al. (1991) utilised cultural measures to evaluate differences in economic performance at the level of nations. Employing samples of 18[11] and 20[12] nations, they found that cultural indices derived from Western[13]

---

11 The 9 'rich' nations (>US$1,300 per capita GNP in 1965): Australia, Canada, West Germany, Japan, the Netherlands, New Zealand, Sweden, the UK, the USA. The 9 'poor' nations: - 'very poor' (US$60-$119 per capita GNP in 1965) India, Pakistan, the Philippines, Thailand, and 'rich/poor' (dividing line of US$1,300 per capita GNP in 1965): Brazil, Hong Kong, South Korea, Singapore, Taiwan.

12 The 18 nations plus two African nations: Nigeria & Zimbabwe.

13 *power distance index*: a society's endorsement of inequality; *individualism*: the tendency of individuals primarily to look after themselves and their immediate families; *masculinity*: an assertive or competitive orientation, as well as a sex-role distinction; and *uncertainty avoidance index*: taps a feeling of discomfort in unstructured or unusual circumstances.

and Eastern[14] investigations of people's values explain more than 50 per cent of the international differences in economic growth rates for the periods 1965-80 and 1980-87. Among the variables, two cultural measures, *consufian dynamism* and *individualism*, account for most of the variance in national economic growth rates. The finding, however, was based on a stepwise multiple regression which is purely a statistical device. This statistical procedure is utilised to maximise the degree of variance (R^2).

Alesina and Spolaore (1997) argue that the benefits of scale derived in large nations may be counter balanced by congestion and co-ordination. There is a "political cost" of large nations because a larger population is likely to be less homogenous. That is the average distance between cultural values and preferences of individuals are likely to be positively correlated with the size of the country. A diverse population is difficult for a central government to satisfy. Easterly and Levine (1997) argue that Africa's high ethnic fragmentation explains a significant part of why these countries have not been able to put in place the public policies necessary for economic growth.

While the econometric work underpinning these studies is not questioned, the policy implications do not follow. In the case of Africa, ethnic fragmentation has been present in those countries for many decades and could have been resolved if it were not for poor governance. If democratic process were in place at the turn of the 20th century then the potential for ethnic conflict would have diminished. Furthermore, if Alesia and Spolaore are right that an ethnically diverse population is difficult for a central government to satisfy, then the issue is less to do with ethnicity and more to do with the quality of governance. In other words, ethnically diverse populations also offer variety in consumption and experiences, and if governments are not able to cope with abroad range of views and bring those views together in harmony then the real problem is the quality of political and community leadership.

A common characteristic of human nature is reluctance to a change. Arrien (1998) describes the human struggle with the issue of multiculturalism: some of us may wish things were the way they once were. For some, a personal comfort zone might dictate a behaviour of "sticking to one's own kind." Some will even resist change, seeing only the difficulties associated with working together with people different from themselves. They see other cultures as threatening and inferior. However, the tide changes. We are going through an evolutionary shift. Without the broader universal understanding of the changes which are occurring, it is all too easy for dominant ethnic groups to feel under threat and to blame the minorities. Educating people in any form is the key. Thus we accept and welcome these changes, and embrace the richness represented by the

14 *Confusion dynamism*: an acceptance of the legitimacy of hierarchy and the valuing of perseverance and thrift; *integration*: an index of degree of tolerance, harmony and friendship a society endorsed; *human-heartedness*: open-hearted patience, courtesy, and kindness; and *moral discipline*: rigid distancing from affairs of the world.

assorted experiences and perspective that flow from this diversity. The greatest challenge for championing diversity is backlash due to fear.

Multiculturalism in Australia and South Australia

Multicultural issue in Australia has been in debate for decades. It continued to evolve in 1980s and 1990s. Through the 1989 *National Agenda for a Multicultural Australia: sharing our future* and the 1992 policy of *Productive diversity* the government attempt to redefine multiculturalism. These policies, unfortunately, for a variety of reasons were unable to secure broad public support. Multiculturalism was in decline when in 1996 many of the institutions crucial to Australian multiculturalism, such as the Office of Multicultural Affairs, were abolished or reduced to insignificance. The rise of the One Nation overshadowed the issue. However, through increased international travel, global media and exposure to other cultures, many Australians became more cosmopolitan and culturally aware. In fact Jones' study (1999) indicates healthy majority of Australians believe that immigration, which closely related to multiculturalism, is good for the economy.

Concerning the reluctance of moving forward, Castles (1999) emphasises that Australia's cultural diversity is "irreversible". Any escape into a nostalgic illusion of an Anglo-centred assimilation is "not only unrealistic but also dangerous, because it blocks the way to a real grasp of what is going on in our fast-changing world." He maintains that what is needed instead of a nostalgic retreat are new forms of multicultural citizenship and democracy, capable of combating the power of uncontrolled markets and huge transnational corporations.

In the era of globalisation, Australia can not avoid the effect of powerful economic, cultural and social factors. As a result, the importance of multicultural issue becomes increasingly realised. In December 1997, the government issued a paper *Multicultural Australia: the way forward* acknowledging the cultural and ethnic diversity of contemporary Australia. Under Australia's federal system the Commonwealth shares responsibilities for cultural diversity policies and programs with States and Territories.

Withers (1998) contends: "Australia has a choice. We can be a small economy or a big economy. We can have a large growing domestic base for our global integration or we can hold back and fall steadily behind." He stated that under present settings Australian population will peak at around 23 million in 2050 and decline gradually thereafter. If fertility continues to fall, and if immigration is held back further than at present, we could peak at a mere 20 million by 2030 and decline fast as deaths exceeds births. South Australia as well as Tasmania will most likely have declining populations even earlier in the new century. Under this scenario, the danger for Australia, as well as for South Australia, is being underpopulated.

A growing population for a developed economy such as Australia will constitute a crucial source of competitive advantage. To achieve a prosper economic growth, a healthy population growth is desirable. This can partly be fulfilled with evaluating Australian immigration policy. The question is what is the optimal ethnic mix to enable Australia to flourish as a multicultural country and how committed Australians are to multiculturalism.

As at June 1996, approximately 8.1 per cent of Australia's population and 7.7 per cent of overseas-born lived in South Australia. At that time the overseas-born represented 23.3 per cent of Australia's total population and approximately 22.3 per cent of the population of South Australia. In 1996-97, South Australia gained 7,205 people through natural increase and 3,480 through net overseas migration. There was an estimated loss of 5,185 people from net interstate migration. In 1997-98 the top five countries of origin (in order) of settlers arrivals to South Australia were the United Kingdom, the former Yugoslavia, New Zealand, South Africa, and India. This compares with the top source countries for Australia of New Zealand, the United Kingdom, China, the former Yugoslavia, and South Africa (DIMA, 2000).

A striking feature of the origins of birth of the population is the Anglo-Saxan domination throughout Australia. In the South Australian region, the Anglo-Saxan domination is slightly stronger. In other words, South Australia, similar to Australia as a whole, is not an ethnically diverse population. Multiculturalism is a function of ethnic diversity and the capacities of all peoples to understand different cultures. While arguably we can immerse ourselves in culture through travel and learning, lack of ethnic diversity will hold us back from cultural integration.

The ethnicity of the population reflects the backgrounds of the first settlers that founded the colony and the immigration policies of successive governments. Reflecting these policies, South Australia is relatively well endowed with Northern Europeans including British and Southern Europeans most notably the Greeks and Italians. Within our neighbourhood, consisting of our closest trading partners in the Asian-Pacific region our community is under-represented by Chinese, South East Asians including Vietnamese and Melanesians. That is, we are under-represented in all countries loosely described as our neighbours.

Lack of ethnicity diversity deprives this region from the potential business networks because the cultures of our neighbours are built on organisations of close family, friends and longstanding employees. Different ways of thinking, new ideas and cultural richness can come from the emersion of peoples with different backgrounds. The potential for conflict arising from differences in values and inequality can be dispersed through strong governance.

Table 7.7
Country of Birth, Persons living in Australia

Country of Birth	NSW	Vic	Qld	SA	WA	Tas	NT	ACT	Aust.
					(Per Cent)				
Eastern Africa	0.09	0.19	0.03	0.01	0.12	0.01	0.01	0.04	0.10
Southern Africa	0.35	0.27	0.26	0.15	0.62	0.16	0.11	0.24	0.31
Northern America	0.43	0.34	0.44	0.33	0.51	0.29	0.68	0.85	0.42
Southern America	0.22	0.16	0.04	0.05	0.07	0.03	0.04	0.25	0.13
North Eastern Asia	2.26	1.15	0.67	0.46	0.65	0.24	0.41	1.28	1.30
China	1.08	0.64	0.22	0.21	0.26	0.08	0.18	0.55	0.62
South Eastern Asia	2.82	2.96	1.28	1.73	2.94	0.52	2.77	2.38	2.42
Viet Nam	1.01	1.26	0.33	0.75	0.58	0.05	0.27	0.75	0.84
Australasia	74.22	73.43	81.40	76.14	70.52	86.66	78.13	75.53	75.56
Australia	72.77	72.46	78.38	75.46	68.27	85.88	76.35	74.35	73.93
New Zealand	1.46	0.97	3.02	0.68	2.26	0.78	1.78	1.19	1.63
Melanesia	0.47	0.19	0.55	0.12	0.10	0.13	0.42	0.45	0.34
Central/East Europe	1.18	1.66	0.49	1.10	0.98	0.37	0.23	1.23	1.11
Northern Europe	5.07	5.19	5.63	9.47	12.43	5.03	4.64	6.36	6.28
United Kingdom	4.78	4.92	5.41	9.22	11.89	4.90	4.42	6.11	5.99
Southern Europe	2.59	4.74	0.86	3.20	2.13	0.51	1.09	2.19	2.72
Greece	0.68	1.41	0.13	0.88	0.20	0.14	0.58	0.47	0.71
Italy	1.09	2.25	0.51	1.91	1.46	0.27	0.32	0.86	1.33
Western Europe	1.11	1.47	1.23	1.76	1.40	1.14	1.16	1.68	1.31
Germany, Fed Republic of	0.54	0.68	0.57	0.93	0.58	0.44	0.56	0.86	0.62
East Mediterranean	0.32	0.55	0.06	0.15	0.06	0.02	0.10	0.09	0.28
Middle East	1.16	0.59	0.08	0.18	0.14	0.03	0.04	0.21	0.58
South Asia	0.87	1.15	0.32	0.41	0.97	0.17	0.45	1.03	0.79
Not stated	6.05	5.41	5.14	4.30	5.52	4.44	6.77	5.40	5.49
Total	**100.00**	**100.00**	**100.00**	**100.00**	**100.00**	**100.00**	**100.00**	**100.00**	**100.00**

Source: IRDB, 1998 and SACES calculations.

The Way Forward

Australia has the potential to grasp the multicultural opportunity. Jupp (1999) indicates nearly half of all people living in Australia were born overseas, or are the children of parents born abroad. Australia is proportionately the world's most intensely immigrant country. But being an intensely immigrant country does not necessarily imply that Australians have a diverse ethnic background. In fact, most Australians' originated from Northern Europe and share similar cultural traits.

One step towards multiculturalism is to integrate Australia more intensely with the Asia-Pacific region. This move would be consistent with the increasing important need of maintaining economic and political stability in this region. To take this step, Australia needs to attain a greater knowledge of the dynamics of modern Asian societies. It is also needs a greater knowledge of Asian languages, indigenous cultural traditions, political, social and economic structures. As at June 1997, 5.3 per cent of 18.53 million Australian population was Asia-born. The number in South Australia is significantly less. These Asian immigrants are themselves one source of this knowledge. Furthermore, their maintenance of links with their countries of origin can also bring the Australian community as a whole in closer contact with Asian societies.

Stromback, et al. (1994) studied South Asian immigrants in Western Australia. They found that almost all respondents had at least family links with their country of origin. There was also a large group who had economic, cultural, religious or political links. The links were more important to the immigrants in business.

These links are a bridge between Asia and Australia. As Asian immigrants use this bridge to support their settlement, Australia can also use this bridge to further develop the relationships with Asian neighbours. It is a bridge on which the knowledge of Asian societies can travel and, to emphasise the purely economic benefits, a bridge which the Australian business community can use in entering Asian markets. Working with cultural diversity is now an important part of business. For example, international tourism is one of the most rapidly growing industries in Australia. In industries as culture sensitive as tourism, labour market diversity, is becoming more and more important.

The State and regional governments have given some recognition to the advantages of multi-cultural communities. In 1999, the State Government launched several initiatives aimed at monitoring government services for multicultural clientele, raising awareness of achieving through diversity, and a range of communications initiatives aimed at the integration of ethnic communities into the general South Australian community. These initiatives are, in principle, an appropriate role for governments, but the main issue remains that until South Australia became ethnically diverse then we will not be fully receptive to the ideas and paths to development practiced in foreign countries.

The Medium for Multiculturalism

Education is a precision tool for building cultural awareness in the society. The tertiary sector is a longstanding means of injecting multicultural experiences into the regional community through intellectual exchange, the recruitment practices for teaching and research staff and, in more recent times, the attraction of students from overseas. The secondary education sector is similarly seeking foreign students and recruiting teachers from broader backgrounds. With particular reference to management training, O'Neil (1998) considers that no professional educational program can achieve distinction without cultural and intellectual diversity because without these characteristics:

- any contemporary education of professionals is simply out of touch with the reality those professionals will face in the world;
- research efforts will have limited applicability in an increasingly diverse world; and
- professional services will not reach many of those most in need and will not be effective and appropriate.

The International College of Hotel Management (ICHM) in South Australia is a prime example of the potential benefits to business of multiculturalism. ICHM attracts between 300 and 400 students per year, of which over 90 per cent are from outside the state. The economic impact of these students and ICHM expenditures are important (possibly of the order of $5 million per annum), but pale in significance along side the potential for future business attributable to the college graduates. When these graduates return home to foreign countries to practice hotel management, they have been fully acquainted with South Australian life style, food and beverage products and established business and social connections with South Australians. SACES (1996) reports that the graduates would have the potential to create additional demand for South Australian food and beverage products of anything of the order of a minimum of $35 million to possibly $70 million over a period of 10 years. That expenditure would support jobs in the order of between 500 and 1100.

Concluding Remarks

A multiculturalist society is a sound basis for economic growth for at least three reasons. Firstly, improved trade relationships. Multicultural societies have a better understanding of overseas business practice and stronger rapport through networks of family, friends and former business colleagues. Secondly, to stimulate economic growth. Multicultural societies create new supply of and demand for diverse commodities. Thirdly, enriched quality of life.

Multiculturalism societies bring diversity in social norms, tastes, styles, etc., that increase choice.

Although Australia is the land of the immigrant, Australians are not ethnically diverse. Accordingly multiculturalism has been superficial experience more so than an emersion in culture. Multiculturalism and immigration are closely related if policies are linked more closely with Australia's neighbours than with our heritage. A policy to increase the degree of multiculturalism in society is not policy of open door immigration. New entrants should be ethnic diverse. They must be able to sustain employment. Although not a comprehensive criteria, new entrants should be able to make a positive contribution to the economy if they (i) meet skill shortages in the region, (ii) develop business through international contacts, or (iii) acquire knowledge and networks locally for employment overseas at some later date as in the ICHM example above.

The above suggests that a policy should:

- promote locally based schools that attract international students;
- advertise local skill shortages overseas involving the promotion of South Australia as a place to live;
- encourage local society to be receptive to multiculturalism; and
- defray relocation costs through loan funding on the basis of a stay for a specified period of time.

Societies that are multicultural tend to be more open and receptive to ideas and adapt more quickly to changed circumstances, and is a quality we need as a region to catch up and stay ahead in the global environment of the new millennium. Education is a key of importance.

The Murray-Darling Basin

The Murray-Darling Basin is one of the Nation's most significant regions covering over 1 million square kilometres of Eastern and South-Eastern Australia, 14 per cent of the total landmass. The river system, which lies at the heart of the Basin includes Australia's three longest rivers, the Darling (2,740 km); the Murray (2,530 km) and the Murrumbidgee (1,690 km) and their tributaries. Irrigation is by far the most significant use of water from the basin, with average annual diversions (1988-89 to 1993-94) of 10,200 Gigalitres. This level of irrigation supports a substantial agricultural sector; the Australian Bureau of Agricultural and Resource Economics estimated that the gross value of agricultural production in the Basin for 1993-94 was $9.4 billion, 39.6 per cent of the Australian total for that year.[15]

15 Quoted on the Murray-Darling Basin Commission website, http://www.mdbc.gov.au/MDBasin/Resources/index.html

Diversions for domestic, industrial, stock and town use are small by comparison to those for agriculture, amounting to 452 GL in an average year. This diversion supports a significant proportion of Australia's population: at the 1996 Census the population was estimated to be 1.96 million, 10.9 per cent of the Australian total.[16] In addition to the persons living in the Basin, the Murray-Darling River also supports the population and industry of Adelaide, providing 40 per cent of Adelaide's water supply in an average year. This means that any decline in the water quality of the River Murray could have significant effects on the South Australian economy, by increasing the cost of drinking and industrial water.

Despite its status as one of Australia's most important environmental assets the Murray-Darling Basin has been systematically mismanaged over the past 150 years, particularly since the significant post-war expansions of irrigation. Fee structures for diverting water did not take into account environmental damage, or externalities caused to other river users. There were also no incentives to move irrigation activity further away from the riparian zone, where it would have had less impact on the water tables (one of the major sources of saline inflows to the river today). On the contrary, many of the government irrigation districts and soldier-settlement schemes were located in regions most susceptible to damage by irrigation. By underpricing water and not making irrigators internalise any impacts on the environment or other water users, government policy encouraged wasteful irrigation and distribution techniques, inappropriate crop choice, and excessive environmental damage.

Salinity is one of the most significant environmental problems facing Australia today. Traditionally much of the attention has been focussed on 'dry-land' salinity, as this affects large areas of Australia's pastoral and cropping land. A recent report by the Murray Darling Basin Commission[17] has found disturbing trends in the salinity levels of rivers in the Murray-Darling basin. They estimated the current total economic cost of river salinity at $46 million per year (MDBC, 1999a, p. vi), and tipped that this would increase substantially, with the annual cost potentially rising to $600 million (in current values) by 2100.[18] The Salinity Audit also found that *"[m]ore than 90 per cent of the salinity impacts are experienced in South Australia"* (MDBC, 1999a p. 22). To give an idea of the scale of these potential impacts, if South Australia continued to face 90 per cent of the impact (which is uncertain), then the annual cost from salinity would be over $500 million, more than the entire gross value of horticultural production in South Australia in 1997-98 and more than $^{1}/_{6}$th of the total gross value of agriculture.

16 *Ibid.*

17 MDBC (1999a), *The Salinity Audit of the Murray-Darling Basin.*

18 *Ibid,* p. 22.

Of particular concern for Adelaide's future water supply is that the MDBC found that:

> "The average salinity of the lower River Murray (monitored at Morgan) will exceed the 800 EC threshold for desirable drinking water quality in the next 50 - 100 years. By 2020 the probability of exceeding 800 EC will be about 50 per cent. ...the cost of one EC unit increase in river salinity at Morgan in South Australia lies in the range of $93,000 to $142,000 per year."[19]

In its 10 year review (MDBC 1999b), the Commission estimated that the salinity strategy had reduced average salinity (measured at Morgan), from 721 EC to 569 EC, comparing averages of 1975-85 with those of 1993-99. In effect, the MDBC strategy has 'bought' 20 years, However, the Commission project a rise, unless further measures are taken, from the current level 570 EC to 790 EC by 2050 and 900 EC by 2100; at that last level, the water would be barely fit for human consumption.

What is to be done? Some of the projected increase in salinity is due to the (long-lasting) effects of old irrigation schemes, and could be reduced by reform of irrigation and water use practices. Such reform could prevent an increase of about 28 EC of the projected rise - another 190 EC increase would be direct flow into the Murray from the Mallee, and 75 EC from flows into catchment tributaries.

As such Australia itself would account for about half of the projected increase in salinity, 26 EC from irrigation and 82 EC from dryland salinity, the government and people of South Australia could consider taking actions without the necessity of obtaining agreement from other States. Clearly, the South Australia community would bear the cost of these unilateral actions; and equity would seem to dictate that not all of the costs should fall on irrigators, as they would be responsible for only a portion of the problem.

An increased concentration of salinity suggests that methods for environmental improvement need to be closely examined. A particular problem with dryland salinity is that is often caused by actions taken generations ago, which means that imposing the costs of environmental improvements on the current farmers is not necessarily equitable. The essential point of reassessment which the increasing impact of dryland salinity poses, is that more government involvement is required.

One positive from these estimates of projected sources of inflow for South Australia is that a considerable proportion is projected to occur in South Australia, which means that action can be taken without the agreement of the other states. The obvious downside of this is that the South Australian

19 *Ibid*, p. vi

community will have to bear much of the costs. This is complicated by the fact that much of the inflow within South Australia is likely to be from dryland salinity, which means that cost recovery from the polluters will be difficult and that abatement methods may be more complicated. An insight from economics is that the chosen method should be the most cost effective one, not necessarily that which removes the particular source of pollution which is at issue. For example, if the only objective were to bring about a reduction in river salinity, then to offset the projected inflows from dryland salinity, the State government could build infrastructure, such as salt interception schemes, or significant tree planting, which reduce or remove the direct source of pollution, or, the best way to address the inflows from dryland salinity may be to purchase water for environmental flows, or to fund salinity reduction works in irrigation districts, either elsewhere in the state or interstate.

There are two basic principles of economics which previous policy on the Murray-Darling Basin has not taken into account. The first principle is that society maximises its welfare when resources are able to be traded, so that they end up in the hands of whoever values them the most. The second principle is that property rights or incentives should be structured so that agents in the economy take into account all of the costs and benefits of their actions, not just those which impact on them directly.

An example of the first of these principles is that if all other things being equal, a water allocation of one ML increases the value of grape production by $200 in the Riverland or $500 in the Barossa then the net welfare of the State is increased by the grower in the Barossa having use of the water. This principle is the reason that economists favour a market system for the allocation of resources, as this is the only systematic way of having people accurately flag the value of a resource to them. Irrigators will not pay more for water than it is worth to them; otherwise, they will lose money. They will, however, be prepared to pay a price for water which (for the last allocation) just adds to their profit.

For a government agency to allocate water rights as efficiently as a market system it would have to possess excellent information about how much each ML of water would be worth to each irrigator in the State and to allocate water on this basis. Obviously no government agency would be able to gauge the values accurately, especially if growers had an incentive to overstate the value they place on water to gain a higher allocation.

With the exception of Victoria and a limited trial run by COAG in the Murray-Darling Basin, water rights are generally linked to property rights, so the only benefit an irrigator gains by increasing the efficiency of their systems is a reduction pumping costs. If water rights were tradeable then irrigators would be able to fund some of the cost of water-saving innovation through selling surplus water rights to other users. Capital expenditure, to improve irrigation efficiency, would be much more financially attractive to irrigators. This is a good example of how environmental outcomes can be improved by moving to a more market-based system.

Tradeable water rights would also mean that, as water rights would be purchased by the users who could produce the highest value from them, higher income would be generated per unit of environmental damage, meaning that there was more wealth available in the economy to deal with environmental problems. A final potential benefit of complete tradeability of water rights is that water utilities and environmental groups would be able to purchase water rights from irrigators for environmental flows. This would improve water quality both through increased flows and through reduced salt inflow due to reduced irrigation.

Turning now to the second basic principle of economics which has not been previously applied in the management of the Murray-Darling Basin, there is currently nothing in place which ensures irrigators face the impact of their actions on others (termed externalities by economists). When irrigators are deciding how much to irrigate, and where to irrigate they primarily consider their own costs and benefits, even though their decisions can have a significant impact on other users of the river system. For an economy to function efficiently all externalities need to be taken into account (or internalised) by those causing them; otherwise excessive activity will occur in those sectors which generate negative externalites, and not enough will occur in those which produce a positive externality.[20]

There are two primary methods suggested by economists to address a negative externality. The first of these is to impose a tax to the value of the negative impact on others. Then irrigators in the Murray-Darling Basin would be charged an environmental levy calculated on the basis of the environmental damage their water use causes. Such an environmental levy would ensure that the full costs of their actions became part of irrigators' decision-making process, so that irrigation would only occur if its benefits outweigh the cost to the irrigator plus the damage it causes. This would then create incentives for irrigators to implement programmes to reduce their environmental damage, such as more efficient irrigation methods, lower water use crops, salt interception schemes etc..

The second method is to assign tradeable property rights for the negative externality, either to polluters or those affected by the pollution. The choice as to whom the property rights are assigned may not much affect the efficiency of this process, but it may have considerable equity implications. In the case where the pollution rights are assigned to the polluter, those affected by the pollution could buy some or all of the pollution rights from the polluter. They will do this up to the point where the cost of buying the pollution rights (which will be

20 Strictly speaking, efficient decisions about externalities require the decision-maker to be faced with the full costs of their actions *on the margin*.

determined by the cost to the polluter of finding alternative disposal methods or reducing activity) is equal to the damage caused to them by the pollution. Similarly if pollution rights are granted to the victims of pollution then they will be prepared to sell those rights to the polluter up to the point where the price they receive equals the damage the pollution causes them; and the polluter will be prepared to buy pollution rights up to the point where the price of the pollution rights equals the cost of either reducing production or using alternative disposal techniques. The costs of operating such a trading scheme are why, for many environmental problems, economists favour the tax (or charge) system discussed in the last paragraph.

There are four mutual non-exclusive policies which the governments could introduce to address the current and potential environmental damage caused by increasing salinity in the Murray-Darling River system. In choosing the balance between different policies the government should assess which deliver the greatest benefit for the least cost, although the equity of any policies implemented should also be of concern. The four potential policies are:

- tax irrigators;
- issue tradeable salinity credits;
- purchase water for dilution flows; and
- government funded capital works.

These have been previously mentioned; a fuller discussion follows. The first and second policies are market-based solutions and the third and fourth are government funded solutions.

Tax the Irrigators

Irrigators are responsible for a considerable share of environmental damage to the Murray caused by human activity. As well as providing funds to governments for environmental improvements in the Murray-Darling Basin, and ensuring that irrigators pay for the full cost of their water use (including the environmental damage which results) a tax on water encourages responsible actions on the part of irrigators. This would be especially the case if a different tax rate were applied to each irrigation district based on the value of environmental damage their water use causes. As inter-State water trading is now occurring, such a tax regime would also encourage a shift in irrigation activity from high-damage districts to low-damage districts. Irrigation activity would switch to those areas which generate the highest net return on irrigation, after allowing for environmental damage. There may be significant equity implications from introducing an environmental tax on irrigators suddenly, as they would have made investment decisions based on existing pricing frameworks. Therefore, any environmental levy should be introduced gradually to allow water users to adjust their behaviour for the increased cost of water without imposing an undue burden on irrigators.

Currently total diversions from the Murray are 10,676 Giga Litres. If all of the estimated costs from salinity were imposed on diverters (including Urban and Industrial water users) the average environmental levy would be $4.30/ML. In order to accurately reflect the damage caused by water use, the level of the tax would have to vary between irrigation districts so this rough estimate would be an average figure, with some irrigation districts paying more and others less.

As farmers tend to be time rich but cash poor, the government could also consider accepting payment in-kind for water taxes: for example planting trees (valued both for land taken out of production and the time taken to plant them), which are known to lower water tables thereby reducing the quantity of salinity inflow into the Murray; or providing labour, equipment, or land to capital works such as salt interception schemes.

Issue Tradeable Salinity Credits

Issuing tradeable salinity credits, where irrigators are given a permit to cause their current level of salinity inflow (or some proportion of it) to the river system, is a method for allocating property rights for pollution (as discussed above). There are several advantages to tradeable salinity permits as a method for addressing the Murray-Darling Basin's Salinity problems. Firstly, their tradeability means that downstream users can reduce the salinity impacts they face by purchasing salinity credits up-stream, and in a market based system this reduction will only occur when the benefits to downstream users are greater than the costs in reduced production up-stream. It also creates an incentive for irrigation activity to shift to areas where it causes less damage.

Purchase Water for Dilution Flows

Another solution to the problem of the environmental damaged caused by irrigation (and one which could be partly funded by the proceeds of an environmental levy) is to purchase water rights to increase dilution flows. The increased water flow would serve to dilute any inflows of salinity to the river, and the reduced irrigation activity would reduce inflows of salinity to the river. Based on current water sale values of $600 per ML, it would cost $64 million to permanently reduce total diversions by 1 per cent. The government could also gain a double benefit from the purchase of water rights, by concentrating its purchase activity on those areas where irrigation causes the most environmental damage.

Government-Funded Capital Works

A final method for the government to improve the water quality of the Murray would be to fund capital works to reduce inflows of salinity. This type of policy would seem to be more appropriate for reducing the effects of dryland salinity, which is often not the result of current actions. If the government were to fund capital works from general revenues to reduce the environmental impact of irrigators there would also be an equity concern, in that the community as a whole would be paying for what are effectively part of the production costs of a private sector industry. The effects on efficiency would be equivalent to the community paying for the coal that BHP uses in its Whyalla steelworks. Of course if the cost of the capital works is funded through a tax on irrigators' water use then this efficiency concern would be addressed. When funding any capital works the government should also ensure that they are the most cost-effective method of achieving the desired salinity reduction. It may be cheaper in some cases to purchase water rights for dilution flows rather than reducing the levels of salinity in-flow to the river.

As the Murray-Darling River System passes through five jurisdictions, and as the Commonwealth does not have the constitutional authority to enforce a national approach, there is a need for cooperation between the states, and between the various levels of government to maximise the nation's welfare. The local communities are also vital to the success of any attempts to fix the river system. Most of the proposed solutions, particularly market based ones, rely on irrigators reacting rationally to changed incentives. If local communities feel excluded from, and disenfranchised by, the policies proposed to prevent a significant further decline in the quality of the river system then they may value the increase in personal satisfaction gained from disrupting the reforms more highly than the incentives to reduce environmental damage. Community groups such as Landcare are also vital to the future health of the nation's rural environment, and if the process of implementing policies for environmental improvements were to reduce involvement in these groups due to feeling of alienation from the decision making process then the net impact could be negative for the environment.

Closing Comments

In this chapter, an attempt has been made to illustrate by example some of the important South Australian endowments. Although by no means a comprehensive economic history, the first section is a reminder that what we are today is in part a function of how we got here. The droughts, depression, protectionist trade policies, poor economic management have suppressed growth and development of this region, but temporarily, giving the impetus and urgency to reform and marking a new path forward.

Although a long way from anywhere, South Australia is drawing closer to the major markets through the gradual decline in transport and communications costs and new technologies that, for example, create controlled climates, and improve the efficiency of mineral extraction, which will over time improve the acreage of arable land.

South Australians are mainly urban coastal dwellers, swelling in numbers only slowly relative to other regions in Australia. Slow population growth reflects longevity, low birth rate and low immigration, and these factors are leading to a gradual ageing of the population. The ageing of the population is not a comparative disadvantage for the region because our trading partners and our competitors are ageing similarly. The main demographic characteristic is that of concern is the lack of ethnic diversity. Until the region can immerse itself in different cultures, we will not be able to fully connect into the international market place. Business linkages will be strengthened and our understanding of the external environment will be stronger, so that our region will not be inhibited from recognising and responding to change.

Finally, we examined one of the States most important endowments: water. The rising salinity of the Murray-Darling river system is one of the most significant environmental problems facing Australia today. Reform is urgent. There are a number of economic policies available to arrest the problem. As the river system passes through five jurisdictions, cooperation among the three tiers of government, various local communities and river water users is a prerequisite to solving this nation-wide problem.

References

Alesina, A. and Spolaore, E. (1997), "On the Number and Size of Nations", *Quarterly Journal of Economics*, November.

Ang, Ien (2000), "Asians in Australia: A Contradiction in Terms?", in *Race, Colour and Identity in Australia and New Zealand*, eds. John Docker and Gerhard Fischer, UNSW Press, pp: 115-130.

Arrien, Angeles (ed) (1998), *Working Together: producing Synergy by Honoring Diversity*, New Leader Press, Pleasanton, California.

Castles, Stephen (1999), "Globalisation, Multicultural Citizenship and Transnational Democracy", in *The Future of Australian Multiculturalism*, eds. G. Hage and R. Couch, Research Institute for Humanities and Social Sciences, University of Sydney, pp: 31-41.

Bos, E., Vu, M.T., Massiah, E., and Bulatao, R. (1994), *World Population Projections, 1994-95*, The International Bank for Reconstruction and Development, The World Bank.

Broomhill, R. (1978), *Unemployed Workers: A social History of the Great Depression in Adelaide*, University of Queensland Press, St. Lucia.

Cope, Bill and Kalantzis, Mary (1997), *Productive Diversity: A New, Australian Model for Work and Management*, Pluto Press, Australia.

Department of Immigration and Multicultural Affairs (DIMA) (1999), *A New Agenda for Multicultural Australia*, Commonwealth of Australia, Canberra.

Department of Immigration and Multicultural Affairs (DIMA) (2000), "Australian Immigration - Multicultural Australia: The Way Forward".
[Online, accessed 9/10/2000]. URL:
http://www.immi.government.au/multicultural

Easterly, W. and Levine, R. (1997), "Africa's Growth Tragedy: Policies and Ethnic Divisions", *Quarterly Journal of Economic*, November.

Franke, R.H., Hofstede, G., and Bond, M.H. (1991), "Cultural Roots of Performance: A Research Note", *Strategic Management Journal*, Vol. 12, pp: 165-173.

Gibbs, R.M. (1990), *A History of South Australia: From Colonial Days to the Present*, Southern Heritage, Adelaide.

Healey, Justin (ed) (2000), "Multiculturalism", *Issues in Society*, Volume 126, The Spinney Press, Australia.

Jones, Frank (1999), "The Sources and Limits of Popular Support for a Multicultural Australia", in *The Future of Australian Multiculturalism*, eds. G. Hage and R. Couch, Research Institute for Humanities and Social Sciences, University of Sydney, pp: 21-29.

Jupp, James (ed) (1999), *Immigration and Multiculturalism*, Committee for Economic Development of Australia.

Library of Congress (1997), "Brazil - A Country Study". [Online, accessed 31/10/2000]. URL: http://lcweb2.loc.government/cgi-bin/query/r?frd/cstdy:@field(DOCID+br0039)

McFarlane, B. (1986), "The Role of Government in the Economic Life of South Australia", in *The State as Developer: Public Enterprise in South Australia*, ed. K. Sheridan, Wakefield Press, Adelaide, pp 4-30.

Meinig, D.W. (1988), *On the Margins of the Good Earth: The South Australian Wheat Frontier 1869-1884*, South Australian Government Printer, Adelaide.

Morosini, Piero (1998), "Managing Cultural Differences: Effective Strategy and Execution Across Cultures in Global Corporate Alliances", International Business and Management Series.

Murray-Darling Basin Commission (1999a), *The Salinity Audit of the Murray-Darling Basin: A 100-year perspective, 1999.*

______________________________ (1999b), *Salinity and Drainage Strategy: Ten years on, 1999.*

Norris, R, (1969), "Economic Influences on the 1898 South Australia Federation Referendum", in *Essays in Australian Federation*, ed. A.W. Martin, Melbourne University Press, Melbourne, pp 137-168.

Norris, R, (1975), *The Emergent Commonwealth: Australian Federation Expectations and Fulfilment 1889-1910*, Melbourne University Press, Melbourne.

O'Neil, B., Raftery, J. and Round, K. (1996), *Playford's South Australia: Essays on the History of South Australia 1933-1968*, , Association of Professional Historians, Adelaide.

O'Neil, John (1998), "A View from the Trenches", in *Working Together: producing Synergy by Honoring Diversity*, ed. Angeles Arrien, New Leader Press, Pleasanton, California, pp: 225-233.

Rich, D.C. (1996) "Tom's Vision? Playford and Industrialisation", in *Playford's South Australia: Essays on the History of South Australia 1933-1968*, eds. B. O'Neil, J. Raftery and K. Round, Association of Professional Historians, Adelaide, pp 91-116.

Schedvin, C.B. (1988) *Australia and the Great Depression*, Sydney University Press, Sydney.

South Australian Centre for Economic Studies (SACES) (1996), *An Economic Impact Perspective on the International College of Hotel Management*, February.

Stokes, G. and Sharp, R. (1986), "South Australia: Governments and Economic Development", in *The Politics of Development in Australia*, ed. B. Head, Allen & Unwin, Sydney, pp 182-208.

Stromback, Thorsten, and Malhotra, Rikshesh (1994), *Socioeconomic Linkages of South Asian Immigrants with Their Country of Origin*, Western Australian Labour Market Research Centre, Bureau of Immigration and Population Research.

Stutchbury, M. (1986), "State Government Industrialisation Strategies", in *The State as Developer: Public Enterprise in South Australia*, ed. K. Sheridan, Wakefield Press, Adelaide, pp 60-9 1.

Vamplew, W., Richards, E., Jaensch, D. and Hancock, J. (1984), South *Australian Historical Statistics*, University of New South Wales, Kensington.

Withers, Glenn (1999), "Creating a Dynamic Australia", in *Immigration and Multiculturalism*, ed. James Jupp, Committee for Economic Development of Australia, pp: 47-57.

Zann, Leon P. (1995), *Our Sea, Our Future: Major Findings of the State of the Marine Environment Report for Australia*, Department of the Environment Sport and Territories, AGPS.

Zann, Leon P. (1996), "State of the Marine Environment: Report for Australia", Technical Summary, Department of the Environment Sport and Territories, AGPS.

Chapter Eight

Human Capital

A regional economy, such as South Australia, aiming at the 'top-end' of the production process to compete in the global market place requires a labour force of highly trained and dynamic people. Skill formation can be acquired from many sources including on-the-job training, but the capacity to innovate falls heavily on the tertiary education sector to attract top staff and top students, and to produce the right sort of graduates to lead our community in the future. The secondary education sector is also a very important preparatory ground for the semi-skilled and technical skilled workforce, and feeder to higher learning institutions. This chapter discusses the importance of human capital and presents a profile of South Australia through descriptive statistics to draw out the major features of the South Australian labour force and form a view about the quality of our human capital relative to other regions.

Evidence on the Importance of Human Capital

In New Growth Theory, knowledge (as embodied in human capital and in technology) can raise the returns on investment, which can in turn contribute to the accumulation of knowledge. Technological change raises the relative marginal productivity of capital through education and training of the labour force, investment in R&D and the creation of new managerial structures and work organisation.

The education system contributes to the key function of: (1) knowledge production - developing and providing new knowledge; (2) knowledge transmission - educating and developing human resources; and (3) knowledge transfer - disseminating knowledge and providing inputs to problem solving.

The recent growth literature has emphasised the importance of education and human capital in the process of economic growth and development. The theoretical literature assumes that the production function of an economy can be expressed as a stable function of aggregate inputs. One of these inputs is human capital, the input associated with the labour force (Sala-i-Martin 1995).

In the US, progress in education has accounted for an estimated one-fourth of economic growth over the past fifty years. In Australia, investment in human capital has taken over from physical infrastructure as the main driving force behind economic expansion in the period since 1930. Human resources will play an even more significant role in development in the future as industrial societies become increasingly knowledge-based (OECD 1997).

Human capital formation is not simply about teachers, curriculum and the education system, but a function of society. Many studies emphasise that quality of education is effected by general health, family values, per capita incomes, society's attitude toward education, job availability and a broad range of pressures influencing student's capacities to achieve. While these are recognised as being important, this chapter draws on crude aggregate statistics to gain general insights into our region's human capital.

Many researchers measure human capital stocks by constructing a measure of average years of schooling. Barro (1991) used school enrolment rates as a proxy for the stock of human capital. Kyriacou (1992) estimated average years of schooling by using a benchmark year and estimates of school enrolments. Sala-i-Martin (1995) measured human capital based on the education attainment of the labour force. From US labour force data for the period 1940 to 1990, he found that the stock of human capital grew twice as rapidly as the average years of schooling.

Current literature reflects the increasing recognition of the role of knowledge and learning as a catalyst for economic development (Knight 1995, OECD 1996b, Cooke and Morgan 1998). In Australia, universities have been a component of regional development policy. This role is extremely important because universities have retained an important role as large institutions that generate significant support infrastructure (Garlick 1998).

Keane and Allison (1999) indicated that institutions of higher education would appear to add value to regional development in at least three ways. First, there are a suite of traditionally identified benefits such as population growth, housing demand, employment opportunities, increased spending and other spin-offs. Second, there are the implicit benefits broadly linked to the growth of the 'knowledge economy'. Specifically, the role of the university in generating information, value adding that information to form knowledge as well as other aspects of teaching and learning. This is now considered to have both tangible and intangible benefits talked about but hitherto unmeasured. These benefits relate to the learning and transfer of knowledge and training that occur in the region. Third, as concepts such as learning regions are proposed as offering flexible and innovative regional responses to rapidly changing economies. These benefits potentially allow universities to make not only a large contribution to the development of their region but also to strategically position that region as a learning region in the knowledge economy.

There is an emphasis on the role of universities in enhancing the stock of human capital. Goddard (1997) lists a range of ways in which this might occur including. These include continuing and professional development to enhance the skills of local managers; locally embedding global businesses by targeted training programmes and research skills; gateway to global knowledge for small and medium sized enterprises (SMEs); producing strategic analysis and leadership within local civic society.

Kanter (1995) believes that the location of universities in regions is a powerful facilitator of these processes: concepts link to research; competence links to teaching and connections link to the transfer to and from a region of people; and networks grown out of universities.

Universities in many countries have traditionally produced raw graduates for a national labour market dominated by large employers, with little concern for small and medium size firms (SMEs) or graduate retention in local labour markets. This model has begun to break down in response to changing patterns of employer demands such as the decentralisation of large corporations into clusters of smaller business units and the greater role of smaller businesses as sub-contractors, suppliers, franchisees, etc. The expansion of higher education provision together with rising numbers experiencing the need to change career later on in life is leading to a growing supply of mature local students for undergraduate and postgraduate programmes (Goddard 1997).

Universities are increasing taking a more active role in economic development. Vital to this participation is that they understand the market segment and inform their teaching activities by its needs. This means not simply responding to currently expressed wants but actively researching the dynamics underlying changing employer needs and treating students as clients and employers as the end customer.

Education Output

Secondary Education

Sociological researchers in Australia and overseas have long been able to demonstrate that participation in post-compulsory education correlates positively with family socio-economic status. Behrens (1978), Rosier (1978) and Williams et al. (1980) show that as occupational status of parents increases, the likelihood of their children participating longer in formal education increases. Power (1984) reports that parental education exerts a considerable influence on whether a young person stays at school to complete a full secondary education. DEET (1987) shows that participation in post-compulsory schooling increases with socio-economic status. The young people from the most advantage socio-economic status background complete year 12 at about twice the rate as those from less advantage background. In the less populous states of South and Western Australia the completion rates of year 12 are slightly higher than the most populous Eastern states.

Total number of schools in Australia during the last decade has declined by 4.7 per cent, from 10,036 schools to 9,590 schools. Among the States and Territories, Victoria, South Australia, and Tasmania contributed disproportionately to the reduction of the schools. Number of schools in South Australia represented 8.9 per cent in 1989 and 8.6 per cent in 1999 of the Australian total. New South Wales increased its share from 30.5 per cent in 1989 and 32.2 per cent in 1999.

The retention rate of secondary school students to Year 12 across the States and Territories in Australia is presented in the following figure. In 1984, the apparent retention rate varied between States and Territories rates from 24.4 per cent in Northern Territory to 79.8 in the Australian Capital Territory. By 1999 these rates had increased significantly across Australia ranging from 52.9 per cent in Northern Territory to 92.5 in Australian Capital Territory. Increasing retention rate is a sign of human capital improvement. South Australia's annual growth of retention between 1984-1999 was 3.08 per cent (from 45.5 per cent to 71.5 per cent) compared to 3.37 nationally (from 45.0 per cent to 72.3 per cent). Broadly, although South Australia's retention rates have improved significantly over the last 15 years, the region's achievements have been out-paced elsewhere in Australia.

The percentage of secondary students staying at school until Year 12 is calculated with the base being the total number of full time Year 10 students. The result is presented in Figure 8.2. The national trend showed a slight increase in numbers of secondary students staying at school. South Australia's Year 11 students, on the other hand, shows a decrease from a high 96 per cent to 90 per cent and Year 12 students decrease from 77 per cent to 68 per cent. The figure for Australia increased from 82 per cent to 88 per cent and Year 12 students is from 67 per cent to 73 per cent.

Figure 8.1
Apparent Retention Rates of Secondary School Students to Year 12, 1984-1999

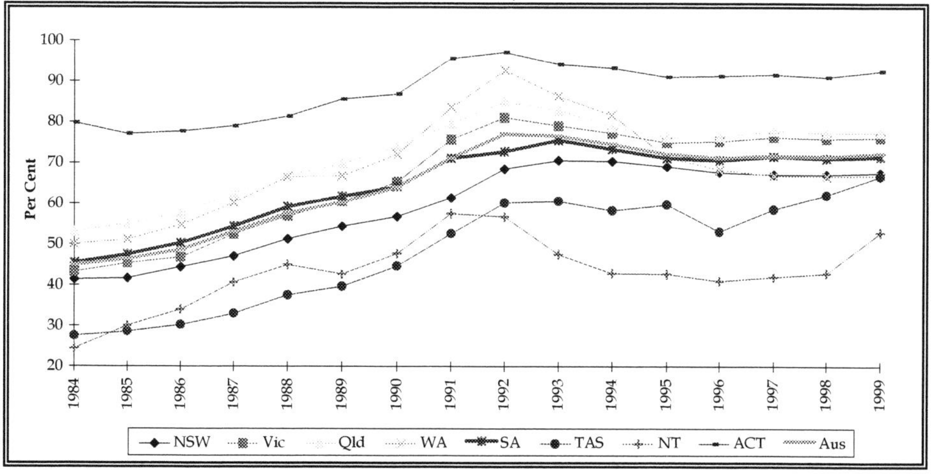

Source: ABS, Cat. No. 4221.0 (Various Years).

Figure 8.2
Percentage of Students Staying at School Year 10 to Year 12, 1989-1999

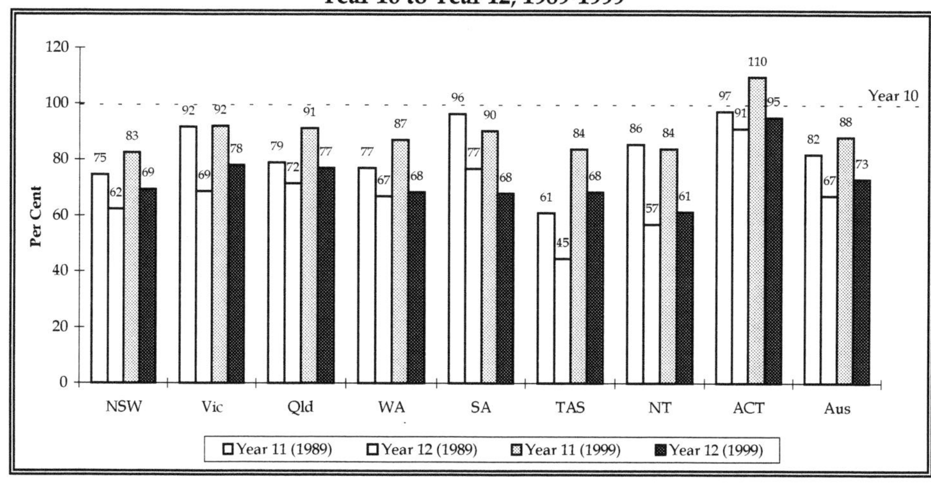

Source: ABS, Cat.no. 4221.0 (Various years).

Full-time secondary student participation rates have changed markedly in 10 years (Figure 8.3). Overall, age 17 year old students contributed the largest increase. South Australia shows significantly larger increases than Australia for 15 and 16 year old students, i.e., 5.1 per cent each. The increases of 17 and 18 year full-time students, however, were below the Australian average.

Figure 8.4 shows that the age participation rates for all age groups except for 19 year olds have increased in the last decade. South Australia participation rate has increased, similarly, but the gap between South Australia and Australia overall has not been significantly reduced.

Figure 8.3
Percentage Change of Full-Time Student
Participation Rate Within Age Group, 1989-1999

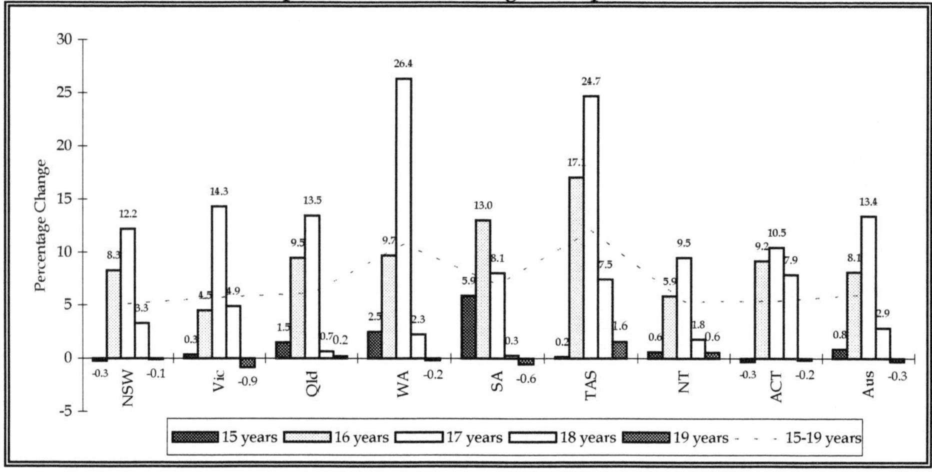

Source: ABS, Cat. no. 4221.0 (Various years).

Figure 8.4
Participation Rate of Full-Time Student within Age Group,
South Australia and Australia, 1989-1999

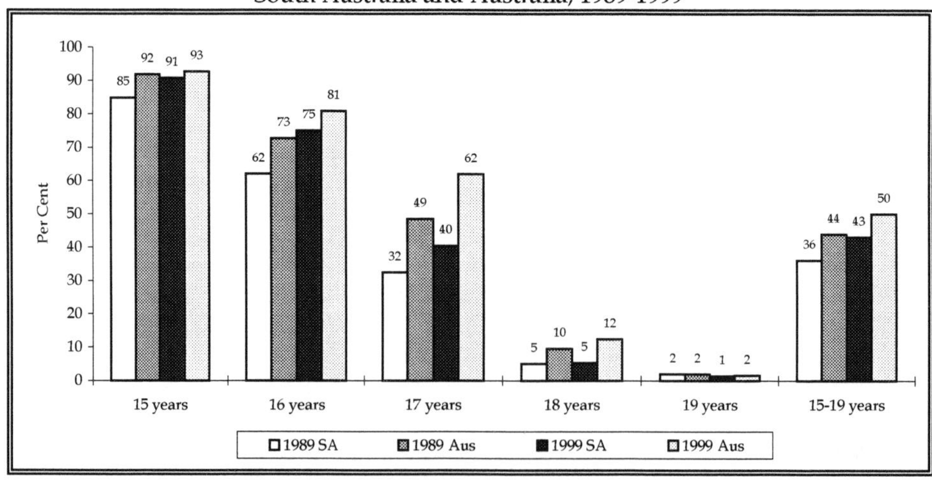

Source: ABS, Cat. no. 4221.0 (Various years).

Higher Education in South Australia

South Australia has three universities - The University of Adelaide, The Flinders University of South Australia, and The University of South Australia. The University of Adelaide was established in 1874, currently has three campuses, nearly 14,000 students or over 12,000 EFTSU[21] and 2,500 staff or over 2,100 FTE[22] (see Tables 8.1 and 8.2). In 1997, the University of Adelaide's expenditure budget was nearly $254 million. The Flinders University of South Australia was established in 1965 and is a single campus university. It currently has over 11,000 students (8,821 EFTSU) and 1,800 staff (1,400 FTE). Its expenditure in 1997 was over 141.5 million. The University of South Australia was established in 1991, has six campuses, over 23,000 students (over 17,800 EFTSU), 2,300 staff (1,847 FTE), and expenditure of over 217 million in 1997.

Table 8.1
FTE[a] Staff Employed by University and Function, South Australia, 1998

University	Academic			Others	Total
	Teaching Only	Research Only	Teaching & Research		
Adelaide	-	397	694	1,047	2,138
Flinders	2	186	513	699	1,400
South Australia	23	169	677	978	1,847
Total	**25**	**752**	**1,884**	**2,724**	**5,385**

Note: a) Full-Time Equivalent.
Source: DETYA (1999a).

Table 8.2
Student Numbers (EFTSUs)[a] by University and Level of Course, South Australia, 1998

University	Higher Degree		Other than Higher Degree			Total
	Research	Course Work	Other Post-Graduate	Bachelor	Other	
Adelaide	1,102	332	493	9,468	623	12,018
Flinders	482	410	149	7,498	282	8,821
South Australia	503	1,056	898	14,694	651	17,802
Total	**2,087**	**1,798**	**1,540**	**31,660**	**1,556**	**38,641**

Note: a) Equivalent Full-Time Student Units.
Source: DETYA (1999b).

21 Equivalent Full-Time Student Units.
22 Full-Time Equivalent.

In the decade between 1989 to 1999 the numbers of tertiary students have increased in every State and Territory (Tables 8.3 and 8.4). During the same period, ten of eleven discipline groups show an increasing trend in Australia. The overall increase is 55 per cent (350,117 to 544,150 EFTSU). The largest increase is Mathematics and Computing discipline group, i.e, 103 per cent. South Australia, however, has increased only 37 per cent (28,601 to 39,125 EFTSU), which is the lowest increase across the nation along with Australian Capital Territory. By the discipline group, the Health Science in South Australia in 1999 has increased 12 per cent, whilst in Australia has increased less, 8 per cent lower. In South Australia, by level of course, the highest contributor of an increase in the number of tertiary students is the Enabling, Non-Award and Cross-Institution program. This is still quite low compared to Australian increase of 254 per cent.

Appendix 8.1 presents the student load by state and discipline group at EFTSU level (Table 8.1.1). The three universities had total enrolments of over 39,125 EFTSU in 1999, which represents 20.9 enrolments per 1,000 population, and 7.2 per cent of national enrolments. These enrolments are the second lowest after Northern Territories (17.4 enrolments per 1,000 population). Australian Capital Territory (ACT) has the highest enrolments of 54.2 EFTSU per 1,000 population. For Australia there are 28.5 enrolments per 1,000 population (544,150 EFTSU).

Administration, Business, Economic, and Law discipline group has the largest enrolments in the region. It represents 22.0 per cent of total enrolments. The same category for Australia is four per cent higher (26.0 per cent). The other 5 of 10 discipline groups make up another 56.4 per cent of total enrolments. They are Social Studies (12.8 per cent), Health Sciences (12.1 per cent), Sciences (10.9 per cent), Humanities (10.6 per cent), and Mathematics and Computing (10.1 per cent). These groups in Australia represent 51.5 per cent of total enrolments (5 per cent below South Australia). The largest difference is the enrolments in Health and Sciences, South Australia is 3.6 per cent higher than national enrolments. Agriculture and Renewable Resources has the lowest enrolments throughout Australia. This discipline group in South Australia has 2.0 per cent enrolments, 0.6 per cent higher than nationally.

Table 8.1.2 in the Appendix 8.1 shows the student load by state and level of course at EFTSU level. Undergraduate enrolments in South Australia, as also shown in other States and Territories, are the largest. The South Australian enrolments, which are 84.1 per cent, are 2.1 per cent above the enrolments in Australia as a whole. South Australia's Post-graduate enrolments are 14.1 per cent, that are 2.0 per cent below Australia's Post-graduate enrolments. The Others enrolments in South Australia are about the same as Australian numbers, only 0.1 per cent difference.

Table 8.3
Percentage Change of Student Load (EFTSU)
by State and Discipline Group, 1989-1999

Discipline Group	NSW	Vic	Qld	WA	SA	TAS	NT	ACT	Aus
	Per Cent								
Humanities	49	32	79	55	17	49	502*	34	50
Social Studies	59	26	123	39	10	66	-43	58	50
Education	-7	-38	24	8	-21	21	-10	-26	-5
Sciences	30	34	69	61	27	8	78	-26	37
Mathematics, Computing	99	90	140	91	96	71	309*	73	103
Visual/Performing Arts	60	38	286	68	29	36	163*	107	69
Engineering, Processing	36	62	39	94	65	159	44*	406	56
Health Sciences	27	58	244	45	30	67	214*	400*	59
Admin, Business, Ec, Law	94	77	81	77	121	45	125	35	84
Built Environment	54	70	48	75	40	25	41*	31	57
Agric., Renewable Resources	34	36	42	-2	25	455	14*	94	36
Total	**52**	**43**	**87**	**58**	**37**	**48**	**85**	**37**	**55**

Notes: (a) Equivalent Full-Time Student Units.
(*) Absolute numbers in 1999 (in 1989 = 0).

Source: DETYA (1999b).

Table 8.4
Percentage Change of Student Load (EFTSU)
by State and Level Course, 1989-1999

Discipline Group	**NSW**	**Vic**	**Qld**	**WA**	**SA**	**TAS**	**NT**	**ACT**	**Aus**
	Per Cent								
Post-graduate[b]	128	82	140	102	50	36	270	83	105
Under-graduate[c]	38	38	77	49	33	50	59	28	46
Others[d]	624	1	500	345	172	96	163	54	254
Total	**52**	**43**	**87**	**58**	**37**	**48**	**83**	**37**	**55**

Notes: a) Equivalent Full-Time Student Units.
b) Higher Doctorate, Doctorate, Master and Other Post-grad.
c) Bachelor, Associate Degree, Other Under-graduate.
d) Enabling, Non-Award, Cross-Institution Programs.

Source: DETYA (1999b).

Labour Force Characteristics

Labour force characteristics, such as employment, unemployment, participation rate, skill and education levels, reflect both the productive capacity and the economic well-being of people in an area.

A region's labour force comprises the civilian population aged 15 and over who are not in institutions and who are either "employed" or "unemployed" as explained below.

Employed persons are those who (1) undertake at least one hour's work for pay or profit during the survey week, or (2) work one hour or more per week without pay in a family farm or business, or (3) are absent from a job or business for such reasons as illness, vacations, or strikes.[23]

Unemployed persons are those who have not worked at all during the survey week, but have during the past four weeks made a definite attempt to gain employment (by applying directly to an employer or a private or public employment agency) and being available for work at the time of the survey.

Individuals unwilling to work or willing but unable to work are not counted as unemployed; they are considered as not in the labour force.

Interpretation of official employment data should not ignore the "invisible unemployed". This includes persons who are working part-time but wish for full-time employment, seasonal workers wishing year round employment, persons who drop out of the labour force after discouraged by unsuccessful attempts in gaining employment, and persons in jobs not fully utilising their skills or training. "Disguised unemployment" or "under-employment" are other terms depicting these situations.

Job Quantity and Employment Growth

Employment growth is one of the most significant indicators of the economic strength and growth of a region. Figure 8.5 shows the South Australian and national employment growths since 1990 for full-time, part-time and total employment. The statistics imply, assuming that unemployment rate differentials change little over time, that job growth in South Australia has been considerably slower than the national rate - indicating weaker economic strength and growth for South Australia.

---

23 The definitions were drawn from ABS.

Full-Time Employment

Figure 8.5
Index of Employment Growth 1989-1999[a]
South Australia and Australia: 1989=100

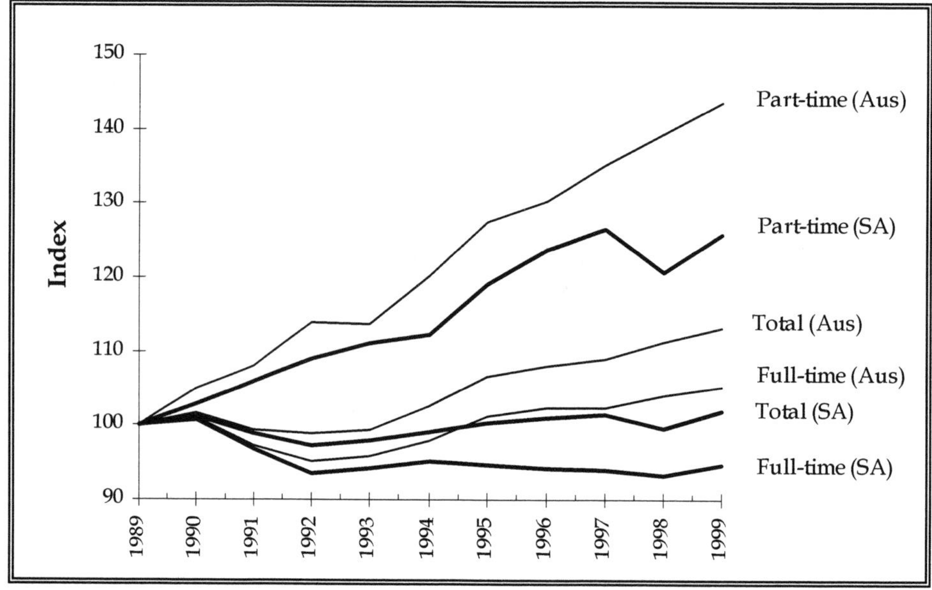

Notes: (a) Annual average of monthly figures.
Source: ABS, Ausstats (Cat. no. 6202.0).

Full-time employment in South Australia experienced negative or no growth virtually over the entire period of 1989 to 1999. After reaching a peak of 500,500 persons in 1990, full-time employment in South Australia plummeted in 1992. This trend follows the national trend. Recovery from this plunge has been slower than the national average. Recent full-time employment was about 470,200 persons - only a slight increase from the low of 464,600 persons in 1992. Over the period of 1989 to 1999, average annual growth of full-time jobs in South Australia was -0.59 per cent - far below the national average of 0.67 per cent.

Part-Time Employment

While growth in full-time employment has been quite slow, growth in part time employment has been quite remarkable, increasing by nearly 50 per cent nationally over the period 1989 to 1999. The growth in South Australia was slower, with an annual growth rate of 2.40 per cent compared with 3.65 per cent Australia wide. Twenty-nine per cent of South Australian jobs in 1999 are part time jobs, up from 23 per cent in 1989. The numbers may at first sight suggest a promising growth of part-time jobs in contrast to full-time jobs, but may in fact be the symptom of the declining availability of full-time jobs, especially in the region.

Total Employment

The total employment growth highlights the slower growth in South Australia relative to Australia. Overall, the employment trends reflect the structural changes in the South Australian labour force: the growth in part-time employment, job shedding of full-time employees (which appears to have slowed) and growth in employment in new industries, but not yet at the scale to absorb job losses.

Employment: Wage and Salary Earners

Wages and salaries are the largest source of personal income and are a major determinant of private consumption and savings. The proportion of employed wage and salary earners to the total employment is presented in Figure 8.6.[24] This proportion has sharply dropped, both in South Australia and nationally, from nearly 90 per cent in 1990. Whereas the proportion for Australia has stabilised in recent years at about 82 to 83 per cent, the proportion for South Australia has been less stable, and has fallen bellow the national figure, to 79 per cent in 1999.

Figure 8.7 presents the index of employed wage and salary earners, both full-time and part-time employed, 1989-1999, for South Australia and Australia. The patterns of indexes are consistent with the patterns of the employment growth indexes. The figure clearly shows the upward trends of part-time employment in this category, both in South Australia and nationally. Full-time employment in this category, however, experienced declining trends from 1990 to 1993 both for South Australia and nationally. Since 1994, the national trend has turned slightly upwards whereas the South Australian trend continued to decline.

Appendix 8.2 presents the index of full-time employed wage and salary earners, and the growth rate by state and territory from 1989 to 1999 (Table 8.2.1). In South Australia in 1999 there were only 89 full-time employed wage and salary earners left for every 100 jobs in 1989. Victoria and Tasmania experienced similar decline. In Australia, there were 101 employed wage and salary earners for every 100 employed persons in 1989. Nationally, the lowest fall in 1992 slowly recovered due to the contribution of better than average wage and salary earners in ACT, Western Australia, and Queensland. At this year South Australia also declined but it was still stronger than Australia. However, while other States and Territories were recovering, South Australia continued to decline until in 1997 reached the worst among States and Territories of only 89 time employed wage and salary earners left for every 100 jobs in 1989. The following year South Australia was on the road of recovery. The growth rate figures show that South Australia declines 1.61 per cent annually, that is the second lowest after Tasmania (-1.86 per cent). Queensland growth rate is the

24 Data do not include self-employed workers and rural farm sector.

largest (+1.82 per cent), and Western Australia is the second largest (+1.35 per cent). The annual growth rate for Australia is +0.10 per cent.

Figure 8.6
Proportion of Employed Wage and Salary Earners to Total Employment
South Australia and Australia, 1989-1999

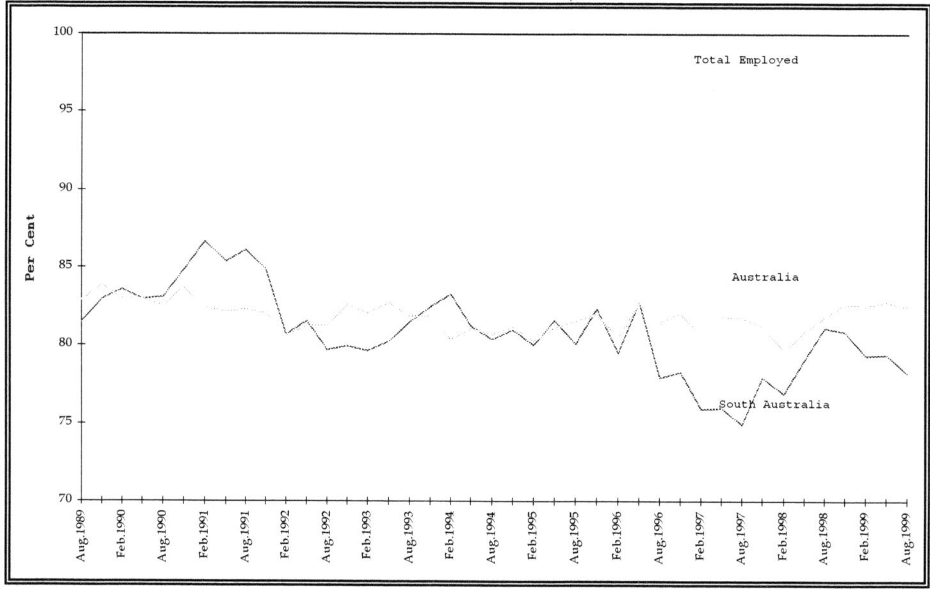

Source: ABS, Ausstats (Cat. no. 6248.0).

Figure 8.7
Index of Employed - Wage and Salary Earners
South Australia and Australia, 1989-99 (1989=100)

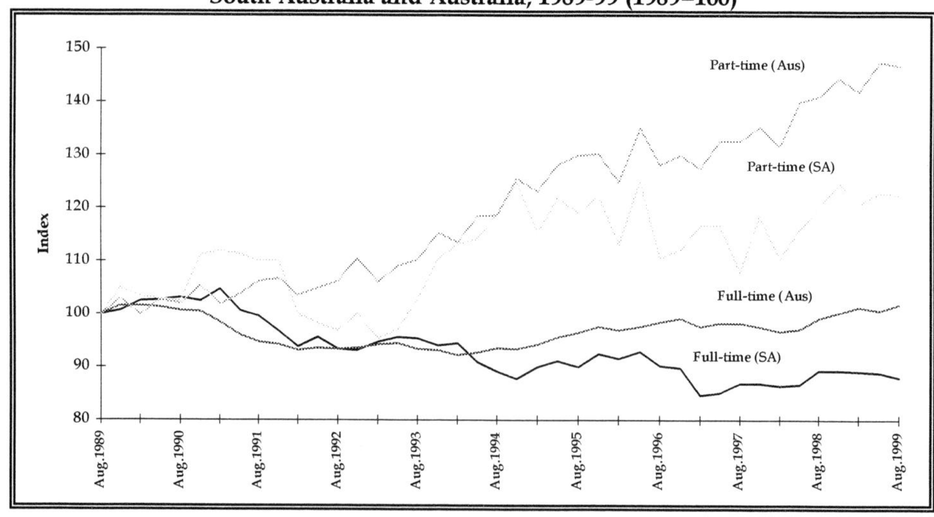

Source: ABS, Ausstats (Cat. no. 6248.0).

The decline in full-time employment is compensated by the increase in part-time employment. This is shown in the index of part-time employed wage and salary earners (Appendix 8.2, Table 8.2.2). For every 100 part-time jobs in South Australia in 1989 there were 122 positions at the end of the period. For Australia the comparative number of positions was 146. The positive annual growth rate in South Australia is still the lowest compared to other States and Territories. South Australia annual growth rate is 1.81 per cent, compared to 3.93 per cent in Australia.

This pattern highlights the changing nature of the labour market, the growth in service, tourism and entertainment sectors of the economy, changing preferences of employers and employees including changing family structures and a greater flexibility and opportunity for combining mixed options of education, training and work.

Employment: Gains and Losses

Figure 8.8 shows the pattern of average annual employment gains and losses for ANZSIC industries. Employment losses have occurred in some sectors of Manufacturing (most severely impacting on male employment), Finance and Insurance, and large losses in Mining and the public utilities of Gas, Water and Electricity.

In South Australia, Construction, Wholesale, and Transport sectors also suffered losses, while nationally, these industries experienced gains.

Figure 8.8
Employment Gains and Losses
South Australia and Australia, 1989-1999

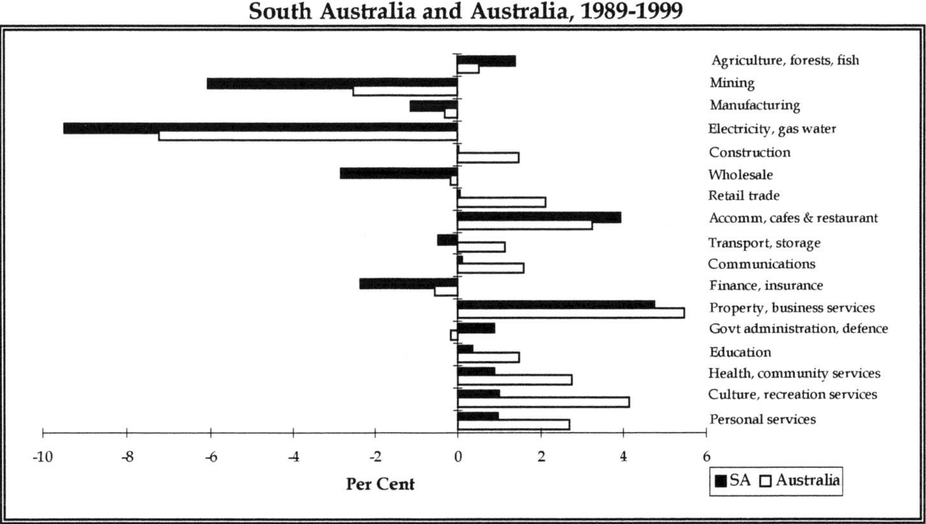

Source: ABS, AUSSTATS (Cat. no. 6291.0).

There have also been strong employment gains, most notably in accommodation (11,400 positions), property and business services (23,800 positions), health (4,600), culture (1,600 positions), and personal services (4,200 positions) over the period 1989 to 1999. This strong employment growth is often part-time, and South Australia has grown more slowly than Australia, except for accommodation.

Taking all "gains and losses" together, and without differentiating between full-time and part-time positions, the "job gain rate" on an annual basis from 1989 to 1999 was 0.17 per cent for South Australia compared to 1.33 per cent for Australia.

Employment: Age Structure

The age structure of the employed labour force is an important determinant of longer-term pressures on an economy. Employment growth must match the increase in the numbers of the working age population (other things being equal) if unemployment is to remain stable or actually decrease. New industries and new technologies require new skills. It is often the case that younger entrants to the labour force are more flexible in adapting to the technologies. The age structure of the population and the labour force has implications for the development of new industries (e.g., multi-media, IT).

Figure 8.9
Age Structure of the Employed Labour Force
South Australia and Australia, 1989 and 1999

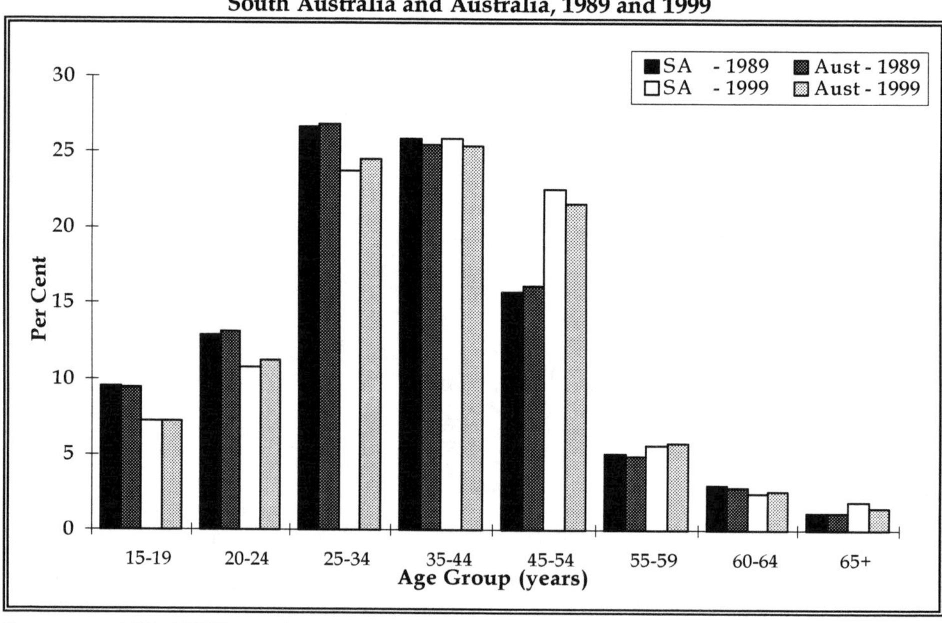

Source: ABS, AUSSTATS (Cat. no. 6291.0).

Figure 8.9 presents age structure of the employed labor force. The South Australian labour force is slightly older than the average for Australia that reflects both slower population growth overall and lower intakes of migrants. It is also noticeable that higher school retention rates during the 1980's have led to a marked decline in school leavers entering the labour force at a very young age. This is an encouraging trend.

The decline of 20-24 year olds and 25-34 year olds in the workforce, to below the Australian average, is primarily the result of outward migration from the State. This reflects more limited career and job opportunities. This is a worrying trend as these age groups are regarded as the core age groups for any economy - core because of more recent qualifications, potential productivity and entrepreneurship.

The Structure of Unemployment

High unemployment, low income levels and out migration the economic development in the region. Unemployment represents a waste of human resources to the economy and the community and it imposes severe costs for the individual, family unit and society. Workers may experience deterioration in their human capital while unemployed. Workers accumulate human capital in employment, which depreciates when they are unemployed. The structure of unemployment and changes to the pool of unemployed persons is an indicator of economic problem areas.

Unemployment by Age Group

The structure of unemployment as a proportion of the relevant age group is different in 1999 than it was in 1989 (Figure 8.10). Except age group 60-64 years, the proportions of unemployed persons to population in the every age group have increased either in South Australia or nationally.

Youth unemployment (15-19 years) remains a serious challenge if only because the proportion of the age group unemployed is large - 13 per cent in South Australia and 11 per cent nationally. Even though the figure shows large increase, the average annual youth unemployment growths were quite low, i.e., 0.14 per cent in South Australia and 0.26 per cent in Australia.

Youth unemployment percentages are considerably higher than unemployment percentages of adult workers. There are several reasons for these. Firstly, teenagers include a large proportion of new entrants into job market associated with searching for satisfactory position. Moreover, many of them begin with accepting part-time employment on temporary basis. Since they generally have fewer responsibilities than adult workers, they experience higher turnover rates in searching for the right jobs. In addition, they lack of experience and on-the-job training, and they tend to be vulnerable to layoffs because of a lack of seniority.

For young persons in South Australia, 20-24 years, the rate of unemployment has slightly increased surprisingly slower than national trend - 0.17 per cent compared to 0.78 per cent. The fact is that the unemployed have aged. There are now 25,300 unemployed South Australians in the age cohorts' 25-34 (13,500) and 35-44 (11,800) when there were 21,000 in 1989. This structural shift in the burden of unemployment more directly impacts on families and family members and increases the demand on community and social support services.

Figure 8.10
Unemployed as a Proportion of the Age Group
South Australia and Australia, 1989 and 1999

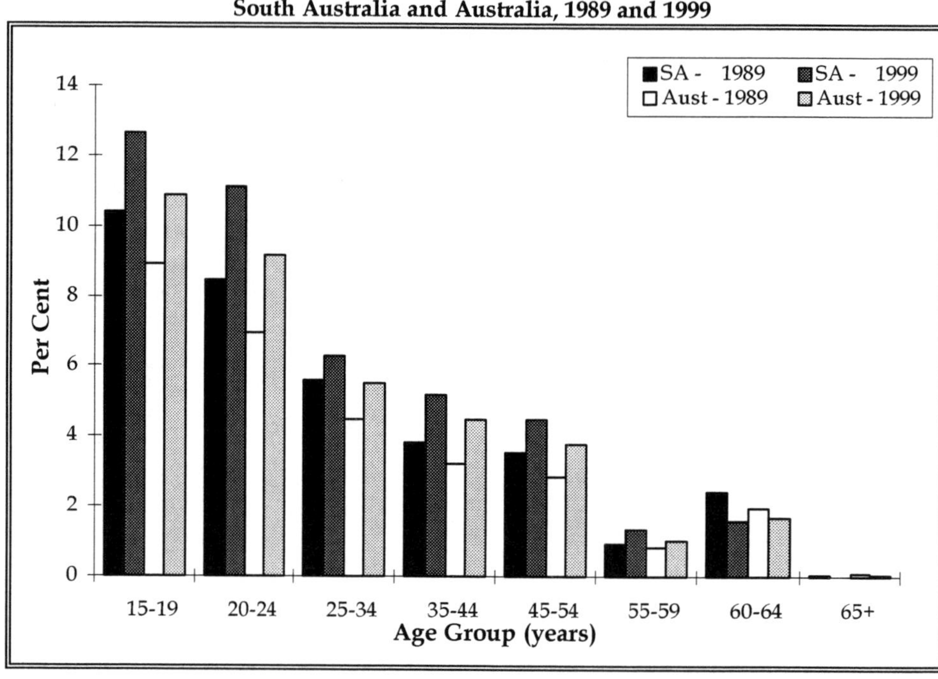

Source: ABS, Ausstats (Cat. no. 6291.0).

In South Australia, the average annual unemployment growth rate for age group 35-44 years is as high as 4.31 per cent, whilst the national rate is 3.36. Persistent higher rates of unemployment in some regions identify a further economic challenge - specifically that the burden of unemployment may be unequally shared and create regional disparities.

Changing Duration of Unemployment

Figure 8.11
Median Duration of Unemployment
South Australia and Australia, 1989-1995

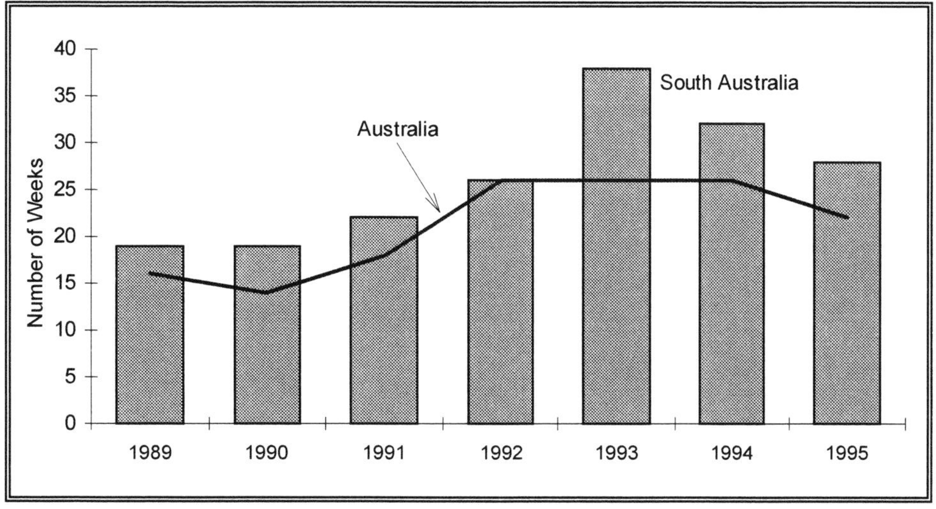

Source: ABS, Datasets (Cat. no. 6291.0).

Extended duration of unemployment erodes the skill level of individuals and contains the seeds of social disillusionment. Structural job losses, in the absence of high rates of labour mobility, frequently result in higher duration of unemployment. Efforts to counter extended duration of unemployment and equip a 21st Century workforce with the skills necessary for new opportunities is an important challenge for the community of South Australia.

The median duration of unemployment in South Australia increased sharply from 19 weeks in 1989 to 38 weeks between 1990 and 1993, but has since declined to 28 weeks in 1995, in concert with the declining trend for Australia (Figure 8.11). It is the case that males tend to experience slightly longer periods of unemployment than females. This is partly explained by the preference for full-time employment, job search activities and a stronger preference (or need) to remain in the labour force. The long-term unemployment either regionally or nationally indicated a raising problem in the job market.

Participation Rate

The participation rate for any group is the labour force expressed as a percentage of the civilian population in the same group. The following table shows the participation rate by gender for South Australia and Australia from 1989 to 1999. Persons participate in the labour force in South Australia are lower than the national trend.

Table 8.5
Participation Rate by Gender
South Australia and Australia, 1989-1999

Year	South Australia (%)			Australia (%)		
	Males	Females	Persons	Males	Females	Persons
1989	74.80	50.60	62.50	75.50	51.30	63.20
1990	75.00	51.10	62.90	75.70	52.20	63.80
1991	74.00	51.40	62.60	74.80	52.00	63.30
1992	73.60	51.00	62.20	74.40	51.90	63.00
1993	72.30	51.00	61.50	73.70	51.80	62.60
1994	71.50	51.90	61.50	73.60	52.60	63.00
1995	71.80	52.30	61.80	74.00	53.70	63.70
1996	71.10	52.90	61.80	73.70	53.80	63.60
1997	71.40	52.60	61.80	73.20	53.70	63.30
1998	70.10	50.70	60.20	72.90	53.90	63.20
1999	69.90	51.20	60.40	72.70	56.20	63.0
Growth	-0.72	0.17	-0.36	-0.38	0.72	-0.01

Source: ABS, AusStats (Cat. no. 6202.0).

Males' participation rates were over 70 per cent, whilst females' participation rates were just above 50 per cent. The participation rates of males have been decreasing over the years since the early period. Females' participation rates, on the other hand, have been increasing, especially the national number. The decline in the males' participation rates are shown both in South Australia and Australia. The increasing trend of females' participation rates have not been enough to compensate the decline in the males' participation rates. The worrying trend in South Australia compared to national pattern is that the decline is faster but the increase is slower.

Skills in Demand

The competitive advantage of the firm, the industry and economic regions will increasingly be determined by the skills of the workforce. Skills are broadly defined to include knowledge, languages and management capability.

So far, this profile has detailed quantitative measures of employment. We turn now to qualitative measures, including skills in demand. Occupational demands are subject to industry output effects plus technology effects. For example, a particular manufacturing industry may reduce its demand for trade persons due to the technology effect, but increase its demand due to increasing output.

Employed persons by occupational groups for the period 1986 to 1996 (Figure 8.12) in South Australia grew at an annual rate of 0.7 per cent compared to the Australian average of 1.4 per cent. Many of the occupations experiencing growth were, however, those that also required professional qualifications and management skills. This trend is consistent with the results of a study, in the US by Howell and Wolf (1992). Skill requirement across the US industries tends to raise the demand for high cognitive skill workers and reduce the demand for low cognitive workers.[25]

The new technologies reduce the number of jobs available for unskilled labour, especially in manufacturing and business services. Declining demand or lower growth for low-skill workers implies that job-opportunities for these workers falls as the mix of employment shifts towards higher cognitive skill workers. This, in turn, suggests that low-skill occupations should show declining shares of employment. And that unemployment should increase for the low-skilled.

Figure 8.12
Employment Growth by Occupational Groups
South Australia and Australia, 1986-1996

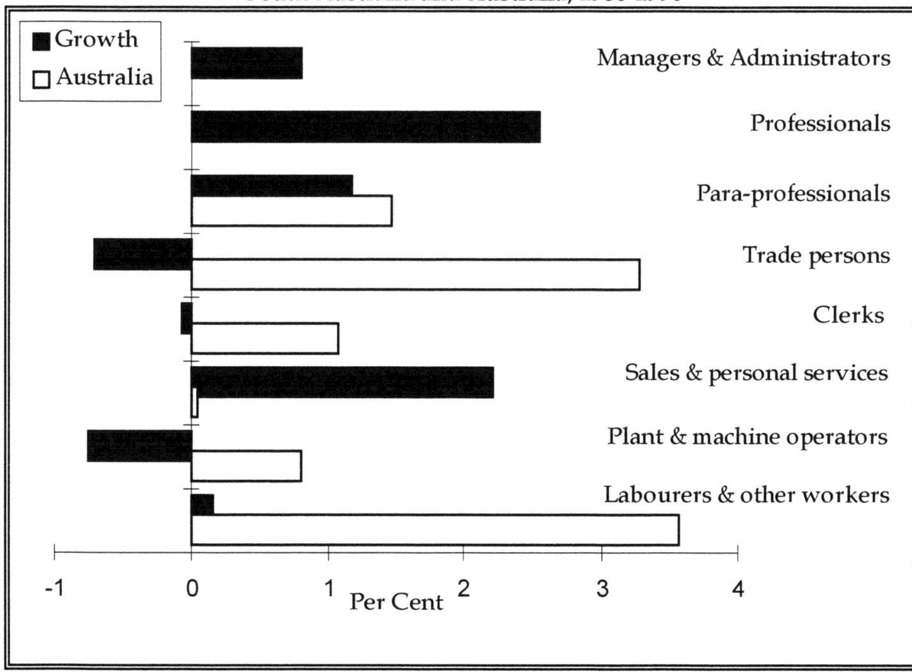

Source: ABS, Datasets (Cat. no. 6291.0).

25 Professional and technical workers (high cognitive skill), managers (moderate-high cognitive skill), clerical workers (low-moderate skill), and operatives and labourers (low skill).

Figure 8.13
Employment Growth by Selected Business & Trade Occupations
South Australia and Australia, 1986-1996

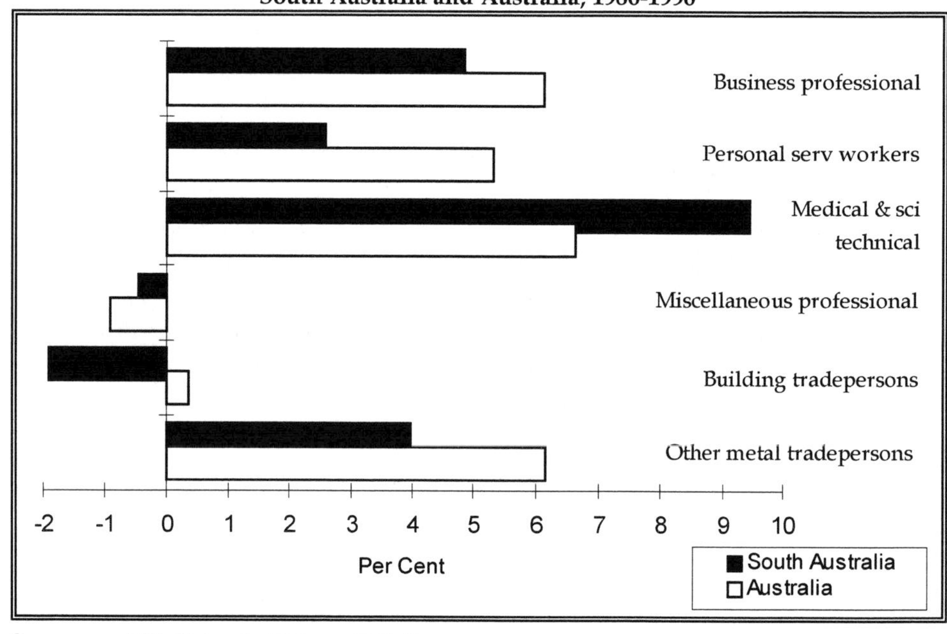

Source: ABS, Datasets (Cat. no. 6291.0).

Business professionals, personal service workers, medical and science/technical officers and other metal tradepersons experienced strong demand (Figure 8.13). The annual growth rate for South Australia was 2.04 per cent. The Australia annual growth rate was 3.35 for the same period. The miscellaneous professional and building tradepersons all experienced declining demand annually for the ten year period, except national employment for building tradepersons.

The application of information technology in industry and regional societies is a potential means to increase the returns to private capital and public investment, respectively. However, a shortage of human capital, especially regionally, has often rendered ineffective attempts to apply new technologies. The real human resources problem for the creation of a knowledge based economy is, therefore, not whether there will be enough jobs, but whether society will produce enough technically trained people to meet the new demand for human capital (Ferné, G, 1996).

Emerging sectors of the economy including information technology, will alter the profile of employment in favour of a "knowledge intensive" workforce. The profile of employment in the emerging software and information technology can be classified as knowledge-intensive. The industry is dependent on a degree qualified labour force.

Figure 8.10 shows the Qualifications in Emerging IT Industry. Graduate occupied half of the employment in IT industry and the other half was shared by Postgraduate (15 per cent), Associate Diploma, Tech/Trade (17 per cent), and Others (18 per cent).

Women Employment

Human resource investments in women have increased relative to those made in men in most countries, proxied by both years of education attained and years of longevity. The shift in the gender composition of human capital formation occurred as women entered frequently into the market labour force, particularly into wage employment outside of the family (Schultz, 1993).

Australia shows a healthy growth of women employment during 1986 to 1996. South Australia has matched or bettered the national annual growth rate for the employment of females in professional occupations. These include the management positions, natural sciences, medical and science technical officers, and business professionals (Figure 8.14).

Figure 8.14
Women Employment Growth by Occupation
South Australia and Australia, 1986-96

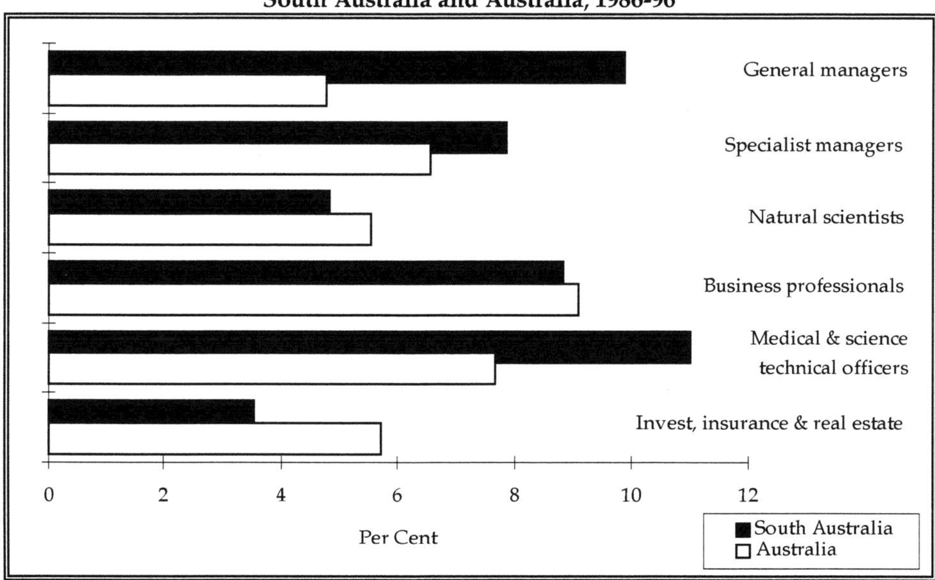

Source: ABS, Datasets (Cat. no. 6291.0).

Participation rate of employed women has increased from 50.6 per cent of the total workforce in 1989 to 51.2 per cent in 1999 (see Table 8.5). Over the same period, consistent with its participation rate, women employment has also increase from 41.4 per cent to 43.6 per cent. However, women full-time employment as a proportion of women total employment has declined from 55.4 per cent to 52.3 per cent in keeping with the slow growth of full-time employment and much stronger growth in part-time employment.

Skill Development

Skill levels within regions represent the human capital the region possesses. This human capital is a factor of production as much as is capital investment. Furthermore, the human capital endowment of a region directly affects the level of current production, which in turn affects the wage productivity of the region. In turn, this impacts upon the growth rate of the region. However, skill level is more important than merely increasing productivity. Skill level is also important in permitting expansion of businesses, either of indigenous firms or for foreign direct investment. The skills accrued within a region give character to the development of the region.

OECD (1994) pointed out that skill shortages weaken economies, limiting their ability to expand and increasing the threat of unemployment. This is particularly relevant at the regional level, since the least skilled workers are the first to be affected by unemployment and underemployment.

More rapid change in markets and technologies makes it relatively more efficient to locate the creation and acquisition of productive knowledge close to the actual productive process. Knowledge and skill developed outside the work situation are increasingly likely to become obsolete before they can be put to use. Firms and schools alike are displaying greater interest in how work itself generates productive competence (Lave and Wenger 1991 and Berryman and Bailey 1992).

Business enterprises have traditionally prefer to minimise their outlay of training so that they will not lose their investment when employees leave. On the other hand, the more rapid obsolescence of work-related knowledge and skill make it more difficult for employers to find exactly what they need on the open market. Enterprise can minimise their training cost and at the same time promote employee development through the strategy of just-in-time learning.

Vocational education, which traditionally has offered practical training for students who were considered to possess relatively low academic ability, now includes strengthening the academic content of vocational classes and making it easier for vocational graduates to pursue further studies at university levels. These changes are intended to attract more intellectually-talented students into vocational programmes, to give them sufficient theoretical grounding to deal with changing technology, and to prepare them for continual problem solving. The blending of vocational and academic education mirrors the convergence of working and learning in the workplace (Stern 1996).

Figure 8.15
A Skilled Workforce Index of Apprenticeships
South Australia and Australia, 1975-1994

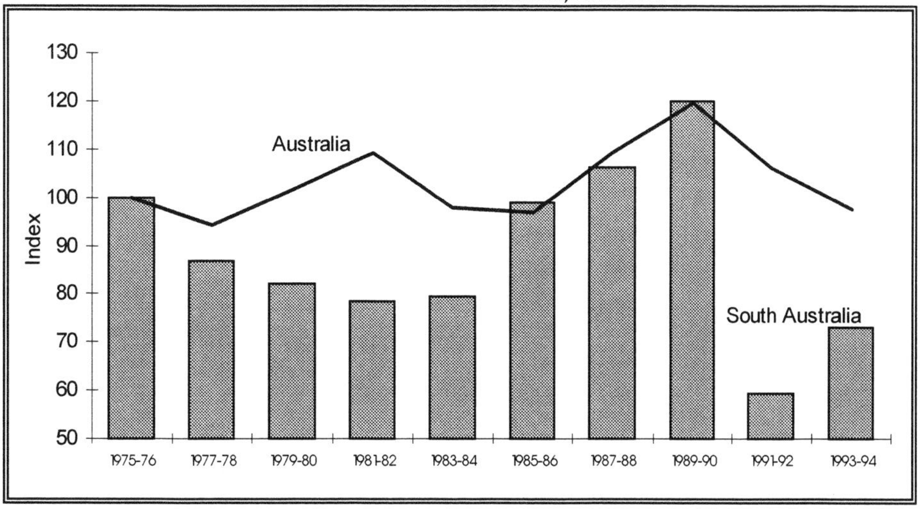

130
120
110
100
90
80
70
60
50
Index
Australia
South Australia
1975-76
1977-78
1979-80
1981-82
1983-84
1985-86
1987-88
1989-90
1991-92
1993-94

Source: DEIR Annual Apprentices Statistics.

Figure 8.16
Index of Trainee Commencement
South Australia, 1989-1995

120
110
100
90
80
70
60
50
Index
1989-90
1990-91
1991-92
1992-93
1993-94
1994-95

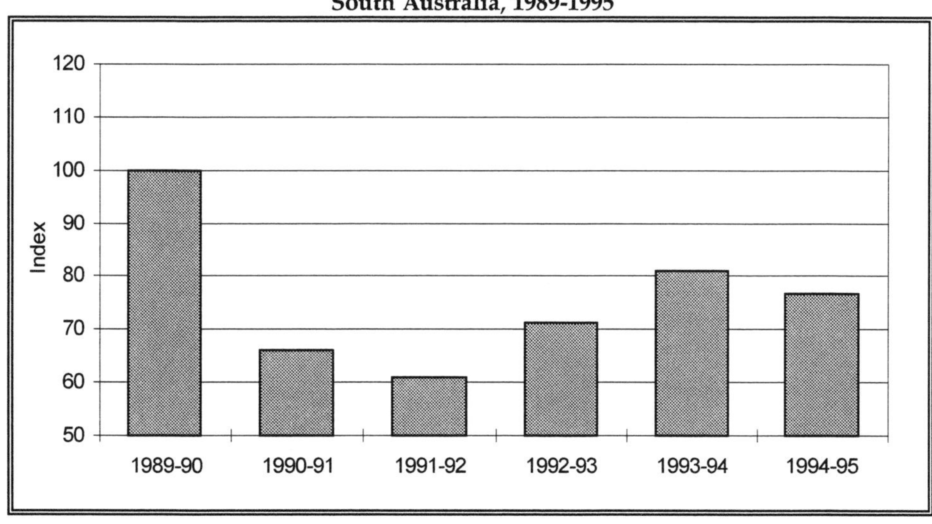

Source: Training Administration Branch, DETAFE.

One approach to assessing social rates of return is to measure the impact of education expenditure and attainment level in society at large on economic growth. A study of 29 countries found education accounting for up to a quarter of economics growth (Psacharopoulos 1984). Another study of 24 countries (7 OECD countries) reached similar conclusions (OECD 1994). The finding that human capital investment can generate economic growth was shown in a study measuring the percentage of the working age population attending secondary school and the effects on productivity levels; it was found to be significant for the entire sample of countries and a sub-sample of 22 OECD countries (Mankiw et al. 1992).

Measuring private rates of return has tended to look at changes in human skills and competencies at the individual or firm level and the impacts on firm performance. A number of studies have been conducted on the effects of on-the-job training on wages and productivity. These point to substantial positive effects on wages, typically ranging from 5 to 15 per cent, as well as positive impacts on productivity (OECD 1996a). One analysis of a large US manufacturing firm revealed that an increase in training expenditure yielded a rate of return for the company of 20 to 35 per cent (Bartel 1995). Other studies have found that the beneficial effects of enterprise training depend on collateral investment in technology (Lynch 1995).

Opportunities for training and skill development have tended to follow economic cycles. In times of recession fewer apprentices and trainees are taken on, when investment and consumer demand have fallen. This pattern, in Australia and South Australia, can be observed in the Figures 8.15 and 8.16, most noticeably in the recession periods (1981-82 and 1991-92). Structural declines in the fortunes of an industry also are manifested in the loss of training opportunities.

The decline in the number of apprentices in training mirrors the fortunes of industry - a depressed Construction sector has resulted in a reduction in training opportunities whereas the Vehicle industry has steadily increased the demand for apprentices to replace outgoing, older employees, and to meet expansion of production and exports. Changing technology has impacted on the Printing trades and several of the Metal trades, including Fitting and Machining. Traineeship programs have been slow to develop, although there are some very encouraging signs of strong industry support from the retail trades and for the traineeship concept.

Skilled Migration

The intake of skilled migrants into the workforce raises the productive capacity and expands the potential output of an economy. Inward migration may be sourced from interstate or internationally. Overseas immigration is estimated to have contributed 40 per cent of Australia's population growth in the post-war period and a slightly higher proportion of the working age population, given the age profile of migrants.

Figure 8.17
Current Intake of Skilled Migrants: Computing and Managerials
South Australia, Actual and Expected

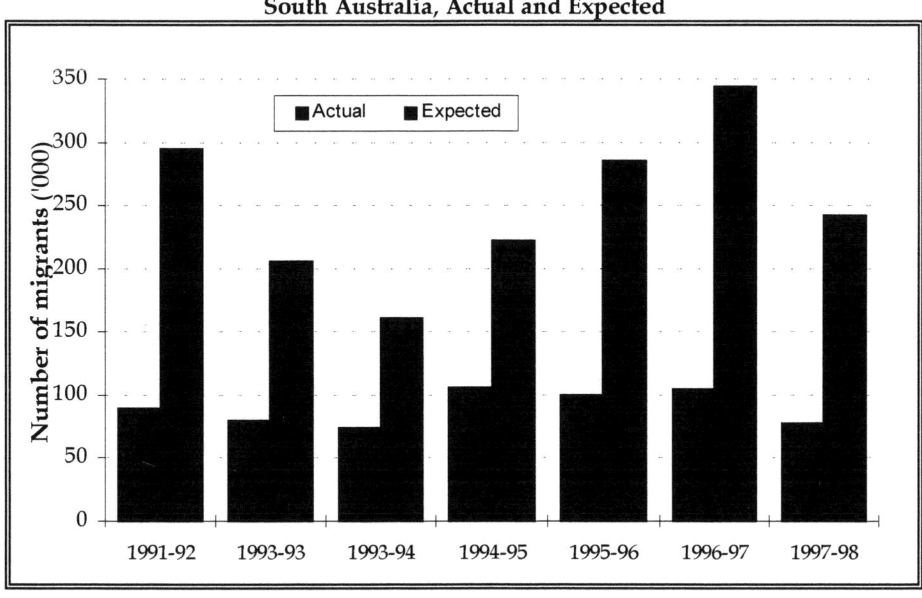

Source: Immigration and Ethnic Affairs.

South Australia has had limited success in attracting skilled migrants to the State in more recent years. The State has attracted less than 4 per cent of migrants since the late 1980s. International skilled migration of those with management or computer professional qualifications and experience represented less than 4 per cent of all skilled migrants by 1998. This is well below the population share of South Australia.

The expansion of new industries and the location of regionally headquartered companies into the State can be expected to exert a "pull effect" on migrant location. It is the case that New South Wales and Victoria combined, have attracted more than 80 per cent of regionally headquartered companies, and 75 per cent of new migrants with computing professional qualifications (compared to 66 per cent of all migrants by occupations going to those two States).

Rate of Skill Formation

The rate of skill formation in an economy is an indicator of the attractiveness of the location for business and migration, an indicator of job and career opportunities (i.e., ability to retain the well qualified) and a partial indicator of the flexibility and responsiveness of education and training systems.

While South Australia is slightly below the Australian average as measured by qualifications held by those in the workforce, the differences are not at all significant, and in fact reflect the "retaining potential of the economy". That is, the share of those with qualifications has fallen marginally as the population has declined. This is perhaps no more than a restatement of the fact that labour mobility is higher for those with qualifications. Those with no qualifications experienced an increase in their relative share over the ten year period.

Figure 8.18
Rate of Skill Formation
South Australia and Australia, 1986-1996

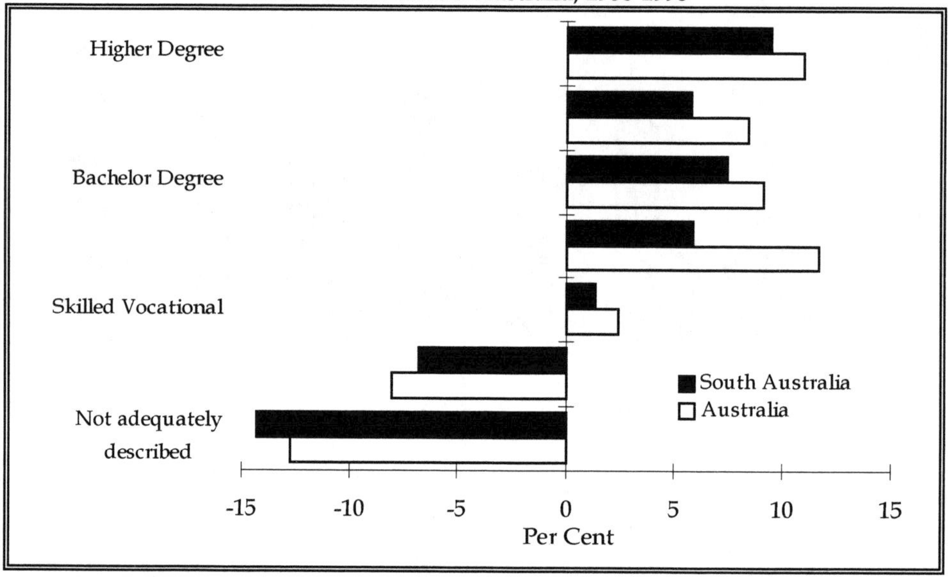

Source: IRDB, 1998.

The rate of skill formation is about that for Australia. The ability to retain those with a higher degree and the degree qualified in South Australia remains the challenge.

Change in Industry Mix

The actual number of employees increased significantly in the property and business services sector and also, but at a slower rate, in the health, education and community services sector. Slow growth in employment or actual losses, characterised the manufacturing sector overall in the period 1989 to 1999. The major industries in manufacturing sector include food and beverages, metal products, and machinery and equipment.

As the number of employment increased, so did the share of gross earnings going to employees from major property and business services. This industry ranked the fourth largest in employment and the third largest in it gross earning shares.

The Retail industry, where Motor vehicle retailing and services are the largest component, ranked second in the number of employment but only the fifth in earning share. The small decreased in its number of employment was not reflected in its earning.

Figure 8.19
Change In Number of Employees[a]
South Australia, 1989-1999

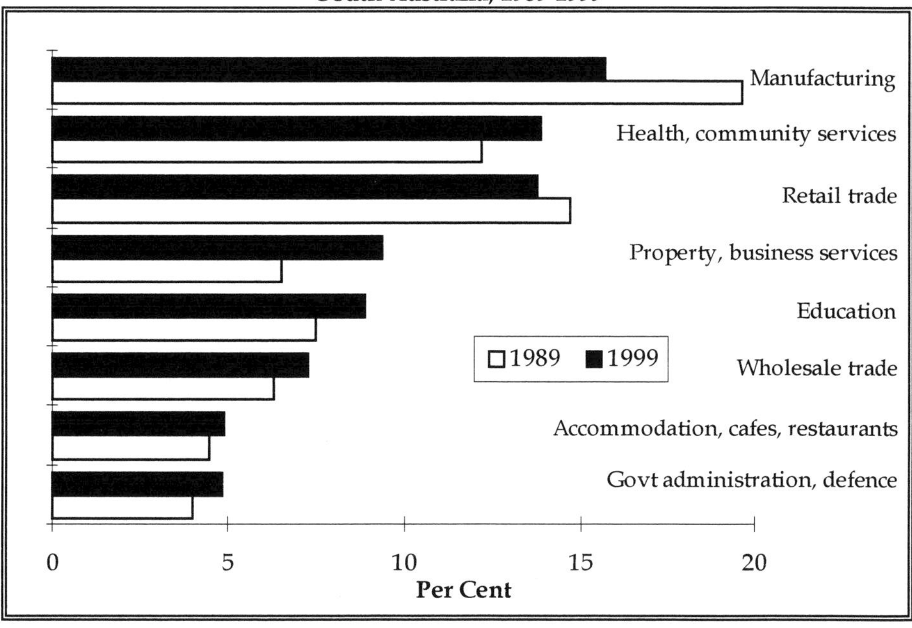

Note: a) As per cent of all employees.
Source: ABS, Ausstats (Cat. no. 6291.0).

Accommodation, Cafés, and Restaurants ranked seventh largest employers, but theirs earning shares superseded by Finance and Insurance which had smaller employee proportion to the employment of total industry.

The increase in the share of earnings for property and business services, education and health is principally the result of an increase in the aggregate number of people employed in these sectors of the economy.

Figure 8.20
Share of Gross Earnings by Selected Industries
South Australia, 1989-1999

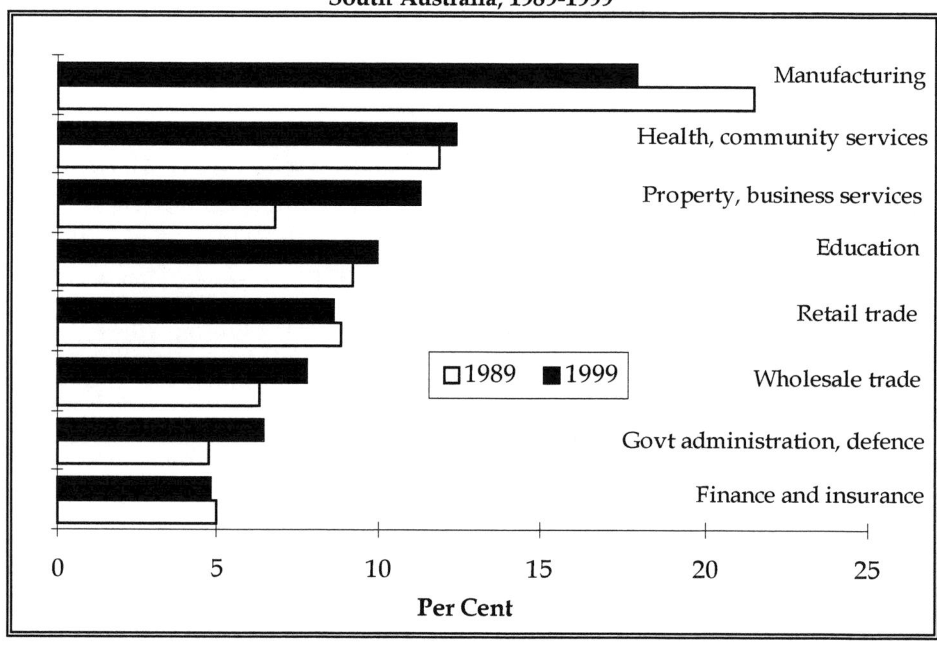

Note: a) As per cent of all industry total gross earnings.
Source: ABS, Ausstats (Cat. no. 6291.0).

Wages and Gender Disparity

Wages and other earnings are an indicator of both costs and demand pressures, potential consumption expenditure and inflationary pressure. Changes in average earnings more particularly, reflect changes in hours worked, overtime and changes in the mix of jobs across industries. Female earnings relative to male earnings are a partial indicator of opportunities and gender disparity.

Full-time adult persons, average weekly ordinary time earnings, have declined from 99 per cent to 94 per cent of the Australian average since 1993 (Figure 8.21).[26] The gap has widened as the mix of jobs has changed across industries and between States. The overall cost competitiveness of the South Australian economy has been advantaged by this trend.

The trend in female earnings as a per cent of male earnings (average weekly ordinary time earnings) in South Australia indicates a narrowing of the income gender disparity.

26 .... Data exclude non-salaries employees.

Figure 8.21
Index of Earnings: Full Time Adult Persons
South Australia and Australia, 1989-1999

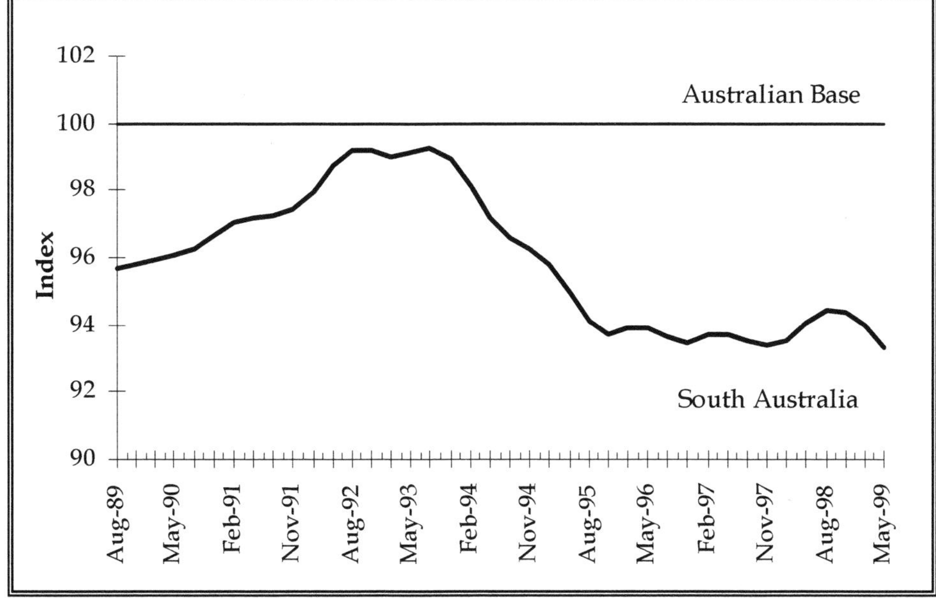

Source: ABS, Ausstats (Cat. no. 6302.0).

Figure 8.22
Female Earnings as Per Cent of Male Earnings
South Australia and Australia, 1989-1999

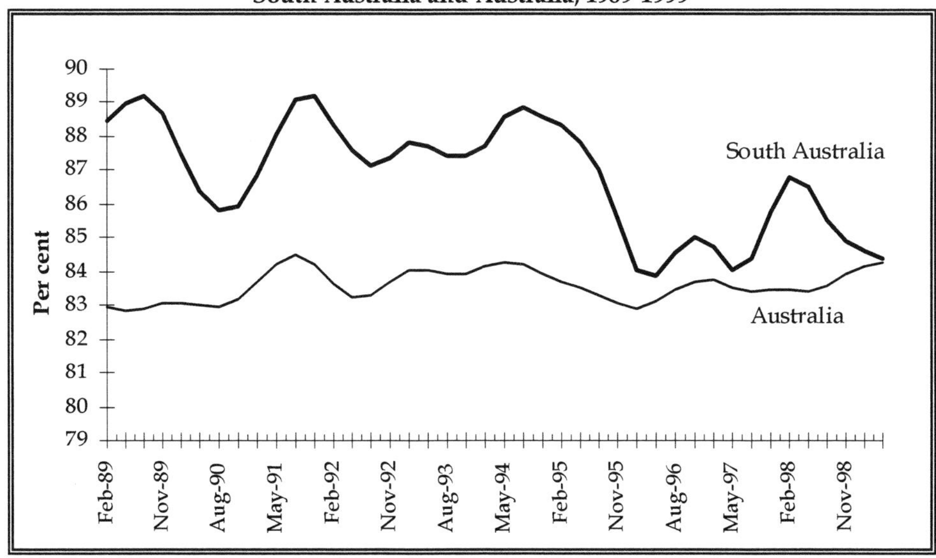

Source: ABS, Ausstats (Cat. no. 6302.0).

Female earnings averaged about 87 per cent of male earnings, the figure for Australia was 84 per cent.

South Australia has performed better than the other states, the primary reason being the above average employment of females in the public sector, the teaching profession and community services sector. In addition, the growth in employment of women in the scientific and business professional occupations will contribute to a narrowing of the existing disparity.

Summary

The importance of human capital in enhancing the economic growth and development of a region has been supported by many researchers in their various studies.

Human capital formation depends on the rate of skill formation through education and post-school training, the rate of growth of employed labour, the skill level of employed labour, and population movements.

Formal secondary and tertiary education are the key forms of investment in the human capital for advanced regional economies such as South Australia. Secondary school student retention rates to Year 12 have been increasing across the nation including South Australia, but the increase in South Australia is slightly slower than nationwide reflecting slower growth of the youth population in South Australia.

In the last decade, full-time student participation rates of 15 and 16 year olds have been higher the national rates. Meanwhile, lower increases of full-time student participation rates above 17 years could mean that they shifted to part-time students and/or employment. At the same period South Australian youth employment has increased faster than nationally.

The tertiary education enrolments per 1,000 population in South Australia is the second lowest in Australia, better only than the Northern Territory. The increase in enrolments over the ten years to 1999 is also slower in South Australia than nationally. This seemingly dismal result is partly explained by a lower proportion of the population in age groups that tend to engage in tertiary education. Overall South Australian's human capital formation through secondary and tertiary education is improving, but the pace is not matched by Australia.

The employment growth in South Australia has been below the national rate. This is shown by the figure of full-time and part-time employed persons and full-time and part-time wage and salary earners. The pattern of employed persons by age group in South Australia is in line with Australian pattern. There are a decline in employment in 15-34 year age groups and an increase in employment of 45-59 year age groups. While overall unemployment in South Australia is higher, the average annual youth unemployment growth is lower. Participation rate in South Australia and Australia has decreased in the last decade. While the male participation rate shows a decreasing trend, females show an increase.

South Australia has been losing population through net movements interstate and overseas; it has only been through natural increase that South Australian population has grown.

South Australia experienced a strong demand in high-skilled labour. This demand has increased in the last 10 years. To meet this demand, in addition to increasing skill through formal education, South Australia also fulfils it through apprenticeships. South Australia is slightly below the Australian average as measured by qualifications held by those in the workforce. The differences, however, are not at all significant. In fact this reflects the "retaining potential of the economy". That is, the share of those with qualifications has fallen marginally as the population has declined

Overall, South Australian human capital has been enhanced significantly over the last decade, but the improvement is below the national pace.

Appendix 8.1

Tertiary Education

Table 8.1.1
Student Numbers (EFTSUs)[a] by State and Discipline Groups 1999

Discipline Group	NSW	Vic	Qld	WA	SA	TAS	NT	ACT	Multi	Aus
Humanities	17,628	13,945	10,651	5,124	4,132	1,095	502	2,849	1,300	*57,226*
Social Studies	18,806	15,669	10,514	6,172	4,992	1,393	390	2,251	1,136	*61,323*
Education	13,259	8,093	9,393	4,004	2,952	1,229	521	787	2,576	*42,814*
Sciences	15,977	15,383	10,602	5,767	4,250	1,263	338	1,608	344	*55,532*
Mathematics, Computing	16,752	18,556	11,469	5,965	3,961	884	319	1,936	376	*60,218*
Visual/Performing Arts	8,504	7,473	4,168	2,400	1,702	851	163	1,139	215	*26,615*
Engineering, Processing	9,500	10,893	4,786	3,071	2,011	755	44	764	38	*31,862*
Health Sciences	14,351	12,987	7,136	4,704	4,715	770	214	400	885	*46,162*
Admin, Business, Ec, Law	47,458	38,820	23,473	14,987	8,596	2,240	827	4,342	770	*141,513*
Built Environment	4,444	3,725	1,965	1,149	1,018	261	41	472	0	*13,075*
Agric., Renewable Resources	2,355	1,739	1,468	789	796	344	14	305	0	*7,810*
Total	**169,034**	**147,283**	**95,625**	**54,132**	**39,125**	**11,085**	**3,373**	**16,853**	**7,640**	**544,150**
Students per 1000 population	**26.2**	**31.1**	**27.0**	**36.2**	**20.9**	**23.6**	**17.4**	**54.2**		**28.5**
Proportion to Australia (%)	**31.1**	**27.1**	**17.6**	**9.9**	**7.2**	**2.0**	**0.6**	**3.1**	**1.4**	**100.0**

Note: a) Equivalent Full-Time Student Units.
Source: DETYA (2000).

Table 8.1.2
Proportion of Student Numbers (EFTSUs)[a] by State and Level Course 1999 (Per cent)

Level Course	NSW	Vic	Qld	WA	SA	TAS	NT	ACT	Multi	Aus
Post-graduate[b]	18.4	16.6	13.0	15.1	14.1	10.0	16.1	20.4	14.2	***16.1***
Undergraduate[c]	79.0	82.7	84.7	82.8	84.1	88.6	73.7	78.0	84.9	***82.0***
Others[d]	2.6	0.7	2.3	2.1	1.8	1.4	10.1	1.6	0.9	***1.9***
Total	**100.0**	**100.0**	**100.0**	**100.0**	**100.0**	**100.0**	**100.0**	**100.0**	**100.0**	**100.0**

Notes:
a) Equivalent Full-Time Student Units.
b) Higher Doctorate, Doctorate, Master and Other Post-grad.
c) Bachelor, Associate Degree, Other Under-graduate.
d) Enabling, Non-Award, Cross-Institution Programs.

Source: DETYA (2000).

Appendix 8.2

Wage and Salary Earners

Table 8.2.1
Index of Full-Time Employed Wage and Salary Earners by State, 1989-1999

Year	NSW	Vic	Qld	SA	WA	Tas	NT	ACT	Aust
	Index (1989 = 100)								
1989	100	100	100	100	100	100	100	100	**100**
1990	101	100	100	103	100	102	104	102	**101**
1991	96	92	96	101	98	98	108	104	**96**
1992	93	86	99	95	103	94	92	105	**93**
1993	94	85	100	95	106	95	93	105	**94**
1994	94	85	99	91	103	89	99	102	**93**
1995	97	87	106	91	106	88	99	102	**96**
1996	98	89	110	91	110	91	106	101	**98**
1997	101	87	110	86	108	92	108	98	**98**
1998	100	87	113	88	111	84	104	101	**98**
1999	102	90	117	89	114	83	109	108	**101**
Growth[a]	0.32	-1.06	1.82	-1.61	1.35	-1.86	0.71	0.04	**0.10**

Note: a) Annual wage and salary earners growth rate.
Source: ABS, Ausstats (Cat. no. 6302.0).

Table 8.2.2
Index of Part-Time Employed Wage and Salary Earners by State, 1989-1999

Year	NSW	Vic	Qld	SA	WA	Tas	NT	ACT	Aust
	Index (1989 = 100)								
1989	100	100	100	100	100	100	100	100	**100**
1990	104	102	103	105	103	96	123	107	**103**
1991	104	106	102	111	108	99	116	114	**105**
1992	105	109	111	100	123	113	122	133	**109**
1993	105	110	116	101	127	122	121	136	**111**
1994	113	118	130	118	132	117	131	140	**120**
1995	125	125	143	119	146	111	118	140	**129**
1996	129	123	146	115	149	124	136	139	**130**
1997	126	129	145	115	170	127	154	149	**133**
1998	133	133	161	118	180	132	147	135	**140**
1999	138	136	173	122	188	139	143	148	**146**
Growth[a]	3.42	3.25	5.77	1.81	6.63	3.46	3.24	3.48	**3.93**

Note: a) Annual wage and salary earners growth rate.
Source: ABS, Ausstats (Cat. no. 6302.0).

References

Bartel, A. (1995), "Training, Wage Growth and Job Performance: Evidence from a Company Database", *Journal of Labor Economics*, Vol. 13.

Barro, R.J. (1991), "Economic Growth in a Cross-Section of Countries", *Quarterly Journal of Economics*, 106(2), pp. 407-442.

Behrens, N. (1978), *Schooling and Work, In Commission of Inquiry into Poverty, School, Community and Work: Urban and Rural Aspects*, AGPS, Canberra.

Benneworth, P. (1996), "The Competitiveness Project: North East Regional Competitiveness", Report 1996. Part 6: Education and Skills Indicators. URL:http://www.ncl.ac.uk/~ncurds/

Berryman, S.E. and Bailey, T. (1992), *The Double Helix: Education and the Economy*, Teachers College Press, New York.

Department of Employment and Education Training (DEET) (1987), *Completing Secondary School in Australia: A Socio-Economic and Regional Analysis.*

Department of Education, Training and Youth Affairs (DETYA) (2000), *Selected Higher Education Student Statistics*, 1999, Canberra.

Department of Education, Training and Youth Affairs (DETYA) (1999a), *Selected Higher Education Staff Statistics*, 1998, Canberra.

Department of Education, Training and Youth Affairs (DETYA) (1999b), *Selected Higher Education Student Statistics*, 1998, Canberra.

Department of Education, Training and Youth Affairs (DETYA) (1998), *Selected Higher Education Finance and Research Expenditure Statistics*, 1997, Australian Government Publishing Services, December 1998, Canberra.

Foray D. and Lundvall, B.A. (1996) "The Knowledge-Based Economy: from the Economies of Knowledge to the Learning Economy", in *The Knowledge-Based Economy*, OECD, Paris.

Garlick, S. (1998), *Creative Associations in Special Places: Enhancing the Role of Universities in Building Competitive Regional Economies*, DEETYA, Canberra.

Goddard, J. (1997a), "Universities and Regional Development: An Overview". URL:http://www.ncl.ac.uk/

Goddard, J. (1997b), "The Local and Regional Role of Higher Education: Comments on the National Committee of Inquiry Report". URL:http://www.ncl.ac.uk/

Healey, Kaye (ed) (1998), "Secondary Education in Australia", *Issues in Society*, Vol. 98.

Howell, D.R and Wolf, E.N. (1992), "Technical Change and the Demand for Skills by U.S. Industries", *Cambridge Journal of Economics*: 16(2), pp. 127-146.

Kanter, R.M. (1995), *World Class: Thriving Locally in the Global Economy*, Simon and Schuster, New York.

Kyriacou, G.A. (1992), "A Cross-Country Estimation of an Aggregate Production Function with Human Capital", Working Paper, Central Bank of Cyprus.

Lave, J. and Wenger, E. (1991), *Situated Learning: Legitimate Peripheral Participation*, Cambridge University Press, Cambridge.

Lynch, L.M. (1995), "Employer-provided Training in the Manufacturing Sector: First Results from the United States", paper presented at the World Bank Conference on Enterprise Training Strategies and Productivity, Washington, DC, June.

Mankiw, G., Romer, D. and Weil, D. (1992), "A Contribution to the Structure of Economic Growth", *Quarterly Journal of Economics*, Vol. 106.

Mincer, Jacob (1993), *Studies in Human Capital*, Aldershot, Hants, England; Brookfield, Vt: E, Elgar.

OECD (1994), *The OECD Jobs Study: Evidence and Explanations*, Paris.

OECD (1996a), *Employment and Growth in the Knowledge Based Society*, Paris.

OECD (1996b), *Transitions to Learning Economies and Societies*, Paris.

OECD (1997), *Regional Competitive and Skills*, Paris.

Power, C. (1984), "Factor Influencing Retentivity and Satisfaction with Secondary Schooling", *Australian Journal of Education*, 28(2) pp. 115-125.

Psacharaopoulos, G. (1984), "The Contribution of Education to Economic Growth", in *International Comparisons of Productivity and Causes of the Slowdown*, ed. J.W. Kendrick, Ballinger Publishing Co., Cambridge.

Rosier, M.J. (1978), *Early School Leavers in Australia*, ACER, Hawtron.

Sala-i-Martin, X. (1995), "Measuring Aggregate Human Capital", Center Discussion Paper No.723, Economic Growth Center, Yale University.

Schultz, T.W. (1993), "Investments in the Schooling and Health of Women and Men: Quantities and Return", *Journal of Human Resources*, 28(4) pp. 694-734.

Sorkin, Alan L. (1974), *Education, Unemployment, and Economic Growth*, Lexington Books, D.C. Heath and Company.

South Australian Centre for Economic Studies (SACES) (1996), "The Contribution of South Australia's Universities to the South Australian Economy", A report prepared for The University of Adelaide, The Flinders University of South Australia, and The University of South Australia.

Stern, David (1996), *Human Resource Development in the Knowledge-Based Economy: Roles of Firms, Schools, and Governments*, Centre for Educational Research and Innovation, OECD.

Thanki, R. (1999), "How Do We Know the Value of Higher Education to Regional Development?", *Regional Studies*, 27(5) pp. 401-17.

Williams, T., Batten, M., Girling-Butcher, S., & Clancy, J. (1980), *School and Work in Prospect: 14-Year-Olds in Australia*, ACER, Hawtorn.

Zann, Leon P. (1996), "State of the Marine Environment: Report for Australia", *Technical Summary*, Department of the Environment Sport and Territories, AGPS.

Chapter Nine

Economic Structure

In this chapter we take a close look at the structure of the South Australian economy and how it has changed over recent years. The structure of the South Australian economy can accurately be described as narrow. This attribute can have positive or negative effects. For example the current industry structure generates a lower per capita level of greenhouse gas emissions with implications for abatement policies (see Chapter 11), but the narrowness reduces the region's resilience to external shocks with the effect of increasing the variability of economic performance.

A Structural Analysis of the South Australian Economy

Introduction

In this section, we use shift-share analysis to explore why South Australia's growth rate has been different from that of the nation as a whole. Shift-share analysis, which has been widely used in Labour Economics, Regional Economics and Urban Economics, is a useful starting point in the analysis of regional growth. It broadly tells us the role of industry mix and the extent to which individual industries have grown relative to their national counterparts (Wood and Bushe-Jones 1989). Shift-share analysis partitions the overall difference in growth rates into two elements. The first is that attributed to differences in the growth rates of the various industries making up the income aggregate. It is obvious that, even if every industry in a state grew as fast as its national counterpart, the state gross domestic product (GSP) would grow more slowly than the national gross domestic product (GDP) if the state happened to contain a disproportionate share of slow-growing industries. The second element, in the difference in growth rates of aggregate income or product, is that attributable to industrial composition.

Blandy et al. (1994) employ shift-share analysis to investigate the differences on industry structure and growth rate of Victorian economy compared to the nation. Moore and Rhodes (1973) use the shift-share technique to evaluate the efficacy of regional policy instruments, whilst Harris et al. (1987) apply it to quantify the displacement effects of substantial inward regional investment. Armstrong and Taylor (1978), Stilwell (1968), and Wood and Bushe-Jones (1989) investigate the influence of industrial structure on differential regional employment growth using a shift-share analysis.

Like location quotient and other economic measures, shift-share is an analytical tool used to evaluate strengths and weaknesses in a local economy using any of a number of variables such as income, output, or employment (LMEA 1995). However, Harris et al. (1987) indicated one of the weaknesses of applying shift-share analysis that is the results gained from shift-share analysis are sensitive to the time period chosen. Shift-share analysis is a comparative static approach that considers conditions only at the beginning and end years of time period analysis. The use of the initial year industrial composition takes no account of changes in industrial composition over the time period. Moreover, the continuous changes in the size of region's total industry or employment over the time period are not taken into account. In addressing this problem, the analysis will cover sub-periods in addition to the full-time period.

South Australia Industry Structure

This section presents the descriptive statistics of South Australian industry structure. These statistics show how the South Australian economy relative to Australia as a whole. More specifically it will focus on the South Australia share of the national GDP.

Table 9.1 presents the South Australia share of the national output by industry. It compares the share of nearly 2 decades ago with a recent year. Unfortunately for South Australia, the overall data shows that its share has changed for the worse over the time. An average share of all industry has declined from 7.6 per cent in 1982-83 to 6.9 per cent in 1998-99. Agriculture, Manufacturing, Electricity, Gas and Water, Health and Community Services, and Personal and

Other Services were among the industries that shared significantly above the average of all industries in both representing years. Agriculture share was the largest and increasing from 9.9 per cent (30 per cent higher than the average) to 12.04 per cent (75 per cent higher than the average). Manufacturing share increased from 8.3 per cent to 8.8 per cent. Electricity, Gas and Water increased its share from 7.7 to 9.8 per cent. Health and Community Services, and Personal and Other Services industries decreased their shares of the national output, following the average share pattern. Below average shares included Finance and Insurance, Property and Business Services, and Mining industries, this last being by far the lowest contributor. These industries' shares were not only below the average, but also decreasing over time except the Mining industry. Finance and Insurance decreased its share from 6.1 to 5.4 per cent. Property and Business Services' shares decreased from 5.9 to 5.4 per cent. Mining industry increased its share one and half points from 2.3 to 3.8 per cent. Construction industry was doing well by sharing slightly above the average (7.7 per cent) at the beginning of the period but then at the end of the period declining to below the average (5.9 per cent).

The prominence of Manufacturing industry is evident of South Australia's industrial structure. This industry was accounted for 17.1 per cent of GSP in 1998-99, decreased from 19.8 per cent in 1982-83. The low share of Finance and Insurance industry sector in 1982-83 (1.2 per cent of GSP) has changed significantly in 1998-99, it accounted for more than 4 times its previous share (5.0 per cent of GSP). Another booming industry was Property and Business Services that increased their shares of GSP from 5.0 to 8.5 per cent. Australia also showed a similar trend. Finance and Insurance, and Property and Business Services industries have been booming. But, the dominating Manufacturing industry has fallen significantly from 18.2 per cent in 1982-83 to 13.4 per cent of GDP in 1998-99.

The annual industries' growths in South Australia indicated that only 3 industries of 19 grew faster than the nation's, namely Agriculture, Manufacturing, and Accommodation, Cafes and Restaurants. The overall trend is consistent with the slower growth rate of annual regional GSP than nation GDP in 17 years that is 2.9 per cent for South Australia compared to 3.9 per cent for Australia.

Both regionally and nationally, Finance and Insurance industry grew much faster than the average – over 5 times in the region and over 4 times in the nation. Property and Business Services grew more than twice average in South Australia and nearly double the average in Australia. Retail Trade has, unfortunately, a very small growth, i.e., only one twentieth of the region average. South Australia's Retail Trade share of Australia, as described in the previous discussion, was above average of all industries.

In general, South Australia's industrial structure can be pictured as the region with significantly more concentrated in Agriculture and less in Mining, than the nation. A set of industries under-represented in South Australia, but only mildly so include Wholesale Trade, Accommodation, Cafés and Restaurants, Transport and Storage, Communication Services, Finance and Insurance, Cultural and Recreation Services, and Ownership and Dwelling. Those mildly over-represented are Retail Trade, Education, and General Government.

Tables 9.2 to 9.7 provide further details of some representative industry classifications. The limited dataavailability prevent from fully achieving the consistency of the time frame and type of data. Note that because of these data inconsistency care needs to be taken in comparing the industry values of these representative industries to the corresponding industries in the Table 9.1. Nevertheless, with these limitations, we are still able to picture South Australian economic position within the nation. The descriptions are concentrated on the South Australia's industry share of the national output. The latest data available are presented in these tables. The same choice of data types (for example: gross value, value added, and turnover) is made for South Australia and for Australia.

Agricultural Industry. In 1998, Agricultural sector shared 11.3 per cent to the national GDP (Table 9.2). As shown in Table 9.1, this share has increased to 12.0 per cent. Crops have the largest share of Agricultural sector both regionally and nationally where South Australia shares 14.1 per cent. Pastures and Grasses contribute slightly more, that is, 14.7 per cent. One third of Pastures and Grasses harvested for seed was from South Australia. Meanwhile Livestock Slaughterings and Livestock Products shared only 7.0 and 8.6 per cent, respectively, of national totals.

Manufacturing Industry. The preliminary data of Manufacturing industry for the same period (1998-99), the South Australian contribution shows a slight increase on Table 9.1 (9.0 per cent compared with 8.8 per cent). Among the Manufacturing sector, Food, Beverage and Tobacco industry and Machinery and Equipment industry had both the largest shares and the largest share. They were the only two of nine sub-sector industries that were above the average Manufacturing SA share. Textile, Clothing, Footwear and Leather industry had the lowest share and also the smallest share.

Construction Industry. Australian Bureau of Statistics discontinued its publication on Construction Industry Australia after the last publication in 1988-99 data. Table 9.1 shows that Construction industry in South Australia, which had the lowest annual growth rate (0.12 per cent) has reduced its national share from 7.8 per cent in 1982-83 to 5.9 per cent in 1998-99. The data shows in Table 9.4 supports this contraction trend. During 1988-89 period, South Australia's Construction sector contributed 7 per cent to the national GDP. Within the sector, special trade Construction was the largest contributors to Australia and also held nearly two third of the share in the region.

Table 9.1
South Australia Share to National GDP by Industry, 1982-83 and 1998-99

Industry	Real GSP SA ($m-1996/97 prices)				Real GDP Australia ($m-1996/97 prices)				SA Share (Per Cent)		Growth Rate (%) 1982/83-1998/99	
	1982/83	%	**1998/99**	%	**1982/83**	%	**1998/99**	%	**1982/83**	**1998/99**	**Sth. Aust.**	**Australia**
Agriculture	1,006	4.9	2,075	5.8	10,173	3.7	17,233	3.3	9.89	12.04	2.03	1.56
Mining	299	1.4	843	2.3	13,043	4.8	22,188	4.2	2.29	3.80	1.80	3.46
Manufacturing	4,104	19.8	6,150	17.1	49,481	18.2	70,316	13.4	8.29	8.75	2.01	1.74
Electricity, gas & water	826	4.0	1,258	3.5	10,790	4.0	12,852	2.5	7.66	9.79	1.44	0.79
Construction	1,583	7.7	2,013	5.6	20,578	7.6	34,418	6.6	7.69	5.85	0.12	2.01
Wholesale trade	1,152	5.6	1,630	4.5	15,682	5.8	29,038	5.5	7.35	5.61	1.64	3.22
Retail trade	1,781	8.6	2,238	6.2	20,578	7.6	31,386	6.0	8.65	7.13	0.14	1.76
Accom., cafes & restaurants	356	1.7	822	2.3	4,987	1.8	12,320	2.3	7.14	6.67	5.14	5.83
Transport & storage	1,143	5.5	1,911	5.3	16,109	5.9	28,134	5.4	7.10	6.79	3.24	3.04
Communication services	402	1.9	968	2.7	6,266	2.3	16,435	3.1	6.42	5.89	4.77	5.99
Finance & insurance	251	1.2	1,808	5.0	4,127	1.5	33,756	6.4	6.08	5.36	15.47	16.34
Property & business services	1,033	5.0	3,072	8.5	17,423	6.4	57,441	11.0	5.93	5.35	6.16	7.49
Govt. admin. & defence	872	4.2	1,192	3.3	12,468	4.6	20,731	4.0	7.00	5.75	1.53	3.43
Education	1,245	6.0	1,812	5.0	14,521	5.3	23,789	4.5	8.57	7.62	2.32	3.23
Health & community services	1,615	7.8	2,691	7.5	16,155	5.9	32,156	6.1	10.00	8.37	3.50	4.54
Cultural & recreational services	297	1.4	606	1.7	3,997	1.5	10,239	2.0	7.44	5.92	3.96	5.71
Personal & other services	463	2.2	1,000	2.8	5,256	1.9	12,542	2.4	8.81	7.97	5.59	5.94
Ownership of dwellings	1,674	8.1	3,096	8.6	23,422	8.6	48,373	9.2	7.15	6.40	3.67	4.62
General government	582	2.8	853	2.4	7,320	2.7	11,184	2.1	7.95	7.63	3.09	3.22
All Industries	**20,685**	**100.0**	**36,037**	**100.0**	**272,379**	**100.0**	**524,529**	**100.0**	**7.59**	**6.87**	**2.93**	**3.89**

Source: ABS AusStats Cat no. 5220.0, SACES Calculations.

Non-building Construction sub-sector was only a small part of the economy that contributes 4.1 per cent. It meant that 95.9 per cent of Non-building Construction is from the rest of the States and Territories.

Table 9.2
South Australia Agricultural Sector Share to National Output, 1998

Agricultural Sector	SA Gross Value	Australia Gross Value	SA Share
	$ million	$ million	Per Cent
Crops	2,100	14,848	14.14
Cereals for grain	916	5,784	15.83
Crops for hay	49	214	22.95
Legumes for grain	99	543	18.30
Oilseeds	35	392	8.84
Other crops	1,002	7,916	12.65
Pastures and grasses	90	613	14.70
Cut for hay	66	541	12.17
Harvested for seed	24	73	33.61
Livestock slaughterings	460	6,594	6.97
Livestock products	514	5,979	8.60
Total Agriculture	**3,165**	**28,034**	**11.29**

Source: ABS, Agriculture, Cat. no. 7113.0 (1997-98).

Table 9.3
South Australia Manufacturing Sector Share to National Output, 1998-99

Manufacturing Sector	SA Value Added	Australia Value Added	SA Share
	$ million	$ million	Per Cent
Food, beverage & tobacco	1,515	13,775	11.00
Textile, clothing, footwear & leather	145	3,257	4.45
Wood & paper product	350	4,221	8.29
Printing, publishing & recorded media	343	6,675	5.14
Petroleum, coal, chemical & assoc. products	584	9,577	6.10
Non-metallic mineral product	190	3,383	5.62
Metal product	745	11,208	6.65
Machinery and equipment	2,151	13,883	15.49
Other manufacturing	153	2,315	6.61
Total Manufacturing	**6,176**	**68,294**	**9.04**

Source: ABS, Manufacturing Industry, Preliminary, Cat. no. 8201.0 (1998-99).

Table 9.4
South Australia Construction Sector Share to National Output, 1988-89

Construction Sector	SA Value Added	Australia Value Added	SA Share
	$ million	$ million	Per Cent
General construction	388	6,339	6.12
Building	317	4,608	6.89
Non-building	71	1,731	4.08
Special trade construction	601	7,772	7.74
Total Construction	**989**	**14,111**	**7.01**

Source: ABS, Construction Industry Australia, Cat. no. 8770.0 (1988-89).

Table 9.5
South Australia Retail Sector Share to National Output, 1998-99

Retail Industry	SA Turnover	Australia Turnover	SA Share
	$ million	$ million	Per Cent
Food retailing	4,254	55,866	7.62
Department stores	1,097	12,405	8.84
Clothing & soft good retailing	563	9,244	6.09
Household good retailing	990	14,944	6.63
Recreational retailing	358	7,146	5.01
Other retailing	936	14,073	6.65
Hospitality and services	1,528	22,934	6.66
Total Retail Industry	**9,727**	**136,611**	**7.12**

Source: ABS, Retail Trade, Cat. no. 8501.0 (1999).

Retail Trade Industry. A pattern similar to that of Construction happened in Retail Trade. The industry share has declined over 17 years (Table 9.1). However, unlike Construction industry which its share of the nation output was below the total average, the South Australian Retail Trade industry share was above the total average. Food Retailing sub-sector played the biggest role for holding nearly half of Retail Trade industry turnover (Table 9.5). This was followed by Hospitality and Services and Department Store sub-sectors. The Department Store was also the largest contributor of national GDP in this industry. On the other hand, the Recreational Retailing sub-sector could not quite compete with the rest of Australia. Its share was only 5.0 per cent which is two points below the Retail Trade industry share.

Table 9.6
South Australia Accommodation Sector Share to National Output

Accommodation Sector	SA Value Added	Australia Value Added	SA Share
	$ million	$ million	Per Cent
Accommodation industry[a]	313.4	6,762.6	4.63
Hotels, Motels, Guest houses & Serviced Apts[b]	184.9	4,143.2	4.46

Note: (a) 1997-98; (b) 1999
Source: ABS, *Accommodation Industry*, Cat. No. 8695.0 (1997-98) and *Tourism Indicators*, Cat. No. 8634.0 (March 2000).

Table 9.7
South Australia Cafés & Restaurants Sector Share to National Output, 1986-87

Cafés & Restaurants Industry	SA Turnover	Australia Turnover	SA Share
	$ million	$ million	Per Cent
Taking from meals	120.3	1,886.6	6.38
Takings from ready-to-eat take away food	12.0	196.0	6.12
Takings from accommodation	4.8	60.0	8.00
Sales of beer, wine and spirits	32.2	331.5	9.71
Other retail sales	5.6	57.2	9.79
Other revenue	3.8	52.5	7.24
Total Cafés and Restaurants Industry	**178.7**	**2,583.8**	**6.92**

Source: ABS, Cafés & Restaurants Industry Australia, Cat. no. 8655.0 (1986-87).

Accommodation, Cafés and Restaurants Industry. The Accommodation industry businesses in Australia are concentrated in the Eastern mainland States, with 80 per cent operating in New South Wales, Victoria and Queensland (ABS, Cat. no. 8695.0). This industry in South Australia showed a declining share from 7.1 to 6.8 per cent in the last 17 years (Table 9.1), these shares were lower than the total industry shares in both periods. Tables 9.6 and 9.7 present the Accommodation in 1997-98, Hotels, Motels, Guest Houses & Serviced Apartments in 1999, and Cafés and Restaurants in 1986-87. The Accommodation industry business in 1997-98 contributed only 4.6 per cent to GDP (Table 9.6). The other data on Hotels, Motels, Guest Houses & Serviced Apartments in 1999 showed even lower percentage. Both data indicated that South Australian Accommodation sub-sector is about two and half per cent below its total industry share. Furthermore, its output share also fell below its population share. This industry was propped by the Cafés and Restaurants sub-sector industry which increased the share to 6.8 per cent in 1998-99. The 1986-87 data showed that the Cafés and Restaurant turnover taking from Accommodation, the sales of beer, wine and spirits, and other retail sales were the major contributors of the national GDP. It is believed that they are still the major components in this industry in recent years.

The South Australian Experience: The Shift-Share Analysis Result

The overall growth rate of a region's activity (as measured by total employment or total value added) is a weighted average of the growth rates of the separate sectors or activities making up the region's economy. If the region's growth rate is compared with that of some other area (for example, the entire nation), it is possible to explain the difference in growth rates statistically in terms of two components, "mix" and "competitive". Quantitative analysis of comparative regional growth rates along these lines is called the "shift-share" approach. This approach was apparently first used by Daniel B. Creamer in 1942 (Hoover & Giarratani 1999). The two components, in other studies, are also known as "industry growth" and "industry composition"[27]; "differential shift" and "proportional shift"[28]; "regional effect" and "structural effect". For the rest of the study, we use the terms "industry growth" and "industry composition" shifts.

The industry growth shift is based on different growth rates of individual industries in the region as compared with the nation. It indicates what of the region's growth can be attributed to differences between the actual growth rates of the region and of the national economy.

The sum of these two components over each industry will then give an analysis for regional economy as a whole, the difference between the regional growth, and the growth of the total economy for a specified period. The difference in total growth is therefore the sum of the two components.

Algebraically this can be written in terms of the equation: [29]

$$g^{t^o t} - G^{t^o t} = \left[\sum_i s_i^{t^o}\left(g_i^{t^o t} - G_i^{t^o t}\right)\right] + \left[\sum_i \left(s_i^{t^o} - S_i^{t^o}\right)\left(G_i^{t^o t} - G^{t^o t}\right)\right]$$

where: $g^{t^o t}$ is the South Australian growth over the period t^o to t,

$G^{t^o t}$ is the Australian growth over the period t^o to t,

$s_i^{t^o}$ is South Australian share of industry i in the base year (t^o),

$g_i^{t^o t}$ is the South Australian growth of industry i over the period t^o to t,

27 Industry growth and Industry composition are the terms used by Blandy et al (1994)

28 Differential/Regional shift and Proportional/Structural shift are the terms used by Department of Geography (2000)

29 see Appendix 7.1 for the derivation.

$G_i^{t^o t}$ is the Australian growth of industry *i* over the period t^o to *t*,

$S_i^{t^o}$ is Australian share of industry *i* in the base year (t^o),

For each industry *i*, the sign of each component indicates whether the region is above or below the national average. For the first component, the sign indicates whether the growth rate for that industry is above (+) or below (-) the growth rate for the same industry in the total economy. A region may have locational advantages which enable even nationally slow growing industries to prosper, thus it may have a positive and large total industry growth. For the second component of the equation the sign indicates whether the region relies more (+) or less (-) heavily on that industry to grow. A region with a large proportion of fast growing industries is likely to grow fast and have a positive total industry composition.

The analysis for South Australia has been done on the production side only without any reference to employment. Data for GSP by industry are available since 1982-83 and the most recent data to date are for 1998-99, the analysis limits to this period. To analyse growth, we use constant price estimates so that the measurement reflects changes in the volume of production and is not related to any change in prices.

Using the national deflator to produce constant price estimates for South Australia it was then possible to analyse differences in growth rates between South Australia and Australia over the full period. The results are shown in Table 9.8.

Over the full 17 year period South Australian GSP grew at 74.2 per cent compared with growth in Australian GDP at 92.6 per cent. The fastest growing industry in Australia as well as in South Australia was Finance and Insurance (717.8 per cent and 620.0 per cent, respectively). Property and Business Services also produced a high rate of growth within the state (197.5 per cent) and nationally (229.7 per cent). Mining industry was the third highest contributor of growth in South Australia (181.8 per cent), unlike in Australia, however, this industry grew only 70.1 per cent in 17 years.

Most of the 18.4 percentage point deficiency in South Australia's real output growth, in fact 13.5 per cent, is attributed to differences in growth rates for individual industries when compared with the Australian average. Only four industries in South Australia grew faster than nationally, that were Agriculture ($^+$1.8 percentage points), Mining ($^+$1.6 percentage points), Manufacturing ($^+$1.5 percentage points) and Electricity, Gas and Water ($^+$1.3 percentage points). On the other hand, among the largest negative contributors were Construction ($^-$3.1 percentage points), and Health and Community Services ($^-$2.5 percentage points), Wholesale Trade ($^-$2.4 percentage points) and Retail Trade ($^-$2.3 percentage points).

Table 9.8
Decomposition of Growth in Real Output by Industry
South Australia and Australia, 1982-83 to 1998-99

Industry	Industry Growth	Industry Composit-ion	Total Shift	Growth Over Period (%) 1982/83-1998/99	
	Per Cent	Per Cent	Per Cent	Sth. Aust.	Australia
Agriculture	1.79	-0.26	1.53	106.21	69.40
Mining	1.61	0.75	2.37	181.77	70.12
Manufacturing	1.54	-0.85	0.69	49.85	42.11
Electricity, gas & water	1.33	-0.02	1.30	52.31	19.10
Construction	-3.07	-0.02	-3.09	27.17	67.25
Wholesale trade	-2.43	0.01	-2.42	41.51	85.17
Retail trade	-2.31	-0.42	-2.73	25.70	52.52
Accommodation, cafes & restaurants	-0.28	-0.06	-0.34	130.84	147.02
Transport & storage	-0.41	0.07	-0.34	67.16	74.65
Communication services	-0.42	-0.25	-0.67	140.51	162.28
Finance and insurance	-1.19	-1.89	-3.07	620.04	717.83
Property and business services	-1.61	-1.92	-3.53	197.47	229.68
Government administration & defence	-1.25	0.09	-1.16	36.61	66.28
Education	-1.10	-0.20	-1.30	45.56	63.82
Health & community services	-2.53	0.12	-2.41	66.64	99.04
Cultural & recreational services	-0.75	-0.02	-0.77	103.76	156.13
Personal & other services	-0.51	0.14	-0.37	115.91	138.61
Ownership of dwellings	-1.74	-0.07	-1.82	84.97	106.53
General government	-0.18	-0.05	-0.23	46.47	52.78
All industries	**-13.51**	**-4.84**	**-18.36**	**74.22**	**92.57**

Source: ABS catalogue no. 5220.0 (various years); SACES calculations.

The other component which contributes -4.8 percentage points to the total difference in growth rates is the industry composition. That is to say, South Australia has a larger share of those industries which were growing more slowly, like Retail Trade (9 per cent share but only grew at 26 per cent growth and -0.4 percentage points). Alternatively the state has only a small number of the industries which grew rapidly, such as Mining (1 per cent share, 182 per cent growth and +0.8 percentage points). The Table Appendix 9.1 presents the industry share regionally and nationally.

One of the limitations of this type of analysis relates to the aggregated level of the data used. There are always sub-sectors within each industry which perform at higher or lower levels than the total industry. For example Machinery and Equipment sub-sector industry performs better than overall Manufacturing industry (Table 9.3). The analysis tells us nothing of the contribution of these smaller groups to overall differences in growth. The effects of industry composition are therefore clouded to some extent and of course the same argument is relevant to the contribution of smaller sub-sectors to differences in industry growth rates.

Two Period Analysis

Using a long period of time for the analysis can also mask changes because the analysis relies on the share of industry in the base year and assumes no change to this share over the period of the analysis. Variations in the business cycle can also be reflected in the growth patterns of industry sectors.

For this reason the analysis for South Australia was repeated using the same data but breaking the period into two sub-periods, namely a six year period from 1982-83 to 1988-89 inclusive and a 11 year period from 1989-90 to 1998-99 inclusive. There are valid reasons supporting the choice of June 1989 to break the series. The first of these is evidenced by Figure 9.1 which graphs the GDP/GSP of Australia and South Australia in index form over the full period of the data. In the first period, South Australian index exceeds Australian index.

Figure 9.1
Real GDP/GSP at Factor Cost
Australia and South Australia - 1982-83 to 1998-99

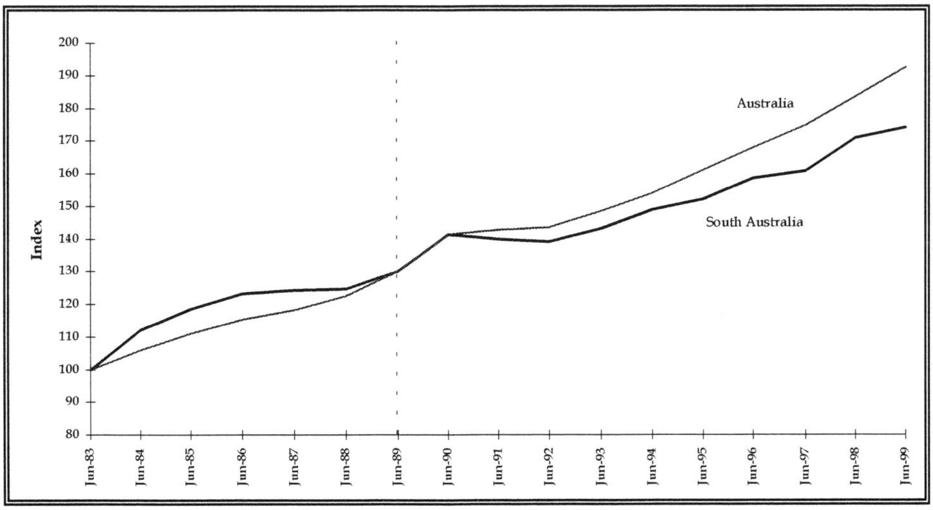

Source: Derived from ABS, Cat. no. 5220.0 (various years)

The first of these periods is a period of high growth with only slight differences between the rates for Australia and South Australia (30.2 and 30.1 per cent respectively, Table 9.9). The difference of 0.1 percentage points in favour of South Australia can be decomposed into the two components. Here again the major part ($^{+}$0.5 percentage points of difference) results from the industry growth. The top two region positive contributors are Mining (+2.2 percentage point) and Manufacturing (+2.3 percentage point). Mining grew rapidly over this period which included the expansion of Roxby Downs. Manufacturing also grew at rates well above the national average.

The industry growth component for this first period is positive (+0.5 percentage points) and counteracts the smaller negative impact of the industry composition factor (-0.4 percentage points). South Australia has a lower than average share of total production, o again the lower share contributes to our slower rate of growth.

South Australia's growth in the second period is slower growth than in the first period, that is, 23.4 per cent compared with 30.2 per cent. South Australia's growth in the second period is also slower than national growth, that is, 23.4 per cent compared with 36.4 per cent. From this state's perspective this is 13.0 percentage points below the national average. This number is relatively high compared to the total favourable shift in period one (+0.1 above national average).

The shift-share analysis for the second period shows an entirely different picture from the first one. The major component of this difference from the national average is the industry growth component. This component contributes a high 12.1 percentage points negative in contrast to the positive contribution (+0.45 percentage points) in the previous period. Only two South Australian industry sectors show growth rates above the national growth namely, Agriculture and Electricity, Gas and Water. These sector growth rates decline nationally. Both sectors are also the only positive contributors of the shift in the region. Among the negative contributors are Manufacturing (-2.1 percentage points), Construction (-1.6 percentage points) and Health and Community Services (-1.5 percentage points). The contribution of the industry composition component is significantly much smaller (-0.8 percentage points). Agriculture and Manufacturing are among those that have unfavourable industry compositions. Meanwhile, Mining and Health and Community Services show favourable industry compositions.

Agricultural sector growth in the second period has been much slower than in the first period both in South Australia and Australia, from 60.1 to 10.4 per cent and 61.6 to -2.7 per cent, respectively. In both periods growth South Australian Agricultural sector has been stronger than the nation. This is shown by the favourable total shift toward the region. Its industry composition contributes to the faster growth in the first period (0.4 percentage points), while its industry growth takes over the contribution in the second period (0.8 percentage points).

Table 9.9
Decomposition of Growth in Real Output by Industry
Differences between South Australia and Australia, 1982-83 to 1988-89 and 1989-90 to 1998-99

Industry	South Australian Real GSP				Australian Real GDP				Shift (%)		
	1982/83	1998/99	Growth	Share (82/83)	1982/83	1998/99	Growth	Share (82/83)	Industry growth	Industry composit-ion	Total
Agriculture	1,006	2,075	106.21	0.0486	10,173	17,233	69.40	0.0373	1.7899	-0.2615	1.5283
Mining	299	843	181.77	0.0145	13,043	22,188	70.12	0.0479	1.6147	0.7506	2.3654
Manufacturing	4,104	6,150	49.85	0.1984	49,481	70,316	42.11	0.1817	1.5361	-0.8455	0.6906
Electricity, gas and water	826	1,258	52.31	0.0399	10,790	12,852	19.10	0.0396	1.3264	-0.0239	1.3025
Construction	1,583	2,013	27.17	0.0765	20,578	34,418	67.25	0.0756	-3.0674	-0.0247	-3.0921
Wholesale trade	1,152	1,630	41.51	0.0557	15,682	29,038	85.17	0.0576	-2.4318	0.0139	-2.4179
Retail trade	1,781	2,238	25.70	0.0861	20,578	31,386	52.52	0.0756	-2.3088	-0.4218	-2.7306
Accommodation, cafes and restaurants	356	822	130.84	0.0172	4,987	12,320	147.02	0.0183	-0.2786	-0.0596	-0.3382
Transport and storage	1,143	1,911	67.16	0.0553	16,109	28,134	74.65	0.0591	-0.4136	0.0695	-0.3441
Communication services	402	968	140.51	0.0195	6,266	16,435	162.28	0.0230	-0.4236	-0.2475	-0.6711
Finance and insurance	251	1,808	620.04	0.0121	4,127	33,756	717.83	0.0152	-1.1870	-1.8857	-3.0727
Property and business services	1,033	3,072	197.47	0.0499	17,423	57,441	229.68	0.0640	-1.6082	-1.9250	-3.5332
Government administration and defence	872	1,192	36.61	0.0422	12,468	20,731	66.28	0.0458	-1.2512	0.0945	-1.1567
Education	1,245	1,812	45.56	0.0602	14,521	23,789	63.82	0.0533	-1.0988	-0.1972	-1.2960
Health and community services	1,615	2,691	66.64	0.0781	16,155	32,156	99.04	0.0593	-2.5294	0.1214	-2.4081
Cultural and recreational services	297	606	103.76	0.0144	3,997	10,239	156.13	0.0147	-0.7529	-0.0191	-0.7720
Personal and other services	463	1,000	115.91	0.0224	5,256	12,542	138.61	0.0193	-0.5081	0.1419	-0.3661
Ownership of dwellings	1,674	3,096	84.97	0.0809	23,422	48,373	106.53	0.0860	-1.7447	-0.0708	-1.8156
General government	582	853	46.47	0.0281	7,320	11,184	52.78	0.0269	-0.1778	-0.0507	-0.2285
All industries	**20,685**	**36,037**	**74.22**	**1.0000**	**272,379**	**524,529**	**92.57**	**1.0000**	**-13.5148**	**-4.8412**	**-18.3560**

Source: ABS catalogue no. 5220.0 (various years); SACES estimates.

Manufacturing should have been a strong contributor to growth based on industry share (18 per cent) and earlier growth rates (23.4 per cent), but the general slow-down in domestic demand during the early 90s had a significant effect. Domestic demand for South Australian Manufactured products is heavily influenced by demand in the Eastern states. A slow-down in those markets is felt quite heavily in this State. After 1992, the wine industry, other processed foods and the automotive industry began to grow in response to an increase in their export markets.

Mining, in spite of tremendous growth in South Australia in the earlier period (162.1 per cent), still has a market share below the national average (40 per cent lower). The plummeting growth in the second period (barely 0.5 per cent), in part, reflects a decline in output from the Cooper Basin. It is the national growth (particularly in Western Australia and Queensland) which continues to outstrip growth in this state causing the relatively poor contribution to the difference in growth.

Electricity, Gas & Water has improved its relative contribution in the second period. Its growth in the first period is 6.5 per cent and in the second period is 39.5 percent, a quite significant increase. This has occurred in response to the downsizing of ETSA and the outsourcing and related reduction in employment of the water segment of this sector. Any increases in exports which may flow from the changes in water policy are likely to benefit the Manufacturing and Business services areas rather than this sector which is confined to the supply and distribution of water. Nationally, by contrast, its high growth in the first period (22.5 per cent) does not continue to the following period, which declines to -3.7 per cent.

The growth of Construction sector has been slower in South Australia since the first period. It falls to 10.2 per cent in the second period after twice as high in the earlier period (26.3 per cent). Nationally, the growth is relative constant if not only a slight increase from 34.3 per cent to 36.1 per cent. The regional decline in growth has been more significant resulting in a negative contribution to the overall difference in growth between nation and state. The industry share has also fallen and below the national average.

Wholesale Trade has grown much slower in the second period both regionally and nationally. The slower growth in the region declined more sharply than the nation. South Australia growth rate has fallen from 28.9 to 6.5 per cent, compared to the decline of the nation's growth from 51.9 to 20.4 per cent. The sector's industry share is slightly below the national average, that reflects the use of interstate buyers both for the Retail Trade and for other areas. Retail Trade has also grown slower, but only slightly. It has made a positive contribution to the difference in both periods with a larger than average share. But it is not enough to compensate a negative contribution with a below national average in growth rate in both periods. The share of the Accommodation, Cafes & Restaurants sector has remained virtually unchanged across the two periods but the growth rate has become higher in the second period even though is still well below the national average.

The Transport & Storage sector has changed from a positive to a negative contribution. This is due only to slower growth in the region compared nationally, since the industry share remains the same. The growth rate has declined a little in the second period, while national growth has improved. The growth change in this sector at both state and national level is the result of increased efficiency following continued micro economic reform in the industry. Among other things, the growth in this state can also be linked to the sharp decline in the Wholesale Trade sector and the need to transport goods to and from the Eastern states. Communication, in spite of expansion in the IT sector, still has smaller than average share (possibly reinforced by the reduction in staffing levels for Telstra in South Australia). The growth rate, although still high, has dropped from above to below the national average. This is not only because the region growth rate has been slower, but also the national growth rate has been faster. At the end of the second period, the positive contribution has changed to negative contribution.

Finance & Insurance and Property & Business Services are both expanding sectors. In each industry the share is below the national average, but both have strong growth rates. Their growths are above the regional and national average, even though only the growth of Property and Business Services in the first period shows higher than that nationally.

The Government Administration & Defence sector has been influenced more by reductions in the level of public employment rather than any changes in defence. South Australia has a lower than average share and this difference has increased due to cutbacks at both the Commonwealth and State level. The sector growth rates in South Australia are also below the national average in both periods. The growth rates both regionally and nationally are much faster in the second period.

Education has both a higher than average share and average growth rate but the favourable difference in the share and growth is decreasing. The increase in the provision of Educational services to international students is a growth area in which would have been greater in other states. It would be expected that this contribution would show a gradual increase in South Australia in future. A move towards higher retention rates at school will also contribute to growth for this sector.

The services sectors, namely Health & Community Services, Cultural & Recreational Services and Personal & Other Services on the whole have shares similar to or above the national average together with growth rates very little different from national rates. The growth in Personal Services sector positively contributes to faster growing sector in the region in the first period. This growth though does not continue to the next period due to national high growth.

Ownership of dwellings has not changed a lot over the two periods although this state has both a smaller share and a lower growth rate than the national averages. General Government expenditure (excluding wages and salaries) has returned to positive growth rates for the second period either regionally or nationally. In South Australia the share for this sector is marginally higher, but the growth rate is below the national average. These result in another negative contribution to the total difference in growth.

Separating the analysis into two periods has given an interesting insight into the growth pattern in this state. Between the two base years there has been some quite changes in the growth and shares of the industry sectors. The differences in the South Australian shares compared with national shares when combined with the national average industry growth rates has turned a small positive ($^{+}$0.5) to a high negative ($^{-}$12.1) component for industry growth. Furthermore, it also has increased a small negative ($^{-}$0.4) to another negative ($^{-}$0.8) component for industry shares. By far the bigger component however has resulted from the slowing down in growth rates for the South Australian industry sectors when compared to the national average. This has been the large contributing factor to the big drop-off in South Australian growth rates in the later period.

Summary

South Australia industry share of national output in the last two decades has been changing. The overall industry share has been falling from 7.6 to 6.9 per cent. The sectors: Agriculture, Manufacturing, Electricity, Gas and Water, Health and Community services, and Personal and Other Services still hold the largest share. On the other hand the sectors: Mining, Finance and Insurance, Property and Business services, and Wholesale trade have shares lower than average.

South Australia's and Australia's industry structures in terms of output are different. In comparison to Australia as a whole, the South Australian economics has a higher share of output in Agriculture, Manufacturing, Electricity, Gas and Water, Education, and Health and Community services, and a lower share of Mining, Construction, Wholesale Trade, Finance and Insurance, Property and Business Services, Government Administration and Defence, and Ownership and Dwelling. Retail Trade, Accommodation, Cafés and Restaurants, Transport and Storage, Communication Services, Personal and Other Services, Cultural and Recreational Services, and General Government have much the same share in South Australia's as in Australia as a whole.

High growth industries in both South Australia and Australia include Finance and Insurance, Property and Business Services, Personal and Other Services, Accommodation, Cafés and Restaurants, and Communication services. None of these industries grew faster in South Australia than in the nation. Low growth industries were Construction, Retail Trade, Electricity, Gas and Water, Mining, Manufacturing, and Agriculture. With Agriculture Manufacturing, and Electricity, Gas and Water grew a little faster in South Australia than in Australia. On average, growth in output in South Australia was lower than in Australia.

South Australia's economy is more concentrated in Agriculture and less concentrated in Mining. A set of industries under-represented in South Australia, but only mildly so include Wholesale Trade, Accommodation, Cafés and Restaurants, Transport and Storage, Communication Services, Finance and Insurance, Cultural and Recreation Services, and Ownership and Dwelling. Those mildly over-represented are Retail Trade, Education, and General Government.

South Australia's growth over the period 1982-83 to 1988-89 was 30.2 per cent and over the period 1989-90 to 1988-99 was 23.4 per cent. That is, the growth in the second period was slower than in the first. For Australia the growth rates were, respectively, 30.1 per cent and 36.4 per cent. That is, South Australia's growth rate was lower than Australia's in both periods. Also, in the second period, the rate of growth slowed for South Australia in contrast with faster growth for Australia.

Shift share analysis is an appropriate tool to diagnose to what extent the poorer performance of the South Australian economy attributable to the differences in its industry structure and to what extent do differences in the growth rates of each industry in South Australia and Australia.

The analysis shows that while industry structure may have played some part in the lower growth of South Australia's relatively poor economic performance, the unfavourable industry growth have played more dominant role. Breaking the analysis into two periods it explains further that the second period is when the South Australian economic more severe. And the favourable industry growth turned to unfavourable.

Appendix 9.1

Shift-Share Analysis Methodology

This appendix present methodology and data processing in applying shift-share analysis of South Australian and Australian growth rates (adopted and modified from Blandy et.al., 1994 and LMEA (1995).

Methodology

South Australian output in industry i is represented as q_i and Australian output in industry i as Q_i. Total output in South Australia is q while total output in Australia is Q.

The South Australian output increment over the period t^o to t in industry i is $q_i^{t^o t}$ and national output increment in industry i is $Q_i^{t^o t}$.

$$\Delta q_i^{t^o t} = q_i^t - q_i^{t^o} \tag{1}$$

$$\Delta Q_i^{t^o t} = Q_i^t - Q_i^{t^o} \tag{2}$$

Regional output growth over the period t^o to t in industry i is g_i and national output
growth in industry i is G_i. Thus the regional growth rate for industry i may be defined,

$$g_i^{t^o t} = \frac{q_i^t - q_i^{t^o}}{q_i^{t^o}} = \frac{\Delta q_i^{t^o t}}{q_i^{t^o}} \tag{3}$$

while the national growth rate for industry *i* is simply,

$$G_i^{t^o t} = \frac{Q_i^t - Q_i^{t^o}}{Q_i^{t^o}} = \frac{\Delta Q_i^{t^o t}}{Q_i^{t^o}} \tag{4}$$

The total economy is the sum of output in industries. The growth in the economy is the share weighted sum of the growth in the component industries. Thus,

$$g^{t^o t} = \sum_i s_i^{t^o} g_i^{t^o t} \tag{5}$$

and

$$G^{t^o t} = \sum_i S_i^{t^o} G_i^{t^o t} \tag{6}$$

are the economy growth for South Australia and nationally, respectively.

Where $s_i^{t^o}$ and $S_i^{t^o}$ are the *base-period* share of industry *i* in the South Australian and national economy, i.e.,

$$s_i^{t^o} = \frac{q_i^{t^o}}{q^{t^o}} \tag{7}$$

and

$$S_i^{t^o} = \frac{Q_i^{t^o}}{Q^{t^o}} \tag{8}$$

Subtracting (6) to (5) yields the difference in the growth rate between South Australia and Australia;

$$g^{t^o t} - G^{t^o t} = \sum_i s_i^{t^o} g_i^{t^o t} - \sum_i S_i^{t^o} G_i^{t^o t} \tag{9}$$

Adding and subtracting $\sum_i s_i^{t^o} G_i^{t^o t}$ term to equation (9) yield;

$$g^{t^o t} - G^{t^o t} = \sum_i s_i^{t^o} g_i^{t^o t} - \sum_i S_i^{t^o} G_i^{t^o t} + \sum_i s_i^{t^o} G_i^{t^o t} - \sum_i s_i^{t^o} G_i^{t^o t}$$

$$g^{t^o t} - G^{t^o t} = \sum_i s_i^{t^o} (g_i^{t^o t} - G_i^{t^o t}) + \sum_i s_i^{t^o} G_i^{t^o t} - \sum_i S_i^{t^o} G_i^{t^o t} \tag{10}$$

Since $\sum_i S_i^{t^o} = 1$ and $\sum_i s_i^{t^o} = 1$, then $\sum_i S_i^{t^o} G^{t^o t} = \sum_i s_i^{t^o} G^{t^o t}$, therefore,

$$g^{t^o t} - G^{t^o t} = \left[\sum_i s_i^{t^o}\left(g_i^{t^o t} - G_i^{t^o t}\right)\right] + \left[\sum_i \left(s_i^{t^o} - S_i^{t^o}\right)\left(G_i^{t^o t} - G^{t^o t}\right)\right] \quad (11)$$

The last equation (11) shows that the growth between two economies, Australia and South Australia, can be decomposed into two term. The first term, the first bracket, is called "industry growth". The second term, the second bracket, is known as "industry composition". The choice of *base-period* shares, in equations (7) and (8), rather than *period-average* shares, or *end-period* shares, is a matter of convenience.

Industry growth is interpreted as differences in growth rates within industry in the two economies. It measures the difference in an industry's growth in the region and that same industry's growth in the nation. For example, the Mining industry is growing much faster in South Australia than it is in the rest of Australia. Thus the industry growth for the Mining industry in the South Australia region would be large and positive. The industry growth is calculated as the difference between regional and national growth rates multiplied by the regional output in that industry. Thus industry growth is actually expressed as an output added or lost in an industry in a region as a result of the industry in the region growing faster (slower) than the national growth rate in that industry.

The following tables are the data sources and the calculation of shift-share analysis for South Australia an Australia as a whole.

Table Appendix 9.1
Decomposition of Growth in Real Output by Industry
Differences between South Australia and Australia, 1982/83 to 1998/99

Industry	South Australian Real GSP				Australian Real GDP				Shift (%)		
	1982/83	1998/99	Growth	Share (82/83)	1982/83	1998/99	Growth	Share (82/83)	Industry growth	Industry composition	Total
Agriculture	1,006	2,075	106.21	0.0486	10,173	17,233	69.40	0.0373	1.7899	-0.2615	1.5283
Mining	299	843	181.77	0.0145	13,043	22,188	70.12	0.0479	1.6147	0.7506	2.3654
Manufacturing	4,104	6,150	49.85	0.1984	49,481	70,316	42.11	0.1817	1.5361	-0.8455	0.6906
Electricity, gas and water	826	1,258	52.31	0.0399	10,790	12,852	19.10	0.0396	1.3264	-0.0239	1.3025
Construction	1,583	2,013	27.17	0.0765	20,578	34,418	67.25	0.0756	-3.0674	-0.0247	-3.0921
Wholesale trade	1,152	1,630	41.51	0.0557	15,682	29,038	85.17	0.0576	-2.4318	0.0139	-2.4179
Retail trade	1,781	2,238	25.70	0.0861	20,578	31,386	52.52	0.0756	-2.3088	-0.4218	-2.7306
Accommodation, cafes and restaurants	356	822	130.84	0.0172	4,987	12,320	147.02	0.0183	-0.2786	-0.0596	-0.3382
Transport and storage	1,143	1,911	67.16	0.0553	16,109	28,134	74.65	0.0591	-0.4136	0.0695	-0.3441
Communication services	402	968	140.51	0.0195	6,266	16,435	162.28	0.0230	-0.4236	-0.2475	-0.6711
Finance and insurance	251	1,808	620.04	0.0121	4,127	33,756	717.83	0.0152	-1.1870	-1.8857	-3.0727
Property and business services	1,033	3,072	197.47	0.0499	17,423	57,441	229.68	0.0640	-1.6082	-1.9250	-3.5332
Government administration and defence	872	1,192	36.61	0.0422	12,468	20,731	66.28	0.0458	-1.2512	0.0945	-1.1567
Education	1,245	1,812	45.56	0.0602	14,521	23,789	63.82	0.0533	-1.0988	-0.1972	-1.2960
Health and community services	1,615	2,691	66.64	0.0781	16,155	32,156	99.04	0.0593	-2.5294	0.1214	-2.4081
Cultural and recreational services	297	606	103.76	0.0144	3,997	10,239	156.13	0.0147	-0.7529	-0.0191	-0.7720
Personal and other services	463	1,000	115.91	0.0224	5,256	12,542	138.61	0.0193	-0.5081	0.1419	-0.3661
Ownership of dwellings	1,674	3,096	84.97	0.0809	23,422	48,373	106.53	0.0860	-1.7447	-0.0708	-1.8156
General government	582	853	46.47	0.0281	7,320	11,184	52.78	0.0269	-0.1778	-0.0507	-0.2285
All industries	**20,685**	**36,037**	**74.22**	**1.0000**	**272,379**	**524,529**	**92.57**	**1.0000**	**-13.5148**	**-4.8412**	**-18.3560**

Source: ABS catalogue no. 5220.0 (various years); SACES calculations.

Table Appendix 9.2
Decomposition of Growth in Real Output by Industry
Differences between South Australia and Australia, 1982/83 to 1988-89

Industry	South Australian Real GSP				Australian Real GDP				Shift (%)		
	1982/83	1988/89	Growth	Share (82/83)	1982/83	1988/89	Growth	Share (82/83)	Industry growth	Industry composition	Total
Agriculture	1,006	1,615	60.55	0.0486	10,173	16,436	61.57	0.0373	-0.0494	0.3557	0.3063
Mining	299	784	162.05	0.0145	13,043	13,999	7.33	0.0479	2.2375	0.7599	2.9974
Manufacturing	4,104	5,066	23.44	0.1984	49,481	55,463	12.09	0.1817	2.2518	-0.3011	1.9507
Electricity, gas and water	826	880	6.51	0.0399	10,790	13,212	22.45	0.0396	-0.6366	-0.0025	-0.6391
Construction	1,583	1,999	26.31	0.0765	20,578	27,652	34.38	0.0756	-0.6170	0.0042	-0.6128
Wholesale trade	1,152	1,485	28.88	0.0557	15,682	23,812	51.85	0.0576	-1.2790	-0.0409	-1.3200
Retail trade	1,781	2,270	27.48	0.0861	20,578	27,956	35.85	0.0756	-0.7208	0.0609	-0.6598
Accommodation, cafes and restaurants	356	440	23.55	0.0172	4,987	6,889	38.13	0.0183	-0.2510	-0.0088	-0.2598
Transport and storage	1,143	1,492	30.51	0.0553	16,109	20,569	27.68	0.0591	0.1561	0.0092	0.1653
Communication services	402	606	50.59	0.0195	6,266	9,094	45.13	0.0230	0.1063	-0.0535	0.0528
Finance and insurance	251	544	116.81	0.0121	4,127	9,827	138.08	0.0152	-0.2581	-0.3258	-0.5839
Property and business services	1,033	1,791	73.40	0.0499	17,423	28,601	64.15	0.0640	0.4614	-0.4787	-0.0173
Government administration and defence	872	892	2.21	0.0422	12,468	13,964	12.00	0.0458	-0.4129	0.0649	-0.3480
Education	1,245	1,334	7.19	0.0602	14,521	16,065	10.63	0.0533	-0.2069	-0.1333	-0.3402
Health and community services	1,615	1,954	21.02	0.0781	16,155	19,769	22.37	0.0593	-0.1058	-0.1443	-0.2501
Cultural and recreational services	297	384	29.22	0.0144	3,997	5,299	32.55	0.0147	-0.0479	-0.0007	-0.0487
Personal and other services	463	585	26.29	0.0224	5,256	6,232	18.56	0.0193	0.1729	-0.0355	0.1375
Ownership of dwellings	1,674	2,251	34.48	0.0809	23,422	32,222	37.57	0.0860	-0.2500	-0.0381	-0.2881
General government	582	553	-5.09	0.0281	7,320	7,202	-1.61	0.0269	-0.0978	-0.0403	-0.1382
All industries	**20,685**	**26,925**	**30.17**	**1.0000**	**272,379**	**354,263**	**30.06**	**1.0000**	**0.4528**	**-0.3487**	**0.1041**

Source: ABS catalogue no. 5220.0 (various years); SACES calculations.

Table Appendix 9.3
Decomposition of Growth in Real Output by Industry
Differences between South Australia and Australia, 1989/90 to 1998/99

Industry	South Australian Real GSP				Australian Real GDP				Shift (%)		
	1989/90	1998/99	Growth	Share (89/90)	1989/90	1998/99	Growth	Share (89/90)	Industry growth	Industry composition	Total
Agriculture	1,879	2,075	10.42	0.0644	17,713	17,233	-2.71	0.0461	0.8445	-0.7153	0.1292
Mining	839	843	0.46	0.0287	18,475	22,188	20.10	0.0480	-0.5644	0.3146	-0.2498
Manufacturing	5,373	6,150	14.47	0.1840	55,945	70,316	25.69	0.1455	-2.0638	-0.4127	-2.4765
Electricity, gas and water	902	1,258	39.48	0.0309	13,341	12,852	-3.67	0.0347	1.3334	0.1519	1.4853
Construction	1,827	2,013	10.19	0.0626	25,297	34,418	36.06	0.0658	-1.6190	0.0011	-1.6179
Wholesale trade	1,530	1,630	6.53	0.0524	24,118	29,038	20.40	0.0627	-0.7271	0.1647	-0.5624
Retail trade	1,824	2,238	22.73	0.0625	22,964	31,386	36.67	0.0597	-0.8705	0.0008	-0.8697
Accommodation, cafes and restaurants	554	822	48.46	0.0190	7,710	12,320	59.79	0.0200	-0.2148	-0.0254	-0.2401
Transport and storage	1,518	1,911	25.89	0.0520	21,274	28,134	32.25	0.0553	-0.3307	0.0138	-0.3168
Communication services	692	968	39.77	0.0237	9,996	16,435	64.40	0.0260	-0.5842	-0.0638	-0.6480
Finance and insurance	1,173	1,808	54.13	0.0402	18,944	33,756	78.19	0.0493	-0.9663	-0.3799	-1.3461
Property and business services	2,348	3,072	30.84	0.0804	39,524	57,441	45.33	0.1028	-1.1653	-0.1998	-1.3650
Government administration and defence	950	1,192	25.53	0.0325	14,326	20,731	44.71	0.0373	-0.6240	-0.0393	-0.6633
Education	1,448	1,812	25.12	0.0496	16,641	23,789	42.95	0.0433	-0.8845	0.0414	-0.8430
Health and community services	2,050	2,691	31.27	0.0702	21,116	32,156	52.28	0.0549	-1.4757	0.2433	-1.2324
Cultural and recreational services	400	606	51.34	0.0137	5,851	10,239	75.00	0.0152	-0.3244	-0.0580	-0.3824
Personal and other services	734	1,000	36.15	0.0251	7,559	12,542	65.92	0.0197	-0.7485	0.1620	-0.5865
Ownership of dwellings	2,462	3,096	25.75	0.0843	34,885	48,373	38.67	0.0907	-1.0888	-0.0145	-1.1033
General government	694	853	22.96	0.0238	8,884	11,184	25.88	0.0231	-0.0694	-0.0069	-0.0762
All industries	**29,196**	**36,037**	**23.43**	**1.0000**	**384,564**	**524,529**	**36.40**	**1.0000**	**-12.1433**	**-0.8218**	**-12.9651**

Source: ABS catalogue no. 5220.0 (various years); SACES calculations.

References

Armstrong, Harvey and Taylor, Jim (1978), *Regional Economic Policy and Its Analysis*, P. Allan, Oxford.

Blandy, R, Carne, S, Johnson, D and Kenyon, P (1994), "Economic Growth and the Victorian Economy: A Medium-Term Perspective", Institute of Applied Economic and Social Research Working Paper Series.

Department of Geography (2000), "Shift and Share Model of Regional Growth", The University of Lethbridge, Canada [Online, accessed 01/08/2000]. URL:http://www.linc.uleth.ca/geo/Shiftshare.htm.

Harris, A.H., Lloyd, M.G., McGuire, A.J. and Newlands, D.A. (1987), "Incoming Industry and Structural Change: Oil and the Aberdeen Economy", *Scottish Journal of Political Economy*, Vol.34(1):69-90.

Hoover, E.M. and Giarratani, F. (1999), "An Introduction to Regional Economics". [Online, accessed 01/08/2000].URL:http://www.wvu.edu/~regional/WebBook/Giarratani.

Labor Market and Economic Analysis (LMEA) (1995). "Kitsap County: Shift-Share Analysis", Branch of the Washington State Employment Security Department. [Online, accessed 31/07/2000]. URL:http://www.kitsap.net/chamber/demographics/kits10.html.

Moore, B. and Rhodes, J. (1973), "Evaluating the Effects of Britain's Regional Economic Policy", *Economic Journal*, March: 87-110.

Stilwell, F.J.B (1968), "Location of Industry and Business Efficiency", *Business Ratios*.

Wood, G.A and Bushe-Jones, S. (1989), "Employment Growth in Western Australia: A Shift-Share Analysis", Economic Programme Working Papers, Murdoch University.

Chapter Ten

Trade

In this chapter we turn to the influence of trade on the growth of the regional economy. Trade enables the region to specialise its production. Trade is also an important medium for exchange of new products, new ideas and knowledge about the external environment which assists a region in the continuous process of renewal and growth. Exports are a means of expanding production and employment beyond domestic requirements, and provides the means to acquire goods and services from foreign countries that cannot be efficiently produced in the region. Building on earlier discussion in this book on the importance of openness of an economy to trade as a driver of regional growth, this chapter examines South Australian trade. In particular, the growth of the tradeable goods sector and the degree of diversity in trade both in terms of production and international markets are examined.

Introduction

Over two centuries ago, David Ricardo emphasised that trade is important to increasing welfare. He showed that even though one country might be (absolutely) more efficient than another at producing every item, there are gains for them both from some specialisation in production and trade, exploiting differences between them in the *relative* efficiency (and hence relative costs) of producing different goods and services.

Australia has not always recognised this principle, but for many decades during the 20th century attempted to gain economic advantages through trade controls such as tariffs and subsidies. By altering the relative prices of traded goods and services, these affected the patterns of both production and of trade. With notable exceptions in the 1920s and 1930s, Australia (and South Australia) have been small to very minor players in most international markets and, as such, lacked the economic clout to be able to affect world prices and thus, terms of trade. It has only been since the 1970s that this fact and the fallacy of protectionist policies have been more generally recognised in Australia, and a more outward-looking trade policy adopted. Consequently, tariffs and other protection measures have been progressively withdrawn over the past quarter of a century. Various other policies, internationally and domestically, have, in turn, affected the composition and direction of Australian exports - for example, policies on exchange rates and industrial relations.

The Australian Constitution prevents State governments from imposing tariff and non-tariff barriers against imports. Trade policy and the traditional mechanisms by which to affect trade (ie., tariffs, quotas etc) are the responsibility of the Australian federal government. Trade policy at the regional level is therefore often confined to the promotion and facilitation of strategic trade development, particularly with regard to identifying and developing export industries. In this respect, the following section examines trends in South Australian trade whilst paying particular attention to the State's export performance in the context of a small regional economy that wields no influence, through regulatory or market mechanisms, on the composition and direction of external trade.

Overall Trend in Tradeable Goods

The openness of a regional economy to international markets significantly influences the extent to which it may potentially experience the consumption, production and employment benefits associated with trade. Openness refers to the regulatory environment governing international trade, or more specifically, the existing level of tariff and non-tariff barriers pertinent to an economy. Although a regional economy may be relatively open in a regulatory sense, there may exist natural impediments that limit a region's ability to engage in international trade activity (i.e., cultural and geographic impediments such as language barriers and geographic isolation).

Several measures of openness exist which indicate the general level of external trade barriers pertinent to an economy, the most relevant of which are direct measures of the general level of tariff and non-tariff barriers. Indicators of the openness of selected OECD markets are provided in Table 10.1 in the form of the average tariff rate and proportion of imports subject to non-tariff barriers (e.g., quotas). From these indicators, it is immediately apparent that regulatory barriers to Australian markets have fallen substantially over time. In short, Australian markets have become more "open" to imports of foreign goods and services. Specifically, in 1988-89 Australia levied the highest average tariff rate (11.2 per cent) of all countries listed in Table 10.1; however, by 1996 trade liberalisation had reduced Australia's average tariff rate to 4.2 per cent - the second lowest of the countries listed: and reduced the proportion of imports subject to non-tariff barriers to a level lower than that of any country shown in the table. Meanwhile, average tariff rates have in fact increased in some countries due to "tarifficiation" of import barriers (ie., replacement of non-tariff barriers such as quotas, which substantially distort trade and reduce market access, with less trade-distorting tariffs in order to increase the transparency of border measures). Australian arguably, therefore, had the lowest trade barriers of these OECD countries in 1996.

Table 10.1
Trade-Policy Indicators 1988-96

	Average Tariff Rate,* All Goods			**Non-tariff Barriers, Import Coverage Ratio**		
	1988-89	**1993**	**1996**	**1988**	**1993**	**1996**
United States	4.4	4.7	5.2	16.7	17.0	7.7
European Union	8.2	8.4	7.7	13.2	11.1	6.7
Japan	4.2	3.6	3.4	8.6	8.1	7.4
Canada	8.7	8.4	12.1	5.7	4.5	4.0
Norway	5.3	4.0	22.3	13.8	11.1	3.0
Switzerland	4.8	4.5	3.2	13.2	13.2	9.8
Australia	11.2	6.6	4.2	8.9	0.4	0.6
New Zealand	10.6	5.7	5.1	11.5	0.2	0.2
Mexico	11.0	12.9	18.0	18.6	17.4	6.9

Note: * Production weighted.
Source: OECD, Indicators of Tariff and Non-Tariff Trade Barriers, 1997, Paris.

Reductions in trade barriers, in most countries, has certainly promoted growth in Australian and South Australian merchandise trade (see Figure 10.1). Given increased market accessibility and that the prices of tradeables now more closely reflect their true costs of production (following reductions in price distorting trade barriers, economic welfare should have risen as an increased quantity and range of commodities were produced (due to gains associated with specialisation in production), traded, and ultimately consumed within the regions. Expanding the range of goods traded is important to raising the economic welfare of consumers with preferences for diversity in consumption.

An important benefit derived from the reduction in trade barriers would be that increased competition placed on local producers should potentially led to gains in aggregate productivity growth.

The fact that South Australian barriers to trade have fallen significantly in recent decades, however, does not necessarily imply an automatic increase in trade activity and thus acquisition of benefits associated with trade. Ultimately, the extent to which a regional economy successfully participates in international trade activity will be reflected in the actual level of trade conducted with overseas markets. Assessments of diversity in South Australian trade both in terms of the commodities traded and geographic markets serviced are made under following separate profiles of South Australian export and import performance. Figure 10.1 illustrates the path of international merchandise trade (sum of international merchandise exports and imports) for both South Australia and Australia from 1988-89 to 1998-99.

Unfortunately, because to the Australian Bureau of Statistics records as imports of a State all international merchandise released from customs control in that State, the absolute level of South Australian international trade as indicated by Figure 10.1 is substantially understated, since a proportion of South Australian imports are imported via the Eastern States. (No similar effect distorts estimates of exports). A rudimentary estimate of actual South Australian international merchandise imports can be derived by applying the Australian ratio of exports to imports for any particular year, to the South Australian level of exports for that corresponding year. Utilising this approach, on average, South Australian merchandise imports are estimated to be 40 per cent higher than ABS estimates per year, for the past eleven years. Consequently, the true absolute level of South Australian merchandise trade (that is, imports plus exports) was substantially higher than indicated by Figure 10.1 (the true aggregate level of merchandise trade may on average have been 20 per cent larger than indicated in the diagram according to our estimates).

Despite the inadequacies of the import data, South Australian merchandise trade as illustrated in Figure 10.1 may be taken as being indicative of the general trend in merchandise trade growth over time. On this basis, South Australia's and Australia's merchandise trade have both grown strongly since 1988-89, effectively doubling by 1998-99. A doubling would be consistent with the performance of the South Australian export sector relative to the national export sector (see later analysis). On the surface, this suggests that both the national and State economies have opened up to international markets (ie., foreign goods and services) in the past decade and are probably experiencing gains from exchange and specialisation in production. Solid growth in merchandise over the past decade is explained not only by trade liberalisation, but a range of factors including terms of trade effects in domestic and foreign markets (for example, the recent low inflationary environment would have improved the relative competitiveness of Australian producers).

Figure 10.1
International Merchandise Trade of Goods
South Australia and Australia - 1988-89 to 1998-99

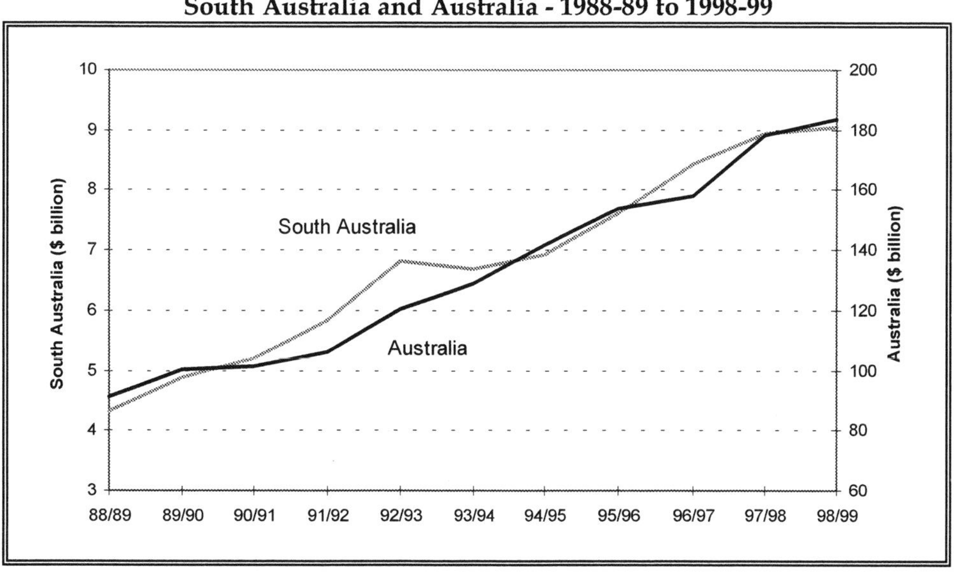

Source: ABS, *AUSSTATS*, International Trade and South Australian Economic Indicators (1307.4)

The substantial increases in the international merchandise trade of Australia and South Australia suggests that trade has become increasingly important to growth of the domestic economy. Figure 10.2 reveals that local economic activity has definitely become more dependent on international markets by illustrating the increased proportion of Gross Domestic Product accounted for by international trade for both South Australia and Australia. This trend would suggest that the scope for the South Australian and National economies to derive the various benefits associated with trade (e.g., exploitation of comparative advantage and economies of scale, increased exposure of local producers to competition and increased generation and diffusion of knowledge) improved. Quantifying these benefits is beyond the scope of this chapter.

In view of the imperfections in State-level merchandise imports data, outlined above, no comparison has been made of international merchandise trade along State lines. The reality is that estimates of merchandise imports and hence total trade will be overstated for some States and understated for others, consequently diminishing the accuracy of any comparative analysis. However, since South Australian merchandise trade has grown in line with the corresponding national aggregate and as South Australia's export sector has certainly performed strongly relative to the national sector, it may be concluded that South Australia's overall trade performance compares favourably to that of other States. (State comparisons of trade performance, particularly in relation to exports, are further explored under the separate assessments of trends in South Australian exports.)

Figure 10.2
International Merchandise Trade as Percentage of GSP or GDP
South Australia and Australia - 1989-90 to 1998-99

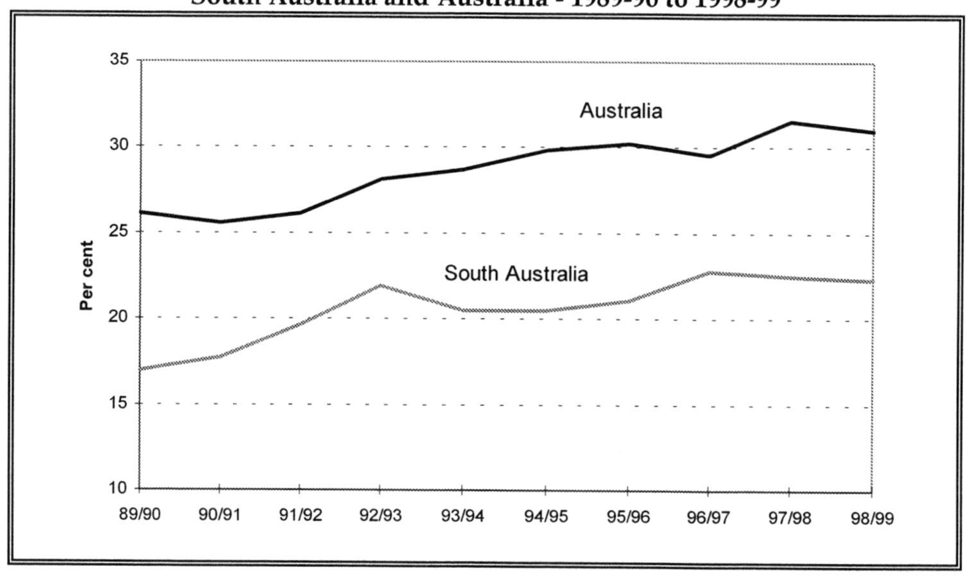

Source: ABS, AUSSTATS, International Trade and Australian National Accounts, State Accounts and South Australian Economic Indicators (1307.4)

Overall Trends in South Australian Merchandise Exports

Exports offer substantial economic development advantages to regional economies through the opportunity to expand production and therefore employment levels significantly beyond the limitations imposed by the domestic market. Such exports would include goods traded to other Australian States; unfortunately the absence of relevant data prevents any further analysis (but it is the case that South Australian imports to other Australian states and territories exceed its imports abroad). Besides, international markets are substantially larger than Australian domestic markets, and therefore present greater economic development opportunities for businesses in regional economies. However, a region's ability to engage individual international markets successfully will depend significantly upon the region's comparative advantages and the presence of competitors within overseas markets.

South Australia's merchandise export performance has been very impressive since the early 1980s (see Figure 10.3), with an the average annual rate of growth of 9.6 per cent. By comparison, average annual growth in Australian exports was 9.1 per cent over the period. Contrary to the impression given by the generally negative view of South Australia's overall economic performance through this period, South Australia's exports increased slightly faster than did total Australian exports. South Australia's export performance was achieved in the absence of the vast mineral wealth that exists in Western Australia and the depth of manufacturing activity in Victoria and New South Wales. The performance of the South Australian export sector relative to other States is depicted in Figure 10.4.

Figure 10.3
Annual Growth in Exports
South Australia and Australia - 1982-83 to 1997-98

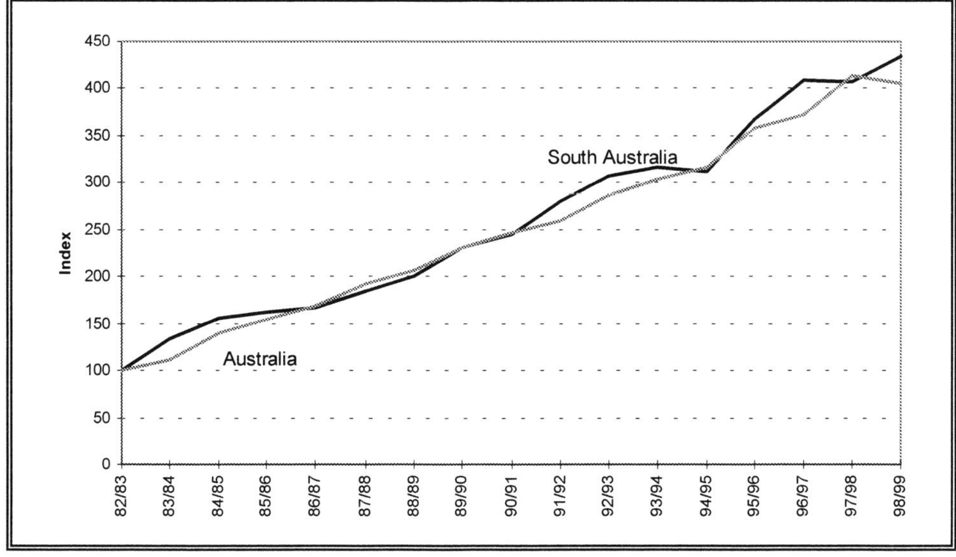

Note:* 12 months ended 31 March, 1998. Prices of the day.
Source: ABS, *AUSSTATS Foreign Trade* and South *Australian Economic Indicators (1307.4).*

Figure 10.4
Index of Merchandise Exports by State: 1988-89 to 1999-00

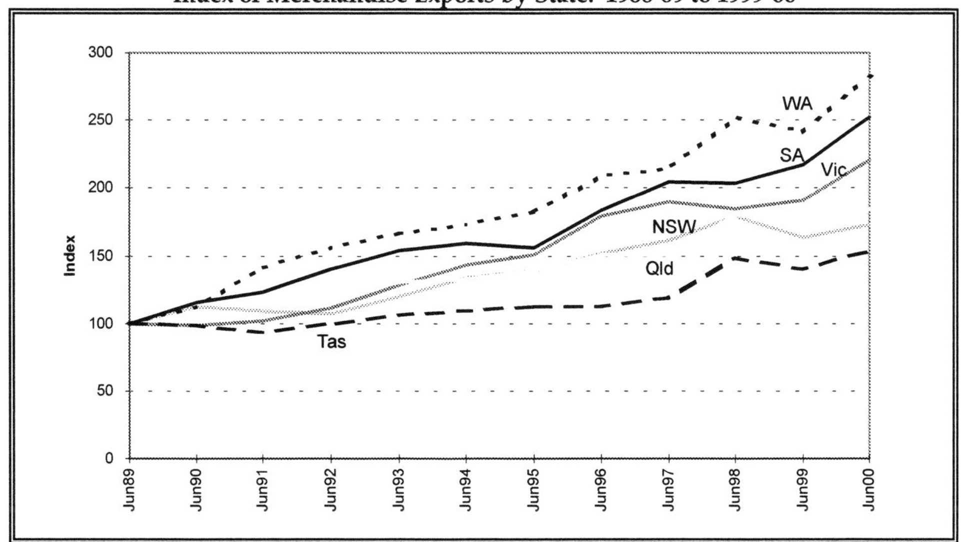

Note: Prices of the day.
Source: ABS, AUSSTATS, International Trade.

In money value, since 1988-89, South Australian exports increased by $2.9 billion, from $2.45 billion to a record level of $5.33 billion in 1998-99. Exports have therefore been an important avenue to substantially boosting local production (economic) activity and to a lesser extent, employment levels and local incomes within export industries, over the past decade.

It should be noted that the data available through the Australian Bureau of Statistics for merchandise exports by State refer only to goods whose *final production* was in that State. Thus, to the extent that South Australia produced goods, which were sold interstate, and *then* incorporated as a component into a good that was later exported, the ABS statistics under-estimate South Australia's contribution to Australia's international exports. By the same token, South Australian international merchandise exports would include a component of goods originally produced interstate.

It is apparent from Figure 10.3 that South Australia's export growth has experienced some significant fluctuations over time. In part, this pattern reflects that external factors significantly influence a large proportion of South Australian exports, a common feature for small regional economies that possess no market power in terms of affecting world prices and thus terms of trade. There are also seasonal factors - rural commodities compose a significant proportion of South Australian exports and are highly dependent on year to year seasonal conditions and international trade cycles.

Figure 10.5
Exports as Percentage of GSP or GDP
South Australia & Australia - 1987-88 to 1998-99

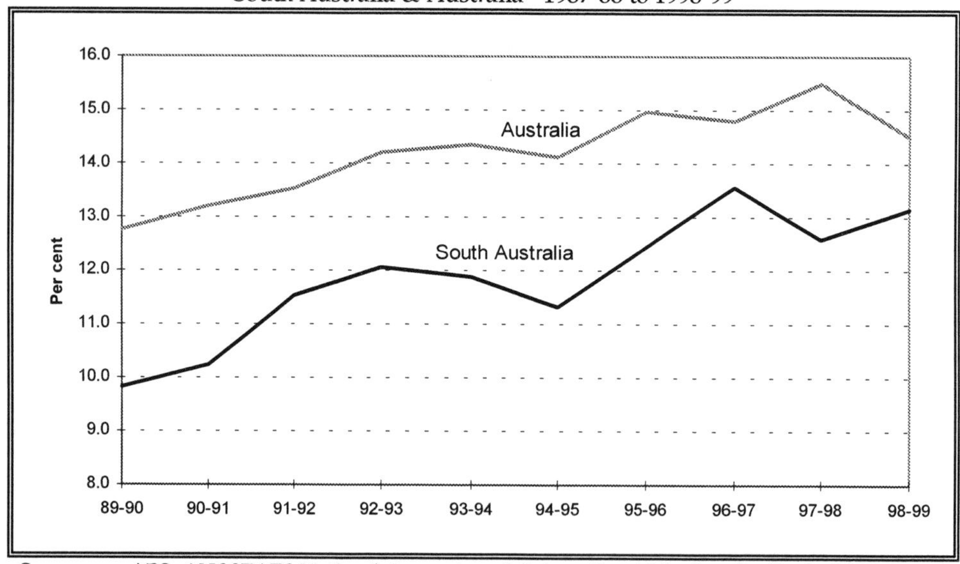

Source: ABS, *AUSSTATS National Accounts* and *International Merchandise Trade (5422.0)* and South *Australian Economic Indicators (1307.4).*

South Australian merchandise exports have grown so strongly in nominal terms (as shown by Figure 10.3), that the export share of Gross State Product has increased over the past decade (see Figure 10.5). That is, merchandise exports have, since the early 1980s, made an increasingly important contribution to the State's economy. By 1998-99, merchandise exports accounted for 13.1 per cent of the State's GSP — closer to the Australian average share of exports, which is boosted by the high export potential of the mineral rich States. In the most recent years, exports shares of GSP/GDP have fallen from highs of 13.6 per cent for South Australia in 1996-97 and 15.5 per cent for Australia in 1997-98. This decline almost certainly is a reflection that strong domestic demand has had increased importance in driving Australian economic growth in recent years.

Figure 10.6 shows the value of exports as a proportion of GSP for all States. The most striking feature is the larger size of Western Australia's export sector relative to other States. In large part this reflects Western Australia's massive endowment of natural resources that has resulted in the development of a substantial mineral and energy industry sector whose production significantly exceeds domestic (Australian) resource requirements and is thus predominantly exported overseas. For example, Western Australia supplied 43 per cent of the world's diamond production (mainly industrial grade), 25 per cent of its ilmenite production, and 18 per cent of its alumina production in 1999 (DME, 2000). Differing endowments of natural resources go some way to explaining differences in the relative size of export sectors across States.

Figure 10.6
Exports by State as a Proportion of State Output
Australian States - 1998-99

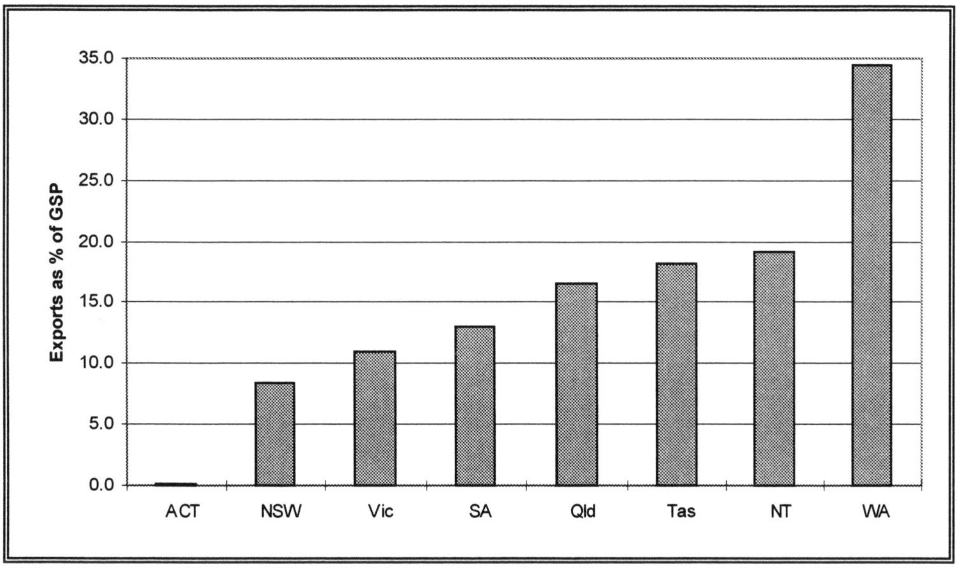

Source: ABS, *AUSSTATS*, National Accounts and *International Merchandise Trade (5422.0).*

Although South Australia appears to have a larger export sector than either New South Wales and Victoria, the two largest States, this does not necessarily imply that South Australia is relatively more successful (Figure 10.6). As a general principle, the smaller the economy the more it exports. (Consider the 'corner solutions', the world economy exports zero, and the household economy exports close to 100 per cent of its product.) That Queensland and Western Australia (both larger than South Australia in economic terms) posses export sectors which comprise a larger proportion of GSP, suggests South Australia trails behind these States in terms of growing its export sector.

From the preceding analysis it can be concluded that the growth performance of the South Australian merchandise export sector has been marginally better than the national sector as a whole and most States over the last decade (see Figure 10.4). An increasing contribution of exports to GSP indicates that not only has export activity become more important to local economic activity in the form of production and potentially employment, but that the State's economy has become increasingly outward oriented. Furthermore, that the South Australian ratio of exports to GSP has moved towards the corresponding national ratio over time implies that exports have been more important to growing the State economy than national economy. However, South Australian exports have grown from a lower level, implying that to some degree South Australian export performance has involved an element of 'catch up' with the National export sector. Nevertheless, the South Australian export sector appears to have performed well since the late 1980s.

Growth in the absolute level of exports does not necessarily capture all the benefits associated with trade. There are important issues related to the diversity of goods and markets, to which we now turn.

Exports by Commodity

South Australia's strong export performance can be better understood by examining the trend in exports by major commodity groups as illustrated in Figures 10.6a and 10.6b. In terms of sales cereal exports have been the largest export item over the last decade. However, growth in wine exports over the period covered has been so strong - at an annual average rate of 25.5 per cent from 1988-89 to 1998-99 - that wine exports are threatening to overtake cereal exports. Whereas wine exports were equal to 15 per cent of the value of cereal exports in 1988-89, this ratio has risen to 74 per cent by 1997-98 despite growth in cereal exports. It should be noted however, that due to confidentiality restrictions, barley exports data are excluded from the cereals commodity group for the latest financial year (1998-99) and therefore exports of this commodity group in 1998-99 are understated, especially as South Australia is the main barley producing State.

Other substantial export performers in terms of average annual growth through the period covered include road vehicles, parts and accessories (18 per cent), machinery (14 per cent), fish and crustaceans (10 per cent) and metals and metal manufactures (8.5 per cent, see Figure 10.7b).

Obviously South Australia's impressive export performance over the last decade has depended significantly upon growth in a narrow selection of commodities - 40 per cent of the growth in total exports between 1998-89 and 1998-99 is solely accounted for by wine and road vehicles, parts and accessories. The concern this pattern may raise is that South Australia's export growth has been too narrowly focused and that overall export performance may be highly sensitive to industry-specific and other exogenous events. For instance, South Australian economic performance may be highly susceptible to a possible downturn in the global wine market given massive recent increases in international plantings of vines. As a small regional economy, South Australia naturally possess a more limited range of natural resources and hence industries with a comparative advantage. However, there are reasons to suggest that South Australian export performance is not overly dependent on specific commodities, or on exogenous factors such as international demand conditions, and that it has not been as narrowly concentrated as initially appears.

Figure 10.7a
Merchandise Exports by Selected Commodity Group*
South Australia — 1988-89 to 1998-99

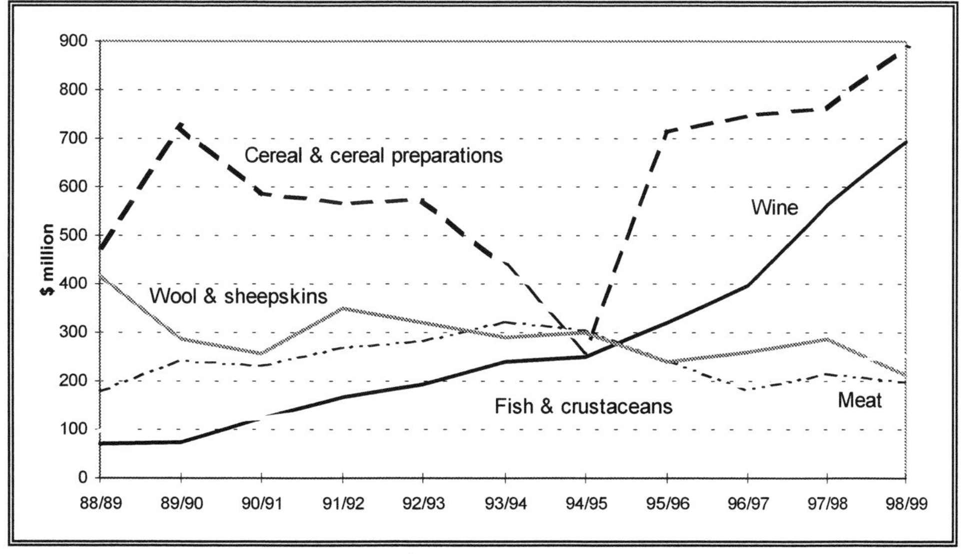

Note: * Data on bulk barley exports are excluded for the 1998-99 financial year but are included for previous years.

Source: ABS, South Australian Economic Indicators (1307.4).

Figure 10.7b
Merchandise Exports by Selected Commodity Group
South Australia - 1988-89 to 1998-99

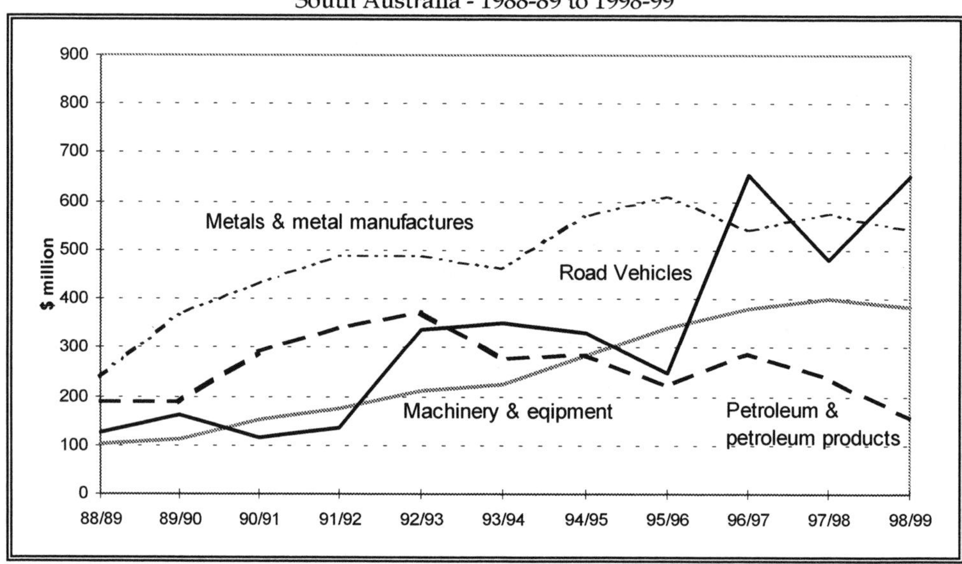

Source: ABS, South Australian Economic Indicators (1307.4).

Perhaps most important is that South Australia's strong export growth in recent years has not been determined simply by favourable exogenous factors; structural changes within the South Australian economy have permitted increased competitiveness of certain sectors of the economy. The best performing export industries in recent years - wine and motor vehicles - have been characterised by concerted efforts in strategic investment and market development by their respective industries. The Australian wine industry for example has become a world leader in research and development investments: the adoption of new technologies has given local producers significant competitive advantages, and export quality has also improved considerably (Anderson, 1999). Furthermore, the industry has actively promoted and developed brand and regional images in overseas markets, especially Europe, to generate demand for the Australian product.

Sustained growth in motor vehicle exports similarly reflects strategic targeting and marketing decisions taken by the local car manufacturing industry over several years. For example, General Motors Holden's Automotive has successfully developed the non-traditional Middle East market for exports of the Commodore. Its experience demonstrates the important benefits that can be derived by strategically targeting markets. In this case, GMHA identified a preference by Middle Eastern consumers for large, spacious and high performance cars like the Holden Commodore rather than smaller (European-Style) cars. Investment in both the manufacturing of left hand drive vehicles and marketing to Middle Eastern consumers resulted in strong export growth to the Middle East despite a climate of global oversupply of motor vehicles.

The overwhelming contributions of wine, road vehicles and cereal exports to total South Australian export growth somewhat mask the extent to which South Australia's export base has in fact broadened over the past decade. Table 10.2 highlights South Australia's fastest growing exports from 1988 to 1997 using slightly older but more comprehensive export data. It can be seen that they include a wide variety of categories. If it were possible in the confines of this chapter to show an even more detailed breakdown of South Australia's exports, the broadening of the base would be even more apparent.

Table 10.2
South Australia's Fastest Growing Exports, 1988 to 1997

Product	1997 ($m)	% Growth 1988 to 1997
Power Generating Equipment	195.0	806
Inorganic Chemicals	17.7	794
Motor Vehicles	634.2	678
Beverages	471.1	597
Paper Products	21.0	415
General Industrial Equipment	33.3	369
Dairy Products	51.8	354
Leather Goods	55.0	344
Confidential Items	520.5	327
Plastics	24.0	252
Professional/Scientific Instruments	23.4	248
Telecommunications/Sound Recording Equip.	18.6	230
Petroleum Products	298.0	151
Miscellaneous Manufactured Goods	48.7	151
Non-Metallic Mineral Manufactures	56.7	142
Specialised Machinery	68.8	136
Non-ferrous Metals	372.3	131
Manufactures of Metals, nes	19.2	123
Electrical Machinery	71.8	116
Iron and Steel	153.2	100
Fish	221.1	100

Source: ABS, Unpublished data from Foreign Trade Database.

To further illustrate the fact that South Australia's overall export performance has indeed depended significantly upon growth in a broad range of commodities other than wine, road vehicles and cereals, we compare South Australian export performance with and without the inclusion of these major commodity items. Including all commodities, average annual growth in South Australia's total merchandise exports from 1988 to 1997 amounted to 9.4 per cent. If we exclude exports of road vehicles, cereal and cereal preparations, beverages (which includes wine) and confidential items (which largely reflects barley) from this result, then South Australian export sector still exhibits robust average annual growth of 7 per cent. Placing this result in perspective, it should be recognised that total Australian merchandise exports grew at an annual average rate of 8 per cent over the equivalent period. The State's strong export performance over the past decade must therefore also largely reflect strong growth in a wide range of smaller commodities whose contribution to growing the export sector has not always been recognised in the face of the contribution of the major commodity items.

Although South Australia's pattern of export growth has not been as narrowly concentrated as initially appears, nevertheless, as is to be expected, the State exports a more limited range of commodities than does Australia. Table 10.3 demonstrates this by showing the proportion of total exports for South Australia and Australia accounted for by the largest (i.e., most important) commodity exports for the respective regions. Whereas the five largest commodity exports accounted for 51 per cent of South Australia's total exports in 1997, 41 per cent of Australia's total exports in 1996-97 were accounted for by the largest five export commodities. This ranking continues as the bundle of commodities is expanded though the difference diminishes.

That a larger proportion of South Australian exports are accounted for by a more limited range of commodities is to a large degree a reflection that as a small regional economy, South Australia possess a limited endowment of natural and other resources as well as factors of production with which to exploit comparative advantages across a wide range of commodities. The diversity of resources and factors of production available at the national level permits the development of a broader range of commodity exports compared to smaller regions. In this sense, South Australian overall export performance (and therefore economic performance given the important contribution of exports to GSP) is more sensitive to individual industry events relative to the national situation. A more revealing assessment of South Australia's export diversity

Table10.3
Concentration of South Australian and Australian Exports

SITC Commodity Group	South Australia 1997 (Per Cent)	Australia 1996-97 (Per Cent)
Top 5	50.9	41.0
Top 10	74.4	59.9
Top 15	85.0	70.7
Top 20	90.3	78.2
Top 25	94.0	84.2
Top 50	99.6	98.4

Source: Compiled by SACES from ABS, Unpublished data from Foreign Trade Database and *International Merchandise Trade (5422.0)*.

Figure 10.8
Australia - Exports by Commodity Groups
Percentage of Total Exports, Year ended January 1998

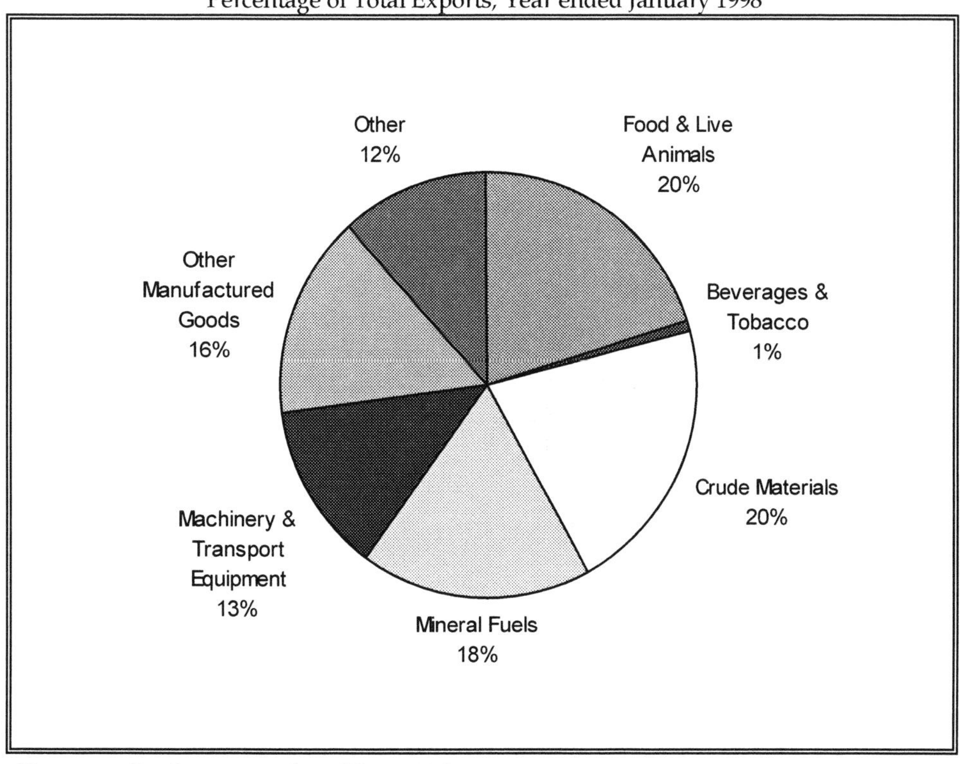

Note: For footnotes refer to Figure 10.9.
Source: Unpublished data from ABS, Foreign Trade Data base.

would be to compare the South Australian experience against other States; however this is beyond the scope of this book.

Finally, it is interesting to examine the breakdown of exports by broad commodity groups between South Australia and Australia in Figures 10.8 and 10.9. The picture of South Australian exports differs from the total Australian picture in several ways. Most notably, South Australia has a higher concentration of exports in the following areas: beverages; machinery and transport equipment; and "other". The higher concentration in beverages reflects, of course, the significant position of the wine industry in this State; the higher concentration in machinery and transport equipment largely reflects the presence of the motor vehicle industry in South Australia; while the high proportion of "other" is largely a reflection of the fact that, within this set of data, barley is captured in the "confidential" component of the export statistics and South Australia is the main barley producing State.

Figure 10.9
South Australia - Exports by Commodity Groups
Percentage of Total Exports, Year ended January 1998

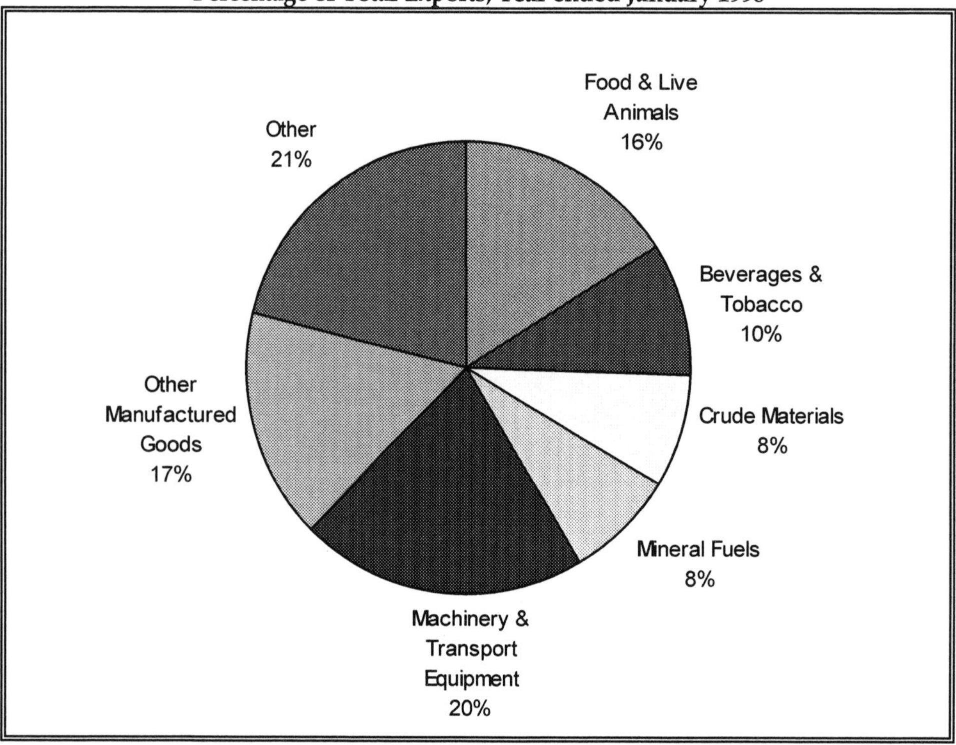

Notes: * "Other" includes products classified as 'animal and vegetable oils, fats and waxes', and 'chemicals and related products', and 'commodities not elsewhere classified' and 'confidential items'.
**" Other Manufactured Goods" comprises those manufactured goods chiefly classified by material, as well as "miscellaneous manufactured articles".

Source: Unpublished data from ABS, Foreign Trade Data base.

South Australian Exports by Country of Consignment

South Australia's export performance may also be examined or presented in terms of the geographical profile of its export markets. An export profile that exhibits a strong focus towards any one region implies susceptibility to economic downturns in that region feeding back into local economic activity (unless of course exporters demonstrate flexibility in switching to alternative markets in such an event). Smaller regions traditionally have a less diversified base of commodity exports and usually a narrower geographical distribution. Assessed against these benchmarks, the performance of the South Australian export sector relative to Australia over the past 10 years has been impressive.

The United States of America and Japan were the two most important individual export markets for both South Australia and Australia in 1998-99. Details on Australian and South Australian exports by selected destinations are shown in Table 10.4. Exports to the United States and Japan accounted for 13 per cent and 12 per cent of total South Australian exports, respectively. Significantly, a substantial proportion of total Australian exports are directed to one individual market - Japan - which receives 19 per cent of Australia exports. That one country accounts for such a large proportion of whole-of-Australian exports suggests that the Australian pattern of export markets may in fact be less diverse than for South Australia.

Table 10.4
Australian and South Australian Exports by Country/Region, 1998/99

	Total Exports ($m) 1998-99		% of Total Exports 1998-99		CAGR* (%) 1988-89 to 1998-99	
	Australia	South Australia	Australia	South Australia	Australia	South Australia
United States of America	7,984	705	9.3	13.2	5.9	14.3
United Kingdom	4,473	476	5.2	8.9	11.2	15.9
European Union	11,629	928	13.5	17.4	6.2	10.1
New Zealand	5,838	386	6.8	7.2	10.0	5.3
Japan	16,566	626	19.3	11.7	3.3	4.8
China	3,948	303	4.6	5.7	12.1	19.3
Hong Kong	3,071	220	3.6	4.1	5.2	14.7
ASEAN	10,403	433	12.1	8.1	10.4	6.0
Total	**85,991**	**5,333**	**100.0**	**100.0**	**6.9**	**8.1**

Note: * Compound Annual Average Growth Rate.
Source: ABS, International Merchandise Trade (5542.0) and South Australian Economic Indicators (1307.4).

From Table 10.5, other major markets for South Australia's exports include the European Union (17 per cent), United Kingdom (9 per cent - the UK also accounts for a substantial proportion of EU exports) and New Zealand (7 per cent).

The diversity and strength of South Australia's recent export performance is further highlighted by the fact that growth in South Australian exports exceeded growth in national exports to all destinations listed in Table 10.5 except New Zealand and the ASEAN group of countries over the period in question. Figures 10.10 and 10.11 illustrate the trends in export growth to these various markets for both South Australia and Australia.

As a bloc, Asian countries represent the largest markets for both whole-of-Australia and South Australian exports. In 1997, Asia took 48 per cent of South Australia's exports, and 62 per cent of those of Australia as a whole. The importance of the Asian market for South Australia's exports has increased significantly over the past 10 years, but South Australia's reliance on the Asian market remains less than Australia's. The greater dependence on the Asian market at the national level can partly be explained by the increased proportion of Australian exports going to Japan.

Figure 10.10
Index of Merchandise Exports by Destination
South Australia - 1988-89 to 1998-99

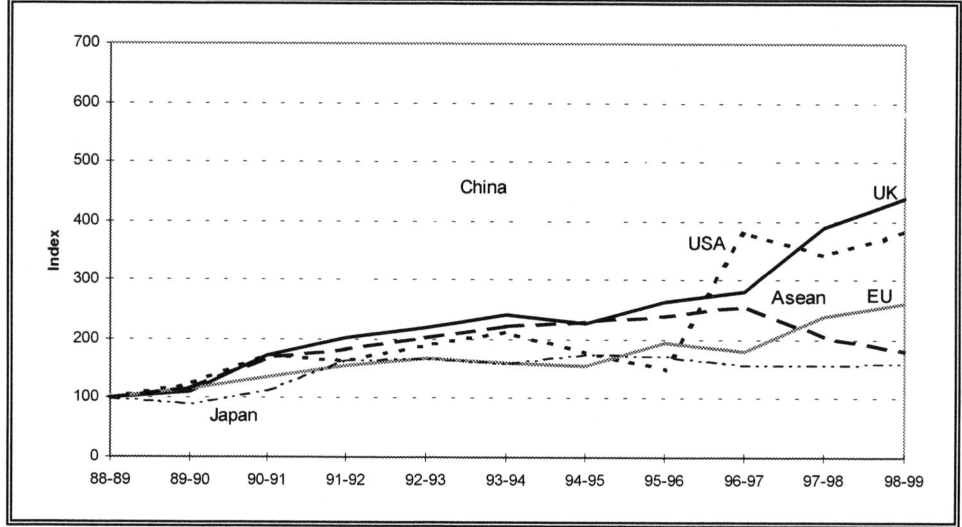

Source: ABS, South *Australian Economic Indicators* (1307.4).

Figure 10.11
Index of Merchandise Exports by Destination
Australia - 1988-89 to 1998-99

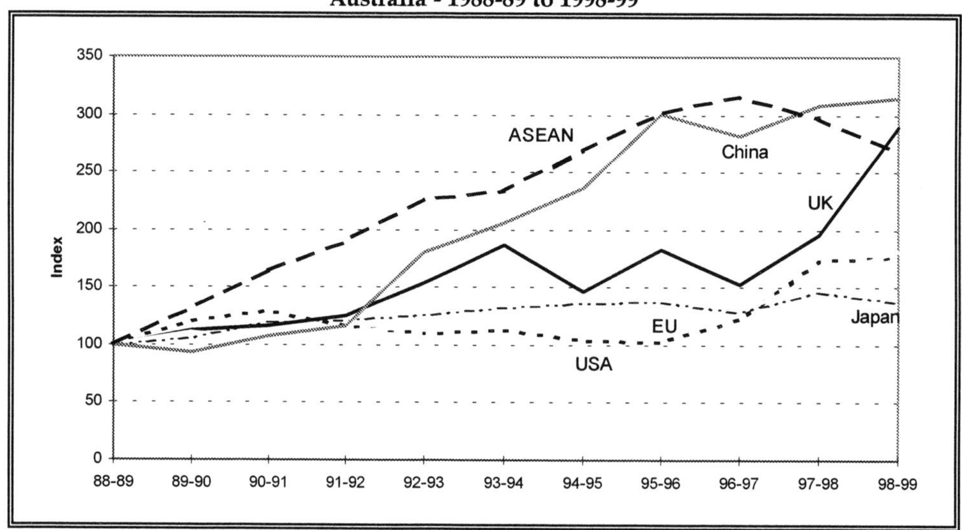

Source: ABS, *International Merchandise Trade* (5422.0).

Figure 10.12
South Australia:
Exports By Major Destination — 1997

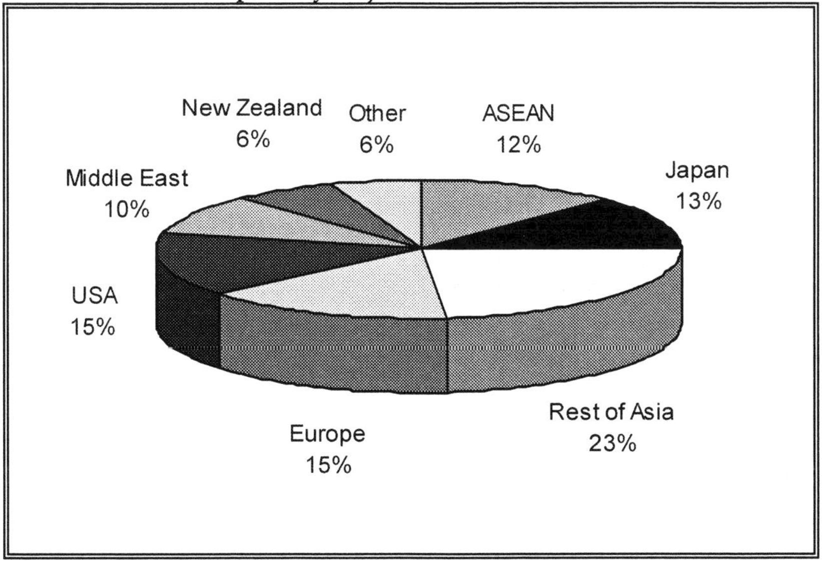

New Zealand
6%
Other
6%
ASEAN
12%
Middle East
10%
Japan
13%
USA
15%
Europe
15%
Rest of Asia
23%

Source: Unpublished data from the ABS, Foreign Trade Database.

Unfortunately, the data in Table 10.5 is not fully comprehensive, excluding several important markets, especially the Middle East and Asia region as a whole. Consequently we turn to Figures 10.12 and 10.13 which reveal an overall geographical distribution of South Australia's and Australia's exports in 1997.

Figure 10.13
Australia: Exports By Major Destination - 1997

New Zealand
7%
Other
7%
ASEAN
15%
Middle East
5%
USA
8%
Japan
20%
Europe
11%
Rest of Asia
27%

Source: Unpublished data from the ABS, Foreign Trade Database.

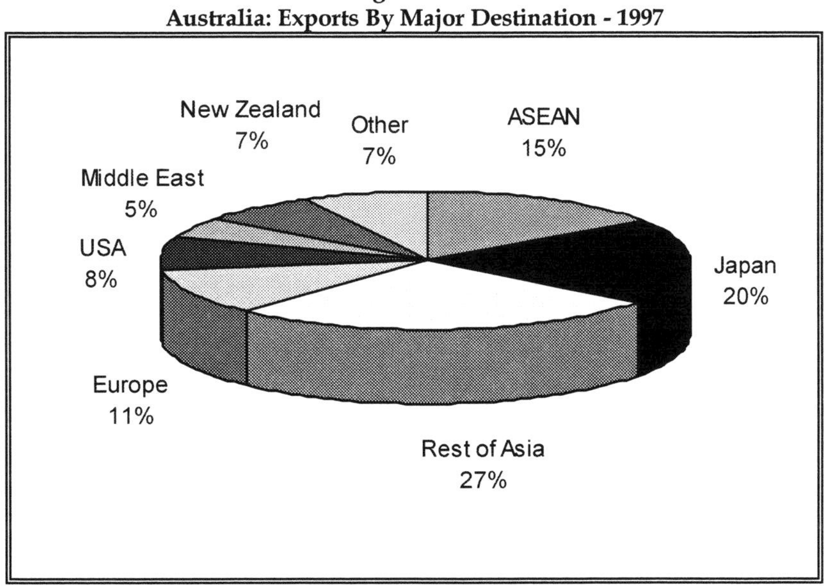

From Figures 10.12 and 10.13 it can be seen that a larger proportion of South Australian exports (10 per cent) go to the Middle East than do Australia's (5 per cent) although the rate of growth in Australian exports to this destination has been much stronger than South Australia's over the 10 years to 1997.

Based on the above analysis, the fastest growing markets for South Australia exports over the past decade have been:

- ***China*** - exports to China have grown by an annual average rate of 19.3 per cent (compared to 12 per cent for Australia) over the eleven years to 1998-99, to $303 million, accounting for 5.7 per cent of all South Australian exports in that year. The main categories of exports in 1997 were various crude materials (such as textile fibres (e.g., wool)) and metalliferous ores and confidential items (perhaps barley?).
- ***United Kingdom*** - annual growth in exports equalled 15.9 per cent from 1988-89 to 1998-99; the UK now accounts for 8.9 per cent of South Australia's total exports (compared to only 4.4 per cent in 1988-89). For the twelve months ended January 1998 'beverages' (i.e., mostly wine) represented 64 per cent of South Australia's exports to the UK.
- ***Hong Kong*** - annual growth of 14.7 per cent over eleven years; Hong Kong now accounts for 4.1 per cent of total South Australian exports which have fallen slightly since the onset of the Asian crisis. Exports are widely spread across food items, crude materials and various manufactured goods.
- ***USA*** - from 1988-89 to 1998-99, exports to the United States have grown on average by 14.3 per cent per year; the US accounted for 13.2 per cent of South Australia's total exports in 1998-99 (compared to 7.5 per cent in 1988-89). For the twelve months ended January 1998, the main export items were 'machinery and transport equipment' (64 per cent of the State's exports to the USA), 'beverages' (10.5 per cent), and 'food' (9.8 per cent).
- ***ASEAN countries*** - i.e., Singapore, Indonesia, Malaysia, Thailand, Philippines, Vietnam, and Brunei. South Australian exports to these countries have increased at an annual rate of 6 per cent since 1988-89 and in 1998-99 accounted for 8.1 per cent of the State's total merchandise exports. The share of South Australian exports to ASEAN has fallen from a high of 14.4 per cent in 1994-95 due to stronger growth in South Australian exports to other regions and decreased ASEAN demand for foreign goods as a result of the negative repercussions associated with the Asian monetary crisis.
- ***South Africa*** - exports have grown 22.2 per cent per annum over ten years to 1997, albeit from a low base, to represent 1.2 per cent of South Australia's total exports in 1997. Similarly, exports to Africa as a whole have increased dramatically over the past ten years, with most of the growth being in the last four years. (In 1997, Africa accounted for 2.3 per cent of South Australia's exports, down from a record 3.5 per cent in 1996.) The main areas of growth in exports to Africa have been in the categories of 'food',

'manufactured goods', including 'machinery and equipment', and 'miscellaneous manufactured articles'.

South Australia therefore has developed quite a different export profile from Australia as a whole over the past ten years. As already mentioned, Asia in 1997 accounted for 62 per cent of Australia's merchandise exports, but only 48 per cent of South Australia's exports. Further, South Australia has increased its export penetration into the USA and the European Union, while for Australia as a whole these markets have declined in importance (from 10.2 per cent (USA) and 14.5 per cent (European Union) of total Australian exports in 1988, to 9.3 per cent (USA) and 13.5 per cent (European Union) of total Australian exports in 1997).

Furthermore, South Australia has been much more successful in targeting exports towards China - a country that holds substantial future economic developments opportunities for business given the massive size of the domestic market due to both its enormous population and rapid economic development of recent years.

The overall picture that emerges from Figures 10.10 to 10.13 and Table 10.5 is one of South Australia having developed more geographically diverse export markets over the past ten years than Australia as a whole. Inter alia, this implies that South Australia is less exposed to a downturn in economic activity in any one area of the world than are some other States. For example, South Australian exports to ASEAN countries declined to a level in 1998-99 30 per cent below their peak in 1996-97 following the Asian monetary crisis. Despite this, the level of South Australia total exports rose 6.5 per cent over this time frame. Had a larger proportion of South Australian exports been directed to these countries, then the associated negative influences on South Australian exports and therefore local economic activity would have been more severe. These recent events in Asia have highlighted the dangers of 'having too many eggs in too few baskets' and the broadening of South Australia's geographic export base in this respect is a positive sign for the future stability of the economy.

Overall Trends in South Australian Merchandise Imports

As stated in the introduction to this chapter, specialisation in production and subsequent trade between regions where comparative advantages in production exist across goods and services, will give rise to increased welfare as the satisfaction of consumption desires is enhanced. Thus, the benefits of trade derive not only from the exportation of goods, which a region produces relatively efficiently, but also from the importation of goods that cannot be produced relatively efficiently within the region. Not only does this raise welfare through increasing the quantity of goods that may be consumed, but also by expanding the possible range and diversity of goods that may be consumed, imports may further raise consumer welfare. Furthermore, the importation of new products (and their subsequent export for that matter) acts as a conduit for accessing knowledge about the external environment and new technologies. In this sense imports are welfare enhancing and do not necessarily entail negative impacts for the local economic environment as often portrayed.

A comprehensive examination of South Australia's trade profile would therefore be incomplete without a thorough analysis of import trends. Unfortunately, due to reasons examined in detail earlier in the chapter, the quality of State merchandise imports data available from the ABS is deficient. The practice of recording international merchandise imports as only those goods released from Customs control in South Australia implies that ABS data does not provide an accurate indication of the aggregate level of State merchandise imports. Because substantial quantities of international goods are imported via interstate, ABS estimates may significantly under-represent merchandise imports, perhaps by as much as 40 per cent for any particular year. Consequently, drawing observations from the pattern of State merchandise imports is fraught with danger and misinterpretation of actual events and trends. The following analysis is therefore highly qualified, and presented as being only indicative of the true situation at best.

Figure 10.14 illustrates the trend in South Australian (via South Australian customs control) and Australian merchandise imports from 1989-90 to 1998-99. It can be stated with certainty that the level of South Australian merchandise imports has increased significantly over the last 10 years. From the graph it also appears that growth in State merchandise imports has been broadly in line with the growth of national merchandise imports since 1989-90. There are reasons to suspect that this trend is representative of the true situation. Firstly, to the extent that South Australian merchandise exports have grown in line with national exports over the last decade and that exports provide a means of financing the consumption of imported goods, then one can expect State imports to have also grown broadly in line with national imports. Secondly, earlier we applied the ratio of national exports to imports to South Australian exports in order to derive an indicative estimate of the true level of State merchandise imports. Applying this methodology to State exports over the last decade would substantially increase the absolute level of imports; however, the trend in adjusted imports over this period would remain in line with the State and national trends illustrated in Figure 10.14.

Solid growth in merchandise imports reflects several factors. Firstly, Australian trade barriers (and therefore South Australian trade barriers) have continued to decline over the last decade (see Table 10.1) promoting Australian market accessibility for foreign producers. So whilst Australian exporters have benefited from declining trade barriers in foreign markets, foreign exporters have similarly benefited from declining Australian barriers to trade. Furthermore, strong growth in exports may have financed increased consumption of imports. On this point it is noteworthy that from a comparison of Figures 10.3 and 10.14, the pattern of growth in South Australian and Australian exports appears to be remarkably similar to pattern of growth in imports. Increased merchandise imports also reflects strong demand and economic conditions locally. Both the national and State economies have experienced strong economic growth over the past decade which would have subsequently further increased demand for imports through generating both higher domestic incomes and increasing local production activity. Increased disposable incomes permit increased levels of consumption thus translating into increased consumption of imported goods and services. Meanwhile, local production in some instances requires imported intermediate inputs, an increase in local production levels would subsequently increase the demand for imports.

Figure 10.14
Index of Merchandise Imports
South Australia* and Australia - 1989-90 to 1998-99

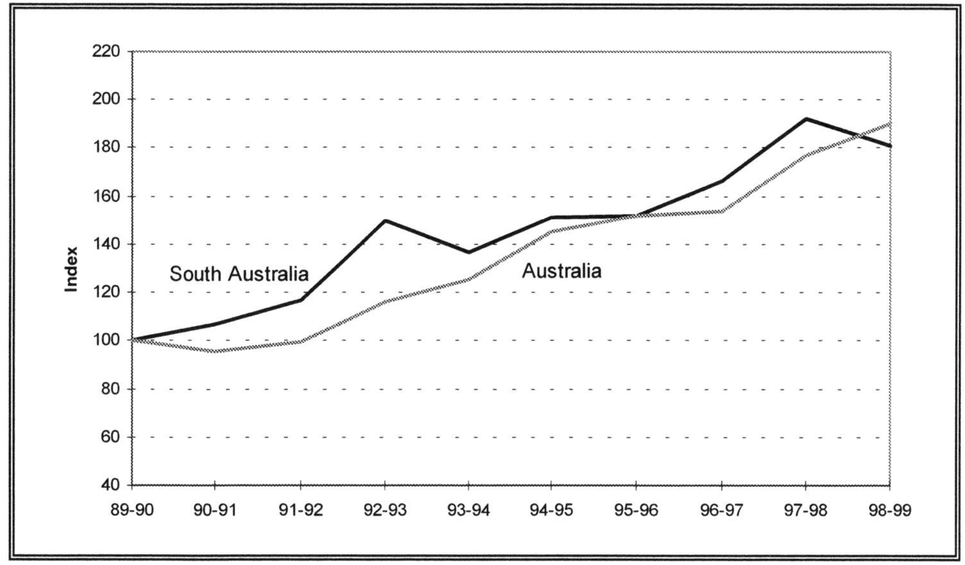

Note: * Refers to imports via South Australian Customs control.
Source: ABS, International Merchandise Trade (5542.0) and South Australian Economic Indicators (1307.4).

It follows that the reasons explaining growth in merchandise imports at both the State and national levels outlined above are broadly similar for both regions. One important difference between the Australian and South Australian pattern of imports is that a larger proportion of South Australian consumption is probably satisfied by imports (at least in terms of diversity) given that the small size of the State economy implies that not all goods can be effectively produced within the region. This may be a particularly important consideration in comparing differences in import patterns between States, whereby larger States (in terms of market size) such as New South Wales rely less on imports to satisfy consumption desires. Whether this translates into differences in international imports between states is difficult to assess because firstly, the unreliability of state merchandise imports data is misleading and state comparisons are therefore unwarranted. Secondly, a majority of such consumption desires are probably satisfied by interstate imports rather than international imports since such goods are produced in interstate markets, unfortunately no data pertaining to interstate imports are collected by the ABS.

The trend towards solid growth in South Australian aggregate merchandise imports over time suggests that imports have been important to satisfying consumption desires and therefore increasing the welfare of South Australian consumers. Primary to this has been the reduction in import barriers which has adjusted the relative prices of imports downwards to reflect their true underlying costs of production allowing consumers to make efficient purchasing decisions and increase consumption through trade. However, trade also permits the consumption of a wider variety of goods than available domestically. Since consumers place value on consuming a variety of goods, diversifying imports leads to further increases in welfare. Furthermore, other benefits may be derived from the consumption of new goods, these include gaining access to new technologies and ideas, and increased knowledge of the external environment. Such benefits from trade are likely to be greater for less developed economies (ie., developing countries) than for a 'mature' economy like South Australia. An example of this process, although in an opposite direction and different form, is the transfer of wine production technologies and ideas from Australian to Southern Hemisphere and Southern and Eastern European producers through the export of viticulture and winemaking consultancy services (also significant in this transfer process is foreign direct investment) (Anderson, 1999).

Assessing the diversification of South Australia's imports over time is of course compromised by the limitations of international merchandise imports data as stated above. If aggregate levels of State international merchandise imports are significantly understated, then data at any disaggregated level will be even less reliable. Keeping this in mind, Figures 10.15a and 10.15b illustrate the trends in South Australian imports of select commodity groups. Similar patterns in the growth of merchandise imports appear to have been experienced by the selected commodity groups. Imports of all commodities seem to have grown to the same degree as total merchandise imports, with the possible exception of petroleum and petroleum products. This could be interpreted as indicating that growth in imports has been experienced across a large range of commodity groups and that South Australian consumption of imports has probably diversified over time. However, according to ABS statistics, 96 per cent of total South Australian merchandise imports in 1998-99 are accounted for by those broad categories of commodities examined in Figures 10.15a and 10.15b. Not only does this deflate any conclusion concerning an increase in the diversity of commodities imported, it also serves to further illustrate that ABS estimates do not capture the full range of commodities imported into South Australia.

Figure 10.15a
Annual Growth in Imports by Selected Commodities
South Australia* and Australia - 1989-90 to 1998-99

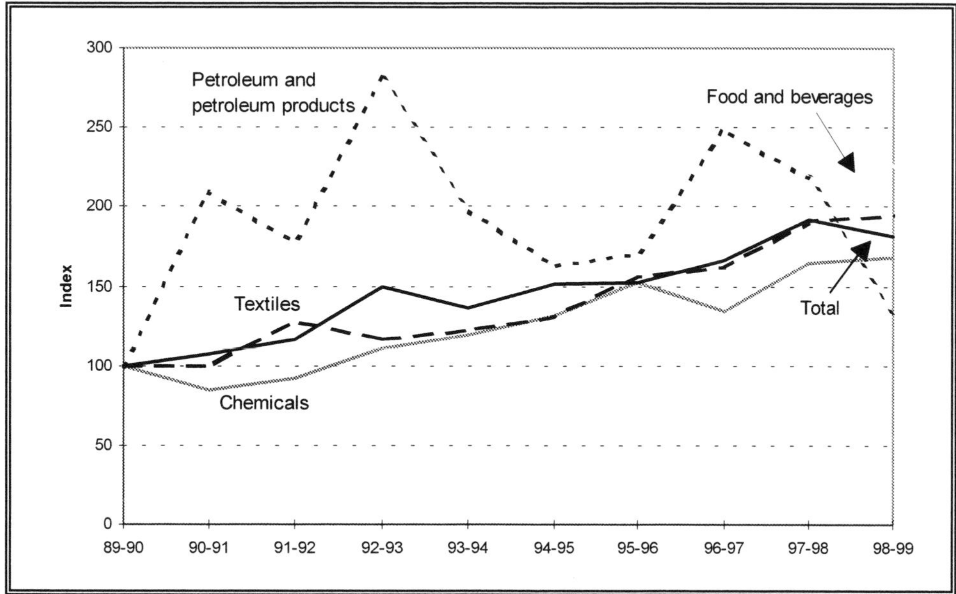

Note: * Refers to imports via South Australian Customs control.
Source: ABS, South Australian Economic Indicators (1307.4).

Figure 10.15b
Annual Growth in Imports by Selected Commodities
South Australia* - 1989-90 to 1998-99

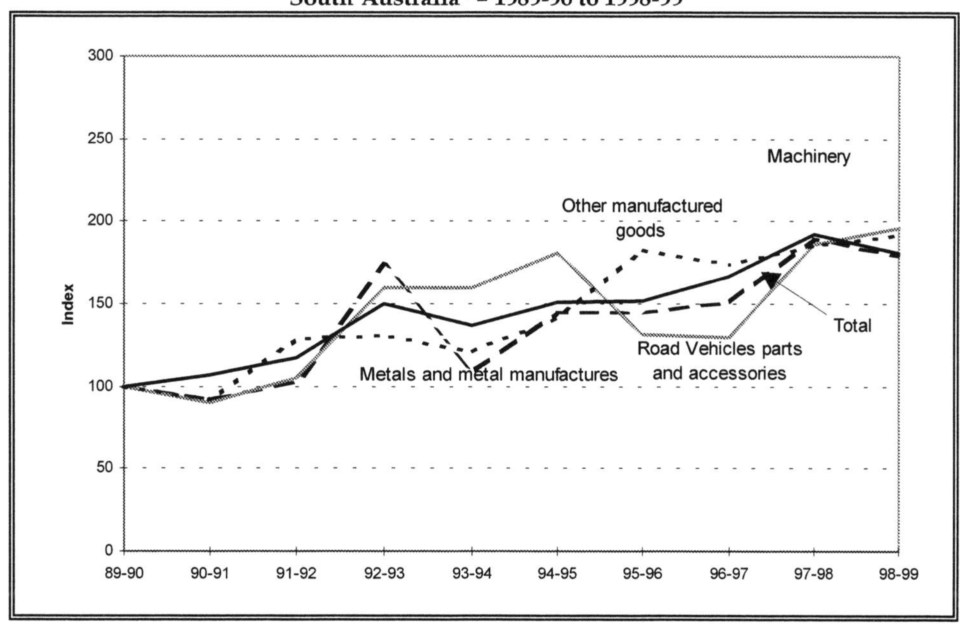

Note: * Refers to imports via South Australian Customs control.
Source: ABS, South Australian Economic Indicators (1307.4).

Despite the limitations of the data, it would appear unlikely that South Australian imports have not diversified over the past decade. During this time, the South Australian economy has become more open to trade (through decreased import barriers) and in a sense more externally oriented as demonstrated by the larger contribution of exports made to Gross State Product. Consequently, the barriers to foreign goods penetrating the Australian market have diminished thus permitting the possibility of a broader range of goods to be traded. Whether or not South Australia has exploited the full benefits offered by diversifying its consumption base will unfortunately remain unclear.

If anything, the import analysis demonstrates the difficulties facing regional economies in terms of thoroughly assessing their trade performance due to data quality issues.

Exports of Services

The analysis of South Australian trade has thus far excluded trade in services - focusing instead on merchandise trade. Services trade would include, for example, consultancy services, health and education services, and international tourism. The exclusion of services is due entirely to the fact that data on services trade are available almost exclusively only on a national basis. This is both unsatisfactory and a pity, since the importance of services to Australian trade has grown dramatically over the past decade or so. Indeed, services exports have grown more rapidly than exports of merchandise goods over time - so that services now constitute a significant component of total Australian exports. An absence of State data pertaining to services prevents any detailed analysis of services trade - although a brief treatment of South Australian services exports is nevertheless provided.

Despite the lack of hard data, there can be no doubt that services exports have also become increasingly important to South Australia - although, as we discuss below, there is reason to believe that South Australia lags the national performance in this area.

To illustrate the extent to which services exports have increased in significance, note that the value of services exports nationally in 1983-84 was $4.9 billion, equal to 20.1 per cent of merchandise exports. By 1998-99, services exports had increased to $25.7 billion, equivalent to 30.2 per cent of merchandise exports. Thus, over the fifteen years from 1983-84 to 1998-99, Australian services exports increased almost 424 per cent, while merchandise exports increased 263 per cent.

On a pro rata basis, however, assuming that South Australia services exports represent the same share of total exports as at the national level, South Australian services exports should have been approximately $1.7 billion in 1998-

99. Anecdotal and partial evidence in relation to South Australia's performance in attracting international visitors and international students - two key sectors of services exports - suggests, however, that South Australia has probably performed below the national average in growing services exports. For example, the proportion of international visitors to Australia who included South Australia in their itineraries declined from 11.6 per cent in 1984 to only 7.6 per cent in 1999. Similarly, 'international visitor nights' spent in South Australia as a proportion of total 'international visitor nights' spent in Australia has fallen from 7.0 per cent in 1986 to 4.2 per cent in 1999. ["International visitor nights" is a measure which is more indicative of visitor expenditure in a location than simple visitor numbers, since it recognises the amount of time spent in a location.]

There is evidence to suggest that South Australia has also lagged in other areas of services exports, including education and health.

It should be noted, however, that South Australia's performance in this area is not by any means entirely dismal. While South Australia has *lagged* the national performance in services exports, it has nevertheless *participated* in the growth of services exports. For example, the number of international visitor nights spent in South Australia increased from an estimated 2.46 million nights in 1986 to around 4.54 million nights in 1999, growth of 84.6 per cent.

Similarly, anecdotal evidence indicates that the number of international students studying in South Australia has increased over recent years.

The bottom line of this analysis, therefore, is that: (i) services exports are increasingly important to the South Australian economy; *but* (ii) there remains a significant challenge to South Australia to grow its services exports.

Conclusion

Despite data limitations on import data and export data on services, there is considerable evidence that the tradeable goods sector in South Australia has expanded strongly over the past 10 years. This growth has been promoted, in part, by declining trade barriers, both in Australia and overseas, which is putting pressure on local producers to improve efficiency and become more innovative and entrepreneurial. A more open economy means that the regions will adapt new products more quickly, have a greater understanding of the external environment in all dimensions and be more exposed to new ideas.

Assessed against national benchmarks, growth in merchandise exports has been particularly impressive since 1988-89. Through specialising in the production of goods and services in which the State possesses a comparative advantage, growth in the export sector has been particularly important to raising local productivity and employment levels, and thus, contributing to overall South Australian economic growth. Importantly, growth in merchandise exports has occurred over a broad range of commodities. Not only does this imply an increasingly stable export sector with the overall performance of the sector being less sensitive to industry specific events, but the benefits associated with exports have been spread over a broad base of the economy and therefore the community. The geographic dispersion of South Australia's exports has also been impressive over the last ten years. However, the South Australian sector does remain highly influenced by exogenous factors such as foreign demand conditions and extreme movements in exchange rates. On the positive side, the diversification of the State's geographic export markets does reduce the overexposure of the sector to possible downturns in any of its major markets and limits any associated negative feedbacks.

Gains from trade do not derive only from exports, but also from imports. Regions export mainly to acquire the means to purchase what they cannot produce economically. Nonetheless, there are some benefits of export production such as the achievement of economies of scale in production which benefits the local markets. Imports are goods and services purchased from outside the region at lower cost than if produced within the region; trade also permits the consumption of a wider variety of goods, further raising welfare of the consumer. Due to data limitations, we can only be certain that South Australian merchandise imports have grown strongly over time in line with the national trend - indicating that South Australia has likely experienced the aforementioned gains from exchange. Nonetheless, given the substantial rise in imports, falling barriers to imports, and recent strength in domestic demand, the South Australian community is almost certainly enjoying a greater diversity of imports.

The increased diversification of imports is an indication that the regional population is broadening its tastes. And the increased diversification of exports, both in terms of products and market destinations, is an indication that South Australians understand more about consumer demands overseas and doing business with foreigners. Given the narrow ethnic representation within the State, South Australia's Anglo-Saxon dominated population has done well to make the trade and business connections that underpin the trade success story. However, the rate of growth of the tradeable goods sector may weaken if we are not able to make the next cultural step from arms length business relations to cultural emersion and integration. The later will enable us to reach a stronger understanding of consumer tastes and business practices in the external environment, more able to read the signals of change and more able to respond to those changes.

References

Anderson, K., (1999), "Australia's Grape and Wine Industry Into the 21st Century", Economic Briefing Report, November 1999, South Australian Centre for Economic Studies. Adelaide.

Department of Minerals and Energy (Western Australia), (2000), Statistics from Department Website, www.dem.wa.gov.au.

Organisation for Economic Co-operation and Development (1999), *OECD Economic Outlook*, December 1999.

Section 3

Case Studies in Regional Development

Chapter Eleven

Climate, Greenhouse Policy and Regional Impact

In this chapter, a case study is offered to provide further insights into the differences between the small regional economy of South Australia and the rest of Australia. The case study deals with national climate change policy. In terms of policy instruments, this chapter suggests that Australia (and South Australia) should adopt tradeable quotas rather than pursue domestic greenhouse gas abatement policies. However, if domestic policies were adopted then South Australia should not follow national policy as the structure of industry and emissions practices in South Australia are different in those of the other regions of Australia. This suggests that there is scope for South Australia to adopt emmissions abatement policies that differ to those of the national policy to effectively address greenhouse gas emissions.

However, before turning to the impacts of climate change policy, two somewhat more basic issues are discussed. Firstly, does climate influence regional economic growth? Secondly, does a change in climate, of the orders indicated by the scientific community, materially effect the South Australian economy?

Climate and Regional Growth

Using data from the Penn World Tables covering 133 countries, Hall and Jones (1996) undertook an econometric study which found that regions in the bands of 45 to 70 degrees latitude above and below the equator receive the highest benefit of climate. They also found that climate is the most important factor influencing long-run economic performance. Typically these countries are European. Iceland, Finland, Norway, Sweden and Denmark all receive more than 145 per cent increment in output per worker due to their location, relative to the median country of Mozambique. Australia is broadly between within this latitude, and setting aside the particular geography of the Australian interior, South Australia reaps the benefit of climate. Most studies other than Hall and Jones find smaller effects of climate on economic growth. Of course degrees of latitude from the equator is not necessarily a good indicator of climatic conditions. Nordhaus (1994) concludes that differences in latitude and climate have small effects on income. A quick scan of the countries near the equator - Zaire, Kenya, Gabon and Uganda - confirm that these countries suffer disadvantages, although Singapore is an outlier. But these observations do not rule out the powerful insights that might be gained from multiple regression analysis.

The effects of climate on long-run economic success are three-fold. Firstly, the effects of climate on capital use. Hot and cold climates require cooling and heating, more specialised infrastructure to deal with weather - induced congestion (e.g., snow) and breakdown (cables etc.), that consume resources otherwise diverted to other productive uses in temperate regions. Secondly, climate appears to effect human productivity. Depression and alcoholism are much more common in extreme climates with high variations in temperatures and length of days. For example, in the Northern Territory, a typical household spends twice as much as a South Australian on alcoholic beverages and tobacco.[30] Diseases spread much more easily in warm, humid climates than in temperate ones. Jones (1997) offers a historical perspective, identifying that the rise of Europe can at least in part be attributed to cooler climates which prevented the worst of epidemics. Thirdly, climate appears to effect human leisure activity. Warmer climates and warmer seasons are more likely to attract tourism and leisure activities, influencing the pattern of investment and consumption.

Given the importance of climate as a factor influencing economic growth of regions it is not surprising that the long-run change in climate, predicted by the scientific community, is of concern to the global community.

The temperature of the earth is influenced by natural phenomena such as solar activity, volcanic eruptions and geothermal activity, and anthropogenic activity through the emission of gases to the earth's atmosphere which adds to the natural greenhouse effect and increases the planet's temperature. Although the

30 Refer Australian Bureau of Statistics, *Average Weekly Household Expenditure*, Cat. No. 6535.0.

scientific community is unclear about the relative importance of the natural versus anthropogenic causes on global warming, the evidence on balance suggests that humans are having a discernible influence on global climate. Climate is no longer an exogenous factor in influencing long-run growth.

World temperature levels fluctuated widely, but increased gradually by about 0.5°C over the last century. Climate change models currently predict that a 50 per cent increase in greenhouse gases will lead to an increase in temperature of between 2 to 5°C. The average increase in predicted temperature has been revised downwards constantly. Indicative is that scientific predictions in 1980 were that the sea level would rise by 8 m over the next century because of global warming; in 1989 predictions were revised downwards to 1 m; in 1990 revised to 65 cm; and in 1993, to 20 cm (Ridley, 1996). Under the business-as-usual case, anthropogenic activity will increase global temperatures by up to 0.2 of a degree per decade (*New Scientist*, 1997).

The consequences of global warming are not distributed evenly around the world, some countries will lose and others will gain. CSIRO has modelled climate change scenarios for locations in Australia, and the predictions are presented in the table below. Although large-scale increases in temperature are not predicted, warming is discernible at between 0.3°C and 1.3°C by 2030. These predictions are significantly lower than predictions for global temperature increases.

Table 11.1
Climate Change Predictions

Australian Region	Local Warming per Degree of Global Warming	Warming in 2030	Warming in 2070
Northern Coast (North of 25°S)	0.9 to 1.3	0.3 to 1.0	0.6 to 2.7
Southern Coast (south of 25°S)	0.8 to 1.6	0.3 to 1.3	0.6 to 3.4
Inland	1.0 to 1.8	0.4 to 1.4	0.7 to 3.8

Source: CSIRO (1996).

If it is assumed that the ground based records of warming and the predictions of global change models are correct, that is, that global temperatures will rise by approximately 2°C over the next few decades, then the potential consequences of such a temperature increase include the following. Firstly, rises in sea levels (it is suggested by 20 cm now) may be caused by thermal expansion of the ocean's upper layers and ice melting. This could result in higher storm surges, increased flooding, coastal erosion and damage to coastal ecosystems and infrastructure. It is suggested that certain lower lying areas may be inundated from climate change. These problems will be greater for developing countries which cannot respond to changes as effectively. Secondly, although attracting debate, the effects in the agricultural sector may be the largest sector of the economy to be affected, given its climate sensitivity. Some countries will benefit from land becoming available for agriculture at higher yields, where other countries will lose land and experience falling productivity and higher costs. In Australia it has been hypothesised that there will be a potential decrease in rainfall, once again affecting the productivity of the agriculture sector, as well as having an impact on flora and fauna. Thirdly, flora and fauna may suffer under climate change, with weed and pest distribution increasing, and plant productivity falling. In Australia especially the risk of fire danger would increase, hence endangering a number of species. Fourthly, additional spending would be required on infrastructure networks in most cities, some of which could involve substantial capital works.

The costs identified above, plus many others, have been used to increase the urgency with which the world should respond to global warming. A general conclusion by many economists is that under a warming of 2.5°C a limited set of damages has been estimated at 1 to 1.5 percent of GDP per year in developed countries and 2 to 9 percent of GDP per year in developing countries. However, abating global warming will also cost huge amounts of money. In general, it has been estimated that holding national carbon dioxide emissions at their 1990 levels will cost approximately 1 to 2 per cent of GDP in the long run in OECD countries. Reducing the level of emissions further would mean higher GDP costs (IPCC, 1995).

However, there will be increased benefits to be derived from air quality improvements. It has been estimated that such non-climate related benefits could offset 30 to 100 percent of abatement costs (IPCC, 1995). It has been seen to be essential to commit to an international agreement on greenhouse gases as soon as possible and to set in place a structure to address the problem. However, to properly address the issue of global warming, the benefits of such warming and the costs of emissions reductions must be considered before assuming that overall there will be a net loss to society. One such critic that suggests that global warming overall is a bonus and not a negative for the earth is Thomas Moore. He suggests that, firstly, the world has previously experienced significant increasing temperature changes, and during such periods economies have blossomed. An example is Europe between AD 800 and 1300. Moore surmises in his historical reflection that cold weather brings stagnation, and sometimes a return to outmoded ways. Secondly, the quality of human health would increase, respiratory and circulatory illnesses would decrease and conversely the chances of acquiring insect-borne diseases would not eventuate, as hypothesised by a number of environmentalists. Thirdly, increased amenity benefits would result from warmer weather, given that humans prefer a hotter climate. Fourthly, energy use overall is hypothesised to fall, given moderately higher temperatures, and fifthly, productivity results would be incurred with less flight and travel delays with warmer weather.

The increase in temperature is likely to have an effect in tourism. Tourists tend to spend more time outdoors than residents and are more vulnerable to the weather. Warming increases the length of the effective summer season and decreases the length of winter seasons. The increase in summer season is likely to be more important than the corresponding decrease of the winter season. On net, global tourism should grow. Mendelsohn (1996)31 predicts that global warming would effect Australian tourism by between -US$0.36 billion to US$0.18 billion.

There is clearly considerable uncertainty over the existence and future economic effects of global warming. However, based on the precautionary principle if the costs of global warming are true, then these global costs would significantly outweigh the costs incurred from being wrong about global warming. In other words, many of the potential disastrous and life threatening consequences of global warming have not been ruled out completely, hence it is better to remain on the safe side and take action now rather than adopt a "wait and see" attitude and take no action at all.

International Climate Change Policy

In December 1997 at Kyoto in Japan, the Parties to the United Nations Framework Convention on Climate Change agreed to a Protocol to reduce global greenhouse emissions. The Protocol was open for parties to sign between March 1998 and March 1999. Australia announced its signature to the Protocol on 30 April, 1998. At the Buenos Aires conference on climate change in November 1998, countries considered workable arrangements for putting the Kyoto principles and objectives into effect including resolution to a number of complex issues for international emissions trading. From the conference emerged the two year Buenos Aires Plan of Action which intends to bring together a number of issues under the broad framework of the Kyoto Protocol for the next conference in The Hague, the Netherlands in November 2000. The Hague conference will be the most important since Kyoto because this conference aims to secure sufficient signatories to the Protocol to trigger the ratification of the Kyoto Protocol. The ratification was planned to happen within 12 months of that conference, but didn't, for a raft of reasons most notably that the Protocol does not capture commitment from developing countries.

Nonetheless, the Kyoto Protocol stands as a key instrument to address global climate change. The Kyoto Protocol set differential emissions targets for developed countries, with a view to *reducing* their overall emissions of such gases by at least 5 per cent below 1990 levels in the commitment period 2008 to 2012.

31 +2.5°C temperature, +8.0 per cent precipitation, and +44 cm sea level change by 2060.

Table 11.2
Emissions Targets

Selected Country	Target by 2012 Relative to 1990
Australia	108
Canada	94
European Community	92
Iceland	110
Japan	94
New Zealand	100
Russian Federation	100
Spain	92
UK & Northern Ireland	92
USA	93

Note: Selected countries only - see Protocol for list of Countries.
Source: United Nations (1997).

As Table 11.2 shows, countries' commitments range from an 8 percentage point reduction in emissions from a 1990 base to a 10 percentage point increase. Australia's target is to contain emissions to an increase of 8 per cent above 1990 levels in the commitment period 2008 to 2012.

This target is widely thought to be a favourable policy outcome for Australia relative to other member countries which are required to meet more onerous targets, have lower emissions per capita and, in some cases, are less able to afford a potential decline in real incomes. Only Iceland has a less onerous target than Australia.

However, these targets are tighter than they seem because of the growth in emissions that has occurred since 1990 to the time in which the targets were agreed. The OECD (1999) reports that between 1990 and 1995 emissions have grown significantly, for example, Australian emissions have grown by 6 per cent placing Australia already close to exceeding the target of 8 per cent to 2012; Canada increased by 10 per cent, exceeding the target of -6 per cent; Japan increased by 8 per cent, exceeding the target of -6 per cent and the United States by 5 per cent exceeding the target of -7 per cent. Where emission levels have fallen, it is usually due to economic decline in transition economies, and in the case of the United Kingdom, to reform in the electricity industry. The targets overall imply reductions that may amount to some 30 per cent. However, the Australian Greenhouse Office, the lead Commonwealth agency on greenhouse matters, states that the 1990 baseline is still being negotiated. If the OECD figures are broadly accurate then global greenhouse policy has a somewhat long road ahead.

Figure 11.1 shows projected global carbon dioxide emissions from fossil fuel combustion over the period 1990-2020. Global emissions are projected to double during this period.

Figure 11.1
Carbon Dioxide Emissions from Fossil Fuel Combustion
1990 to 2020

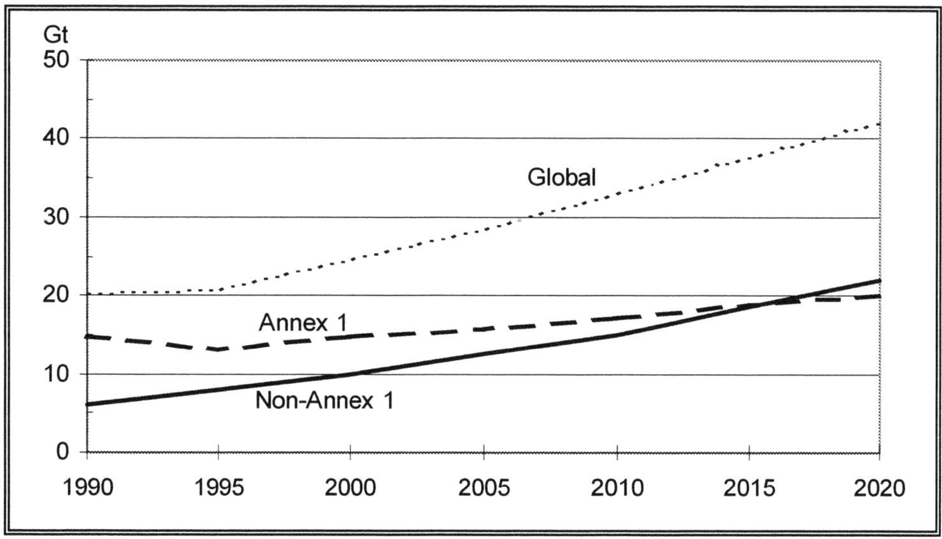

Note: Annex 1 Countries: OECD countries except Mexico, Korea and Turkey, plus Russia, Belarus and the countries of central and Eastern Europe. Non-Annex Countries are mainly developing countries.

Source: ABARE, *Research Report 97.4.*

Global emissions growth projections are driven to a large extent by the developing regions. Emissions are projected to rise at an average rate of 1.34 per cent a year in developed countries, while emissions from developing countries are projected to rise by substantially more - an estimated 3.96 per cent a year. By 2016, developing countries' emissions are projected to overtake developed countries, and by 2020 developing countries will be responsible for 52 per cent of global emissions. The OECD predicts that China and India will be responsible for 38 per cent of global emissions by 2050. These predictions have an important bearing on international negotiations on climate change since the Kyoto Protocol only applies to developed countries. It is for this reason that President Clinton is having difficulty in getting Congress to agree to the United States signing up.

Australia is a relatively small player in greenhouse emissions, accounting for only 1.4 per cent (402 Mt CO_2-e in 1995) of global emissions. However, emissions per capita and per GDP are high, reflecting (i) dependence on coal for electricity generation (ii) emissions intensive industries (aluminium, iron and steel and petroleum products) and (iii) growth in export of these energy intensive products.

Figure 11.2
Greenhouse Gas Emissions & Projections
Australia and South Australia 1996-97 to 2009-10

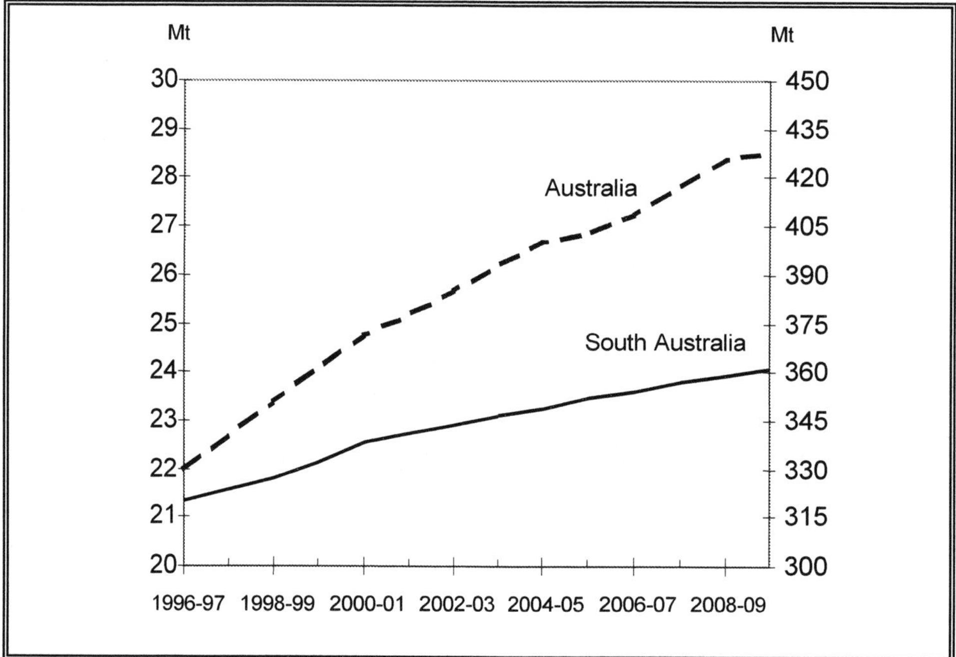

Source: ABARE, *Research Report 97.2* and SA Centre for Economic Studies (1998).

Figure 11.3
Greenhouse Gas Emissions Per Capita
Australia and South Australia 1996-97 to 2009-10

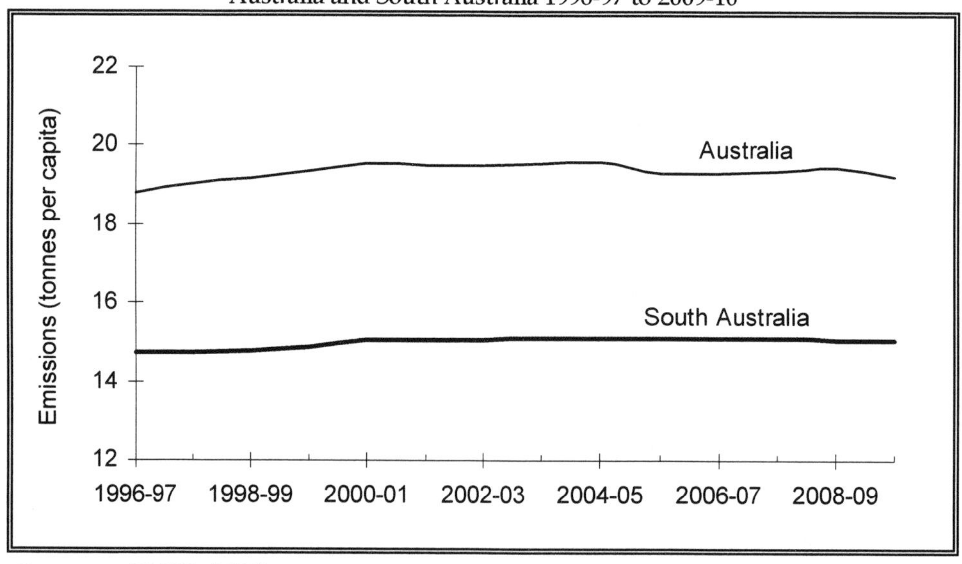

Source: SACES, (1998).

Comparative Australian and South Australian emissions data are hard to come by, but Figure 11.2 traces emissions growth projected for the 14 years from 1996-97 to 2009-10. During this period Australia's emissions are expected to grow by about 29.7 per cent. Interestingly, South Australia's emissions growth is expected to be less than half of that - only 12.8 per cent. The slower growth in emissions from South Australia reflects a slower growth in population and output relative to Australia.

Emissions per head of population are also lower for South Australia than for Australia (Figure 11.3), reflecting that South Australia is a 'cleaner' State than nationally. Two key factors work to South Australia's advantage, namely, (i) the higher proportion of use of 'clean' fuels for electricity generation particularly natural gas, and (ii) the structure of the South Australian economy particularly in that there is no energy intensive alumina production and that agriculture is still relatively more important in South Australia than nationally. In addition, South Australia imports electricity from the Interconnection grid.

Australian Government Initiatives

In the absence of the adoption of greenhouse policies, that is, under the business-as-usual case, Australia's emissions would grow by 43 per cent by 2012 relative to emissions in 1990. Following the first two UN conferences (Rio de Janeiro 1992 and Berlin 1995), national climate change policies have been implemented which are expected to reduce emissions growth to 28 per cent by 2010 relative to 1990 emissions levels. In November 1997, the Prime Minister announced a new set of policy measures which built and expanded upon the original climate change package. These initiatives are expected to result in emissions levels of 448Mt CO_2-e by 2010, 18 per cent higher than in 1990. This package goes beyond the 'no regrets', minimal cost policies.

The gap between announced policies and the target is 10 per cent (that is, 18 per cent emissions growth compared with target of 8 per cent). How Australia will bridge this gap is not yet clear, as there have been no further greenhouse policy announcements. Apparently the gap may be handled through some combination of (i) re-estimation of calculations for emissions associated with land clearing and carbon sinks (e.g., forests) as these estimates carry very broad error bands and are argued to overstate current emissions growth estimates, (ii) adoption of market based policy initiatives such as the introduction of a carbon tax or an emissions trading system and (iii) State and/or local government based greenhouse policy initiatives.

The major climate change initiatives announced in November, 1997 include:

(1) Boosting the use of renewable energy, which involves setting mandatory target for electricity retailers to source an additional 2 per cent of their electricity from renewable energy sources by 2010.

(2) Establishing a Commonwealth Greenhouse Office, responsible for delivery of Commonwealth greenhouse programmes.

(3) Accelerating energy market reform. Efficiency standards for fossil fuel electricity generation will be implemented by 2000, ensuring Australia adopts best practice. Accelerated energy market reform will deliver both economic and environmental, particularly greenhouse benefits.

(4) Improving the fuel efficiency of our car fleet. The Government will negotiate with the automotive industry to secure a 15 per cent fuel efficiency improvement target by 2010 over business as usual. There will be mandatory, model specific, fuel efficiency labelling.

(5) Implementing national energy efficiency codes and standards for buildings, appliances and industrial equipment. Energy efficiency codes and standards will be developed that will take us to best practice standards.

(6) Fostering growth in plantation forestry and native revegetation to act as a sink for greenhouse gas. Plantations 2020 vision involves trebling the plantation estate by 2020. This will complement the Bush for Greenhouse programme which will force partnerships between the corporate sector and landholders through the corporate funding of revegetation projects.

(7) Extending the successful voluntary industry Greenhouse Challenge Programme to allow greater uptake by industry. More than 1,000 large and medium companies will participate by 2005. An innovative Greenhouse Allies program for smaller businesses is to be included in the Challenge.

(8) Supporting the extensive uptake of the worldwide Cities for Climate Protection campaign by Australian Local Governments. Through the campaign Local Governments will work with their communities to reduce emissions through increasing energy efficiency, and developing creative transportation, waste management and building policies.

Harrington in ABARE (1999) indicates that the energy sector accounts for 79 per cent of Australia's greenhouse gas emissions of which electricity generation accounts for 55 per cent, transport 17 per cent and the remainder is fugitive. Consequently, he argues, power generation will be called on to lead the way in achieving effective national greenhouse mitigation. However, on marginal cost principles of emissions abatement this view does not follow. It is plausible that a minimum cost approach to reaching the Kyoto target may not rely so heavily on power generation, but moreover, it may be cost effective for Australia to buy the right for some other country to reduce emissions because they can achieve the outcome cheaply. It is increasingly accepted in global forums that economic instruments (such as tradeable permits and carbon taxes) are more effective than regulations and standards for controlling greenhouse gas emissions. As the OECD (1998) state "economic instruments allow firms and households to meet environmental goals in a least-cost way, whereas regulations often lock-in technologies or market practices that turn out to be inefficient".

Even a cursory review of the Australian greenhouse policies would suggest that many of these policies are regulatory in nature or involve setting mandatory national standards. These policies have the potential to impose higher than necessary resource costs on industry and the general community, and are likely to erode at least part of the trade advantage secured by Australia and Kyoto. There is no reason to expect least-cost outcomes if each State adopts the same approach to its contribution to reduce greenhouse emissions or if each State is required to contribute to greenhouse emissions reduction on an equi-proportional basis, particularly as some States, such as South Australia, are projected to have significantly lower per capita emissions than nationally. The same argument follows at the industry and community levels.

Australia has not adopted, at this time, economic instruments for the abatement of greenhouse emissions. However, substantial research on emissions trading has been undertaken, for example (ABARE, Research Report 98.1), indicating the viability of such systems and guidelines for global emissions trading is a key issue at the next UN Framework Convention on Climate Change in The Hague.

Economic Impacts

Australia

OECD world economic models estimate that the cost of emissions reductions would range from 0.6 to 1.7 per cent of GDP in OECD countries and from 1.2 to 2.3 per cent in non-OECD countries. Overall, the level of world GDP would be lower by 0.9 to 1.8 per cent in 2050. These costs are, of course enormous, but such models do not take into account the benefits of less global warming.

The agreement reached at Kyoto to set differential country targets for emissions will work in Australia's favour. This outcome reflects that Australia's emissions target of 8 per cent *growth* compared with emissions *reductions* for most of the developed countries means that (i) the task (and the resource cost implications) are less onerous for Australia and (ii) given Australia's relatively high wealth per capita, the sacrifice made by Australians will bite less hard than for the less wealthy countries. The relatively lower resource cost of implementing policies to reduce emissions growth will mean that the price of Australian produced goods and services will rise, but, by a lesser amount than other developed countries, and by implication, confers an international trade advantage for Australia. South Australia will, of course, share the national advantage conferred through the international negotiations on targets.

In addition, as per capita levels and predicted growth rates of emissions are lower for South Australia than nationally, the resources required by South Australia to contribute to reducing the national target should be less thereby conferring a trade advantage for South Australia relative to Australia. That is, South Australia may receive a double win.

The impact of greenhouse gas abatement policies on the Australian economy has been simulated using ABARE's model of the Australian economy and 18 other regions comprising the rest of the world. The model, known as MEGABARE, was used by ABARE to advise the Australian Government leading up to negotiations at the Kyoto Conference, and the model has been refined with new information made available post-Kyoto.

The economic impact of greenhouse policies is estimated relative to the business-as-usual case. This case refers to emissions growth that is projected from economic production and technological change that would have occurred in the absence of the adoption of policies and initiatives to abate greenhouse gas emissions to the year 2012. Under the business-as-usual case, it is assumed that Australia's real GDP grows at the average annual rate of 2.5 per cent, population grows at 1.5 per cent and emissions grow at 1.9 per cent. These assumptions are

Table 11.3
Unilateral Country Emission Reduction Targets - Impact on GDP

Country	Percentage
Australia	-0.52
New Zealand	-2.15
United States	-0.06
Canada	-1.41
Japan	-1.90
European Union	-1.02
EFTA	-1.35
Republic of Korea	0.03
China	1.04
Taiwan	0.09
Indonesia	-0.77
Other ASEAN	-1.02
India	0.00
Mexico	-0.55
Brazil	-0.01
Rest of America	-0.38
former Soviet Union	-0.21
Central European Assoc.	-0.22
Rest of World	-0.02

Source: MEGABARE model.

underpinned with specific growth rates for various energy-intensive industries, in particular, coal, oil, gas, iron and steel and non-ferrous metals.

Two scenarios are presented: unilateral country targets and international tradeable quotas.

Under unilateral country targets, Annex B countries to the Protocol achieve emission reduction targets by adopting domestic greenhouse gas abatement policies, regardless of the abatement cost differentials which exist between regions.

Under this scenario, the real GDP of Annex B countries is projected to decline by 0.86 per cent less than it would have otherwise been in the absence of greenhouse gas abatement policies. Country specific results are presented in Table 11.3. Australia's real GDP is projected to decline by 0.5 per cent, smaller than the average for Annex B countries and significantly less than for New Zealand (decline of 2.2 per cent) and Japan (decline of 1.9 per cent). Hence, the economic impact of Australian emissions reductions required under the Kyoto Protocol are less severe than for many other Annex B countries, but are nonetheless significant.

At the industry level, the most significant reduction in output occurs in the Australian non-ferrous metals industry. Output is projected to decline by about 33 per cent relative to the business-as-usual case. In absolute terms, this means that output from the industry by 2012 is limited to approximately the current levels of production. Production of non-ferrous metals (which includes aluminium smelting) requires large inputs of electricity. Electricity generation in Australia is coal intensive and so large abatement costs are passed onto the non-ferrous metals sector via increased electricity charges.

Coal output is projected to decline by about 25 per cent, relative to the business-as-usual case. This result reflects a decline in demand for coal both domestically and by foreign countries, notably Japan.

Australian output of chemicals, rubber and plastics is projected to increase by around 26 per cent relative to the business-as-usual case. This result reflects that the Australian industry is less emissions intensive relative to the same industries in other Annex B countries. Australian output of manufacturing, agriculture and processed agriculture is also projected to rise relative to business-as-usual.

Under the international tradeable quota scheme, Australia buys quota from the former Soviet Union and Eastern Europe. It is cost effective for Australia to buy quota and adopt greenhouse policies to reduce emissions by 11.4 per cent rather than adopt domestic greenhouse gas abatement policies to achieve the emissions target. In other words, Australia buys the right to emit greenhouse gases and other Annex B countries implement abatement policies which would enable Annex B countries collectively to achieve the overall target set at Kyoto.

The impact of international tradeable quota on the real GDP of Annex B countries is projected to be a reduction of 0.21 per cent, relative to the business-as-usual case. Country specific results are presented in Table 11.4. Australia's real GDP is projected to decline by 0.1 per cent, which, within the parameters of the modelling is not significantly different from no impact.

Table 11.4
Tradeable Quotas - Impact on GDP

Country	Percentage
Australia	-0.08
New Zealand	-0.49
United States	0.06
Canada	-0.06
Japan	0.00
European Union	-0.17
EFTA	-0.04
Republic of Korea	0.09
China	0.37
Taiwan	0.08
Indonesia	-0.08
Other ASEAN	-0.10
India	0.03
Mexico	-0.04
Brazil	0.07
Rest of America	-0.05
Former Soviet Union	-2.94
Central European Assoc.	-3.08
Rest of World	0.04

Source: MEGABARE model.

At the industry level, the most significant reduction in output occurs in the Australian non-ferrous metals industry. Output is projected to decline by about 21 per cent in 2012, relative to the business-as-usual case. In absolute terms, growth of the industry is impaired but does not contract. The competitiveness of the industry is eroded relative to other regions where electricity used as an input to the industry is less dependent on fossil fuels, and accordingly the industry declines. However, the impact is less than under the previous scenario. In absolute terms, this result implies that industry growth is contained to about a third of what it would have otherwise been in the absence of greenhouse gas abatement policies.

South Australia

The impact of greenhouse gas abatement policies on the South Australian economy has been simulated using the Centre's FED-SA economic model of the South Australian economy and the rest of Australia. (The FED-SA and MEGABARE models were interconnected for this study). As with the economic impact on Australia, two scenarios are presented - unilateral country targets and international tradeable quotas.

The economic impact is measured relative to the business-as-usual case. In general, it is assumed that South Australian real GSP grows by 1.5 per cent, population grows by 0.5 per cent and emissions grow by 1.3 per cent each year. Specific assumptions are also made on the growth of the energy-intensive industries.

Under the unilateral country targets, South Australia's real GSP decreases by 0.26 per cent or about $106 million relative to the business-as-usual by 2012. This result is a minor impact on South Australia, and significantly less than the impact on Australia.

The iron ore, non-ferrous ores, coal and basic metals industries are projected to reduce output relative to the business-as-usual case, but given the rate of underlying growth in the South Australian economy, all industries continue to grow relative to current production levels. The slowing of growth relative to business-as-usual reflects the significant adverse impact of greenhouse gas abatement policies on international trading partners, most notably Japan.

The South Australian chemicals industry increases output relative to the business-as-usual case.

Under the international tradeable quota scheme, South Australia's real GSP increases by about 0.1 per cent or about $42 million by 2012.

This is a favourable result for South Australia, and is in contrast with the results for Australia where real GDP declines.

The iron ore, non-ferrous ores, coal and basic metals industries reduce output relative to the business-as-usual case. These output reductions are mild, and in absolute terms, international tradeable quotas slow the growth of these industries by only about one quarter by 2012.

The relatively favourable result for South Australia reflects a differing economic structure (see Figure 11.4). Compared with Australia, South Australia has a (i) less emissions intensive manufacturing industry, reflecting particularly the absence of alumina production, (ii) uses a cleaner mix of fuel for electricity generation including the import of about 30 per cent of domestic demand from the Interconnection grid, (iii) a larger agricultural sector and (iv) smaller mining sector. This structure requires a less resource intensive response to greenhouse gas abatement and enables South Australia to secure a trade advantage relative to the rest of Australia.

In addition, South Australia is less trade exposed to Japan relative to the rest of Australia. Japan is an emissions intensive country relative to most other countries in the world. As its economy contracts in response to greenhouse gas abatement measures, South Australia feels the trade impact less so than does the rest of Australia.

Figure 11.4
Economic Structure — South Australia Compared with Australia

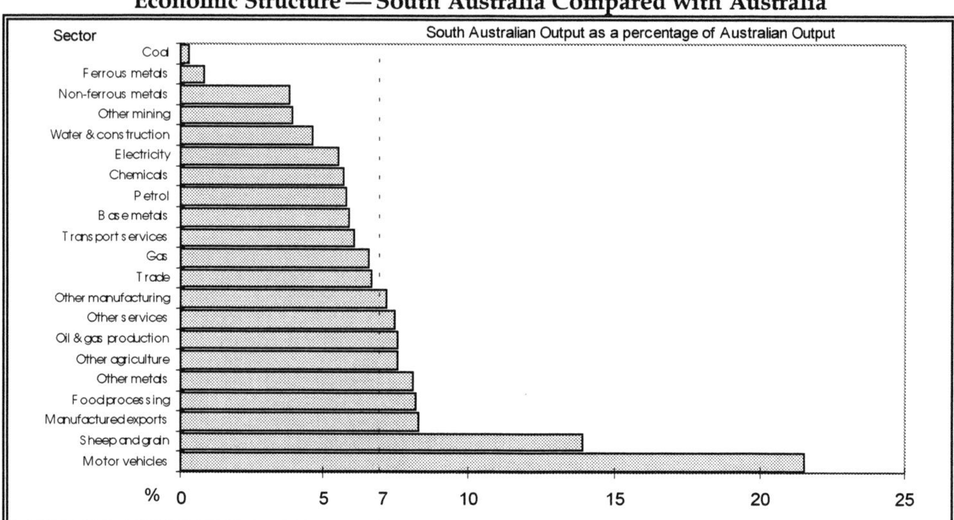

Regional Policy Issues

Per capita emissions for South Australia are significantly lower than for Australia as-a-whole and are expected to remain so through to 2010. Figure 11.5 shows that per capita emissions for South Australia are also lower than Victoria and Queensland and substantially lower than Western Australia.

If Australia were to adopt a scheme of international tradeable quotas, then the issue for South Australia is to agree with the Commonwealth and the other States on its share of the purchase cost of the quota. In general this agreement would be uncontentious from South Australia's perspective if the share were measured according to emissions per capita. However, if national greenhouse gas abatement policies are adopted instead of international tradeable quotas, then the issue for this region is more complex.

As indicated above, lower level emissions and lower expected growth of emissions are a reflection of the structure of the South Australian economy. While the structure of the economy is clearly advantageous from the point of view of conserving the natural environment, the downside is that reducing greenhouse gas emissions consistent with nationally determined policies may be harder for this region to achieve relative to more intensive emission regions. That is, the marginal cost of abatement may be higher for South Australia than for other regions. The implication being that the resource cost per capita to achieve the national target will be higher for South Australia.

Figure 11.5
Growth of Per Capita Greenhouse Gas Emission From The Energy Sector
Australia and Selected States - 1988-89 to 2009-10

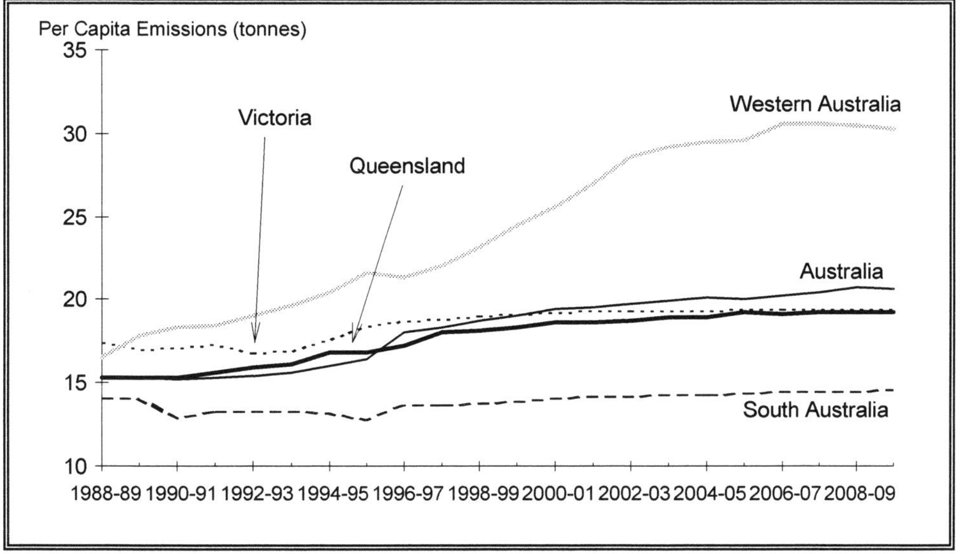

Source: Derived from ABARE and Centre for Economic Studies data and ABS, *Demography*.

By adopting the national strategy on greenhouse emission abatement, this region may be placing itself at a relative disadvantage. South Australia does not need to travel along this path.

Under the international tradeable quota scheme Australia would buy emissions quota. Countries that have low abatement costs would adopt greenhouse policies and countries that have high abatement costs would buy permits to emit gases instead of implementing abatement policies. Following this approach, an emissions trading scheme at the national level, would provide the flexibility needed to identify actions to achieve target emissions reductions which involve the least resource cost.

The framework for a national emissions scheme would be quite similar to the international scheme. The Centre understands that the Australian Greenhouse Office (AGO) has responsibility to Federal Cabinet for submitting a recommended course of action on the implementation of a national emissions trading scheme. A framework for such a scheme is to be developed in consultation with the States.

While, in principle, there are several versions of the scheme, basically, quota would be allocated to each State and then the State could trade quota at the market clearing price. As South Australia is a low emission region, there is a reasonable expectation that the region should be able to sell quota. The value of this quota may be a significant source of revenue for the State and possibility for the South Australian Government, depending on how the scheme is administered. However, the possibility of South Australia being a seller of quota rests on the method for allocating the initial quota endowment. To secure the best outcome for South Australia and, in particular, to ensure recognition as a low emission State, the South Australia Government should take steps now to ensure that an appropriate methodology is adopted.

Alternatively, South Australia may wish to consider directly purchasing the right to emit greenhouse gasses from the Eastern European Bloc or from other countries with low marginal abatement costs. The payment of cold hard foreign exchange would be a transparent and least cost method of achieving the global objective of saving this planet from ourselves.

Summary

The effect of anthropogenic activity on climate is one of the most important long-run issues for regions and, moreover, for the global community.

The relationship between climate and regional economic growth is difficult to measure and measurements vary between studies. However, there is broad acceptance that climate effects capital use, human productivity and leisure activity. With the exception of the far North, South Australia's climate is an advantage for the region.

The scientific community has found evidence that the global climate is warming, due to both natural and anthropogenic causes. Predicted effects of global warming include rising sea levels, changes in weather patterns, changes to flora and fauna, changes to human productivity and health and consequent effects on public and private expenditure programs and policies. These changes can be beneficial or damaging. Overall, the consequences of climate change are unclear, but if warming is unabated then the long run consequences might be catastrophic. As the 'downside' might be so disastrous, the global community (or at least the developed countries) has adopted the precautionary principle, committing resources to emissions abatement even though the effects of global warming are currently unclear. On the basis of this principle, developed countries have agreed to a set of targets that limit the growth of emissions.

Australia's target is to limit the growth of CO_2 emissions to 8 per cent by 2012, relative to 1990.

In broad terms, there are two types of policies that could be adopted to abate greenhouse gas emissions: an international tradeable quota scheme or unilateral targets underwhich each country would adopt emissions abatement policies. The analysis presented in this chapter concludes that international tradeable quotas is the best option for Australia (and South Australia) as it is cost-effective for Australia to buy the right to emit gases while other countries such as Eastern Europe sell that right and use the funds to commit resources to upgrade facilities such as electricity generating plants.

If domestic policies must be adopted in each country then Australia has a more costly task to reach its targets. The Australian government has a set of national policies for greenhouse gas abatement. The South Australian economy is a low emissions region relative to most other regions in Australia, and the expected growth in emissions per capita is low. South Australia should not be forced into adopting national policies to achieve the national target. Recognition should be given to the green State, and abatement policies should only be adopted if the resource cost is lower than some alternative policy in other States.

References

ABARE, (1999), *Outlook 1999: Commodity Markets and Resource Management*, March.

ABARE (1998a), "Emissions Trading in Australia: Developing a Framework", Research Report 98.1, March.

ABARE (1998b), *International Trading in Greenhouse Gas Emissions*, May.

ABARE (1998c) *Outlook 1998: Commodity Markets and Resource Management*, February.

ABARE (1997a), *Climate Change: Australia's Second National Report under the United Nations Framework Convention on Climate Change*, November.

ABARE (1997b), "The Economic Impact of International Climate Change Policy", Research Report 97.4, June.

ABARE (1997c), "Energy: 1997 Predictions", Research Report 97.2, June.

Environment Australia (1995), *Australia's National Greenhouse Gas Inventory*.

Environment Australia (1998), *Climate Change - The Enhanced Greenhouse Effect*.

Environment Australia (1997), *Framework Convention on Climate Change - Outcomes of the third session of the conference of the parties*, Kyoto, 1-10 December 1997.

Hall, R.E., and Jones, C.I. (1996), "The Productivity of Nations", National Bureau of Economic Research, Working Paper 5812, November.

Intergovernmental Panel on Climate Change (IPCC), (1995), Second Assessment Report, Working Paper III, Cambridge University Press, Massachusetts.

Jones, P., (1997), *The European Miracle*, Cambridge Press.

Kyoto Protocol to the United Nations Framework Convention on Climate Change, Final Version, 1998.

Mendelsohn, R. (1996), "The Impact of Global Warming on Pacific Rim Countries", in *The Economics of Pollution Control in the Asia Pacific*, eds. R. Mendelsohn and D. Show.

Mendelsohn, R. and Show, D. (eds.) (1996), *The Economics of Pollution Control in the Asia Pacific*.

National Greenhouse Gas Inventory Committee (1995), *National Greenhouse Gas Inventory 1995*, Australia.

National Greenhouse Gas Inventory Committee (1997a), "Land Use Change and Forestry Workbook for Carbon Dioxide from the Biosphere", Workbook 4.2, Revision 2, Australia.

National Greenhouse Gas Inventory Committee (1997b), *National Greenhouse Gas Inventory 1995*, Environment Australia, September.

National Greenhouse Gas Inventory Committee (1997c), "National Greenhouse Gas Inventory Land Use Change and Forestry Sector 1988-1995", based on Workbook 4.2., Australia.

Nordhaus, William D. (1994), *Managing the Global Commons: The Economics of Climate Change*, MIT Press, Cambridge Massachusetts.

OECD (1998), *Economic Outlook*, OECD Publications, Paris, June.

OECD (1999), "Policy Changes Arising from Climate Change", in *Economic Outlook*, OECD, Chapter V, June.

Ridley, Matt (1995), *Down To Earth - A Contrarian View of Environmental Problems*, IEA, London.

Ridley, Matt (1996), *Down To Earth II: Combating Environmental Myths*, IEA, London.

Ridley, M. (1997) *Down To Earth II Contrarian View of Environmental Problems*, IEA, London.

South Australian Greenhouse Committee Renewable Energy Working Group (1995), *Towards the Renewable Energy Target for South Australia.*

Chapter Twelve

The Relaunch of Woomera

The revitalisation of Woomera rocket range and potential industry developments in the Salisbury region of South Australia provide an interesting and relevant case study. The development of the Woomera spaceport by the Kistler Aerospace Corporation will be the world's first commercial facility for launching reusable space vehicles. Woomera is geographically remote, both from the location of Australian economic activity and the foreign investors' technology base. In addition, the harsh physical environment is not attractive to workers. If new knowledge spillovers are to occur, then it is likely that these will occur through some non-physical clustering or, as termed in this chapter, information clustering.

Building on a commissioned project assignment between the Centre and the Kistler Aerospace Corporation, this chapter presents findings on the economic impact of the investment in the Woomera region and investigates the theory and empirical evidence for information clustering. In addition, an assessment is made of the potential for new knowledge spillovers from the revitalisation of Woomera, and the capacity for new knowledge to be captured by firms in South Australia in contrast with being captured by the foreign investor's technology base.

The Rise and Decline of Woomera

The history of the development of Woomera is well documented in Buchanan and Edwards (1998) and in Morton (1989), the later taking a defence perspective.

Spurred on by the frighting destruction of Germany's V1 and V2 rockets, Britain was keen to acquire new knowledge on the integration of atomic weapons and rockets. The UK, having a land mass too small for rocket testing turned to consider the potential for sites in the two largest Commonwealth countries namely Canada and Australia. Canada was eliminated because the climatic conditions would make it too difficult to recover rockets. In April 1947, the UK-Australia Joint Project came into existence and Woomera was born. Over the 50 years since its creation, Woomera's role changed from a rocket and military testing support base in the 1950s - early 1970s to its current mission as a residential support area for the Joint Defence Facility, Narrungar. During the first decade and a half of the operation at Woomera, Britain and Australia used the massive industrial complex, which was once a munitions factory, at Salisbury, South Australia, as the back bone for the Weapons Research Establishment. The establishment was responsible for the design and manufacture of missiles and target vehicles for testing at Woomera.

Morton (1989) estimates that from 1947-48 to 1979-80 the joint project cost about $3.2 billion of which the UK share was about $1 billion and the Australian share was $2.3 billion in 1986 dollars. Although not a large sum in the context of the respective defence budgets over a 30 year period, the Joint Project involved significant R&D spending and was an important component in the overall push in Britain to raise military R&D spending over the decade post Second World War. The Chifley government propounded the benefits of the Joint Project in terms of recalling the desperate days of 1943 when Britain had denied Australia armaments to use in the Pacific theatre, the Chifley government was keen to acquire new generation weapons for use in any future war. The relocation of weapons research to the Woomera and Salisbury regions would, in addition, bring new industries and additional foreign investment of about $1 billion and associated additional employment in Australia arising from that expenditure. Other benefits included the bringing forward of improved telecommunications in the outback and the stimulation of the development of the Woomera township including access to education for Aboriginal children.

As Morton points out, Australia's involvement could have been regarded as a remarkable bargain because Australia had negotiated full access to experimental data. However, the technology transfer did not happen to any significant extent. Within the context of the analytical applications of the first section of this book, of Morton's arguments are re-interpreted to enable consideration for the potential of South Australia's future in the space industry.

Firstly, the defence industry in the newly formed satellite settlement of Salisbury, just North of Adelaide, was reorganised in 1955 just prior to scaling up the joint project at Woomera. The reorganisation was designed to reduce the influence of the British partner thereby fostering the development of the fledging Australian high-tech defence and related industries. However, the reorganisation had the effect of discouraging the British from setting up the design teams in Australia. London retained the R&D agenda and the control, which put Australia in the position of supplying the answers to R&D topics set for them. Australia did not have the critical mass of technological knowledge to meet the requirements and computing and communications systems were not sophisticated in those days for intensive knowledge exchange. Consequently the program fell back to using Woomera as a test range with the design work being done mainly from London. In essence, Australia should have waited until the British firms moved into Salisbury to capture the technology, and, having moved too quickly, there was very limited opportunity to successfully work with the British firms from their base in Britain because the computing and communications technology of the era was not sufficiently advanced for the intensity of the knowledge transfer required. An 'innovative milieu' failed to develop as external firms were not sufficiently encouraged to establish in SA, nor were policies put in place to build links between those firms which did locate in SA and the existing players in the state economy.

Secondly, some technology transfer was unsuccessful because of the problem of efficient scale economies. In the case of precision optics, the production runs were too small and discontinuous for a small scale fledging firm. This was a reflection of the demand characteristics of the region at the time - the demand for the production from Woomera was not sufficient to sustain the operation and there were very limited domestic private markets to fall back to. This reinforces the importance of having a range of (potential) clients and links with the broad economy for the successful development of firms providing specialised sub-contracting or business services.

Thirdly, Australia did not use the technology that was developed at Woomera and therefore did not acquire the deep knowledge that comes from adapting and modifying technology. There were some important exceptions, for example, the target aircraft, Jindivick, which met an identical need for both countries. However, most of the projects that were developed at Woomera were not used by the Australian defence force. Australian tended to buy the US alternatives because they were more suitable to Australia's defence operational and strategic needs. Australia therefore did not capture the flow-on benefit of using technology it had developed. It did not gain the depth of experience that comes from adopting the technology for local conditions and making the ongoing micro-inventions that come from the familiarity of using a technology.

Fourthly, some of the most costly projects had no direct value to Australian defence. While it was conceivable that Australia might wish to possess a nuclear arsenal for which it had the technical competence to manufacture, the need for this technology both from a defence strategy and a global community safety point of view was very doubtful.

Fifthly, some projects such as the Black Knight and Blue Streak launched in the early 1960s were not only dubiously relevant to the defence of Australia, but, as the Menzies Cabinet realised as early as 1957, were not very remarkable weapons.

The summation of these points is that the mismatch between Australian defence expenditure and defence needs and the inability to 'receive' technology arising inadvertently from the reorganisation of Salisbury in 1955, meant that instead of a bargain, Australia subsidised the British R&D defence program. More importantly, the plan to create an indigenous missile and space industry did not happen and the failure to find a continuing use of the Range meant that the capital equipment, buildings, workshops, plant and airfield were ran-down and the expertise dissipated when Woomera was all but closed down.

Not all was lost in the quest for technology transfer. There are success stories, which contribute to the understanding of South Australia's future development of the space industry. Although, tiny compared with the major Australian migration program at the time especially the recruitment of university staff from overseas, there was a flow of scientific and technical brainpower to South Australia. A small number of firms did establish subsidiaries or branches at Salisbury, and Fairey, British Aerospace, Hawker and Thorn EMI survived after the closure of the joint project. Fairey's survival rested on several characteristics: the initial advantage came from staff with specialised skills not generally available in Australia and ability to achieve economic production runs of specialised target cameras developed by the Weapons Research Establishment at Salisbury. The firm was a versatile engineering company capable of "jobbing" their way into related markets for the specialised civilian projects (capturing teaching aids and scanning systems for geographical survey companies), and moved to Adelaide in 1986. A further benefit of technology transfer is the expertise in rocket and propulsion, aero-ballistics, data reduction, fine mechanisms, advanced optics and electronics developed at Salisbury which was inherited by the current DSTO and flowed into many of the all-Australian defence projects such as over-the-horizon radar.

Woomera Today

During the mid 1990s, as Buchannan and Edwards (1998) have recorded, Woomera continued to be used for testing aircraft and weapons. The Stack Fragmentation trials, the Japanese ALFLEX trials, the NASA sounding rockets and the amateur AUSROC launch have been undertaken. However, Woomera is a much smaller town today than in the 'hay days' of the early to mid 1960s, and although the town still retains a unique identity it is gradually converging and retreating into the outback, looking more like the other regional towns as the years pass. Some selected statistics help to illustrate these socio-economic characteristics.

In the 'hay days' of the early to mid 1960s, Woomera's population approached 6,000, but the population had declined to 1,244 persons (plus 99 overseas visitors) by the 1996 Census. The population had fallen 23 per cent from the previous Census, 5 years earlier. By 1996, the slightly larger towns of Coober Pedy and Roxby Downs had populations of 3,075 and 2,674 respectively with Port Augusta having a population of 14,206. Woomera's population age distribution is similar to other towns in the Far North - Coober Pedy, Roxby Downs and Leigh Creek - although younger than for Port Augusta and South Australia as a whole: Woomera has 73.8 per cent of its population under 40 years compared with 57.3 per cent for South Australia. These age profiles are characteristic of a 'frontier settlement'.

Of the Far North towns only Woomera and Coober Pedy have a significant portion of the population originating from overseas: in 1996, 24.6 per cent of Woomera's population originated from North America and 21.7 per cent of Coober Pedy's population originated from Europe. Despite the British presence in Woomera, the UK and Irish population are now under-represented relative to the State. The cultural mix helps to retain the uniqueness of Woomera. It is common to see both left and right hand drive vehicles on the town's roads and American traditions and holidays are observed with the residents trick or treating on Halloween and Fourth of July Parade and celebrations.

Table 12.1
Selected Areas - Age Distribution - 1996 Census

	Woomera	Coober Pedy	Roxby Downs	Leigh Creek	Port Augusta	South Australia
0-9	260	399	580	211	2,299	193,366
10-19	141	336	290	137	2,082	196,274
20-29	239	335	611	159	2,065	203,210
30-39	279	439	636	247	2,332	221,716
40-49	183	488	346	161	1,997	208,581
50-59	97	550	148	59	1,423	144,983
60-69	42	398	39	12	1,060	115,861
70+	3	130	24	18	948	138,531
Total	**1,244**	**3,075**	**2,674**	**1,004**	**14,206**	**1,422,522**

Table 12.2
Selected Areas - Region of Birth
Census 1996 - Percentage Distribution

	Woomera	Coober Pedy	Roxby Downs	Leigh Creek	Port Augusta	Far North SSD	South Australia
Australia	56.5	57.2	82.7	87.4	87.6	75.0	75.7
Other Oceania, Antarctica	0.9	1.0	1.5	0.7	0.4	1.0	0.8
Total Oceania, Antarctica	57.3	58.3	84.2	88.1	88.0	76.0	76.6
Europe Other	2.6	21.7	1.7	1.0	2.4	7.9	7.1
UK & Ireland	6.7	4.1	5.6	4.8	4.3	4.8	9.5
Middle East & N Africa	0.0	0.1	0.1	0.0	0.0	0.1	0.4
SE Asia	0.9	1.1	0.5	0.3	0.3	0.6	1.8
NE Asia	0.5	0.4	0.0	0.0	0.0	0.2	0.5
Southern Asia	0.6	0.1	0.0	0.0	0.1	0.1	0.4
Nth America	24.6	0.3	0.5	0.0	0.1	3.0	0.3
Sth & Central America	0.5	0.1	0.0	0.0	0.0	0.1	0.2
Africa (excl. Nth)	0.0	0.1	0.3	0.0	0.1	0.1	0.3
Other	0.0	1.7	0.6	0.6	0.3	0.9	0.0
Not Stated	6.4	12.0	6.5	5.2	4.4	6.4	3.0
Total	**100.0**	**100.0**	**100.0**	**100.0**	**100.0**	**100.0**	**100.0**

Table 12.3
Selected Areas - Educational Institution Attended
Census 1996 - Percentage Distribution

	Woomera	Coober Pedy	Roxby Downs	Leigh Creek	Port Augusta	Far North SSD	South Australia
Pre-school	1.9	0.9	2.5	2.8	1.3	1.3	1.2
Infant/Primary	13.4	11.3	14.8	14.8	13.4	10.6	10.6
Secondary	3.7	3.4	3.3	5.6	5.5	2.4	5.8
TAFE	1.4	3.2	2.8	4.1	2.8	2.1	2.4
University	3.4	0.6	1.4	1.4	0.9	1.2	3.3
Other	1.1	0.4	0.3	0.0	0.3	0.4	0.5
None	67.0	65.9	68.4	67.2	69.1	63.6	71.8
Not Stated	8.0	14.4	6.4	4.2	6.7	18.3	4.4
Total	**100.0**	**100.0**	**100.0**	**100.0**	**100.0**	**100.0**	**100.0**

Woomera, Roxby Downs and Leigh Creek all had income levels higher than the state average. Levels of income varied between the areas of study with Roxby Downs having more persons with higher income levels while Coober Pedy had a larger proportion at the lowest levels.

The proportion of persons in employment in these three centres is higher than the state average and correspondingly the proportion who are unemployed is lower. There was also a smaller proportion who were not in the labour force. Total employment in the Far North rose over the period from 1986 to 1996 while the total level of unemployed persons declined. Most were employees with a fall in the number of employers and self-employed.

The main industry in the region is mining influenced by Roxby Downs and Leigh Creek. The large numbers in government administration and defence are influenced by activities at Woomera although the numbers in this industry have declined since 1986. Other industries to exhibit growth include health and

Table 12.4
Far North SSD - Employment By Industry - Census 1986, 1991 and 1996

Industry	Persons			Percent		
	1986	1991	1996	1986	1991	1996
Agriculture, Forestry & Fishing	342	360	299	7.7	6.0	6.0
Mining	854	996	1034	19.3	16.5	20.6
Manufacturing	78	210	138	1.8	3.5	2.7
Electricity, Gas & Water Supply	12	23	15	0.3	0.4	0.3
Construction	428	304	393	9.7	5.0	7.8
Wholesale & Retail Trade	301	543	415	6.8	9.0	8.3
Accommodation, Restaurants etc.	242	357	373	5.5	5.9	7.4
Transport and Storage	195	214	143	4.4	3.6	2.8
Communication Services	77	68	49	1.7	1.1	1.0
Finance, Property & Business Services	303	318	456	6.9	5.3	9.1
Government Admin. & Defence	532	465	411	12.0	7.7	8.2
Education	274	304	286	6.2	5.0	5.7
Health & Community Services	166	382	575	3.8	6.3	11.4
Cultural & Recreation Services	29	41	42	0.7	0.7	0.8
Personal & Other Services	391	551	179	8.9	9.2	3.6
Non-classifiable & Not Stated	193	884	216	4.4	14.7	4.3
Total	**4,417**	**6,020**	**5,024**	**100.0**	**100.0**	**100.0**

community services, trade and construction. The main occupational groups are tradespersons (influenced particularly by the mining activity at Roxby Downs and Leigh Creek) together with the intermediate production and transport workers and labourers. Professionals and associated professionals are also dominant occupations in Woomera and Roxby Downs. The level of employment in manufacturing is only 3 per cent compared with the state average of 15 per cent. Retail trade as would be expected is associated with the larger centres, particularly Port Augusta. Tourism contributes to the retail activity in Coober Pedy which is really the main area of interest to tourists within the region of study. The opal diggings and the underground living are of particular attraction. Building approvals are somewhat sluggish overall except in Roxby Downs and Port Augusta. The expansion in the former has given the non-residential sector a boost in 1997.

The brief socio-economic profile of Woomera suggests the following. Although Woomera is only about $^1/_5$ of the size it was in the hay days of the early to mid 1960s and is smaller than the main Far North regional centres of Roxby Downs, Coober Pedy and Leigh Creek, the town has retained some characteristics unique to the region and to the State which enable it to remain fertile and receptive to regional development and growth, although this potential is likely to have diminished some what since local activity was further reduced by the closure of Nurrungar. The American population, still important in Woomera, opens the town to overseas friends and relatives and projects cultural Americanism through regular festive events and ways of life. The remaining test site facilities attract, albeit at low levels, overseas parties of specialists conducing experiments and tourists curious about the high security, high tech past. The town's population is at least as well educated as South Australians generally, and unemployment is low. Reflecting the past population peaks, the general facilities of the town - roads, parks, recreation facilities and shops - are 'oversized' relative to the current population and could accommodate population growth without major problems.

Re-Launch of Woomera

In late 1997, the prospects of a new investment in space technology gave rise to the hopes of re-launching Woomera. The Kistler Aerospace Corporation proposed the establishment and operation of a commercial launch service within the Woomera Prohibited Area. The launch service would offer customers the means to deploy communications satellites and other payloads in low and medium earth orbits.

Kistler Aerospace Corporation is designing and building a small fleet of re-useable space launch vehicles, known as the K-1. These vehicles, which are being developed and built at Kistler's base in Seattle, involve an investment in excess of $1 billion. At Woomera, there is to be a phased investment. The first facility will consist of prefabricated buildings anchored to concrete pads, removable vacuum flasks and storage tanks. Standard industrial equipment will be used to handle and transport the K-1 vehicles. An existing hangar at Woomera airport will be used for payload preparation. As the launch rate increases, steel framed buildings will be constructed at the launch site and specialist handling equipment will be employed. Construction of the launch facility requires acquisition of land.

Ground operations are typical of those involved in heavy industry. Vehicle maintenance involves standard cranes and fork-lifts to manipulate vehicles and electronic diagnostic equipment to assess their status. Small amounts of solvents, lubricants and industrial gases such as nitrogen and helium will be consumed.

Vehicles will be fuelled at the launch pad using Rocket Propellant 1 a highly refined form of kerosene, and an extremely cold, liquid form of oxygen as the oxidiser. Pumping these liquids, while requiring specified procedures and training, is a usual industrial operation.

Flight operations begin with engine ignition at the launch pad. Launch and ascent are similar to that for expendable vehicle launches - other than both stages return to the landing area immediately adjacent to the launch facility. The first stage returns within ten minutes of launch. The second stage returns approximately 24 hours after launch.

The returning vehicle stages rely on parachute and airbag systems to slow their descent and provide a soft landing. Crews at the landing site recover the stages and transport them to the processing facility to begin the cycle again.

The K-1 will be operated from a launch facility at Ashton Hill, located North West of Woomera within the Woomera Prohibited Area.

Other sites had been considered in the United States, French Guiana and elsewhere in Australia - however, Ashton Hill site offers the benefits of existing infrastructure, including that associated with previous launch activities, unobstructed launch corridors, adjoining flat plain for economic vehicle landing and recovery, nearby Woomera township to provide accommodation for launch and processing personnel, few environmental constraints and a relatively harmonious civil society of joint Aboriginal and European settlement.

At the time of writing, serious problems have emerged in the market for communications satellites. As reported in *The Advertiser* (1 April, 2000), there are four separate proposals for launch facilities around Australia which are fighting for a slice of the $400 billion international satellite industry. There is an oversupply of launch technology and there is some indications that expected payloads are not materialising. The recent failure of Iridium, a communications company with over 60 satellites established in 1997, is evidence of overcrowding in the market and may shake the confidence of potential investors. Nonetheless, the Kistler Aerospace proposal, eventually successful or not, provides the opportunity to consider what are the potential economic benefits of an investment in space technology for the small regional economy of South Australia.

In 1998, Kistler Aerospace Corporation commissioned the Centre to, inter alia, estimate the economic impact of the proposed new investment on the South Australian economy. The Centre used its Computable General Equilibrium (CGE) model, FED-SA, to estimate the impacts, which are presented below.

Kistler Aerospace Corporation has kindly given permission to the Centre to report the impacts on the South Australian economy, but the capital cost, operations expenditure, profitability and assumptions concerning the repatriation of profits remain confidential. Methodology and modelling assumptions which drive to results are detailed in the appendix to this chapter.[32] Estimates of the outlays and revenues of the project were modelled in two segments; the construction phase and the operational phase.

The construction phase draws labour into South Australia. The state's work force increased for the duration of construction (of one year) by 0.03 per cent or around 210 workers (Table 12.5), of which 110 jobs are created directly. Real GSP in South Australia increases by 0.04 per cent, or about $12 million, with negligible change in real GDP at the national level. South Australia's real GSP gain is smaller than the proposed annual expenditure, representing mainly the direct value-added component.

The construction phase benefits the South Australian economy through the direct investment expenditure with the services sector gains occurring through additional non-residential construction. Export-orientated industries such as agriculture, mining and manufacturing lose slightly from the real exchange rate effect associated with the additional demands of construction, and the Balance of Trade consequently worsens.

At the industry level, the beneficiary from the investment in launch services is the construction industry - output increases by 0.22 per cent in South Australia and by 0.03 per cent in the rest of Australia. Agriculture, mining and manufacturing sectors in South Australia and the rest of Australia contract slightly. The reduction in output reflects the effect of labour being drawn away from these sectors to be utilised in the construction sector. The impacts are minor. Of the other 61 sectors in the South Australian and Australian economies there is no significant (positive or negative) impact on industry.

32 The modelling work was undertaken by Glyn Wittwer and Melissa Bright who were employees of the Centre at that time.

Table 12.5
Economic Impact of the Construction Phase (Change from Base Case)

	South Australia	Rest of Australia	Australia
Macroeconomic			
Real GSP, GDP($m)	12.0	-12.0	0.0
Real Consumption($m)	2.0	-2.0	0.0
Employment (FTEs)	210.0	-210.0	
Broad Sectoral Outputs (% change)			
Agriculture	-0.05	-0.03	-0.04
Mining	-0.03	-0.02	-0.03
Manufacturing	-0.02	-0.01	-0.01
Construction	0.22	0.03	0.05

Source: FEDERAL-SA projections.

The construction phase of this project, as with any investment phase, boosts the host State for only as long as the construction activity lasts. The operational phase is far more important than the construction phase because it is ongoing each year over the economic life of the launch services. The economic impact of the operational phase is in the section that follows.

Table 12.6
Economic Impact of the Operational Phase (Change from Base Case)

	South Australia	Rest of Australia	Australia
Macroeconomic			
Real GSP, GDP($m)	40.0	-15.0	25.0
Real Consumption($m)	26.0	-5.0	21.0
Employment	480.0	-480.0	
Broad Sectoral Outputs (% change)			
Agriculture	0.05	-0.90	-0.88
Mining	0.07	-0.04	0.01
Manufacturing	0.12	-0.02	0.08
Construction	0.13	0.52	0.48
Communication	1.86	0.97	1.10
Personal Services	0.17	-0.25	-0.21

Source: FEDERAL-SA projections.

By the time the launch site is near full operation, South Australia's real GSP increases by about $40 million relative to the base case (i.e., without the launch site). Interstate, real GSP of the other States decreases by about $15 million reflecting a diversion of resources away from those States to South Australia. The net effect of these State transfers of resources is an increase in Australian GDP of about $25 million or 0.005 per cent. Given the size of the launch project relative to aggregate Australian economic activity, this is a significant positive result.

Real consumption in South Australia increases by $26 million, and increases at a rate which is higher than the increases in employment. The implication being that real consumption per capita increases, that is, South Australians are wealthier.

There is a slight decline in real consumption (of about $5 million) for the rest of Australia, but the percentage change is lower than the percentage change in employment. The implication being that per capita consumption increases for the rest of Australia. That is, for those who remain in the other States, the average level of wealth is higher. This outcome reflects that although resources are drawn away from other States those resources (mainly labour) are less productive, and find high valued activities in South Australia through engagement, either directly or indirectly, in the Kistler launch service.

Employment in South Australia increases by 480 jobs. As explained earlier in this section national employment is fixed, so the employment arises in South Australia from the attraction of labour from other States. In practice it is reasonable to expect that additional net employment will be created as some occupations will draw from the pool of unemployed.

Table 12.7 summarises the impact of the Kistler operational phase on employment, by main categories. Broadly, direct employment by Kistler of 135 operational staff will increase total employment in the region by 2.7 per cent. The flow-on impacts bring total employment creation to 5,505 jobs. Although it is difficult to ascertain the location of the flow-on employment, the Centre expects that the regional location of employment to be high particularly in the regional towns of Woomera, Roxby Downs and the neighbouring area.

The main industry to benefit from the project is the communications industry, where output increases by 1.86 per cent in South Australia and by 0.97 per cent in the other States. Nationally, the communications sector increases output by 1.10 per cent. Almost all industries in South Australia benefit from the project, with output rising by between 0.02 per cent and 0.17 per cent. The table above shows that the more important beneficiaries are manufacturing, construction and personal services. The increases in output are attributable to the flow-on effects of higher incomes from those who work on site at the launch facility. Nationally, output increases, the most significant increases being in the communications and manufacturing industries.

Table 12.7
Employment Impact By Occupation

Employment Category	Total Employ ment	Employment Generated by Kistler		Total Employ ment
	1996[1]	Direct[2]	Indirect[3]	2003[4]
Managers & Administrators	375	11	26	412
Professionals	610	19	21	650
Associate Professionals	613	28	11	652
Tradespersons & Related Workers	933	27	91	1,051
Clerical & Service Workers	824	26	58	908
Intermediate Production & Transport Workers	672	12	70	754
Labourers & Related Workers	783	12	68	863
Inadequately Described & Not Stated	215	-	-	-
Total	**5,025**	**135**	**345**	**5,505**

Sources:
1 ABS Census - refer Table 15. Far North SSD.
2 Based on Kistler communication of 6 May, 1998.
3 SACES FED-SA projections.
4 Excludes the effect of restructuring of Aust-US Defence services expected in the region.

Overall, the economic impact of the investment in launch facilities at Woomera is estimated, during the construction phase, to increase South Australian GSP by about $12 million and employment by about 210 jobs, and, during the operational phase, increase South Australian real GSP by about $40 million and employment by about 480 jobs. Within the context of the overall size of the South Australian economy these impacts are not large. On the other hand, the nature of the investment and the potential for new knowledge to spill-over into local firms for broader applications of the technologies could be substantial.

In chapter 5, consideration was given to factors that may lead to the development of clusters in the high-tech sector, and this may enable us to form a view as to the likelihood of a cluster developing as a result of Kistler Aerospace's investment in Woomera. Most of the factors suggest that this is not likely to occur. First, the primary South Australian investment will be in Woomera, an area without the quality of life or transportation infrastructure usually required to sustain a cluster requiring skilled labour. Secondly, all of the development work on the re-useable launch vehicle will occur in Washington D.C., hence the investment will not result in an increase in the pool of skilled high-tech labour in South Australia. Thirdly, the fact that the development work occurs in Washington means that any new companies which are created as a result of innovations in the development process will occur in Washington. Fourthly, as the majority of Kistler's operations are located in Washington it will not encourage the development of a cluster in South Australia by enabling the development of specialised suppliers of business services. Finally, there do not seem to be any structures in place which could integrate the activity at Woomera into the broader regional economic community to form an 'innovative milieu'. In conclusion examining the proposed investment in the light of economic theory on regional development suggests strongly that the only benefits to SA will stem directly from the investment; there will be no 'spin off' benefits, nor any impact on the locational choice of high-technology industry.

Summary

The assessment of the potential to revitalise the Woomera rocket range provides an interesting case study of the shifting sands of high technology industry. In the late 1940s, Australia and South Australia in particular, had the opportunity to attract a high-tech rocket and military testing industry which potentially had major spillover benefits to defence, electronics, communications and other high-technology industry. Looking back over the 50 years since the inception of the UK-Australia joint project there is some evidence of the lasting success of the investment, but the benefits could have been for greater. There were several problems or misjudgments: (i) the British were discouraged (inadvertently) from setting up design teams in Salisbury which were necessary for knowledge transfer to local firms; (ii) very few Australian firms could achieve economies of scale from production runs; (iii) Australia did not use the technology developed at Woomera and hence did not "learn by doing"; (iv) some products did not fit well with defence strategy or global community safety; and (v) some projects were not very remarkable weapons.

Woomera today is a much smaller town than in the 'hay days' of the rocket launching. And it is known now more for hosting Kosovo refugees. Nonetheless, Woomera still manages to retain a unique identity. With almost three quarters of the population under 40 years old, it has the characteristic of a 'frontier settlement'. The infrastructure, albeit dated, is 'oversized' for the town and thereby capable of expansion. Overall the town remains receptive to regional development and growth.

There are prospects of a new investment in space technology which offers hope of re-launching Woomera. Kistler Aerospace Corporation is designing and building a small fleet of re-useable space launch vehicles which would use the old Woomera launching facilities as the base for Kistler's operations. The new investment would bring employment to the region and boost the State's GSP.

However, the main interest for this region is in whether the high-tech investment has important spillover benefits to Woomera and to other regions in the state such as Salisbury, just North of Adelaide. The assessment in this chapter is that such spillovers are unlikely. The main mitigating factors against significant knowledge spillovers are (i) the remoteness of Woomera is not appealing for a professional workforce; (ii) most knowledge intensive development work is expected to occur in Washington D.C. hence there is no mechanism for knowledge transfer; (iii) there is little opportunity for firm clustering or creation of related or supporting service industries; and (iv) there is no structure for the integration of firms into the broader regional economic community to form an 'innovative milieu'.

Appendix 12.1

Modelling Investment in Woomera

The Centre's Computable General Equilibrium (CGE) model, FED-SA, was used to estimate the impact of developing a launch facility at Woomera. CGE models allow the analyst to predict the overall impact that technological changes in one group of industries, communications for example, may have on industries in other sectors, namely manufacturing, agriculture and services.

Estimates of the outlays and revenues of the project have been modelled in two scenarios, one depicting a construction phase, the other an operational phase. For each scenario, labour is assumed to be fixed at the national level, but it moves between regions in response to regional differences in economic outcomes. This accords with available evidence that wage differentials and unemployment differentials have varied little between regions since 1985. State and Territory shares of the national population, however, have changed significantly over this period. See, for example, Wittwer and Bright (1997).

The modelling results presented entail a comparative-static analysis. The operational phase involves a long-run setting in which capital stocks have time to adjust to equilibrate rates of return across industries. In the construction phase, capital stocks are exogenous and rates of return endogenous.

Capital and operating costs and revenues for the first 5 years of the project, were advised by the Kistler Aerospace Corporation. The costs and revenues are a sub-set of estimates presented in Kistler's business plan (Kistler, 1996). The Centre understands that the remaining costs and revenues are attributable to the Nevada, USA, operations for this launch service.

Key assumptions underpinning the estimated economic impact are as follows: Launch site costs ($40 million) are 50 per cent labour/25 per cent materials/25 per cent equipment; vehicle 1 costs are 65 per cent labour/35 per cent materials; vehicle 2-5 costs are 35 per cent labor/65 per cent materials; vehicles will be sold to Kistler Woomera Pty Limited; all of 1999 revenue will be generated from the Australian site; from 2000-2005, 40 per cent of revenue will be generated from the Australian site; 60 per cent will be generated from the Nevada site; operational labour costs are 75 per cent U.S. personnel during the testing phase and full operations labour will commence with 75 per cent U.S personnel and reduce to 25 per cent within 5 years; and operational profit repatriated to the United States is 80 per cent of total operational profit.

Some of the assumptions above warrant further explanation, as follows. The space vehicles are assumed to be developed and constructed in the United States and imported to Australia. As the cost of the vehicles is fully financed by Kistler, there is no impact on Australia's trade balance. Accordingly, the space vehicles neither add to nor detract from Australian economic activity. In practice some assembly costs may be undertaken in Australia, but this activity is assumed to be minor and to the extent that it does imply that the economic impacts for Australia and South Australia are conservative.

The proportion of profits from the Woomera launch operations will be repatriated to the United States is assumed to be 80 per cent. Economic impacts may be over or understated depending on whether the profits repatriated are, respectively, higher or lower than that assumed. The Woomera launch operation is estimated to be highly profitable even when 80 per cent of the profits are repatriated. Within the CGE modelling framework, economic activity expands until the rate of return in the space industry equilibrates with normal returns to capital. Accordingly, the repatriation of profits is an important assumption, and drives the economic outcomes.

The Centre understands that an interstate company, would undertake the construction of the launch facility. Although the company is expected to draw on interstate staff for the project most of the labour, particularly semi-skilled and low-skilled, is expected to be drawn from the Woomera regions.

The construction of the launch site increases the level of construction over what would otherwise occur in South Australia. The Centre uses a medium-run setting, in which labour moves between regions in the model (i.e., South Australia and the rest of Australia) although employment is fixed at the national level. Capital stocks in each industry are fixed. Typically, in a construction phase, the region in which the activity takes place will gain through the direct increase in activity, while other regions may lose out slightly through a diversion of resources, with negligible net national effect.

Externalities (or spillovers) should not be confused with economic multipliers generated by an activity - particularly when the regional impact of a project is being considered. Multiplier effects are not an externality. Multipliers are summary measures of economic linkages. For example, it is often stated that an investment project, as well as employing a certain number of people itself, will generate additional employment in other industries. A typical statement is that "one job in X will 'generate' Y additional jobs elsewhere in the economy". Similarly, it is claimed that a project will generate economic investment elsewhere in the economy, additional to the investment associated with the project itself - so the project will result in a large addition to State economic activity.

Governments often use evaluation techniques based on multiplier analysis when considering the impact of major projects of their jurisdictions, with the results used to identify 'additional' gains to the economy and to justify government assistance. Typical output multipliers quoted are in the range 1.1 to 2.5, implying that one dollar of investment will generate an increase of between 1.1 and 2.5 dollars in Gross State Product. Some studies use significantly higher multipliers.

Multipliers, as simply measures of linkages, can measure a net gain to the economy only to the extent that their demand on resources for associated activities can be met from resources which otherwise would not be used. They do not consider possible alternative uses of such resources. If an expansion of one industry can occur only by bidding resources away from another industry, then there is no net multiplier effect. Indeed, the initial expenditure itself will increase activity only if it involves a more efficient use of resources. In particular, the alternative uses of government funds used to assist the investment are usually ignored. These funds may have greater value (or even higher multipliers) used in other ways or if left in the hands of taxpayers.

Nevertheless, for a particular region, multipliers can measure a net gain to the extent that the resources attracted come from outside the region, and at no cost to the region. However, there will be losses to the region from which the resources are attracted to offset the gains for the region to which they move. Whether these are gains to the nation depends on whether those resources moved as a result of 'artificial' inducements or as the result of changes in the competitive environment. However, the question is whether there are gains to the nation as a whole when the movement of jobs is the result of specific inducements provided by government.

References

Buchanan, H., and K., Edwards, (1998), *Woomera: The First Fifty Years 1947-1997,* Unpublished booklet.

Kistler Aerospace Corporation, (1996), *Business Plan,* August.

Morton, P., (1989), *Fire Across the Desert: Woomera and the Anglo-Australian Joint Project 1946-1980,* AGPS Press Publication.

Wittwer, G. and Bright, M. (1997), *The Effects of a Mining Boom on the South Australian and Australian Economies,* South Australian Centre for Economic Studies.

Chapter Thirteen

Globalisation and Inter-governmental Fiscal Transfers to Local Government

This chapter turns to a fiscal policy topic, namely, the allocation of funds from national to local government.

Earlier chapters in this book developed the theme that globalisation is raising the importance of regions and diminishing the role of the nation-state. The pressure increasingly being exerted on regions to respond globalisation is adding an extra degree of complexity to inter-governmental management. An important part of inter-government management is the system of transfers of funds from national to lower tiers of government. In this chapter, we consider what globalisation means for inter-governmental fiscal transfers to local government units (LGUs) - the government closest to the regions.

Part of the discussion focuses on comparisons between Australia and Japan. The Japanese system of inter-governmental fiscal transfers to local government emphasises allocations based on expected regional needs in contrast with Australia's system which is based on reported actual needs. Japanese local government plays a greater role in regional communities relative to their counter parts in Australia. The Japanese system has several shortcomings attributable to centralism but the allocation of funds to local government draws on a detailed methodology to assess relative needs which more accurately reflect the needs of local government relative to Australian local government. The Japanese method offers the potential for funding prospective regional economic development strategies including stabilisation and counter-cyclical policies. The benefit of this approach must be weighed against additional administrative burdens associated with dealing with many LGUs and more complex information needs.

Inter-governmental Management

Inter-governmental management is changing. The roles of multi-national and sub-national bodies are becoming more important, community groups and private sector actors are becoming more widely and deeply involved. Simultaneously, interaction between the actors is becoming less authoritative and more co-operative. The increasing number of important actors in governing and providing public services increases the complexity of inter-governmental management and challenges the systems of governance (OECD, 1997).

The implications for managing across levels of government are far reaching, and new public sector reform strategies are being designed and implemented in the most advanced economies. The main elements of these reforms are:

- devolution of authority and enhanced flexibility: authority is being decentralised through the transfer of responsibilities to lower tiers of government, or deconcentrated by re-locating central functions from central offices to regional offices. Devolution offers regions the flexibility needed to respond to regional specific issues in ways which regions see best to deal with them;
- increasing emphasis on client and service orientation: a re-evaluation of decision-making from the point of view of the student, customer and other recipients of the output provided. The concept covers notions such as 'value for money', 'one stop shop' and 'client empowerment';
- strengthening capacity for developing strategy and policy: these capacities are being designed for the identification of medium-term objectives and the formulation of plans to strengthen relationships with key stakeholders, and to draw resources and manage risks consistent with achievement of those objectives;
- introducing competition: as a means of creating market based incentives in contrast with administratively determined incentives to encourage efficiency and responsiveness in service delivery; and
- focusing government on outcomes: principally by re-assessing public expenditure and revenue programs in terms of price, quantity and quality. Under this concept, government buys outputs from its agencies or alternatively buys those services from private sector sub-contractors.

Fiscal pressures are at the heart of these reforms, forcing attention on efficiency, private sector participation and the roles of respective tiers of government.

There is an emerging view that sub-national governments may be better disposed than national governments to adopt features of the new public sector management such as service quality initiatives, the use of market-type mechanisms and performance management. The reason being that numerous relatively smaller government units encourage competition and choice, and that the public service is then closer to the community. There is evidence from Japan, in the health and education sectors, that local government generates innovation and entrepreneurship (OECD, 1999). Although difficult to measure there is empirical evidence that fiscal centralisation is significantly associated with a weaker record of economic growth (see for example Castles, 1999). Those who mount the counter-arguments see the need for central government to ensure adequate macro-control and the need for the coherent formulation and application of policy. Centralists would also point out that the disposition of local government to innovation and entrepreneurship is variable because local government does not have a strong skill base.

Striking the right balance between central and local government is complex, and draws on an intimate understanding of the degree of intensity of the effect of globalisation on the region and the region's readiness to respond to the development challenge. In broad terms, the right balance involves:

- encouraging more autonomy at lower levels of government while providing overall direction;
- allowing for differentiation through flexibility, yet ensuring some minimum degree of uniformity; and
- catering for more responsiveness to local needs, but not to the detriment of efficiency and economy.

Some of the instruments of policy that may be employed to achieve the balance are:

- adjusting financial and administrative controls away from detailed, top-down requirements and towards broadly agreed frameworks and ex-post, result-oriented instruments;
- developing co-ordination and consultation mechanisms for a more comprehensive and coherent approach to target-based governance and which fit the cultural context and the "style of relationship" in each sector; and
- promoting accountability and control procedures to enable greater participation by citizens.

The broad public sector finance aggregates indicate that the devolution of authority is translating into smaller central government relative to other tiers of government. Chart 13.1 shows the change in the composition of public employment since 1985. The trend across the OECD countries indicates that the central government's share of public employment is declining. Australia is consistent with this trend. However, the trend is not uniform, there are notable exceptions.

Chart 13.1
Share of Total Government Employment by Level of Government

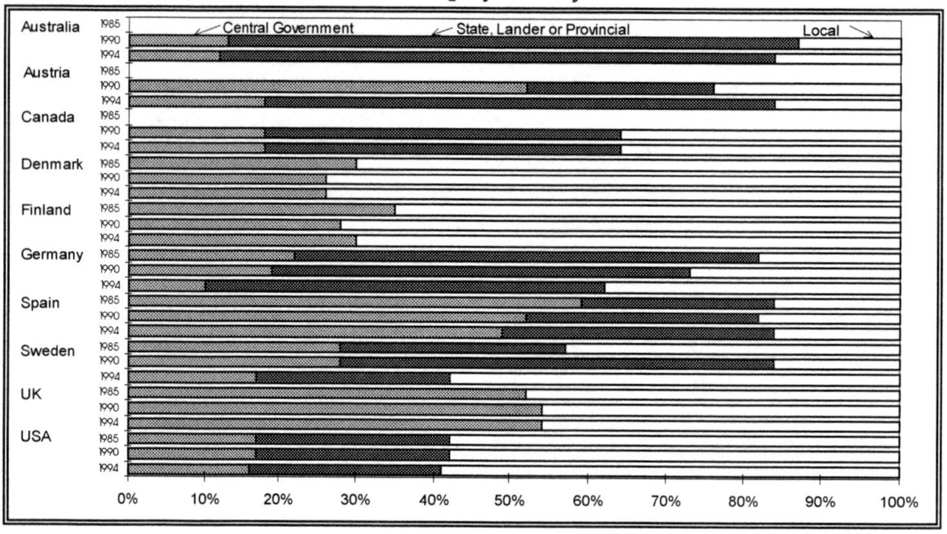

Central Government
State, Lander or Provincial
Local

Australia 1985 1990 1994
Austria 1985 1990 1994
Canada 1985 1990 1994
Denmark 1985 1990 1994
Finland 1985 1990 1994
Germany 1985 1990 1994
Spain 1985 1990 1994
Sweden 1985 1990 1994
UK 1985 1990 1994
USA 1985 1990 1994

0% 10% 20% 30% 40% 50% 60% 70% 80% 90% 100%

Source: OECD, *National Accounts*.

Inter-governmental Fiscal Transfers — Principles

Rationale

Inter-governmental management has many facets, and the policies and procedures that govern the allocation of national government revenue to lower tiers of government are an important component. The quantum of funds transferred is a clear measure of the importance of these transfers. In the 1998-99 year, the financial transfer from the Commonwealth was approximately $22.1 billion of which $2.1 billion was received by South Australia. The changing nature of inter-governmental relations and the importance of this fiscal component, suggest that there is room to reconsider fiscal arrangements between Australian tiers of government. Transfers to local government are the most important as the regions served by local government are those most effected by globalisation.

In most countries, local governments draw at least part of their revenue from a higher tier of government through a system of inter-governmental transfers. The literature on fiscal federalism (see, for example, Broadway et al (1993), Shah (1994) and Rosen (1995)), suggests several economic rationales for inter-governmental fiscal transfers.

Firstly, inter-governmental fiscal transfers address vertical fiscal imbalance. In most countries, the national government is assigned the major tax bases, leaving insufficient revenue resources to the sub-national governments for covering their expenditure needs. Inter-governmental transfers are therefore needed to balance the budget at the LGU level. The choice of assignment of major revenues to national government and the assignment of expenditure responsibilities to LGUs is a world-wide debate between the 'centralist' and 'localist' approach.

Table 13.1 shows the extent of vertical fiscal imbalance. In Australia, local government draws about 22 per cent of its revenue from higher tiers of government (7 per cent from the State and 15 per cent from the Commonwealth) whereas local government in Japan draws 37 per cent of its income from the national tier of government in the case of Prefectures and 33 per cent of income in the case of Municipalities.

Secondly, transfers address horizontal fiscal imbalance. On the one hand, some jurisdictions may have access to natural resources or other tax bases not available or inferior in other jurisdictions. They may also have higher income levels than those in other jurisdictions. That is, there are differences in fiscal capacities. On the other hand, some jurisdictions may have greater expenditure needs, because they have high proportions of poor, old or young population, or because they need to maintain national airports and harbours. The net fiscal disability, measured by the gap between fiscal capacity and fiscal need, is often caused by these factors and, it is argued, should be addressed by central government transfer. In many countries, the central government accepts an obligation to maintain a minimum standard of public service in all the LGUs. Regions without sufficient resources to reach this minimum level are subsidised. Going further, under the principle of Horizontal Fiscal Equalisation (HFE), each jurisdiction provides government services at a level not appreciably different from that of other jurisdictions, without having to impose taxes and charges at levels appreciably different from those in other jurisdictions.

Thirdly, transfers address inter-jurisdictional 'spill-over' effects. The provision of a public service in one jurisdiction may be of benefit to a neighbouring jurisdiction. Examples are pollution control (water or air), inter-regional highways, higher education (graduates may leave for other regions to work), fire departments (may be used by neighbouring areas), etc. Without reaping all the benefits of these projects, a local government tends to under-invest in such projects. Therefore, the central government needs to provide incentives or financial resources to address the problem of under provision.

Table 13.1
Sources of Revenue

		Australia		Japan	
		States	**Local Government**	**Prefectures**	**Municipal-ities**
Own Source	- Taxes	39	55	31	36
	- Other	26	23	32	32
Grants from	- National Govt.	35	15	37	28
	- State Govt.		7		5
		100	**100**	**100**	**100**

Source: OECD (1997), 1993 year.

Separate from the Broadway et al. (1993) framework, is the rationale that inter-governmental fiscal transfers assist regional economic development. This may involve providing benefits to poorer regions by central governments targeting infrastructure, education, training and other nationally agreed objectives.

The first two general rationales above lead to a need for untied or general purpose transfers whereas the remaining rationales imply tied or specific purpose transfers. It is therefore a fundamental point that the desired *structure* of inter-governmental fiscal transfer involves payments which are both general and specific purpose in nature.

Methodology

The methodology for determining the allocation of revenues varies significantly across countries, but the characteristics of good revenue transfer schemes are not contentious. In particular, the methodology used for the allocation of revenue should have regard to the following characteristics:

- *Degree of dependency*: simple schemes suffice where small transfers are involved, but larger transfers require more attention to detailed methodology;
- *Efficiency*: to promote incentives for the LGUs and the community to use funds efficiently across regions and across functions;
- *Equity*: to promote the allocation of funds to standardise the level of well being across regions and individuals within regions, for all services required;
- *Data availability*: to enable calculation from data that is readily and reliably available;

- *Flexibility*: to have the capacity to modify the methodology in response to changing socio-economic circumstances and the availability of improved data;
- *Readily understood*: to reduce the burden of learning and interpreting complex methods and promote transparency in decisions regarding revenue allocation;
- *Enforceable and secure*: to minimise the scope for misuse and misappropriation of funds; and
- *Acceptable*: readily acceptable to governments and the community, reflecting social and cultural norms of the respective country.

Given the context of changing inter-governmental management, the next two sections examine the role of LGUs in Australia and Japan and their systems of funds transfer. Finally, options for change in Australian intergovernmental fiscal transfer systems are examined.

The Roles of LGUs in Australia Compared with Japan

International Comparison

Any international comparison of inter-governmental fiscal transfer systems should begin with an understanding of the differing economic, social, cultural and political conditions prevailing in these countries. The brief socio-economic profile captured by Table 13.2, illustrates that Japan is quite different from that of Australia. With more than 6 times the population of Australia and within a much smaller land mass, the density of Japanese population is far greater. The population is also more broadly dispersed throughout the land than in Australia. The Japanese economy is far larger and, importantly, material wealth per person is considerably higher than for Australia. Japan is more industry-oriented whereas Australia is service oriented. Japanese people live slightly longer, and the age profile is slightly older. And longevity of the population has risen quickly: in 1935, life expectancy was only 46.9 years for men and 49.6 years for women. Statistically, the Japanese population is ageing faster than anywhere else in the world (CLAIR, 1997).

Even within this brief and very general profile its clear that the tasks for LGUs are very different. Higher incomes have implications for the expected standard of service required by Japanese. Higher population densities in both rural and metropolitan areas suggest a greater potential for achieving economies of scale in delivery of LGU services and the ability for LGUs to product differentiate. The population size suggests that waste collection and treatment is a far larger issue than in Australia and that the size of concentration of industrial processes suggests that industrial waste is also a major LGU issue. The fast rise in life expectancy combined with a reduction in household size and diminution of the family care culture, all occurring in recent decades, suggests that aged care provision is a major issue in Japan.

Table 13.2
Japan-Australia Profile

	Japan	Australia
Population		
Total (million, 1997)	126	19
Density (psns/km^2, 1997)	333	2
Urbanisation (% of popn)	78	85
Income		
GDP (US$ million, 1997)	4,202.6	391.0
GDP Growth (% 1990-97)	0.8	3.7
GNP/capita (US$)	37,850	20,540
Production (%)		
Agriculture	2	4
Industry	41.5	31
Services	56.5	65
Life Expectancy		
Males (yrs, 1996)	77	75
Female (yrs, 1996)	83	81
LGUs		
Number (1997, 1998)	3,232	831
Dependency (% 1996, 1998)	30.8	17.0

Local government structures and functions are vastly different across countries and regions within countries. These differences need to be understood because they will influence the fiscal transfer system from national to local government and the assessment of those systems.

Structure

The structure of government, and in particular the number of tiers of government, is usually related to geographical conditions, population levels and the degree of centralisation/control exercised by the national government. There are broadly two systems, of government, namely, Federal and Unitary systems. In Federal systems, there are (at least) two tiers of government that have constitutionally entrenched guarantees of their existence and of their autonomous powers. The structure of sub-State/sub-Provincial governments can vary, and their existence is usually in the power of the State/Provincial government level to decide. In Unitary systems, both regional and local government units are created but both structures and the degree of autonomy exercised by them are subject to national government legislation alone. This system of government is more complex and multi-layered in nations where

Unitary systems are adopted than in Federal systems. By this measure, Japan is a typical Unitary system and Australia is a typical Federal system.

Japanese Prefectures and Municipalities vary widely in terms of population and area. Japan's 47 Prefectures range in population from Tokyo Metropolis (To-kyo-to) with more than 10 million, to Tottori Prefecture with just 600,000; and in size, from the Hokkai-do region with an area exceeding 80,000 km^2, to Osaka Prefecture with a little under 2,000 km^2. The Municipalities exhibit even greater variety: they range from Yokohama City with a population in excess of 3 million, to Aogashima village in Tokyo, or Tomiyama village in Aichi Prefecture - both with populations below 200. As for variations in area, Ashoro Town in Hokkaido covers as much as 1,400 km^2, and Takashima Town in Nagasaki Prefecture covers only 1.5 km^2.

The number of Prefectures has remained unchanged since the system was adopted during the Meiji Period (1868-1912). Prefectural areas are based on the local administrative units instituted under ancient statues during the 8th century, as well as the relationships that existed between the Shogunate government and each area's local clan during the Edo Period, which began in 1603. As a result the areas are well established in the minds of the Japanese people.

However, there is a growing view that the size of the Prefectures should be reviewed to match changes in the economic reality brought about by Japan's post-World War II economic growth. The number of Municipalities has steadily decreased since the end of the Second World War, mainly to improve local financial viability by enlarging fiscal scale. Many towns and villages merged in the mid 1950s following the central government's introduction of legislation promoting municipal mergers, and the number of Municipalities fell by about 50 per cent from a previous high of some 10,000. This led to improvements in their administrative and financial capabilities, and helped to promote the growth of local autonomy and the urbanisation which followed, as Japan entered its boom years. From then on, mergers took place according to realities and requirements of municipalities. As of March 1997, there are 3,232 Municipalities.

Soon after his inauguration in 1996, Prime Minister Ryutaro Hashimoto outlined three-and-a-bit challenges that Japan must tackle in the context of Japan's broad agenda for decentralisation: administrative reform, devolution of authority, deregulation (and he also indicated an interest in relocating the capital city!). As the local public sector accounts for about 16 per cent of GDP in 1995 and employed over 3 million people and is one of the most regulated and centrally controlled sectors of the economy (Ter-Minassian, 1997), then the challenge is both substantial and potentially beneficial.

Local government in Australia is similarly heterogenous across the States. Population densities, land use and differing functions between State and local government are a characteristic of Australian local government. For example, in Victoria, New South Wales and Queensland services such as electricity and water and urban public transport have been provided at the local government level but these are customarily the State's responsibility in South Australia.

Table 13.3 provides some indication of differences in local government in Australia.

Functions

A striking difference between the Australian and Japanese local government is, in the case of the later, the broader carriage of functions and the substantially larger fiscal responsibilities.

In 1995-96 Japanese local government spent ¥23.0328 trillion (CLAIR, 1997), or, using exchange rate of the day and adjusting for population size, equivalent to expenditure $9,400 per capita. By contrast, South Australian local government expenditure was about $475 per capita (MAG, 1995). Japanese local government has a far greater level of fiscal responsibility for its regions than does local government in Australia.

Although the role of Prefectures and Municipalities in Japan are different from that of State and Local Government in Australia, a disaggregation between these tiers assists in making comparisons between the 'third' tiers of government in each country.

Table 13.3
Local Government Across the States

State	No. of LGUs	Average Population Per Unit	Average Area (Km²)
New South Wales	176	33,320	4,555
Victoria	210	21,082	1,083
Queensland	134	21,888	12,888
South Australia	122	11,795	8,065
Western Australia	138	11,764	18,300
Tasmania	46	10,119	1,473
Australia	831	20,808	9,244

Source: Commonwealth of Australia, (1998).

Table 13.4
Expenditure Shares for each Level of Government
(Percentage of Total Public Expenditure)

Function	Japan		Australia		
	National	Local	National	State	Local
General public, public order & safety	23	77	42.64	52.45	4.91
Defence	100	-	100	-	-
Education	24	76	32.65	67.23	0.12
Social security, welfare & housing	53	47	87.02	10.26	2.72
Economic affairs	23	77	100.00	90.09	21.78
Other	...	...	90.57	12.74	-3.32
Total			**70.18**	**34.33**	**2.54**

Notes: ... indicates data not available.
Data refer to the following years: 1992 for Japan, 1998-99 for Australia.

Table 13.4 shows what proportion each tier of government spends on major public sector functions. Common to Japan and Australia is that all expenditure on defence is carried out by the national tier of government. But the commonality stops there. Compared to Australia, Japanese local government spends proportionately more than the national government and, in particular, more on public services, public order and safety, health, social security and economic affairs and less on education.

Table 13.5
Local Expenditure by Function (% Shares)

Function	Japan			Australia		
	Total Local Govts.	Prefec-tures	Municip alities	Total Local Govts.	State	Local
General public service, public order & safety	18.9	17.3	20.6	15.36	15.06	17.84
Social security & welfare	10.6	6.0	15.5	5.25	5.10	6.48
Health	5.7	3.7	7.8	17.20	19.02	2.21
Education	20.1	25.0	14.8	20.76	23.23	0.40
Economic affairs	34.0	36.2	31.7	25.63	20.83	65.16
Debt services	8.0	7.2	8.8	11.52	12.03	7.29
Other	2.8	4.7	0.8	4.29	4.73	0.63
Total	**100.0**	**100.0**	**100.0**	**100.0**	**100.0**	**100.0**

Note: Data refer to the 1990 year.
Source: For Japan: Ter-Minassian (1997), p. 311. For Australia: ABS Cat. No. 5501.

Responsibilities of Japanese local government include family and resident registration; building and management of day-cares, kindergartens, primary and secondary schools, libraries, public halls and similar facilities; the construction, maintenance and management of refuse and sewerage disposal facilities, water supply and sewerage works; the development and improvement of roads and parks; and police and firefighting services. Local government plays a significant role in the growth of society as a whole, as well as in the stability and improvement of people's daily lives.

In contrast to the sectional administration of the central government's ministries and agencies, local government provides comprehensive services in its administrative region, for example, local development and cultural policies.

The services provided at the Local Government level in South Australia are broadly indicative of LGU services in most States. Although there are some notable exceptions, for example, water and sewerage services provided in Queensland and electricity services provided in New South Wales. Other than expenditure on administration, the major categories are transport and communication (road construction and maintenance), recreation and culture (includes parks and gardens), and housing and community services (includes garbage collection).

International comparisons of LGU functions are complicated by the varying degrees of coverage and efficiency of the services provided. In South Australia, for example, some LGUs services are not required (for instance, maintenance of foreshores is only relevant for beach-side LGUs). Secondly an important element of local government is diversity. A local community may choose a broad range of services offered or a LGU and it may choose to provide limited services. A difficulty arises where ratepayers in one LGU who have decided on limited services, have the opportunity to free-ride on the services of a neighbouring LGU, which ultimately bears the financial burdens. For example, the provision of public goods (for instance, parks and gardens, public place amenities, libraries) are available for use from residents outside of the responsible LGU.

Overall, Japanese local government services are broader than those of South Australia and have a greater role in the allocation of expenditures for promoting Japanese economic growth and development. Nonetheless, importantly, the role of regional development is not necessarily a reflection of local government expenditures but fiscal control. That is, Local-National and Local-State linkages are important in influencing the attraction and retention of National and State public expenditure in regional areas in addition or in association with LGU spending and taxing priorities.

Issues in Revenue Allocation

The Australia and Japanese systems for the allocation of revenue from national government to local government are described in some detail in appendix 13.1 to this chapter. In general, the main characteristics of the systems are as follows. In Japan, there are three basic types of grants to local government of which the Local Allocation Tax (LAT) is the most important. The LAT is an unconditional, general purpose revenue-sharing grant, accounting for about 50 per cent to 60 per cent of all transfers from the national to local government.

The main purpose of the LAT is to equalise the fiscal capacity of local governments, and the approach to equalisation is quite similar to the Australian system of General Revenue Assistance to the states.

An important difference between the Australian and Japanese systems is that Japanese local government fiscal needs are determined on the basis of estimates, that is, projected needs. "The Local Finance Plan forms the concrete basis for estimating the level of such needs " (CLAIR, 1997). Although highly centralist in its approach, the important element of the assessment is that there is a far greater emphasis on planning and development because there is a large financial incentive to submit quality plans.

Japanese central government is heavily engaged in the determination of local revenue and expenditure, and the central and local budgets are closely linked through the Local Public Finance Program. The Local Allocation Tax and the local borrowing program play an important role in balancing estimated local revenues and expenditures. The LAT is a unique mechanism for national-local coordination of fiscal policies. As a macroeconomic policy tool and a means of achieving horizontal fiscal equalisation, the LAT is a powerful instrument. Allocations are based on estimates local revenues and expenditures for the forthcoming year, enabling central and local planning for efficiency gains, new policies and new economic development initiatives. The process removes a considerable degree of uncertainty at the local level about availability of revenues and financing. However, its shortcomings lie in the excessively tight expenditure controls, lack of freedom of local governments to determine local tax rates and the problems of dependence of local government on grants and borrowing's.

Reform debate has concentrated in recent years on fiscal centralisation. The theoretical foundation for the advantages of decentralisation lay in Brennan and Buchanan (1980) and Tiebout (1956) and are based on the view that political competition between various fiscal jurisdictions would minimise the opportunity for 'rent' extraction by government. Also, there is an argument that the central government faces softer budget constraints because of the greater opportunity for deficit spending through public borrowing and seigniorage. There is fairly strong empirical evidence on the tendency of the public sector in Japan to expand faster than in less centralised economies as a result of higher revenue and expenditure centralisation (see Moesen, 1993, for example).

Although much is owed to the Commonwealth Grants Commission in terms of basic ideas, at the level of detailed methodology, relatively little guidance is available for the distribution of local government grants. The reasons are: (i) at the Commonwealth tier of government, there is a very large pool of funds which is sufficient for the Commonwealth to fully equalise the position of the financially weaker States. By contrast, the total pool made available for distribution by the Local Government Grants Commission (LGGC) is far less than would be required to fully equalise; (ii) the distribution is subject to a minimum grant for each Council laid down by Commonwealth legislation, which impedes fiscal equalisation; and (iii) the much larger number of entities (75 in South Australia as against 8 States and Territories) would make the application of the Commonwealth Grants Commission's complex methods quite administratively burdensome. An important consequence is that the SA Grants Commission relies heavily on its own judgements in meeting its legislative obligations.

Issues concerning the overall structure of the LGGC's methodology, (as distinct from its detailed application in specific areas) are as follows:

Capacity to Equalise: The total grant available for distribution is less than required for full equalisation and there is a minimum grant required under Commonwealth law. This imposes major constraints on the Commission's ability to apply equalisation principles. The general approach of the Commission has been to calculate what the grants "should be" on an equalisation basis and then impose the constraints.

Symmetry Between the Revenue and Expenditure Calculations: There are major differences between the revenue and expenditure sides of the Commission's calculations. Differences in revenue-raising capacity are reflected in both positive and negative figures relative to the "standard" - the former reflecting below average raising capacity and the latter above average. On the other hand, relativities in expenditure needs are, in effect, assessed only over a certain range and are reflected in positive figures only. This asymmetry is undesirable in principle. One of its consequences, in practice, is to disadvantage those Councils which have relatively high revenue-raising capacity and relatively high expenditure needs as against those in the opposite position.

Revenue Areas Subject to Assessment: While the Commission makes assessments for quite a large number of expenditure areas, there is only one revenue area which is assessed, namely property rates. This reflects, of course, the dominance of rates in local government revenues, that being the only tax power granted by State Parliament to local government. However, if there were other revenues which were significant and there was reason to believe that there were significant differences between Councils in their relative capacities to raise revenue, then it would be appropriate for them to be examined. By the way of example, it may be that the quite different position of the Adelaide City Council compared with others with respect to the raising of revenue from car parking should be taken into account.

Capital Expenditures and Facilities: The Commission's assessments of relative expenditure needs (as reflected in the nature of the disability factors) have been largely confined to the recurrent, rather than the capital, side of Council finances.

Given the fiscal equalisation at the local Government level is relatively new, and given that it has been very partial, it is highly likely that large differences between Council areas in the availability and standard of those public facilities for which Local Government has been responsible will exist, for example between wealthier residential areas and others. Where facilities have been built in less wealthy areas, they are more likely to have required borrowings, with effects on annual Council budgets through interest changes. It is also obviously the case that, as a general rule, faster growing Councils (often in outer suburban areas) will require greater levels of capital expenditure than others.

Annual Fluctuations in the Commission's Assessment and in Grant Levels: Grants payable to individual Councils may vary from year to year for a number of reasons, including:

- changes in the total funds available from the Commonwealth;
- changes in the assessed relative revenue or expenditure needs of Councils; and
- changes in methodology.

The first factor is beyond the Commission's control. In relation to the second factor, a preliminary analysis suggests that there are significant changes over time in property values in particular and these do significantly affect the Commission's results. Thus exploring the possibility of introducing a system which averages that over a period of years. In relation to the third factor, the Commission is, at this stage, unable to predict the magnitude of changes which might be made as a result of the regular 5 year review by the Commonwealth. The Commission has not fully adjusted to changes of one kind or another made previously. This reflects the Commission's caution in limiting annual changes in grant payments to individual Councils. One possibility is to permit the Commission to examine the possibility of permitting larger annual adjustments for councils which are less dependent on fiscal equalisation grants as a source of revenue.

The Scaling Back of Assessed Grants to Fit the Limited Aggregate of Funds Available: There is a very large gap between the funds actually available for distribution and amounts which would be required to fully equalise. The procedure generally used by the Commission has been to "scale back" each Council's assessed grant (subject of course to the minimum per capita requirement) on a proportionate basis. One of the effects of this is to give equal weighting, as it were, to the needs of Councils whose positions are above average to those whose positions are below average.

The current procedure has the virtue of simplicity. The Commonwealth legislation refers to Councils being able to operate "at a standard not lower than the average standard of other Councils in the State". It could, perhaps, be argued that it would be more consistent with this to give greater weighting to those Councils in a below average position - i.e., there would be less than a proportionate "scaling back" for such Councils. A stronger and arguably preferable variant on this would be to give greater weighting still to those Councils whose relative needs are greatest.

Issues of detailed calculations for LGUs in South Australia are as follows.

Rateable Capacity of Councils: The number of Councils using site values rather than capital values is small and declining and the Commission's intention is to continue to base its calculations on capital values as a matter of pragmatic judgement. The first part of the calculation, based on population numbers, is appropriate in broad principle.

However, the second part which is based on property numbers may be problematic. To illustrate the issue here consider two Councils with exactly the same population and aggregate property values, the only difference being that for some reason (possibly merely historical) Council A has more properties than Council B. Under this part of the formula, Council A will receive a higher grant because the average valuation per property will be lower than that assessed for Council B. It is possible that in practice the opposite should be the case - e.g., Council A may have a higher capacity to raise revenue than Council B as it may have more properties subject to minimum rates.

It is the case that in some areas Council expenditures might be more closely related to property numbers than population numbers but, where that is so, it is appropriately taken into account in assessing relative expenditure needs.

Property Values and Capacity to Pay: The foregoing discussion has left aside a more fundamental issue, which has often been raised with the Commission. The argument is that property values do not adequately reflect the capacity to pay of Council residents and that other measures such as incomes or value of production should be used. This view is most commonly put by the representatives of Councils in certain rural areas where property values, as determined by the Valuer-General, remain relatively high, but farm incomes are low or even negative in some cases (reflecting seasonal conditions or particular commodity markets at the time). The argument is advanced that property values are an unrealistic measure of capacity to pay in these kinds of instances.

As one example of an alternative approach, in 1991 the Commonwealth Grants Commission produced a report on the Interstate Distribution of General Purpose Grants for Local Government. It suggested that an appropriate approach might be to consider three classes of ratepayers - commercial/industrial, residential and rural - separately. The following procedure was used:

- for commercial/industrial, property values were retained;
- for residential property, incomes were used;
- for rural properties, farm income averaged over a period formed the basis of assessment.

The issue can be considered in terms of three options:

- basically to retain the present system based on aggregate property values;
- to use different measure of capacity to pay altogether (e.g., incomes) either in lieu of in addition to property values; and
- to continue to base the assessments on property values, but to take more specific account of Council's actual rating policies and practices.

Expenditure Areas Not Covered: Conversely, however, there may be other expenditure areas, not currently considered, in which Councils suffer different levels of cost for the provision of a standard service level.

As a related point, some expenditure areas currently treated in one expenditure function (especially Administration) cover a large proportion of Council budgets and some improved precision in the model's calculations may be achieved by dividing these expenditures into small defined categories.

Roads: When the relative contributions of each of the expenditure functions to the total grant allocations are examined it is clear that the functions relating to roads expenditures are amongst the most significant.

Clearly, the most important factors which impact on Council's road costs are the length of the road network under its control and whether those roads are sealed or unsealed. These factors are currently taken into account in the Commission's methodology.

There are, however, other factors which impact on Councils' roads expenditures, when they are compared one with another, such as width of road pavement, usage, terrain, proximity of suitable road-making materials etc.. Information is needed from Councils on the significance of these, and any other factors, influencing the cost of their roads. The emphasis is on whether, and if so to what extent, costs faced by individual Councils or groups of Councils differ from others.

Economies of Scale: Within the Commission's current expenditure calculations there is no factor to take account of economies of scale in the operation of Councils. That is, an individual Council's expenditure need is calculated by reference to the standard cost of the service provision (the average cost across all Councils). It is clear, however, that, while some Councils may be able to achieve savings in the cost of delivering services by taking advantage of economies of scale, there are many areas where smaller Councils can neither achieve these nor step back from providing services.

In unpublished work, the SA Centre for Economic Studies formed a view that diseconomies of small scale do exist for Councils at the small end but then there is a "flattening" out. Specifically, administration expenditures per head decline significantly up to a Council population of about 5,000 to 10,000 or so and then tend to "flatten out" at about $100 per head.

Some caution needs to be taken in interpreting these figures as they may be affected by different organisational structures and accounting practices as between larger and smaller Councils. It seems likely, for example, the smaller Councils will tend to place more of their expenditure in the "administration" category, while in larger Councils the equivalent expenditure would be allocated more to specific functional areas. This aspect of the data requires further examination.

The inclusion of some measure of diseconomies of small scale in the Commission's calculations is questionable. Where Councils have had reasonable opportunity to amalgamate with other Councils and have chosen not to do so, the argument for increased grant funding allocation on the basis of diseconomies of small scale is unconvincing. Contracting out, possibly to an adjacent LGU, can also reduce the costs of smallness in scale. The Commission may thus confine any consideration of this issue to those Councils which, by reason of geography or other factors, cannot reasonably be regarded as being in this position. A distinction between metropolitan and non-metropolitan Councils may well be relevant here - not only in terms of amalgamation choices available but also in terms of access to "contracting out" possibilities and such like.

Input Costs: The isolation factor currently included in the Commission's expenditure assessments relates to the increased cost, in a general sense, faced by Councils which are distant from Adelaide compared with those in or near Adelaide.

In considering this issue it is useful to consider Council expenditures not by function but in terms of the ***kinds*** of goods or services purchased by Councils. Thus, some of the cost categories would be: wages and salaries; fuel; road making and repair materials; equipment purchase (cars and trucks, earthmoving equipment, computers etc.); office accommodation; communications; and travel.

Arising from revised taxation arrangements including the introduction of an Australian Goods and Services Tax, the Commonwealth and the States entered into a new Intergovernmental Agreement on the Reform of Commonwealth - State Financial Relations. As part of the ongoing process of reform of Commonwealth - State financial relations, the Commonwealth Grants Commission (CGC) is required to undertake a number of specific projects, two of which are of significance to regions, namely:

- The Commonwealth has requested the CGC to provide a report into the distribution of Commonwealth funds for fundamental projects that affect indigenous Australians, by March 2001. The inquiry will review the relative needs of indigenous Australians for programs including health, education, housing and employment, training and infrastructure that are funded directly by the Commonwealth or indirectly through the States or local government; and
- The CGC is reviewing Commonwealth General Purpose Grants to local government under the *Local Government (Financial Assistance) Act 1995.* Grants are distributed on an equal per capita basis between the States (excluding identified road grants that are distributed on historical shares) and on fiscal equalisation principles within States (minimum grant entitlements apply for each municipality). The report will assess the effectiveness of achieving fiscal equalisation within each State and is due by June 2001.

Both projects provide the opportunity for regions to develop a dialogue with the Commonwealth that leads to stronger recognition to regional disabilities and the growing role of regional government in assisting regions to respond to globalisation.

Conclusion

Globalisation of the economy is intensifying regionalism and diminishing the role of the nation-states. New public sector management reforms are gradually being implemented across OECD countries which are responding to globalisation by devolving fiscal control to lower tiers of government and encouraging greater participation of multi-national and sub-national bodies and community groups in government decision making. The increase in the number of players and the change in the respective powers of those players in the field of inter-governmental relations makes the management of relations much more complex. As inter-governmental fiscal transfers from central to lower tiers of government involve vast sums of money, these transfers play an important role in inter-governmental relations. As large flows of funds create strong incentives for good or bad economic behaviour, then it is important that the mechanisms for such transfers are designed to meet the specified social objectives.

The Commonwealth government has, by OECD standards, a relatively sophisticated system for the allocation of funds to the States. However, the system for allocation of funds to local government is still quite simplistic. The justification offered for a simplistic approach is on the grounds that there is 10 fold more local governments than State governments, and the allocation of funds to local government is not as large in the context of public finances generally.

Unlike Australia, Japan is not a Federalist system, and decisions over the allocations of funds to lower tiers of government are highly centralised. The degree of vertical fiscal imbalance is also an issue. However, the role of local government is much larger and enables regions to better position government to deliver public services that will assist these regions to compete in the global market place. Decentralisation of fiscal responsibility is gradually taking hold in Japan since the policy was adopted by the Japanese government in 1995. Importantly, allocations of funds to local government are based on expected incomes and expected expenditures. Under this system, incentives are created for local government to consider closely economic development initiatives that will assist their regions to grow and the central government has the means to rationalise between those initiatives where there is potential for inter-regional overlays or duplication as well as to identify development gaps.

Globalisation and the new inter-governmental relations that rely on decentralisation and broader participation by other economic agents are leading to greater not lesser shared fiscal responsibilities between tiers of government. Co-ordination and co-operation are at a premium. On this basis, devolution of responsibilities to local government in Australia will follow Japan, whereby central government will need to develop closer relations with local government in addition to maintaining its relationship with state government. This is a departure from the hierarchal system whereby Commonwealth tends to communicate with the States and these communicate with local government. This departure does not diminish the role of the State but changes the role whereby the three tiers of government form a network - an organisational structure akin to the network of collaboration between firms - that seeks to position their regions and their local industry for competition in the global market place. The opportunity for dialogue on these issues currently exists in the context of the CGC's ongoing process of reform of Commonwealth - State financial relations.

Appendix 13.1

Revenue Allocation to Local Government

Japan

Of the three basic types of grants to local governments, the Local Allocation Tax an unconditional, general purpose revenue-sharing grant, is by far the most important transfer. The Local Allocation Tax accounts for, in 1990, about 50-60 per cent of all transfers from the national to local government or 15-20 per cent of total revenue. Local taxes account for 37 per cent of local revenue, total transfers account for 35 per cent, non-tax revenue is 20 per cent and bond finance is 9 per cent.

The major purpose of the Local Allocation Tax is to equalise the fiscal capacity of local governments, and the transfers are designed to take into account the inherent differences in both revenue raising capacities and expenditure needs of local governments. The approach is very similar to the Australian system of General Revenue Assistance to the States.

The Local Allocation Tax is linked to national tax revenues as follows: 32 per cent each of Income Tax, Corporation Tax and Liquor Tax revenues, 24 per cent of Consumption Tax and 25 per cent of Tobacco Consumption Tax revenues (Article 6 of the Local Allocation Tax Law). In practice, the amount does not always agree with the amount obtained by specified percentages of national tax revenues. When local revenue sources are expected to be insufficient through yearly formulation of the Local Finance Plan, the central government may borrow to fund the Local Allocation Tax, bring forward tax allocations, or increase/decrease the total amount of the tax.

Of the annual total set aside for Local Allocation Tax, 94 per cent is distributed to equalise the differences in individual financial capability as described earlier; the remaining 6 per cent is set aside for extraordinary cases such as natural disasters.

The amount of ordinary allocation is in principal the difference between an authority's basic fiscal needs and its basic fiscal revenues (revenue shortfall), as determined by a fixed formula (stipulated by law or Cabinet order). An authority's basic fiscal needs are determined by reference to a specific calculation of each service item. The Local Finance Plan forms the basis for estimating the level of such needs. Therefore, some authorities with more revenues than needs, Tokyo for example, are not eligible for the Local Allocation Tax.

The calculation uses a model Prefecture with a population of 1.7 million and a model Municipality with a population of 100,000 adjustments are then made for population, area and regional characteristics. To calculate income, a percentage is set of the estimated total income each authority is likely to receive, based primarily on past annual receipts. The percentages, 80 per cent for Prefectures and 75 per cent for Municipalities, are used because any prediction of need cannot reflect the various authorities' individual circumstances. Just as importantly, if a 100 per cent figure were used it would take away from local authorities all freedom of choice in how they spend the money, and discourage them from building reserves (which would automatically be lost in the coming year's calculation).

When the aggregate revenue shortfalls of individual authorities as determined by the foregoing method do not match the total amount of the ordinary Local Allocation Tax, the two figures are brought in line by multiplying adjustment rate to each authority's revenue shortfall.

In the case of Special Allocation Tax, in accordance with a Ministry of Home Affairs ordinance, it is distributed to each authority whose revenue shortfall has not been tracked by the basic fiscal needs.

Australia

The flow for Commonwealth government payments to State/local general government is shown in Figure 13.1.1. Payments to other levels of government (excluding Special Purpose Payments (SPPs) 'through' the States except for local government general purpose assistance grants) accounted for around 22 per cent of the total outlays of the Commonwealth general government sector in 1997-98.

These payments also accounted for around 39 per cent of the total revenue of the State general government sector and for around 17 per cent of the total revenue of the local general government sector.

The pattern of Commonwealth and State revenue raising and expenditure responsibilities is longstanding. Both the Commonwealth and the States have the legal capacity to levy taxes, the only exception being customs and excises which the Australian Constitution reserves for the Commonwealth. The States derive own-source revenue form a range of sources, the most important of which are payroll taxes and taxes on property, including stamp duties.

The merits of imbalance between the revenue raising and expenditure responsibilities of different tiers of government attract debate: One point of view (Commonwealth, 1998) is that advantages to Australia as a whole of a national taxation system are considerable, from both an economic and an administrative perspective. In Australia, a certain level of VFI is also necessary

Figure 13.1.1
Impact of Commonwealth General Government Payments to Other Levels of Government 1997-98 (Estimated)

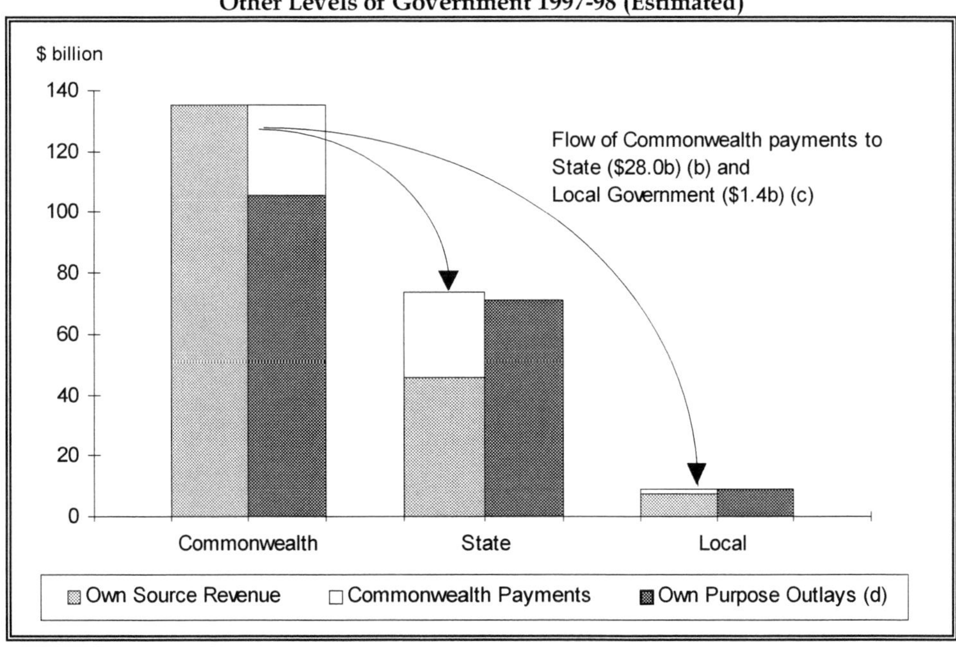

Source: Commonwealth of Australia, 1998.

if the Commonwealth is to distribute payments to the States in accordance with the principle of horizontal fiscal equalisation. The provision of grants to the States in the form of SPPs is a means for the Commonwealth to pursue its policy objectives in areas where the States are the primary service providers. Another point of view is that the extent of VFI is often been criticised on the grounds that it reduces government accountability. Accountability is considered to be best served when the level of government responsible for expenditure is also responsible for funding that expenditure through taxes. However, in practice, State governments are accountable for their budgetary decisions at the margin. The States raise around 58 per cent of their total revenue, and increases in State taxation. Financial market scrutiny also has a bearing on a government's accountability for its spending decisions. There is also the argument that national systems of tax administration and collection are sound if they are contracted by the States to collect revenues for them at rates they determine. Otherwise, they are sources of dependency which constrain State flexibility and innovation.

General purpose assistance to local government has been provided by the Commonwealth since 1974-75. Under current arrangements, the Commonwealth provides general purpose assistance to local government in the for of local government financial assistance grants and local government untied road funding. This assistance is paid to the States as Special Purpose Payments (SPP) on the condition that the finds are passed on to local government.

General purpose assistance is provided to local government authorities under the *Local Government (Financial Assistance) Act 1995.* Under the Act, the Treasurer is responsible for determining the annual increase in Commonwealth general purpose assistance paid to local government. The Act provides for general purpose assistance to be increased each year by an escalation factor, which reflects the underlying movement in general revenue assistance provided to the States.

The Commonwealth provided an estimated $1.229 million in local government general purpose assistance in 1998-99.

Table 13.1.1 sets out the payments of general purpose assistance to local government in 1997-98 and 1998-99.

As in the past, the interstate distribution of local government FAGs for 1998-99 will be on an equal per capita basis, using the State populations at 31 December in the previous financial year.

Table 13.1.1
General Purpose Assistance for Local Government
1998-99 - $ million (estimated)

	NSW	VIC	QLD	WA	SA	TAS	ACT	NT	Total
1998-99									
Financial Assistance Grants	288.1	211.4	156.8	82.8	67.7	21.6	14.1	8.6	581.1
Identified Road Grants	109.6	77.9	70.8	57.7	20.8	20.0	12.1	8.8	377.7
Total General Purpose Assist.[(a)]	397.7	289.3	227.5	140.5	8.5	41.6	26.2	17.5	1,228.8

Note: (a) Total general purpose assistance is the actual cash payment that the State receives on behalf of local government in the given year. It is equal to the estimated entitlement for that given year adjusted for an over or under payment from the previous year.

There are around 120 SPPs. In most cases SPPs are subject to conditions reflecting Commonwealth policy objectives or national policy objectives agreed between the Commonwealth and the State. It is because of the conditions attached to SPPs that they are sometimes called 'tied grants'. Such may include: i) general policy requirements on States (for example, that the States provide free public hospital treatment to Medicare patients as a condition of receiving hospital funding grants); ii) a requirement that a payment be expended for a specified purpose (for example, housing assistance for homeless people); iii) meeting broad Commonwealth-State agreements covering principles and program delivery mechanisms (for example the Commonwealth-State Housing Agreement); and iv) conditions of joint expenditure programs including project approval, ,matching arrangements (for example, dollar-for-dollar contributions) and performance information.

SPPs also include some payments, which are not subject to conditions. These typically relate to revenue sharing arrangements or compensation (either for the transfer of responsibilities or for other Commonwealth action).

In accordance with the South Australian Local Government Grants Commission Act 1992, revenue allocations were made to 69 Councils, the Outback Areas Community Development Trust and 5 Aboriginal communities eligible for grants.

The grants were allocated to communities as small as 70 people (the Nepabunna Community Council) and communities as large as 145,429 people (the Onkaparinga City Council - a large metropolitan council in Adelaide).

The South Australian Local Government Grants Commission, like its counterparts in other States, recommends the distribution of two sets of Commonwealth grants to local government, namely: i) Financial Assistance Grants (A$68.3 million in 1998-99); and ii) Identified Local Road Grants (A$20.9 million in 1998-99).

Both sets of grants are distributed according to various principles laid down by the Commonwealth, but the methodology differs between the two sets of grants.

The principles for the grant allocations that underpin the methodology employed by the Commission in the distribution process are as follows.

Horizontal Fiscal Equalisation: The general financial assistance component will continue to be distributed using a horizontal equalisation or needs based approach, which aims to compensate councils with below average revenue raising capacity and above average costs of service provision.

Effort Neutrality: In assessing grant levels for individual councils, the Commission takes no account of the policies and practices of those councils. Thus individual policy on rate setting, service provision and standards, and level of debt and reserves have no impact on the grant outcomes.

Minimum Grant: The minimum grant entitlement is the amount that councils would be entitled to if 30 per cent of the general financial assistance component was distributed between councils on a per capita basis.

Other Grant Support: Grants from sources other than the Commission are treated by the inclusion approach, with a separate revenue function calculated for them, providing that they are not received for special effort on the part of the council.

Aboriginal and Torres Strait Islander: Financial assistance is allocated to councils in a way which recognises the needs of Aboriginal and Torres Strait Islander people within their boundaries.

Identified Road Component: Local road grants are distributed according to the relative road expenditure meeds of each council and to preserve its road assets. Factors including road length, type and usage are considered.

The methodology involves the assessment of differences in the fiscal capacity and needs of Councils. To do this, comparisons are made between the position of each Council and an average, or "standard" position. That assessment may be positive or negative relative to that standard. For example, Councils with above standard capacity to raise revenue will receive a positive assessment. Councils with above average expenditure needs will receive a positive assessment and those with below average needs will receive a negative assessment.

The aggregate of the positive and negative assessments in each revenue and expenditure areas will, in principle, net to zero (although in some cases it may not do so precisely for technical reasons). It is to be emphasised that whether a particular Council has a positive or negative assessment in a particular area, (or in aggregate), the size of that assessment is in no way a measure of the adequacy or otherwise of the financial policies or efficiency of that Council. It is purely a measure of the financial capacity or needs of that Council ***relative to others*** and is calculated quite independently of its own financial policies or practices.

From the formulae, the populations of individual Councils and of all Councils combined enter heavily into the calculations. The effect of this, in principle, is to equalise the fiscal positions of Councils to the standard ***in per capita terms***. This is subject both to the fact that the aggregate levels of funds available for distribution between Councils is insufficient for this purpose, (see discussion below under the heading "Scaling Back"), and to policy decisions of individual Councils. To enable this principle to be achieved and again to achieve internal consistency throughout its assessments, the Commission eliminates the ***per property*** element (which has in the past been part of its assessment of rateable capacity).

Reference has been made above, and more detailed reference is made below, to assessments being made relative to an "average" (or "standard") position. Such averages are calculated by aggregating data for all Councils combined - e.g., the average tax rate referred to in the next section of this paper is calculated by aggregating the rate revenue of all Councils and the capital values of rateable properties in all Councils and dividing the second aggregate into the first. These might be referred to as weighted averages as distinct form simple averages, which would be obtained by calculating the relevant ratio for each Council separately and when averaging the results.

In respect to the "weighting" which should be given to the revenue and expenditure sides of assessments, there is no pre-conceived weighting system. The approach is to assess differences in relative capacity and need in each area and then to aggregate the results and to determine grants based thereon. The relative "importance" of revenue and expenditure items in the overall results thus flows naturally out of the calculations and is not predetermined in any way.

The Commission is of the view that allocations to individual councils should only fluctuate mildly on an annual basis due to the fact that the main drivers; the units of measure, the population and the standard cost will not vary greatly from year to year.

References

Brennan, G. and Buchanan, J., (1980), *The Power to Tax: Analytic Foundations of a Fiscal Constitution* Cambridge: Cambridge University Press.

Broadway, R.W. and Hobson, P.A.R. (1993), *Intergovernmental Fiscal Relations in Canada,* Canadian Tax Foundation Tax, Canadian Tax Paper No. 96.

Castles, F.G. (1999), *Decentralisation and the Post War Economy,* Centre for Economic Policy Research, ANU, Discussion Paper No. 399, March.

Commonwealth of Australia (1991), "Taxation and the Fiscal Imbalance between Levels of Australian Government", Commonwealth, State and Territory Working Party on Tax Powers, October.

Commonwealth of Australia (1998), "Federal Financial Relations 1998-99", *Budget Paper No. 3,* May 1998.

Council of Local Authorities for International Relations (CLAIR) (1997), *Local Government in Japan,* Third Edition, February.

Klein, J.R., (1998), "A Strategic Approach for Donor-Assisted Counter Corruption programs", in *Governance Innovations in the Asia-Pacific Region,* eds. G. Bhatta and J.L. Gonzalez III.

Legaspi, P.E., Cabo, W.L. and Jouquin, E.T. (1996), *Local Economic Promotion in the Philippines,* Local Government Centre and Public Administration Promotion Centre.

Local Government Grants Commission - South Australia (1997), "Review of Methodology", Discussion Paper, November.

Local Government Grants Commission - South Australia (1998a), *Annual Report 1997-98.*

Local Government Grants Commission - South Australia (1998b), "Summary of Outcomes for the 1997-98", Review of Methodology, July.

Ma, J. (1997), *Inter-governmental Fiscal Transfer: A Comparison of Nine Countries,* World Bank, May.

Ministerial Advisory Group (MAG) on Local Government Reform (1995), *Reform of Local Government in South Australia: Councils of the Future,* June.

Moesen, W.A., (1993), *Community Public Finance in the Perspective of EMU in Commission of the European Communities,* The Economics of Community Finance, European Economy, Vol. 5.

Morgan, P.J. (1999), "Japanese Economy - Outlook for Growth in 1999", in *Outlook 1999,* Australian Bureau of Agricultural and Resource Economics - Commonwealth of Australia, March.

OECD (1997), *Managing Across Levels of Government,* OECD Publications, Paris.

Rosen, H.S., (1995), *Public Finance,* 4th Edition, Illinors: Richard D. Irwin, Inc.

Shah, A., (1994), *The Reform of Intergovernmental Fiscal Relations in Developing and Emerging Market Economies,* Policy and Research Series No. 23, Washington D.C.: World Bank

Ter-Minassian, T. (1997), *Fiscal Federalism in Theory and Practice,* International Monetary Fund, Washington.

Tiebout, C.M., (1956), "A Pure Theory of Local Expenditure", *Journal of Political Economy 64.*

Yonehara, J. (1993), *Financial Relations Between the National and Local Governments,* Tokyo, University of Tokyo Press.

Chapter Fourteen

Economic Co-operation

Since Adam Smith's explanation of early European industrialisation, the theoretical framework of economics has been built on the notion of competition. When economic co-operation was introduced much later, the notion was associated with the evils of collusion, that is, firms would conspire to fix prices and extract extraordinary profits from consumers. However, the tide turns, co-operation is not necessarily bad if the extraordinary profits are used to fund innovative R&D necessary for the next technological leap. Co-operation between firms is not necessarily bad if synergies are created between them which better position local firms for global competition.

In this final chapter, we take a look at two initiatives in South Australia that have involved economic co-operation for the purpose of bring parties together to create the synergies for innovation and growth. The first is the water industry which appears to have been successful so far in creating clusters of firms to co-operate for growth. The second is the Multi-function Polis, an innovative milieu, which eventually got off the ground but in a form that is considerably diluted relative to the initial grand plan.

Although economic co-operation is not the whole picture of economic success and growth, this chapter is based around the importance of co-operative relationships in order to reinforce work at earlier chapters relating to good governance, clusters and milieus.

The Nature of Economic Co-operation

Before examining the details of the two initiatives, there is a need to define the nature of economic co-operation. Economic co-operation is defined as special relationships between at least two entities (firms, governments or any other entity in the community) that are (i) beyond normal market transactions involving buying and selling and (ii) involve some permanence either by long term contracts or a strong sense of civic fabric that binds parties to achieve common objectives. There are other definitions, but this definition serves, at least, the purposes of this chapter.

In every society there is a set of institutions that either create or destroy opportunities for economic development. The structure of incentives guides these institutions to make the transition from where they are today to where they want to be in the future, a creative distruction which involves a process dismantling the old and replacing with the new. A fundamental element that influences both the speed and direction of economic development is the process of building and maintaining relationships for economic co-operation. What binds partners are opportunity, common vision, compatible or complementary strengths and culture.

While economic co-operation arises automatically through trade and incidentally as a by-product of the general course of business activities between governments, firms and individuals, an important element comes about through a strategy. In particular, we consider the strategy of economic co-operation in three forms:

- a partnership between government and a major multinational corporation. For example, the contract between the SA Government and EDS for the outstanding of information technology services and commitment by EDS to foster the economic growth of the industry;
- a cluster of firms in the same industry group that co-operate to complete in an external market. For example, the South Australian defence industry cluster which consists of a number of defence, electronic and related high-technology firms and government to share information abut the national and international industry developments; and
- a milieu of organisations across different industries, government, universities and community groups that aim to create synergies by

working co-operatively toward a set of broad objectives spanning economic, social and cultural aspects. Silicon Valley is an example.

These relationships can involve a few or many parties. Partnerships, clusters and milieus represent steps on the ladder from less complex to more complex sets of relationships. A region not able to benefit from partnership arrangements is unlikely to be successful at the more demanding and more managerially intensive relationships necessary to form clusters and milieus.

In general, there is agreement (see, for example, Camagni (1993), Birley et al (1991)) that economic co-operation is motivated by the following benefits:

- increased profits or sales appears to be the most important and readily identifiable benefit;
- market knowledge is mainly an unanticipated spin-off of co-operation activities. Economic co-operation tends to be based on concrete things;
- gaining new customers and suppliers both locally and overseas; and
- product development, and in particular the exchange information of technology and production processes.

Economic co-operation does not always work (Korczynski, 1994). Firstly, there is the important problem of the additional time needed to develop and service the relationships. Secondly, there are administrative and legal costs associated with defining and managing intellectual property and the potential loss of competitiveness associated with disclosing commercial secrets. Thirdly, there are potential and difficulties in the personalities of the key representatives.

The potential loss of control over business outcomes, and concerns about trust between parties are also important problems, and add to the uncertainty and uneasiness in dealing with other parties.

All parties have a role in managing the relationships and a large part of the success is attributable to the strength of the communication between the parties. A role of governments in facilitating economic co-operation would involve the following. Firstly, recognising that governments have a role. Secondly, governments should provide information to agents where those agencies are not able to access information or due to the public good nature of information firms tend to under-access available stock. Thirdly, improve the level of skills in relationship building and maintenance and importantly orderly exit from relationships once they have run their natural course. Fourthly, bringing potential partners together.

Water Industry

Background

When the current South Australian Government took office in 1993, most of the States had already reached the intensive stage of microeconomic reform of government enterprises. And national competition policy was just around the corner. Burdened with the financial impact of the State Bank collapse, the South Australian government searched for big ticket Budget savings items. Outsourcing of government services promised significant efficiency gains. Within two years, the government had, among other initiatives, outsourced whole-of-government information technology services to EDS, established an Electronic Services Business and outsourced water and watewater services to a private sector consortium led by a French water company[33], known locally as United Water.

Smith and McGuire (in SACES Economic Briefing, July 2000) describe the strategy behind the water outsourcing initiative, the contractual deliverables and the challenges that remain. The contract with United Water consists of two important components, namely, cost-effective operations and maintenance of the water supply system and implementing a set of initiatives to facilitate the growth of the water industry.

The structure and culture of the South Australian water industry, at the time United Water was established in 1996, were heavily dominated by the (then) Engineering and Water Supply Department (E&WS). The E&WS covered almost all functions in the industry: the water and wastewater service provider, the water regulator and the dominant product designer. The industry was almost one dimensional. More specifically, the industry was characterised as a series of sub-component suppliers clustered around the E&WS. The E&WS was then a department of state and as such had a public service culture - process oriented, inward focused with little business acumen and strongly engineering skills dominated. Importantly, the industry lacked the expertise to develop new products and market those products outside the state.

Growing the Industry

The E&WS underwent a major structural change. In addition to outsourcing a major set of functions to United Water, Riverland Water was selected to construct a Build, Own, Operate and Transfer scheme for water treatment plants to supply filtered water to country areas. The E&WS was corporatised and the regulatory functions were transferred to another government agency. The 'game keeping' was separated from 'poaching', and the 'poaching' was outsourced. The old poacher became the SA Water Corporation and the new corporate body developed skills in contract management, strengthened its role in community

33 (Then) known as Compangné Générale des Eaux (now) Vivendi Water.

issues and in the provision of water policy advice. And the culture changed, at least slightly, away from engineering to policy and management.

Apart from accepting a contract to achieve cost efficiencies in the delivery of water and wastewater products, United Water accepted the task of growing the industry. In essence, this meant lifting the objectives of the small and fragmented band of water firms from local to national and international horizons. The task involved facilitating the upskilling of firms to enable them to develop new products and using United Water's global industry network to identify markets and organise the industry to market the products overseas either on a firm basis or in consortia with firms with complementary skills.

Although it is very difficult to measure the benefits of such policies, there is evidence that the water industry in South Australia has grown. Smith and McGuire report a strong trend in the industry's growth. The lag between the starting development date of 1996 reflects the long term nature of product development.

As Smith and McGuire point out, establishing a closer relationship between the R&D community and the water industry is fundamental to the development of new products and sources. The players in this relationship are the water industry, academic and R&D communities.

An important part of building the relationship was the establishment of a water industry cluster.

The development of the water industry cluster was completed by early 1998. The reference group, as it was known then, consisted of 40 water industry organisations and individuals. At that time there were efforts to establish an incorporated association, and an interim Board of Management was formed with representation from several local companies, United Water, North West Water and the SA Water Corporation. The association later became known as the Water Industry Alliance (WIA).

The principle aim of the WIA is to facilitate the development and growth of the water industry in South Australia. The benefits of being a member of the cluster, as articulated by the WIA are:

- access to market information and opportunities;
- assistance in the formation of strategic alliances to approach those opportunities; and
- access to relevant education, training and awareness programs.

Figure 14.1
Increase in Net Exports Relative to 1995 Net Exports,
South Australian Water Industry 1996 to 1999 (In 1996 Prices)

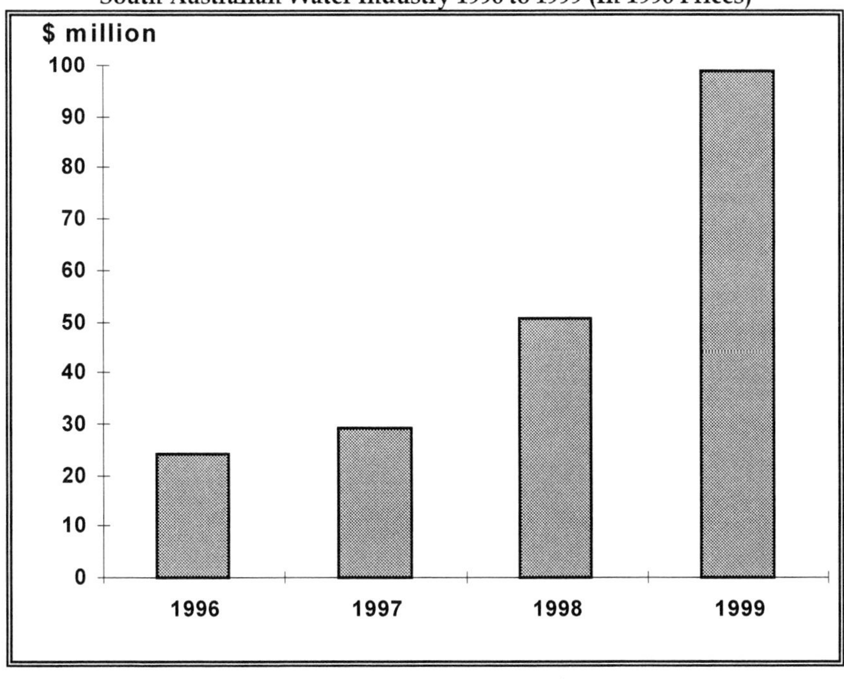

Source: Smith and McGuire in SACES Economic Briefing, July 2000.

There are two other incorporated associations in the water industry: the Australian Water and Wastewater Association and the Irrigation Association of Australia. However, the WIA differentiated themselves from these associations on the basis that these associations represent national not local interests and that neither has a specific economic development focus.

Connected to the cluster are a number of initiatives jointly developed by United Water and the SA Water Corporation. United Water presented a series of seminars aimed at providing water industry members with information about international developments. For example, the economic crisis which gripped SE Asia in 1997 put governments under fiscal stress as tax revenues plunged. There was concern locally that the fiscal response of the SE Asian governments may be to substantially cut public expenditure programs for upgrading water facilities which in turn would adversely effect opportunities for the local water industry to capture market opportunities. United Water brought in specialists from the parent company in France to offer global perspectives. Assessments of the SE Asian markets were undertaken and alternative markets in Latin America and sub-Saharan Africa were considered.

While the water industry cluster has been formed and the intensity of the network has accelerated since incorporation of the WIA, there remain a few dark clouds over the relationship. Firstly, United Water is a relatively tiny component of the parent company's activities, and global corporate strategy will be determined in France. This means that the level of resources committed to the 'Adelaide branch-office' will be a function not only of the return on the investment but the strategic priorities of the parent. United Water in Adelaide may not get heard.

Secondly, the relationship between the two big players, United Water and the SA Water Corporation, has its tensions. Most of these tensions would be relieved if both players stick to the rules, namely, 'you do your job, and I'll do mine'. More specifically, there is some concern to ensure that SA Water Corporation keeps away from the business of try to capture markets overseas. They do not have a comparative advantage in the market knowledge as this is rightly the responsibility of United Water. But the rules are not that simple. How does the SA Water Corporation know if United Water is doing their best in capturing markets for local players. It could be argued that the competitive spirit of United Water will ensure that it will try its hardest because it is in their interests to profit maximise. However, as previously suggested United Water operate under 'constrained' optimisation, constrained by corporate head office priorities. SA Water Corporation need to be sure they know enough about markets and marketing to be comfortable with United Water's advice.

Thirdly, clusters work best in the business of information exchange because this activity is less prone to power-play. But the WIA does more than that. At least implicitly, this cluster is involved in the organisation of the smaller players in the industry to collaborate amongst themselves and with the big players. Asymmetric information and superior management inevitably lead to a degree of dominance. Is the structure of the industry stable or will United Water take over the best of the little players and discard the rest? Without a thorough analysis one could not reasonably advance a prediction. But there are some interesting trade-offs to consider. (i) A profit maximiser may tend to buy firms that have big potential and where the value is not currently captured in the share price. On the other hand, the purchase of local firms may engage United Water in veritical integration which may not consistent with their corporate strategy (either locally or corporate head office). (ii) What is the corporate culture of United Water - is it an aggressive and ruthless player, interested in taking the best local talent and the new ideas from local firms. This could be construed to be a description of certain attitudes in the South Australian information technology industry. On the other hand, it may be the case that United Water is genuinely interested in collaboration because the small players can offer a specialist service which United Water cannot efficiently undertake in-house.

Fourthly, the basis of the relationship between SA Water and United Water is that United Water has the dual responsibility of the water and wastewater services operation and growing the industry. The contract between them specifies performance criteria, with penalties for falling short. The contract is confidential, and not without good commercial reasons. But the lack of transparency is an invitation for government scrutineers to question the basis of the relationship - are there hidden subsidies, is there a moral dilemma. The government would be just as embarrassed as United Water for non-performance so what does this mean for incentives for disclosure. Are there some trade-offs distorting the allocation of resources within the industry. For example, to fund the economic development initiatives it is possible to improve the rate of return on the outsourced operations and maintenance by adjusting upwards the agreed fee. These are remarks, speculative gestures to bring out the complexity of the relationship, and there is nothing that could not be properly managed. As the United Nations (1999) argue "transparency is the most important requirement for sustaining such a partnership" because transparency "helps to remove many negative effects that partnership itself may cause".

With a horse race that will run for 15.5 years, it will be interesting to see what unfolds. Nonetheless, what can be said at this time is that the industry is growing, and the cluster process appears to be the growth engine.

MFP: Innovative Milieu or Real Estate Muddle

Background

Deep in the urban jungle of Adelaide, just 12 km North of the central business district, you can observe the remains of the Multi-Function Polis - the lost city of high technology. In the late 1980s and 1990s, in the minds of the social architects, this city was a hive of new ideas and high-tech concepts. A merging of Australian and Japanese business culture. A place of thinking at the frontiers of knowledge in fields important to a prospering global community in the 21st century. But by the mid 1990s an imbalance of power had emerged between the bureaucrats, the real estate agents and the technologists. The priorities become muddled, visions become foggy and the new ideas evaporated. The MFP was never, of course, created, in its original conception. Although the State government did proceed with a regional and urban development project, known as Mawson Lakes, a residential enclave for middle income families.

Following the themes of this chapter, we consider the nature of economic co-operation that underpinned the initiative. But, in addition, we will take the perspective of the analyst, brought-in to undertake a regional economic assessment and to advise on the merits of proceeding with the initiative. Regional economic assessment involves the use the economist's standard tool kit of evaluative techniques. Its true importance is the capacity of these techniques to 'bring it together' and highlight the relevance and the contribution of the component parts and sub-initiatives that make up the whole project. It is a tool for guiding the formulation of proposals. Too often, in contrast, economic assessment techniques are used for spelling out, ex-post, the implications of decisions made on other criteria.

The economic evaluation of the feasibility of a city is unusual for several reasons. Firstly agglomeration of activities in urban settlement patterns tends to 'just happen' for non-specified reasons. The so called New Location Theory argues that the agglomeration of urban settlement is the outcome of two opposing forces: centripetal forces and centrifugal forces. Centripetal forces bind settlements and draw in resources and centrifugal forces repel or dispurse economic activity. These forces are explained in some detail in the chapter of Cities and Towns. With all of these things going on, the evaluation of an urban settlement becomes very problematic.

Secondly, agglomeration can occur through the co-incidence of events or the result of exploration. Urban planning tends to be broad brush - concentrating on the utilisation of existing conditions for hosting future economic activity. The density of the agglomeration, the nature of activity and the distribution of income are a function of the decisions of pioneer settlers. A chance event which has long range implications. Consider for example what would Adelaide be like today if the allocation of land to the early settlers had been less generous, or the division of land had been based differently than on a 'first in, first served basis'.

Thirdly, urban agglomeration can also happen as a by-product of some external event or policy. California's industrial base was established, ground-up, from a decision by the US government to position defence forces on the West coast to enable America to participate in the Pacific theatre of world war two. California did not make a policy decision to attract industry, nor was it in the same way as Gerschenkron (1952) described the way in which Russia adopted national development policies involving the government in direct public investment and the banks in financial development assistance in all attempt to stimulate Russian's catch up to the newly formed industrialised economies of Western Europe.

By contrast, the MFP concept was about creating a special set of conditions sufficiently strong enough to mobilise targeted industries to the specified location. There was no co-incidence of natural events nor some major external factor to drive agglomeration. In every sense, the MFP was to be a designer product for a niche market, and in every sense a clearly ambitious venture.

The Vision of the Innovative Milieu

In 1987, the Japanese Ministry of International Trade and Industry (MITI) proposed to the Australian government that the two countries collaborate to build a new kind of city in Australia with extensive Japanese involvement. Although a vaguely conceived concept that combined high technology and high leisure facilities, the MFP was held out to be of huge benefit to Australia particularly in the sense of holding out new ways organising to extract profits from new technologies. For the next eleven years, until 1998, the MFP concept was debated until it was officially abandoned by the South Australian

Government. In 1996, building on a set of feasibility studies, the Centre for Economic Studies prepared a cost-benefit study on the MFP, initially for input to a Commonwealth review conducted by the Commonwealth Bureau of Industry Economics (BIE) and then as an aid for the State Government's decisions over the future of the MFP. The study, as far as, the Centre can determine is the last major economic feasibility study done prior to the final decision to abandon the project. Although the debate was protracted, Baines (1999) suggests that the debate was lost well before then, in fact "it took less than a year for the initial potential to be lost" because "as a nation Australia was unable to embrace the possibilities inherent in the project".

The original concept was proposed by the Japanese in January 1987 at the 9th Australia-Japan Ministerial Committee meeting headed by Minister Tamura of Japan's MITI. The proposal was sketchy but was described as a forum for international exchange in the Pacific region, would feature high technology industries and new lifestyles for work and leisure that would look ahead to the 21st century, significant in size possibly between 20,000 and 200,000 people of overseas origins and be a locus of cultural exchange between Japan, Australia and other countries particularly ASEAN nations. Australia, at the time saw the MFP more as a facility than a city, but MITI formulated a concept plan in September 1987 which reaffirmed the larger dimensions of the project and identified major participating Japanese corporations.

Mouer and Sugimoto (1990) admirably articulate the debate. They identify "the idea of building an MFP with considerable Japanese involvement has become an extremely sensitive issue which is positioned on the emotional cutting edge of Australia". At that time there were calls from various quarters including Camillari and McKay that the benefits were real and Australia needs to respond creatively to them, but others argued that a little attention had been directed to how the income generated by the MFP would be linked to the Australian standard of living. Morris - Suzuki's comments warned that technopolises and science cities had generated a range of problems within Japan. Concerns were expressed about the distribution of income, ownership and the reputation of multi-national corporations to manoeuvre around local legislation. Another plank of worries was based on racism, both in the sense of 'antipathetic racism' characterised by 'I hate those bloody Japs' and in the sense of 'stereotyping racism' which guided by the sentiment that "all Japanese are the same".

Nonetheless, in June 1990 the Federal Government announced that the MFP preferred site would be the Gold Coast, but later that year following tensions over land values the runner-up, Adelaide, was the endorsed site. Subsequent to a feasibility study, the Federal Government formally approached the Adelaide project in July 1991 and allocated initially $12 million, and then a further $40 million in March 1992. During the period 1991 to 1996 there were a long list of administrative and organisational announcements and assessment reports, but the Japanese lost enthusiasm subsequent to a visiting delegation in late 1991 and the Commonwealth phased out funding for the project subsequent to the findings at the May 1996 BIE report. From that point on, the project became a state-based regional and urban development project.

Economic Evaluation

In July 1996, the Centre for Economic Studies completed a commissioned assignment to evaluate the costs and benefits of the project from a State, in contrast with national, perspective.

By this time that this evaluation was being undertaken, the MFP was described, in essence, as an economic and business development initiative, or more particularly, as an economic and business *transformation* initiative of benefit to Australia as a whole and especially to South Australia as the geographic home base.

What particularly distinguished the MFP from other economic development initiatives is that (i) the focus is on new and emerging technologies and on the promotion of education and training; (ii) an explicit aim to combine economic with social and environmental considerations to support the development of a model of a 21st Century Community; and (iii) the development of an urban settlement which incorporates and show-cases new products and consumer technologies and the integrated organisation of community and social activities around education facilities in an environmentally and cultural sensitive manner.

On the basis of a big stack of assumptions, the economic evaluation of the project seemed favourable, although the net benefits were sensitive to the assumptions. Considerable effort had been expended on the real estate development. In place was the design of the urban layout including the artificial lakes, removal of the sheep burial pits, the road access and positioning of the development area relative to the adjacent university campus and the proposed industrial site. The State government agencies questioned, and rightly so, the impact of the new residential development on the land values and other nearby residential developments. There was considerable analysis done. However, a key problem was the assessment of the Telstra and related high technology, business opportunities. The quantification of the benefits was much more difficult than other segments of the project. Analysis of the benefits was a bit like assessing the probability of access through a revolving door. In essence, Telstra had a national investment plan for 'roll out' of fibre optic cables, and the intention was to spread the investments around the regions partly for operational reasons and also so that Telstra would be seen to be equitable. The later being akin to an undisclosed Community Service Obligation. From a national perspective, which is usual for a sound economic evaluation, the location of the investment does not matter except for cost-effectiveness reasons. However, the MFP project involved attracting a higher share relative to that which South Australia would have received in the normal course of events. The normal 'entitlement' was not a disclosable item.

Remarks

The agglomeration of urban and industry settlement tends to happen through the fundamental economic forces of comparative advantage. The MFP concept was clearly ambitious, aiming to create an artificial economic environment from 'greenfields', that was sufficiently attractive to mobilise targeted industry to a specific location North of Adelaide. In this sense the MFP was a designer product for a niche market.

The economic assessment of the MFP Stage I Development was particularly difficult task. Defining the precise nature and bounds of the project, the estimation of costs and benefits and, importantly, the sensitivity of those estimates to the underlying assumptions were both problematic and precarious. It was very clear from the point of view of an external party looking in on the state of play of the project several years after initial planning that most of the intellectual effort had been directed toward the design of the urban development and very little of the effort directed toward the intellectual and innovative aspects of the IT&T business. The project was dominated by the urban developers, maximising opportunities for big profits from selling real estate.

The economic assessment, although rubbery, showed that there were positive signs that the region would benefit from the project.

While its easy to criticise after the event, there are some worthwhile issues that warrant thought by government and industry leaders when they (and I suggest they do) try it again.

Firstly, if Baines (1999) and others are right, the respective governments should have moved far more quickly to either proceed with or dismiss the project proposal. Lengthy delays in the decision making process turned the Japanese government away, and, linked to that, discouraged other overseas corporate investors. From that point, the project diminished from being of national significance to regional significance. Of course, moving slowly is necessary if one is on unsure ground, inexperienced in dealing with such ambitious projects.

Secondly, the strength of the economic co-operation between the main parties was not in balance. There were problems with differing cultures earlier in the project, and then later, at the local level, real estate development led industry development and technological innovation took the back seat.

Thirdly, the project was clearly ambitious because it was starting from a greenfields site. The MFP was a designer product for a niche market. The level of effort required to meet requirements of the project was enormous. And the local players were lacking sufficient depth of experience in the new game.

Fourthly, the project was also ambitious from the point of view of the number of participants in the collaborative effort. As previously explained, then MFP as a milieu, is at the top end of the spectrum in terms of intensity of economic co-operation.

Conclusion

Partnerships between government and multi-national corporations, clusters of firms and innovative milieus are three examples of special relationships for economic cooperation. These relationships go beyond the normal market transactions of buying and selling and involve long term commitments.

Shifting up the spectrum from partnerships to clusters to milieus involves increasingly complex relationships which rely much more heavily on trust, shared vision, clear roles for each party, transparency in decisions and mutual respect for (intellectual and physical) property. This is an intensive, high level management process requiring very strong communication. These relationships can be fragile, and, are subject to the changeable factors that drive the creation and maintenance of these relationships (such as changing market opportunities which require different inputs from partners).

The SA Government's water industry and MFP initiatives are two practical examples of these special relationships. In terms of the complexity of the relationships for economic cooperation, both the water industry and MFP initiatives are ambitious but the latter initiative is far more so. The water industry initiative which is now about one-third of the way through its 15 year life, has shown to be successful as a means of transforming the culture of a department of state and growing the water industry. By the time the MFP was implemented, most of the true benefits of initiative had been lost. The shear ambitiousness of the level of economic cooperation needed to make the grand plan work is the root cause of its decline. The (high) level of economic cooperation required was not attained which led to long delays in the decision making process turning off the Japanese investors and others and to imbalances between parties (real estate vs business development).

References

Baines, C. (1999), *Multifunction Polis: Lost City of Opportunity*, Doctor of Philosophy Thesis, University of Adelaide.

Birley, S., S. Cromie and A. Myers (1991), "Entrepreneur Networks: Their Emergence in Ireland and Overseas", *Inernational Small Business Journal*, Vol. 9, No. 4.

Bureau of Industry Economics, (1996), *Evaluation of Commonwealth Support for MFP Australia*, AGPS.

Camagni, R. (1993), "Inter-Firm Industrial Networks: The Costs and Benefits of Cooperative Behaviour", *Journal of Industry Studies*, Vol. 1, No. 1, pp. 1-15.

Gerschenkron, A. (1952), *Economic Rachwardness in Historical Perspective in The Sociology of Economics Life*, edited by Mark Granovetter and Richard Swedberg, Boulder, Colorado: Westview Press, 1992.

Inkster, I. (1991), *The Clever City: Japan, Australia and The Multifunction Polis*, Oxford University Press, Australia.

Korczynski, M. (1994), "Low Trust and Opportunism in Action: Evidence on Inter-Firm Relations from the British Engineers Construction Industry", *Journal of Industry Studies*, Vol. 1, No. 2, pp. 43-64.

Mouer, R.E. and Sugimoto, Y. (1990), *The MFP Debate: A Background Reader*, La Trobe University Press.

United Nations, (1999), *Building Partnerships for Good Governance*, New York.

Chapter Fifteen
Advancing the Regions

In this final chapter, we attempt to bring together the main themes of the book and describe the main factors that influence the development of regions.

The Context

The progressive integration of international markets, reflecting the relaxation of protectionist trade policies and declining costs of transport, communication and access to information, is driving fundamental change in the competitiveness of regions.

The change is so fundamental and far reaching that there can be no doubt that some regions will decline and others will rise. This book has sought to present current thinking on factors that may influence regional economic development and identify strategies and policies that governments, industry and the community can adopt to take charge of their regions. South Australia and its sub-regions have been the focus, but the principles and case studies have broader applications.

Throughout this book we refer to a 'region'. This term has no precise meaning because the definition of a region is essentially purpose driven. The purposes can reflect government policies which are defined by the border of a jurisdiction or common socio-economic characteristics or common products. Similarly, a 'small' region is a fluid term which can cover Australia, South Australia or something smaller such as the Riverland or the Green Triangle. But common to all small regions is the tendency to be heavily influenced by the external environment.

Regional economic development is a broad expression, reflecting not just growth of incomes, but the quality of life. Although difficult to measure, this concept embraces health, learning, experience, variety, work and leisure quality, security and confidence about the future. Regional economic growth is a narrower concept compared with regional economic development. The most common measure of growth is Gross State (or Domestic) Product per capita. Despite a range of measurement problems this measure is widely used because it is relatively easy to calculate.

World economic growth has tended to be stable at around 2 per cent per annum over most of the 20th century. There are mixed views about whether the developing countries are catching up to the advanced countries, but this is considerable evidence that regions within countries are converging.

In 1870, Australia was the world's richest economy, in terms of income per capita, but Australia has not matched the pace of economic change over the past 130 years. Although a broadly affluent society, South Australia has not kept pace with Australia. Being a small regional economy, South Australia has limited levers to pull to stimulate the catch up process, but small regional policies can make a difference. Targeted industry assistance is not the answer. Microeconomic reform policies are a stronger stimulus, but most importantly regions need to recognise that the global dynamics are changing.

Globalisation consists of two elements which describe the nature of interconnection between regions. The first element is intensified trade interdependence, that is, the growth of imports and exports between countries. The second element involves integration, a quality shift, in that global entities organise production, distribution and consumption in various countries, the strategies and policies of which are governed by global laws and international trade practices, independently of nation-states.

No-one argues that globalisation is not happening, but the evidence of the extent of trade interdependence seems stronger than for market integration. However, the former can be considered to be a prerequisite for the latter, and, that being accepted, means that nation-states will gradually loose control to the international corporate bodies and the regions that host them.

Regions are emerging as the natural units of competition, defined less by the economies of scale in production but rather by an ability to match the changing and diverging tastes of consumers through small production runs of specialised products. A region, more so that a nation-state, has a (i) clear identity and is not defined arbitrarily by a border; (ii) produces an array of products which are linked by common inputs or processes, and is (iii) networked with markets but with fewer points of contact which facilitates co-operation and collaboration and reduces information costs.

There is an overwhelming sense that small regional economies are being increasingly exposed to powerful external factors. Regions will need to assess the impact of global forces on them. They must charter a course, find a new passage to growth by building on their regional advantages, and hope that they are smart and nimble enough to survive and prosper in a rapidly changing global environment.

A Framework For Regional Economic Development

Since Adam Smith gazed over the dawn of early industrialisation in Europe, theories to explain why regions grow have been submitted and elevated to 'laws' only to be demolished. While the literature as a whole may seem something of a disappointment, there seems to be some consensus building from the many studies published during the 1990s.

In this book we have attempted to take a cross section of the vast array of contributions to the literature on regional economic growth. While this literature cannot be adequately dealt with in a single chapter, the contemporary theory can perhaps be circumscribed by three overlapping pieces of wisdom. The first piece of wisdom, ascribed to Eric Jones, is that economic growth is like a combination lock. Certain things must be in place before it happens. A region may have some of the 'right' factors, but if one or more of the remaining factors is missing or insufficient then the others may not be enough to permit sustained growth. This emphasises the role of substitutes. For example, if you do not have the human capital and you can not wait 20 years to develop it, then hire it from another region.

The second piece of wisdom, ascribed to James Ridel, is that regions should do what comes naturally. His insights are drawn from the East Asian growth miracle. Economic growth has been fostered because workers, business people and the community have been left alone to get on with the job. They have seen the virtues of keeping their children at school for longer and progressively trained them so that they are able to ride the escalator of higher valued production. Relaxation of government control and reduced market intervention seem to work.

The third piece of wisdom, ascribed to Mancur Olson and discussed at some length earlier in this book, is that 'big bills are left on the sidewalk'. There are opportunities. They have not all been picked up through arbitrage. Some things about our society are holding us back, we are not on the production frontier. It is not so much the size of our populations or our technologies or our natural resource endowments that are holding us back. Borders of public choice that dileneate economic institutions and policies are what make the difference. Institutions and policies create a system of incentives for good and bad economic behaviour. Our institutions and policies are what we make of them, and they reflect our society and culture, how hard we work, the way we organise to produce, how we conduct our relationships with others, and our attitudes to development of ourselves and the others.

The main themes in the contemporary regional economic growth literature can be separated into two sets: those themes which describe factors that are basic to understanding regional growth and those which offer a deeper more fundamental understanding upon which policy prescriptions can be developed.

Labour productivity, capital productivity, the role of export and domestic demand, critical events and triggers, product life cycles and natural endowments are all relevant basic factors that describe why some regions grow and others do not. But these factors offer little by way of guidance on how to improve regional growth; they are the proximate causes, not the deeper more fundamental factors that drive growth. At best, they point to the need for diversification of economic activity, low cost and efficient infrastructure, cost-effective government services, a need to exploit export markets particularly where the domestic or local market is too small to reap economies of scale. These are useful hints for the policy maker, corporate adviser and community leader, but there is no prescriptive power in the analysis.

There are some now generally accepted observations about regional development that offer a deeper understanding of factors that influence growth, and point to ways in which regions can catch up and match the pace of the leading regions.

Firstly, in a globalised world, promoting regional development is increasingly a key element in promoting national development. Inter-regional linkages often have overtaken national linkages as the focal point of economic and social development opportunities. People appear to be establishing a stronger attachment to their regional and community bases - in contrast to national and State governments - as a source of support in the face of increased uncertainty, instability and stress associated with competing globally.

Secondly, regional development is about more than economic development. While the word 'sustainability' has usually been attached to environmental and natural resource issues, in its widest sense, it encapsulates all factors that affect the capacity of a regional economy to remain viable and vibrant - whether these relate to natural resources, the skills base of the region, its administrative and political support systems, the vitality of its sports, or strength of cultural and social cohesion.

Thirdly, regional development critically depends on the regions leading the process of developing strategies and plans for realising their potential or redressing the factors that have been pulling them down. This does not imply that regions and communities can do it all for themselves. Rather, the international evidence points to the fact that regions which have turned around their fortunes, or who have most fully capitalised on new opportunities arising from global change, have done so in large part by recognising that they have themselves the capacities needed to influence their future economic and community development. What they need is collaboration and support from State and national governments.

Fourthly, there's nothing unique about the drivers of regional development, although differences in the relative significance of some of them have emerged as a result of both the rapid growth of the information economy and changes in broader economic factors. That is, like all economies, regional economies basically grow or decline according to the demands for, and supply of, the natural and human resources they have access to, and the investments that businesses are prepared to make in them as a result. The expansion of the wine industry within the Riverland region is a case in point.

Fifthly, the more fundamental drivers of regional development, those that enable regions to catch up and stay ahead, lay in the institutions, policies, social and cultural values of the community, and the way in which firms and individuals organise to work together and relate with the external environment. Those factors form the structure or framework within which incentives are created for good or bad economic behaviour. The stronger the incentives for good economic behaviour the more likely:

- individuals will work near full levels of effort and potential;
- individuals and firms will co-operate and collaborate;
- resources will be devoted to productive outcomes, and less likely that resources will be devoted to rent seeking, subversive behaviour, protracted legal actions, crime and destruction; and
- there will be trust in the society.

Finally, what recent research emphasises, more so than in the past, is the role of regional leadership, the increased significance of innovation and technology transfer at regional level, the significance of not just education and skills development but also adaptability to changing needs and demands, and the significance of the development of strategic clusters and networks as a basis for the development of industry.

Among the most important factors common to the discussion above is good governance. Governance is about the exercising of political, economic and administrative authority to manage a region's affairs comprising a complex range of mechanisms, processes, relationships and institutions through which citizens and groups articulate their interests, exercise rights and obligations and mediate differences. Government promotes economic development through efficient government, effective civil society and a successful private sector. Governance does not down play the role of government in promoting regional growth, but recognises that government is but one of several important stakeholders. Governance is a partnership between the three tiers of government, the community and the private sector characterised by inclusiveness, experience sharing, strategy, capacity building, consensus building and continuous improvement.

Institutions and political organisations have an important role in the determination of national and regional policy. Regions whose governments are able to react quickly and responsively to the changing economic circumstances have tended to generate higher rates of growth. Whereas governments which are in 'gridlock', and unable to influence policy to any major extent, often occur in countries and regions with low rates of growth and relative incomes. Government policies and strategies that better position regions for competing globally involve:

- increasing the role of the most responsive sector of the economy, the private sector, to provide services;
- facilitating the exchange of information between stakeholders through information networks, conferences and clusters;
- government procurement of leading technologies to assist in fostering economies of scale for infant industries;
- gathering, analysing and disseminating information about the environment external to the region when that information has multiple purposes and uses for units in regions;
- encouraging a participatory approach to regional decision making through transparency and clear criteria;
- diversifying regional activity (limited only by sustainable long term outcomes) by adopting immigration polices drawing on people to supplement shortages in skills, international business networks and entrepreneurial skills and linking to existing regional activities;
- matching accountability with control, and devolving government activity by deconcentrating (central government represented at the

regions) and decentralising (transfer of responsibilities to lower tiers of government and semi-government or non-government bodies);

- providing incentives for good economic behaviour by rewarding excellence, and, just as importantly, rewarding significant and sustained improvements;
- up-skilling the community particularly in technology, entrepreneurship, management, professional ethics and relationship building. Education should be promoted as a life-long experience; and
- promoting the region by show-casing, marketing, staging events and creating a distinctive feature or feeling about the region.

In the context of South Australian economic policy, some of the above elements warrant emphasis:

- accentuation of regional and State identity through cultural diversity, broadening the production base and lifestyles. A greater emphasis on immigration of diverse groups of peoples with capacity to generate incomes though partnerships (business or community). Visual differentiation is also important;
- policies to promote regionalism, and, in particular, clarifying the roles of national, State and local government in regional development including strengthening fiscal transfer systems to local government;
- raising the level of community debate over regional development issues by hosting international conferences. That is, adopting the view of looking for the people with answers, rather than trying to solve problems locally; and
- adopting stronger incentive based methods for allocating resources. The establishment of a fund for supporting best practice in each of the key issues for the region.

With few exceptions, assistance to industry is not an effective means of promoting economic development, or of improving the standard of living of Australians as a whole. However, common-good policies - such as innovation and infrastructure investment - motivated by competitive pressures are likely to have generally beneficial effects. A key problem with direct assistance to industry is the secrecy of the activity.

The extent to which an economy engages in trade, free from restrictions such as tariffs and quotas, is known as the openness of an economy. Although there has been much anecdotal information that suggests that countries open to trade grow faster, only recently have economists been able to establish the connection empirically. Openness is important because it (i) permits specialisation and expansion of production beyond domestic demand, (ii) external competitive pressure is exerted on domestic industry to improve efficiency, (iii) investment decisions are likely to improve because revenue flows are based on world prices which is a better reflection of the opportunity cost of resources; (iv) and capital mobility is likely to improve because funding decisions can based on the most efficient use of those funds. Importantly, openness also plays a more fundamental role in promoting growth. The more open an economy is to trade and other international economic transactions, the more receptive it is likely to be to new knowledge and innovation.

There are several other factors which have been examined to consider their contribution to regional growth. The degree of regional autonomy is understood to promote growth as decisions are best made by those whom decisions affect. The quality of life has intuitive appeal as a basis for attracting economic activity. However, higher incomes and quality of life are interconnected, and there is no clear evidence of the causal link. Education has an important role in growth. The precise role will vary from region to region, depending on the level of economic development. In advanced economies, such as South Australia, high quality secondary and tertiary education is critical. The tertiary sector has a major role in promoting global partnerships with the aim of facilitating research and development and the conversion of ideas to commercial opportunities. Most studies confirm the importance of the link between growth and research and development to growth because of the high degree of 'spillover' benefits from high technology firms.

Factors that influence the choice of location of high technology firms that regularly are identified in studies are (i) the presence of similar firms, (ii) strength of the local market, (iii) low wage rates, (iv) defence expenditure and (v) presence of research parks. Climate is significant for electronics component manufacture. Sustaining a cluster of high technology firms is influenced by the size of the domestic market (customers and suppliers), the capacity to sub-contract on a local basis, the degree of local inter-firm co-operation and strength of local scientific and technical links.

An innovative milieu is a cluster of innovative firms with strong linkages to the broader macro and political economy of the region. There is a strong role for regional governments (state and local) to address factors that may inhibit the development of an innovative milieu. In particular (i) improving the resource endowments of the local economy by physical or human capital investment, (ii) improving the flexibility of the local economy, (iii) encouraging the development or entry of specialised business services, (iv) building the educational and research capacity of the region, and (v) building connections within the milieu.

Amongst the high technology developments is e-commerce, which is worth a special mention as it has such an important influence on regions. Recent Australian studies have calculated the impact of e-commerce on the States and Territories. The estimates suggest that the growth of all States and Territories would be boosted by the use of e-commerce. Those States and Territories which have a relatively low share of commodity exports (the ACT, Victoria and SA) experience the greatest benefits, and those with a high share (WA and the NT) the least. This result is largely driven by assumption that relatively low productivity gains for these sectors are more than off-set by the estimated appreciation of the Australian dollar. If the actual impact on the exchange rate is neutral or the Australian dollar depreciates then the benefits for these lagging state and territories will be much higher.

The potential for disintermediation to concentrate economic activity in the major financial centres, Sydney and Melbourne, could qualify these results. For example, if book retailing were to become substantially an e-commerce based industry, nationally there would be a drop in activity and employment in book retailing, an increase in activity in the wholesale trade and transport sectors, increased activity in other sectors of the economy as the resources previously devoted to book retailing are invested elsewhere, and an increase in consumption in other areas as prices for books have fallen therefore consumers can spend more income on other consumption goods. At the national level this should increase GDP (unless all book consumption switched offshore, in which case the net result would be uncertain) however this is not necessarily the case for a region within the country. In this example the increased employment in wholesale trade and part of the increase in transport would be more likely to occur in Sydney or Melbourne than in Adelaide, as South Australia receives a disproportionately low share of private investment. It is also quite possible that the reinvestment of resources previous invested in book retailing would occur elsewhere.

There is also the possibility that there could be tax erosion from South Australia due to increased use of e-commerce, for example the growing use of internet share broking services could lead to the transfer of stamp duty revenue away from the smaller states. Similarly if the concentration of economic activity in the larger states increased due to e-commerce, as described above, then this could reduce tax revenues from sources such as payroll tax for the governments of smaller states. This would mean that governments in these states would face the invidious choice of either reducing government services or increasing other forms of taxation, both of which are likely to reduce community welfare.

South Australia: A Small Regional Economy

One of the most notable characteristics about South Australia that it is highly urbanised State within a highly urbanised country. Almost three quarters of total employment in South Australia is found in the capital city, and 80 per cent if you include outer Adelaide. Changes in the pattern of urban settlement show some mixed trends, but there is a clear drift away from rural areas across Australia and South Australia is consistent with this trend. An interesting trend is the growth of small to medium sized towns, reflecting life style for those attracted to country living with urban amenities.

South Australia is a region of regions. Recent survey work by SACES shows that within the State's six provincial cities, there is a general perception of decline although the Riverland is an exception. These regions understand that the external environment is changing, but policies and programs by the three tiers of government were not helping sufficiently.

The pattern of urban settlement reflects the outcome of centripetal and centrifugal forces. These forces will strengthen or weaken according to a broad array of factors. Globalisation is a major influencing factor, and so is the ageing of the population. The effect of technology is unclear.

What we are today is in part a function of how we got here. The droughts, depression, over protectionist trade policies, poor economic management have suppressed the growth and development of this region, but temporarily, giving the impetus and urgency to reform and marking a new path forward.

Although a long way from anywhere, South Australia is drawing closer to the major markets through the gradual decline in transport and communications costs and new technologies that for example create controlled climates, and improve the efficiency of mineral extraction, which will over time improve the acreage of arable land.

South Australians are swelling in numbers only slowly relative to other regions in Australia. Slow population growth reflects longevity, low birth rate and low immigration, and these factors are leading to a gradual ageing of the population. Population ageing is not a comparative disadvantage for the region because our trading partners and our competitors are ageing similarly. The main demographic characteristic is that of concern is ethnicity. Until the region can immerse itself in different cultures, we will not be able to fully connect into the international market place. Business linkages will be strengthened and our understanding of the external environment will be stronger so that our region will not be inhibited from recognising and responding to change.

The rising salinity of the Murray-Darling river system is one of the most significant environmental problems facing Australia today. Reform is urgent. There are a number of economic policies available to arrest the problem. As the river system passes through five jurisdictions, cooperation between the three tiers of government, various local communities and river water users is a prerequisite to solving this nation-wide problem.

The importance of human capital in enhancing the economic growth and development of a region has been supported by many researchers in their various studies. Human capital formation depends on the rate of skill formation through education and post-school training, the rate of growth of employed labour, the skill level of employed labour, and population movements.

Formal secondary and tertiary education are the key forms of investment in the human capital for advanced regional economies such as South Australia. Secondary school student retention rates to Year 12 have been increasing across the nation including South Australia. However, the increase in South Australia is slightly slower than nationwide. The tertiary education enrolment for every 1,000 population in South Australia is the second lowest after Northern Territory. The increase in ten years is also slower in South Australia than nationally. Overall South Australian's human capital formation through secondary and tertiary education is improving, but the pace is not matched by Australia.

The employment growth in South Australia has been below the national rate. This is shown by the figure of full-time and part-time employed persons and full-time and part-time wage and salary earners. The pattern of employed persons by age group in South Australia is in line with Australian pattern. There are a decline in employment in 15-34 year age groups and an increase in employment of 45-59 year age groups. While overall unemployment in South Australia is higher, the average annual youth unemployment growth is lower. Participation rate in South Australia and Australia has decreased in the last decade. While the male participation rate shows a decreasing trend, females show an increase.

South Australia has been losing population through net movements interstate and overseas; it has only been through natural increase that South Australian population has grown.

South Australia experienced a strong demand in high-skilled labour. This demand has increased in the last 10 years. To meet this demand, in addition to increasing skill through formal education, South Australia also fulfils it through apprenticeships. South Australia is slightly below the Australian average as measured by qualifications held by those in the workforce. The differences, however, are not at all significant. In fact this reflects the 'retaining potential of the economy'. That is, the share of those with qualifications has fallen marginally as the population has declined.

Overall, South Australian human capital has been enhanced significantly over the last decade, but the improvement is below the national pace on the measures chosen.

South Australia industry share of national output in the last two decades has been changing. The overall industry share has been falling from 7.6 to 6.9 per cent. The sectors: Agriculture, Manufacturing, Electricity, Gas and Water, Health and Community services, and Personal and Other Services still hold the largest share. On the other hand the sectors: Mining, Finance and Insurance, Property and Business services, and Wholesale trade have shares lower than average.

South Australia's and Australia's industry structures in terms of output are different. In comparison to Australia as a whole, the South Australian economics has a higher share of output in Agriculture, Manufacturing, Electricity, Gas and Water, Education, and Health and Community Services, and a lower share of Mining, Construction, Wholesale Trade, Finance and Insurance, Property and Business Services, Government Administration and Defence, and Ownership and Dwelling. Retail Trade, Accommodation, Cafés and Restaurants, Transport and Storage, Communication services, Personal and Other Services, Cultural and Recreational Services, and General Government have much the same share in South Australia's as in Australia as a whole.

High growth industries in both South Australia and Australia include Finance and Insurance, Property and Business Services, Personal and Other Services, Accommodation, Cafés and Restaurants, and Communication services. None of these industries grew faster in South Australia than in the nation. Low growth industries were Construction, Retail Trade, Electricity, Gas and Water, Mining, Manufacturing, and Agriculture. With Agriculture Manufacturing, and Electricity, Gas and Water grew a little faster in South Australia than in Australia. On average, growth in output in South Australia was lower than in Australia.

South Australia's economy is more concentrated in Agriculture and less concentrated in Mining. A set of industries under-represented in South Australia, but only mildly so include Wholesale Trade, Accommodation, Cafés and Restaurants, Transport and Storage, Communication Services, Finance and Insurance, Cultural and Recreation Services, and Ownership and Dwelling. Those mildly over-represented are Retail Trade, Education, and General Government.

South Australia's growth over the period 1982-83 to 1988-89 was 30.2 per cent and over the period 1989-90 to 1988-99 was 23.4 per cent. That is, the growth in the second period was slower than in the first. For Australia the growth rates were, respectively, 30.1 per cent and 36.4 per cent. That is, South Australia's growth rate was lower than Australia's in both periods. Also, in the second period, the rate of growth slowed for South Australia in contrast with faster growth for Australia.

Shift share analysis is an appropriate tool to diagnose to what extent the poorer performance of the South Australian economy attributable to the differences in its industry structure and to what extent do differences in the growth rates of each industry in South Australia and Australia.

The analysis shows that while industry structure may have played some part in the lower growth of South Australia's relatively poor economic performance, the unfavourable industry growth have played more dominant role. Breaking the analysis into two periods it explains further that the second period is when the

South Australian economic more severe. And the favourable industry growth turned to unfavourable.

Despite data limitations on import data and export data on services, there is considerable evidence that the tradeable goods sector in South Australia has expanded strongly over the past 10 years. This growth has been promoted, in part, by declining trade barriers both Australian and overseas which is putting pressure on local producers to improve efficiency and become more innovative and entrepreneurial. A more open economy means that the region will adapt new products more quickly, have a greater understanding of the external environment in all dimensions and be more exposed to new ideas.

Assessed against national benchmarks, growth in merchandise exports has been particularly impressive since 1988-89. Through specialising in the production of goods and services in which the State possesses a comparative advantage, growth in the export sector has been particularly important to raising local productivity and employment levels, and thus, contributing to overall South Australian economic growth. Importantly, growth in merchandise exports has occurred over a broad range of commodities. Not only does this imply an increasingly stable export sector with the overall performance of the sector being less sensitive to industry specific events, but the benefits associated with exports have been spread over a broad base of the economy and therefore the community. The geographic dispersion of South Australia's exports has also been impressive over the last ten years. However, the South Australian sector does remain highly influenced by exogenous factors such as foreign demand conditions and extreme movements in exchange rates. On the positive side, the diversification of the State's geographic export markets does reduce the overexposure of the sector to possible downturns in any of its major markets and limits any associated negative feedbacks.

Gains from trade do not derive from exports, but from imports. Regions export mainly to acquire the means to purchase what they cannot produce. Nonetheless, there are some benefits of export production such as the achievement of economies of scale in production which benefits the local markets. Imports are goods and services purchased from outside the region at lower cost than if produced within the region; trade also permits the consumption of a wider variety of goods, further raising welfare of the consumer. Due to data limitations, we can only be certain that South Australian merchandise imports have grown strongly over time in line with the national trend - indicating that South Australia has likely experienced the aforementioned gains from exchange. Nonetheless, given the substantial rise in imports, falling barriers to imports, and recent strength in domestic demand, the South Australian community is almost certainly enjoying a greater diversity of imports.

The increased diversification of imports is an indication that the regional population is broadening its tastes. And the increased diversification of exports both in terms of products and market destinations is an indication that South Australian's understand more about consumer demands overseas and doing business with foreigners. Given the narrow ethnic representation within the State, South Australia's Anglo-Saxon dominated population has done well to make the trade and business connections that underpin the trade success story. However, the rate of growth of the tradeable goods sector may weaken if we are not able to make the next cultural step from arms length business relations to cultural emersion and integration. The later will enable us to reach a stronger understanding of consumer tastes and business practices in the external environment, more able to read the signals of change and more able to respond to those changes.

Various case studies highlighted differences between South Australia and other regions.

1. *Climate Change Policy*

The effect of anthropogenic activity on climate is one of the most important long-run issues for regions and, moreover, for the global community. The relationship between climate and regional economic growth is difficult to measure and measurements vary between studies. However, there is broad acceptance that climate effects capital use, human productivity and leisure activity. With the exception of the far North, South Australia's climate is an advantage for the region.

The scientific community has found evidence that the global climate is warming, due to both natural and anthropogenic causes. Predictions about the effect of global warming are rising sea levels, changes in weather patterns, changes to flora and fauna, changes to human productivity and health and consequent effects on public and private expenditure programs and policies. These changes can be positive or negative. Overall, the consequence of climate change are unclear, but if warming is unabated then the long run consequences might be catastrophic. As the 'downside' might be so disastrous, the global community (or at least the developed countries) has adopted the precautionary principle. That is, to adopt a policy to commit resources to emissions abatement even though the effects of global warming are currently unclear. On the basis of this principle, developed countries have agreed to a set of targets that limit the growth of emissions. Australia's target is to limit the growth of CO_2 emissions to 8 per cent by 2012, relative to 1990.

In broad terms, there are two types of policies that could be adopted to abate greenhouse gas emissions: an international tradeable quota scheme or unilateral targets under which each country would adopt emissions abatement policies. The analysis presented in this chapter concludes that international tradeable quotas is the best option for Australia (and South Australia) as it is cost-effective for Australia to buy the right to emit gases while other countries such as Eastern

Europe sell that right and use the funds to commit resources to upgrade facilities such as electricity generating plants.

If domestic policies must be adopted in each country then Australia has a more costly task to reach its targets. The Australian government has a set of national policies for greenhouse gas abatement. The South Australian economy is a low emissions region relative to most other regions in Australia, and the expected growth in emissions per capita is low. South Australia should not be forced into adopting national policies to achieve the national target. Recognition should be given to the green State, and abatement policies should only be adopted if the resource cost is lower than some alternative policy in other States.

2. *High Technology Industry*

The assessment of the potential to revitalise the Woomera rocket range provides an interesting case study of the shifting sands of high technology industry. In the late 1940s, Australia and South Australia in particular, had the opportunity to attract a high-tech rocket and military testing industry which potentially had major spillover benefits to defence, electronics, communications and other high-technology industry. Looking back over the 50 years since the inception of the UK-Australia joint project there is some evidence of the lasting success of the investment, but the benefits could have been for greater. There were several problems or misjudgments: (i) the British were discouraged (inadvertently) from setting up design teams in Salisbury which was necessary for knowledge transfer to local firms; (ii) very few Australian firms could achieve economies of scale from production runs; (iii) Australia did not use the technology developed at Woomera and hence did not 'learn by doing'; (iv) some products did not fit well with defence strategy or global community safety; and (v) some projects were not very remarkable weapons.

Woomera today is a much smaller town than in the 'hay days' of the rocket launching. And it is known now more for hosting Kosovo refugees. Nonetheless, Woomera still manages to retain a unique identity. With almost three quarters of the population under 40 years old, it has the characteristic of a 'frontier settlement'. The infrastructure, albeit dated, is 'oversized' for the town and thereby capable of expansion. Overall the town remains receptive to regional development and growth.

There are prospects of a new investment in space technology which offers hope of re-launching Woomera. Kistler Aerospace Corporation is designing and building a small fleet of re-useable space launch vehicles which would use the old Woomera launching facilities as the base for Kistler's operations. The new investment would bring employment to the region and boost the State's GSP.

However, the main interest for this region is in whether the high-tech investment has important spillover benefits to Woomera and to other regions in the state such as Salisbury, just North of Adelaide. The assessment in this chapter is that such spillovers are unlikely. The main mitigating factors against significant knowledge spillovers are (i) the remoteness of Woomera is not appealing for a professional workforce; (ii) most knowledge intensive development work is expected to occur in Washington hence there is no mechanism for knowledge transfer; (iii) there is little opportunity for firm clustering or creation of related or supporting service industries; and (iv) there is no structure for the integration of firms into the broader regional economic community to form an 'innovative milieu'.

3. *Inter-governmental Fiscal Management*

Globalisation of the economy is intensifying regionalism and diminishing the role of the nation-states. New public sector management reforms are gradually being implemented across OECD countries which are responding to globalisation by devolving fiscal control to lower tiers of government and encouraging greater participation of multi-national and sub-national bodies and community groups in government decision making. The increase in the number of players and the change in the respective powers of those players in the field of inter-governmental relations makes the management of relations much more complex. As fiscal transfers from central to lower tiers of government involve vast sums of money, these transfers play an important role in inter-governmental relations. As large flows of funds create strong incentives for good or bad economic behaviour, then it is important that the mechanisms for such transfers are designed to meet the specified social objectives.

The Commonwealth government has, by OECD standards, a relatively sophisticated system for the allocation of funds to the States. However, the system for allocation of funds to local government is still quite simplistic. The justification offered for a simplistic approach is that there is 10 fold more local governments than State governments, and the quantum of funds to local government is not as large in the context of public finances generally.

Unlike Australia, Japan is not a Federalist system, and decisions over the allocations of funds to lower tiers of government are highly centralised. The degree of vertical fiscal imbalance is also an issue. However, the role of local government is much larger and enables regions to better position government to deliver public services that will assist these regions to compete in the global market place. Decentralisation of fiscal responsibility is gradually taking hold in Japan since the policy was adopted by the Japanese government in 1995. Importantly, allocations of funds to local government are based on expected incomes and expected expenditures. Under this system, incentives are created for local government to consider closely economic development initiatives that will assist their regions to grow and the central government has the means to rationalise between those initiatives where there is potential for inter-regional overlay or duplication as well as to identify development gaps.

Globalisation and the new inter-governmental relations that rely on decentralisation and broader participation by other economic agents is leading to greater not lesser shared fiscal responsibilities between tiers of government. Co-ordination and co-operation are at a premium. On this basis, devolution of responsibilities to local government in Australia will follow Japan, whereby central government will need to develop closer relations with local government in addition to maintaining its relationship with state government. This is a departure from the hierarchal system whereby Commonwealth tends to communicate with the States and these communicate with local government. This departure does not diminish the role of the State but changes the role whereby the three tiers of government form a network - an organisational structure akin to the network of collaboration between firms - that seeks to position their regions and their local industry for competition in the global market place. The opportunity for dialogue on these issues currently exists through the Commonwealth Grants Commission's ongoing process of reform of Commonwealth - State financial relations.

4. *Economic Co-operation*

Partnerships between government and multi-national corporations, clusters of firms and innovative milieus are three examples of special relationships for economic cooperation. These relationships go beyond the normal market transactions of buying and selling and involve long term commitments.

Shifting up the spectrum from partnerships to clusters to milieus involves increasingly complex relationships which rely much more heavily on trust, shared vision, clear roles for each party, transparency in decisions and mutual respect for (intellectual and physical) property. This is an intensive, high level management process requiring very strong communication. These relationships can be fragile, and, are subject to the changeable factors that drive the creation and maintenance of these relationships (such as changing market opportunities which require different inputs from partners).

The SA Government's water industry and MFP initiatives are two practical examples of these special relationships. In terms of the complexity of the relationships for economic cooperation, both the water industry and MFP initiatives are ambitious but the latter initiative is far more so. The water industry initiative which is now about one-third of the way through its 15 year life, has shown to be a successful mechanism for both transforming the culture of a department of state and for growing the water industry. By the time the MFP was implemented, most of the true benefits of initiative had been lost. The shear ambitiousness of the level of economic cooperation need to make the grand plan work is the root cause of its decline. The (high) level of economic cooperation required was not attained which led to long delays in the decision making process turning off the Japanese investors and others and to imbalances between parties (real estate vs business development).

As a final word, and in the spirit of a leading economist of the 1940s, Schumpeter, economic growth is a process of creative destruction. The continual process of replacing the old with the new is facilitated by a culture of innovation combined with entrepreneurship in a sound framework where the quality of life broadly defined is advanced and shared by all.

Index